**Eastern U.S.
Edition**

RADIO
ON
WHEELS™

Eastern U.S. Edition

RADIO ON WHEELS™

by Paul Rocheleau

BERKLEY BOOKS, NEW YORK

The Publisher and the Author both
strongly advise the reader not to
use this book while driving a
motor vehicle.

RADIO ON WHEELS
EASTERN EDITION

A Berkley Book / published by arrangement with
the author

PRINTING HISTORY
Berkley edition / July 1991

ISBN: 0-425-12860-1

A BERKLEY BOOK ® TM 757,375
Berkley Books are published by The Berkley Publishing Group,
200 Madison Avenue, New York, New York 10016.
The name "BERKLEY" and the "B" logo
are trademarks belonging to Berkley Publishing Corporation.

PRINTED IN THE UNITED STATES OF AMERICA

10 9 8 7 6 5 4 3 2 1

There is only one person that this book could be
dedicated to — my wife, Elaine.
She gave the initial encouragement to start
the project, then once it began devoted all her energies to making
it succeed. She is the true hero of this project.
Thank you, darling.

Acknowledgments

In the time it took to produce this guide many helpful hands were extended through either words of encouragement or well-performed tasks. Regardless if the help was contracted or given in friendship, the people mentioned below showed a belief in the project for which we are most appreciative. We extend to them our warmest thanks.

The person that gave the most to this project both in time and effort is Kimberly Rennie. Kimberly joined the project at its beginning and became responsible immediately for computerizing the project. Data bases, programs, computer design work, and general assisting in all facets of the project were the tasks she did and did in an exemplary manner (most of this while she was a full-time college student). Following closely behind in time spent and responsibilities taken on was our son Joseph. Without his careful attention to detail and accuracy the project would have suffered greatly. Next we would like to thank Elaine's sister Ann Archey and her daughter Karen, who came in during times of excess work loads and performed the numerous mundane tasks that take so much time and energy.

When I work in my real profession (photography), I have the enviable position of working with many talented people. Many of those people were shown prototype designs and gave their expert advice on how to improve them. One designer I have to give special thanks to is David Larkin. Not only was he a catalyst in initiating me into action, but also offered invaluable expert opinion on design concepts. And on top of that, the poor bloke had to endure my incessant checking of radio stations as we drove to our photography locations.

Special thanks to three friends that made such a contribution to the project. First, Sabra Elliot, who we will forever be indebted to for presenting and advocating our project to the editorial board of The Berkley Publishing Group. Second, Blake and Pauline Gardner, who through suggestions and great moral support helped get us through some of the tougher times.

To our editors at Berkley, Natalee Rosenstein, Jill Dinneen, and Bill Harris, thanks for all that we saw you do, but extra thanks for all that was done in the background that we were not aware of. There is always more effort that goes into these projects than is readily noticed.

To Phil Ruderman, Steve Powell, and Sandy Powell, thanks for all the efforts in making the city skyline graphics interesting and fun. To another computer whiz, Jean King, thanks for taking a complex project and making it work.

Last but not least, we want to thank all the people in the radio industry who were so helpful in filling out questionnaires and taking time to talk to us on the phone when we had specific questions. And definitely we cannot forget the musicians that make the music we all listen to. It would be a very empty world if music did not exist.

Contents

Introduction

The idea for this radio guide originated from the same frustration that many of you have had while traveling for business or pleasure in unfamiliar territory. Wanting to listen to the radio, you start to scan the dial for a radio station that will give you an hour or so of your favorite tunes before you lose the signal. In searching for that station you find that one-third of the stations are on commercial break, so you have no idea if they are playing your type of music. Do you get lucky and find something satisfactory, or do you settle for a station that is at least close to what you want? If you do momentarily compromise, do you end up re-scanning in ten minutes, and if in a major city do you want to re-scan through twenty or more signals? The next problem encountered is not knowing where the signal is coming from. Is the tower thirty miles behind you so that in another ten minutes the signal begins to fade? The seek button on a radio might find you a song you like, but not necessarily a station you care for, or one whose signal you can anticipate having for a comfortable period of time. Therefore, we decided to develop a radio guide that you, the motoring public, could use to alleviate the frustrations of playing radio roulette.

Recognizing a problem is an important first step, but finding a solution is the difficult part. In the case of this radio guide, more than two years transpired before the idea of a linear approach utilizing the interstate highway system was conceived. This idea seemed to approximate as much as possible the actual use of a car radio on an extended trip. Text alone would not accomplish a solution to all problems, so to supplement the text it was decided to create an interpretive map at the top of the page. Metropolitan areas, with so many signals to choose from, necessitated having their own section in the guide. More graphics were incorporated in the design, so if you were driving alone and were momentarily stopped you could scan the pages quickly.

Problem number two was the question of what to include in the guide. The first major issue was whether or not to include the AM band. Because of space considerations and the limited listenership of AM versus FM, we originally decided to make the guide strictly FM. Within a year of gathering data we saw the error of our decision and decided that the AM band did have much to offer and could not be completely neglected. Again because of space considerations we had to be selective about what AM stations to include. The most logical choices were the talk, news, and clear-channel stations, which are those AM stations given the allowance to broadcast at full power during the evening hours.

While decisions about the AM band were in the making, the question of what to include or exclude from the numerous FM stations across the country also had to be settled. Since we were primarily making a guide for a mobile audience, we made the decision to eliminate very weak stations because their signals would not carry far enough to be practical for someone moving at 55 miles an hour. An exception was made in major metro areas, where it was felt that linear movement would be at a minimum. Of major concern was determining how far left and right of the interstate we would go to include stations. Very powerful Class C stations were brought in from up to sixty miles away. Moderately powerful Class B stations were included if within forty miles of the interstate. And the moderate power Class A stations had to be within twenty miles to get a listing. Since FM transmission is line of sight, topography also became a factor in determining whether stations should be included.

With all the programming and services provided by radio stations, the primary goal was to go beyond being just a format guide and introduce more detailed information about the stations. Public stations in particular had so much programming to offer that to just list them as either classical, jazz, or eclectic was to do a disservice to the stations and listeners. Commercial stations, with their traffic reports and news teams, were also providing the public with more than just music.

One area of programming that we decided to include that we knew was going to be very labor intensive and difficult to portray easily was news programming. The importance of knowing when a station was giving a news broadcast was made evident one day when driving home from Boston. There was a major happening in the world that we were trying to get informed about and it seemed that every station we tuned in did not have a news broadcast at the logical top of the hour. If we had known which station in the area gave a newscast, and at what time, we would have been most grateful.

To gather the information needed a survey was sent to each radio station listed in the book. In thanks to the men and women in the industry, the response rate was excellent and the information provided superb. What did not come by mail was then solicited by phone. All stations were provided an equal opportunity to provide us with data.

In conjunction with the data gathering, field tests of the design were taking place. Approximately 20,000 miles were logged in two vehicles checking the accuracy of the entries as they related to their placement on the page, signal power, and other technical criteria. It must be admitted that this was the fun part of the project. Some might question the wisdom of spending so much time on the road when theoretically you should be able to calculate signal projections from power and antenna heights. This is true, but not being engineers ourselves we felt more comfortable double-checking what theory said should happen. And in doing the checking we always managed to find some quirks that necessitated some change in our station placement or inclusion.

It is hoped that our efforts have resulted in a radio guide that is both informative and easy to use. This being the first edition, we realize there will be some inaccuracies that will have to be corrected, and we welcome suggestions from our readers and the radio industry. A cautionary note about radio formats though: some radio stations may change their formats in reaction to trends. We have made our best efforts to have the latest information about what each station is playing, but in the time that we close pages and the book is printed and distributed things can change in the radio industry. We will keep up with those changes and update these guides periodically.

One last note: If you are driving alone do not attempt to use this book while in motion. If you are in a city wait for the next red light or traffic jam, and if you are on the interstate wait till you have to stop for gas or coffee. We want you to be around to buy the updated version!

HOW TO USE THE GUIDE

PAGE ENTRY EXPLANATION

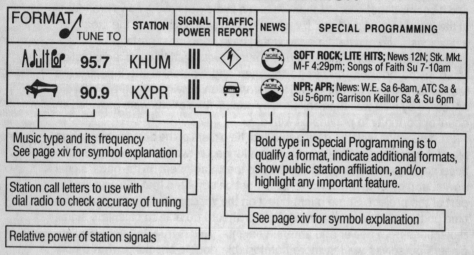

FORMAT ♪ TUNE TO		STATION	SIGNAL POWER	TRAFFIC REPORT	NEWS	SPECIAL PROGRAMMING
A♪ult♪♪	95.7	KHUM	‖‖	◈	(MORE)	**SOFT ROCK; LITE HITS;** News 12N; Stk. Mkt. M-F 4:29pm; Songs of Faith Su 7-10am
🎹	90.9	KXPR	‖‖	🚗	(MORE)	**NPR; APR;** News: W.E. Sa 6-8am, ATC Sa & Su 5-6pm; Garrison Keillor Sa & Su 6pm

Music type and its frequency
See page xiv for symbol explanation

Station call letters to use with
dial radio to check accuracy of tuning

Relative power of station signals

Bold type in Special Programming is to
qualify a format, indicate additional formats,
show public station affiliation, and/or
highlight any important feature.

See page xiv for symbol explanation

ROAD PAGE MAP EXPLANATION

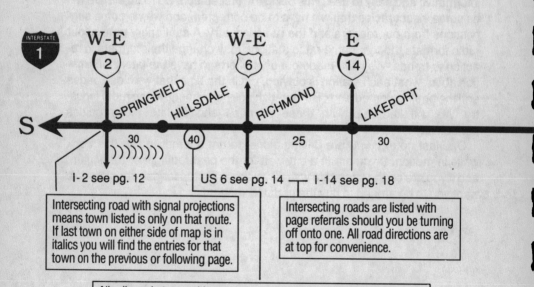

INTERSTATE 1

W-E ②   W-E ⑥   E ⑭

S ◄─── SPRINGFIELD ── HILLSDALE ── RICHMOND ── LAKEPORT ───

30))))))))) ④⓪ 25 30

I-2 see pg. 12   US 6 see pg. 14 ── I-14 see pg. 18

Intersecting road with signal projections
means town listed is only on that route.
If last town on either side of map is in
italics you will find the entries for that
town on the previous or following page.

Intersecting roads are listed with
page referrals should you be turning
off onto one. All road directions are
at top for convenience.

All mileage between cities are averaged air miles. In the Northeast and
southern California strong stations (three bars) project a good signal 35
to 50 miles. In the rest of the country three-bar stations project up to 90
miles. Use these figures to estimate how far to look ahead for stations.

METRO PAGE EXPLANATION

The map immediately below is a visual representation of what is taking place in a metro area.

Central city Alpha has the major portion of stations. The surrounding cities or towns (A,B,C,D,E,F) comprise the remaining amount of signals placed in the metro area.

METRO   ALPHA

N

D

NW   NE

E

W — C   CENTRAL CITY "ALPHA"   F — E

B

SW   SE

A

S

GREENVILLE

From the road map below notice that as you leave Greenville the signals from Metro Alpha are now reachable. At this point it is advisable to leave the road pages and open to Metro Alpha.

As you enter Metro Alpha from the south you can look for listings of three-bar stations. All three-bar stations from central city and surrounding towns A,B,C,&F should be receivable. Given your location in the very southern section of the metro area, the three-bar stations from towns D&E may have some difficulty being received and it is very unlikely that the two-bar stations will come in from those locations.

Two-bar stations from towns C&F may also be difficult to get. Depending on the distance, two-bar stations from central city and town B should be receivable in the vicinity of town A.

Not all metros are picture perfect so there will be variations in what signals are receivable. If you keep a mental picture of the map you can anticipate what stations will be available as you enter from any compass point. Generally, though, stations from the opposite compass points are going to be trouble until you get closer to the central city.

INTERSTATE 1

GREENVILLE

GREENVILLE

25

SEE METRO ALPHA   NORTH   SEE METRO BETA

SOUTH   SOUTH

N

Signal Projection

Interlocking Metros mean you are referred from one Metro to the other without going back to the road pages.

Symbols

Adult Popular/Adult Contemporary: Music for the tastes of a general adult-aged audience

Contemporary Hits: Playing a variety of currently produced rock, dance & rap music

Album-Oriented Rock: Rock with less chart emphasis, maybe some heavy metal, and classics from the 60's, 70's, 80's.

Classic Rock: Album rock from the 60's, 70's, 80's. Think of the Woodstock Generation

Progressive, New & Heavy Metal: The cutting edge of contemporary rock. Usually played on college radio

Country & Western: Music with a southern and country touch

Oldies: Popular rock from the 50's & 60's. Classic hits extends the range and introduces classic rock type selections

Rhythm & Blues: Soul and what the industry calls urban contemporary. Black-oriented current music

Soft Adult Popular: Slower tempo than adult popular with less current music and more hits from the 70's & 80's

Easy Listening: Including big band, mellow music, soft vocalization and more instrumentals

Classical: Solo, chamber, symphony, opera, music from the great composers (can be a public or commercial radio station)

Jazz: Traditional, big band & vocal, usually with some blues programming

ek-lek′-tik Eclectic: Stations mixing formats evenly. Can range from a 50/50 classical/jazz station to a community station playing everything under the sun

Lite Jazz: New-age type of instrumental music. Stations usually program in some traditional jazz

College: Most colleges play progressive rock and a general eclectic playlist. Remember colleges have semester breaks and summer vacations which put some off the air at those times.

Spanish Speaking: Music can range from Latin salsa to Mexican rock to a variety of Spanish-flavored music

Religious: This incorporates Christian contemporary, Christian music, southern gospel, Black gospel and inspirational preaching

All News: Usually all news until later in the evening when most turn to a talk format

Talk-News/Talk: Primarily talk but giving emphasis to news by giving two newscasts an hour

AM Clear Channel: These stations maintain full power in the evening and can project a signal at night 750 miles away by bouncing their signal off the ionosphere

Powerful Station: Will project a good signal 40 to 80 miles from tower

Medium Power: A good signal projects 15 to 30 miles depending on topography

Weak Station: Signals project 5 to 10 miles. Usually found in larger metro areas. Usually are college or community stations playing varied music format

Traffic Reports: Usually in metro areas. Stations giving morning and afternoon commuter traffic conditions

Traffic Advisories: Stations giving information for local interstates about severe weather (snow, tornado, etc.) and other hazardous road conditions

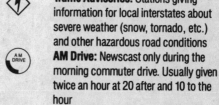

AM Drive: Newscast only during the morning commuter drive. Usually given twice an hour at 20 after and 10 to the hour

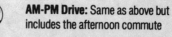

AM-PM Drive: Same as above but includes the afternoon commute

AM Drive Plus: Same as AM Drive above but with some additional newscasts listed in Special Programming column

 AM-PM Drive Plus: Same as above but including the afternoon commute

 News on the hour: News throughout the day. Morning and afternoon drives might have two newscasts during an hour. Some stations also have a newscast on the half hour. See Special Programming for information

 Same as above, but with newscast starting at five to the hour

 Same as above, but with newscast starting at ten to the hour

 Same as above, but with newscast on the half hour

 Continuous News Programming: Usually from 5am to 10pm

 Newscasts are at odd times: They are listed in Special Programming column

 Extended Newscast from 6-9am and 4-6pm: Usually public stations airing All Things Considered, MonitoRadio, Marketplace, Morning Edition, BBC & Pacifica News. See also Special Programming for other newscasts during the day and on weekends

 Same as above, but news block is from 6-9am and 5-6pm

 **Same as above,** but news block is 6-8am and 4-6pm

 Same as above, but news block is 6-7am and 5-6pm

 Same as above, but news block is 6-8am and 5-6pm

 Same as above, but news block is 6-7am and 4-6pm

 Spot News: News interjected anytime during the programming day as events dictate

COMMON ABBREVIATIONS

Agri.	Agriculture News Service
ATC	All Things Considered
Amer.	American
APR	American Public Radio
Bus.	Business
CLASS.	Classical
Comm.	Community
Ctry.	Country
Ctdwn.	Countdown
F	Friday
H.S.	High School
hr.	Hour
hrly.	Hourly
Mktplace.	Marketplace
M	Monday
Morn.	Morning
NPR	National Public Radio
Prgsv.	Progressive
Pub. Aff.	Public Affairs
R & R	Rock & Roll
Sa	Saturday
Spts.	Sports
Stk. Mkt.	Stock Market
Su	Sunday
Thu	Thursday
Tu	Tuesday
U.	University
W	Wednesday
W.E.	Weekend Edition

INTERSTATE SECTION

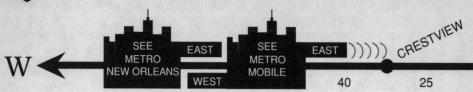

INTERSTATE 10

FORMAT ♪ TUNE TO		STATION	SIGNAL POWER	TRAFFIC REPORT	NEWS	SPECIAL PROGRAMMING
SEE NEW ORLEANS METRO PAGE 204						
SEE MOBILE METRO PAGE 200						
CRESTVIEW/FORT WALTON BEACH AREA						
TOP40	98.1	WWSF	‖‖			
TOP40	99.5	WKSM	‖‖	🚗	🕐	Morning Humor
👢	92.1	WMMK	‖	⚡	🕐	Sa Nite House Party 7pm; Ctry. Ctdwn. Su 9am; Nashville Live Su 7:30pm
👢	104.7	WAAZ	‖‖			
☀OLDIES	105.5	WYZB	‖	⚡	AM DRIVE	Morn. Humor; Supergold Sa 7pm–12M; Dick Clark Su 6–10pm
✝✝✝	90.1	WTJT	‖			
DE FUNIAK SPRINGS AREA						
Adult Pop	102.3	WWAV	‖			
👢	103.1	WQUH	‖	◇	AM & PM DRIVE	Farm Weather; North Florida Crop Report; Agri. Business Reports
🛋	88.1	WUWF	‖‖		MORE	JAZZ M–F 10pm–1am, Sa 11pm–12M, Su 11pm–1am; News: W.E. 7–9am, ATC 4–5pm
BONIFAY AREA						
Adult Pop	97.7	WTBB	‖	◇	🕐	CTRY.; Spts.: Gators, Bucs, High School
Adult Pop	106.7	WKMX	‖‖	🚗	MORE	News 10:50am, 11:50am; Spts.: U. of AL; Beach Weather; Church Service Su Morning
TOP40	96.9	WDJR	‖‖	◇	🕐	ADULT POPULAR; Morn. Humor

DE FUNIAK SPRINGS   BONIFAY   MARIANNA/PANAMA CITY   CHATTAHOOCHEE   TALLAHASSEE   E

25   30   20   40

FORMAT ♪ TUNE TO		STATION	SIGNAL POWER	TRAFFIC REPORT	NEWS	SPECIAL PROGRAMMING
MARIANNA/PANAMA CITY AREA						
Adult Pop	99.7	WOOF	|||	⚡	AM & PM DRIVE	Stk. Mkt. 5:05pm; Spts. News 6:20am, 5:50pm
TOP40	105.9	WILN	|||	🚗		Morn. Humor; Top 40 Ctdwn. Su 8am–12N; Spts.: Football, Local, MSU, NFL
TOP40	107.9	WPFM	|||	⚡		**ALBUM ROCK;** Morn. Humor
🤠	92.5	WPAP	|||	⚡	SPOT NEWS	Ctry. Ctdwn. Su 8am–12N
🤠	95.5	WTVY	|||	⚡	🕐	Ctry. Ctdwn. Su 3–7pm; Nashville Live Su 7–11pm; P. Harvey M–F 8am, 12N, 4pm
🤠	100.9	WJAQ	||			
🤠	102.3	WPHK	||		🕐	Spts.: U. of Florida
OLDIES	98.5	WFSY	|||	⚡	AM DRIVE	**CLASSIC HITS**
OLDIES	103.5	WBKL	|||	⚡	MORE	News 10 after the hr; A Closer Look from Cornell U. 12:10pm; Memory Min. 7:10am
🎹	88.7	WRWA	|||		MORE	**NPR; EZ; JAZZ;** News: W.E. Sa 7–8am, ATC Sa & Su 4–5pm; Opera Sa 12N–3pm
🎹	90.7	WKGC	|||			Gulf Coast Community College
✝✝✝	91.1	WJNF					
CHATTAHOOCHEE AREA						
TOP40	97.3	WJAD	|||	⚡	MORE	News also :48 hrly; Open House Party Sa 7pm–12M; Rick Dee's Top 40 Sa 6–10am
Lite Hits	100.7	WGWD	||			

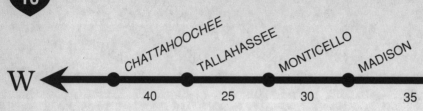

Interstate 10

W ← CHATTAHOOCHEE • TALLAHASSEE • MONTICELLO • MADISON
40   25   30   35

FORMAT ♪ TUNE TO	STATION	SIGNAL POWER	TRAFFIC REPORT	NEWS	SPECIAL PROGRAMMING
TALLAHASSEE AREA					
Adult Pop 98.9	WBGM	‖‖			
Adult Pop 103.1	WUMX	‖	🚗	A.M. DRIVE	Morn. Humor; Casey Kasem Su 8am–12N
🎸 104.1	WGLF	‖‖	⚡	A.M. DRIVE	**ALBUM ROCK;** Morn. Humor; Spts. News 7:20am, 5:50pm
🤠 94.9	WTNT	‖‖	⚡	A.M. DRIVE	Morn. Humor
🤠 99.9	WHKX	‖	⚡	A.M. DRIVE	Morn. Humor
☀️OLDIES 95.9	WTMG	‖		MORE	Morn. Humor; News 10am; All-Request Amer. M–F 9pm–1am; Pub. Affairs Su 8am
R&B 101.7	WIQI	‖			
E❄Z 104.9	WMLO	‖		🕐	Wall St., Mkt. & Bus. Reports 6am–10pm; Bus., Wall St. Wrap-ups 4:30, 5, 5:30pm
🎹 91.5	WFSQ	‖‖			Orchestra Concerts M–W 8–10pm; Jazz Su 12N–5pm; Swing Sa 6–10pm
NEWS 88.9	WFSU	‖‖	⚡	MORE	**NPR; APR; INFORMATION** M–F 5am–2am; News: W.E. Sa 8–10am, Su 8–9am
Talk 1450	WTAL	‖	🚗	MORE	News on the hr. & 1/2 hr, Updates 5–6pm; Stk. Mkt; Spts.: High School, Auburn
MONTICELLO AREA					
🎸 106.3	WTUF	‖			**OLDIES**
🤠 92.9	WAAC	‖‖	⚡	🕐	P. Harvey M–F 8:30am, 12:06, 5:30pm; Spts. News 7:30am, 4:30pm, Racing 7:30pm
🤠 107.1	WSTT	‖			
Lite Hits 101.9	WJPH	‖	⚡	🕐	News also on the 1/2 hour; Agri. Reports

4

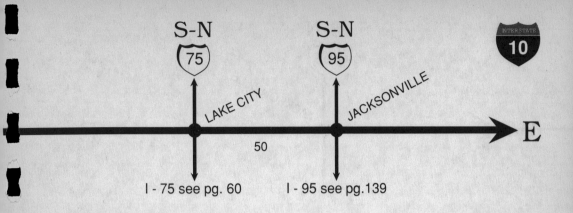

I - 75 see pg. 60   I - 95 see pg.139

FORMAT / TUNE TO		STATION	SIGNAL POWER	TRAFFIC REPORT	NEWS	SPECIAL PROGRAMMING
MADISON AREA						
Adult Pop	95.7	WQPW	‖	⚡	AM & PM DRIVE	Morn. Humor; Public Affairs Su 7–8am
R&B	104.9	WIMV	‖			
✝✝	101.1	WAFT	‖‖	⚡	MORE	News :55 11am, 12, 2, 3pm; Facts & Fellowship M–F 5:30pm; Thru the Bible 12:25pm
LAKE CITY AREA						
Adult Pop	94.3	WNFB	‖‖	🚗	🕐	
🎸	103.7	WRUF	‖‖			U. of Florida
🎩	98.1	WQHL	‖‖	⚡	🕐	Spts.; Christian Program
🎩	102.1	WQLC	‖		AM & PM DRIVE	
🎹	89.1	WUFT	‖‖	⚡	MORE	**NPR; APR;** News: W.E. Sa & Su 8–10am, ATC Sa 5:15–6pm; Jazz M–F 9–11pm, Sa 5–8pm
✝✝	90.5	WYFB	‖‖			
JACKSONVILLE AREA						
Adult Pop	96.1	WEJZ	‖‖	🚗	AM DRIVE	
Adult Pop	102.9	WIVY	‖‖	🚗		Morn. Humor; After Dark (Jazz/Urban) Su–F 9pm–1am; JAXX Jazz Su 8am–12N
Adult Pop	106.3	WKBX	‖	⚡	🕐	**HOT ADULT POPULAR; TOP 40;** Spts.: U. of GA; Timewarp (Oldies) M–F 12N–2pm
Top 40	95.1	WAPE	‖‖			
Top 40	99.9	WNFI	‖‖	⚡	AM DRIVE	Amer. Top 40 Su 8am–12N; Direct Hits Su 9–11pm; UK Chart Attack Su 11pm–12M
JACKSONVILLE AREA CONTINUED ON NEXT PAGE						

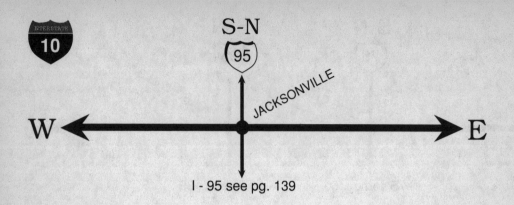

S-N
95
JACKSONVILLE

W ◄━━━━━━━━━━━━━━━━━━━━━━━━━► E

I - 95 see pg. 139

FORMAT ♪ TUNE TO	STATION	SIGNAL POWER	TRAFFIC REPORT	NEWS	SPECIAL PROGRAMMING
CONTINUATION OF JACKSONVILLE AREA					
TOP40	101.5	WHJX	‖‖			**R & B**
🎸	104.5	WFYV	‖‖	🚗	AM DRIVE	Morn. Humor; Dangerous Exposure Su 11pm
🎸☮	100.7	WIOI	‖‖	🚗	AM DRIVE	Morn. Humor
🤠🎵	92.1	WJXR	‖	🚗	🕐	Morn. Humor; Spts.; Swap Shop & Auction Sa AM; Farm Reports M–F 5:30am
🤠🎵	93.5	WLKC	‖		🕐	Fish. Report 7:30am, 4:45pm; P. Harvey 12:45pm, 8:45pm; Spts. News 6:30, 9:30am
🤠🎵	99.1	WQIK	‖‖	🚗	MORE	News 3:50, 4:50pm; Morn. Humor; Hit Kicker Sunday Magazine 6:30–7am
🤠🎵	107.3	WCRJ	‖‖	🚗	AM DRIVE	Top 30 Sa 6–9am; Sunday Sunrise 7:30am; Ctry. Music Top 10 Su 10pm
☀OLDIES	96.9	WKQL	‖‖	🚗	AM DRIVE	Dick Clark Su 8pm–12M; Daily Nooner M–F 12N; 60's at 6pm M–F; 70's at 7pm M–F
R&B	92.7	WZAZ	‖	🚗	AM DRIVE	Morn. Humor; Mark Little (Talk) Su 4pm
E ✿ Z	90.9	WKTZ	‖‖	◈	🕐	
🎹	89.9	WJCT	‖‖		MORE	**NPR; APR; JAZZ; BIG BAND;** The Metro/Interview/Variety M–F 4am
✝✝✝	88.1	WNCM	‖	◈	🕐	**CHRISTIAN CONTEMPORARY**
✝✝✝	88.7	WJFR	‖		AM & PM DRIVE	
✝✝✝	91.7	WNLE	‖‖	◈	🕐	**SOUTHERN GOSPEL; SACRED;** Minirth-Meier Clinic 1pm; Bible Conf. Time 11am
TALK	600	WOKV	‖	🚗	MORE	**NEWS;** Stk. Mkt. 6:50, 7:50, 8:50am, 5:50pm; Spts.: U. of FL, Dolphins, Magic
NORTH OR SOUTH ON I-95 SEE PAGE 139					

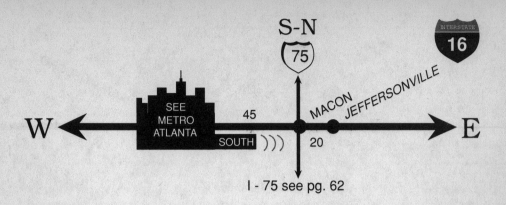

FORMAT ♪ TUNE TO		STATION	SIGNAL POWER	TRAFFIC REPORT	NEWS	SPECIAL PROGRAMMING
NORTHWEST TO ATLANTA SEE PAGE 166						
MACON AREA						
Adult Pop	107.9	WPEZ	‖‖	◇	🕐	Lunchtime at the Oldies M–F 12N–1pm; Request Oldies M–F 7–10pm; Sprgld. Sa 7pm
Top40	99.1	WAYS	‖‖	◇	AM & PM DRIVE	Opn. Hse. Prty. Sa 7pm–12M; C. Kasem Top 40 Su 10am–2pm; Hitline USA Su 11pm
Top40	101.7	WPPR	‖	◇		R. Dee's Top 40 Su 10am; S. Shannon Ctdwn. Sa 9pm; J. Landers Ctdwn. Su 8pm
🎸	106.3	WQBZ	‖		AM DRIVE	Electric Lunch M–F 12N; Psych. Psupper M–F 6pm; Concert Calendar M–F 4:35pm
👢	97.9	WKXK	‖	◇	🕐	Morn. Humor; Spts.: U. of Georgia
👢	104.1	WYAI	‖‖	🚗	AM DRIVE	Local Ctry. Ctdwn. Sa 7–10am; NASCAR Ctry. Su 8–11am; Public Affairs Su 5–8am
👢	105.3	WDEN	‖‖	◇	🕐	Inside Macon Su 2pm; American Ctry. Ctdwn. Su 10am; Top 30 Su 8pm
☀OLDIES	107.1	WQXM	‖	◇	AM & PM DRIVE	Morn. Humor; Solid Gold Sa 7pm–12M; US Hall of Fame Su 5–10pm
R&B	100.1	WFXM	‖	◇	AM DRIVE	Morn. Humor; On the Phone with Tyrone M–F 7:45am; Inside Middle Georgia Su 6am
R&B	100.9	WPGA	‖	◇	🕐	Pillow Talk M–F 9pm–12M; All Night Theatre M–F 12M
🎹	88.1	WJSP	‖‖	◇	MORE	**NPR; APR; JAZZ** Sa 9am–12N; News: W.E. Sa & Su 8–10am; Thistle & Shamrock Sa 8pm
✝✝✝	91.3	WJTG	‖‖		🕐	Unshackled M–F 6:30pm; Focus on the Fam. M–F 8pm, Sa 6pm; Su. Sounds 4:05pm
✝✝✝	91.5	WPWB	‖‖		🕐	Focus on the Family 8am, 7pm; Minirth-Meier Clinic 1pm; In Touch 9am, 8pm
✝✝✝	93.3	WVFJ	‖‖	◇	🕐	Focus on the Family M–F 10:30am; Point of View M–F 2pm; In Touch M–F 9:05am, 9pm

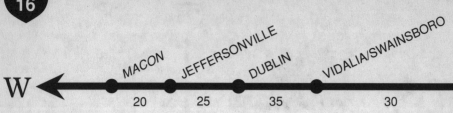

W ← MACON — JEFFERSONVILLE — DUBLIN — VIDALIA/SWAINSBORO

20   25   35   30

FORMAT / TUNE TO		STATION	SIGNAL POWER	TRAFFIC REPORT	NEWS	SPECIAL PROGRAMMING
JEFFERSONVILLE AREA						
🤠	96.7	WVMG	‖		SEE S.P.	News 7am, 12N, 5pm; Stk. Mkt. 6:45am, 12:15, 5:15pm; Ctry. Today Su 6pm
🎹	89.7	WDCO	‖‖	◇	MORE	**NPR; APR; JAZZ** Sa 9am–12N; News: W.E. Sa & Su 8–10am; Thistle & Shamrock Sa 8pm
DUBLIN AREA						
Adult Cor	92.7	WKKZ	‖	◇	🕐	Morn. Humor; Sprgld. Sa 7pm–2am; Cruisin' Amer. with Cousin Brucie F 10pm–1am
Top40	95.9	WQZY	‖‖	◇	🕐	P. Harvey Daily 8:30am, 12:06pm; C. Kasem Su 12N–4pm; Memories F 6–10pm
VIDALIA/SWAINSBORO AREA						
Top40	97.7	WTCQ	‖		SEE S.P.	News 7:45, 11:45am, 4:45pm; Top 40 Ctdwn. Su 8pm; Munster Man M–F 7pm
Top40	98.1	WJAT	‖		🕐	News also on the 1/2 hr; C. Kasem Su 7am; Rick Dee Su 6pm; Dr. Demento Su 10pm
🤠	92.5	WLYU	‖	◇	SEE S.P.	News 7am, 12N, 5pm; Spts.: Local, Georgia Southern U., Falcons; Ctry. Ctdwn. Sa 10am
🤠	103.9	WXRS	‖	◇	🕐	Morn. Humor; American Farmer M–F 12:20pm; 4H Sa 11:30am
☀OLDIES	101.7	WKTM	‖	◇	🕐	Classic Cafe M–F 12N–1pm; Lost Lennon Tapes Su 5pm; Dr. Demento Sa 10pm–12M
CLAXTON/STATESBORO AREA						
Top40	100.1	WMCD	‖	◇	SEE S.P.	News 7:30, 8:30am, 5:30pm; Stk. Mkt. 7:30am, 6:15pm
Top40	104.9	WHCG	‖		AM DRIVE	Dave Sholin's Insider Sa 6–10am; On the Radio Su 4pm; The Ctdwn. Su 5pm
🤠	107.1	WCLA	‖	◇	🕐	Morn. Humor; Stk. Mkt. 12:20pm; Spts.: Local, U. of GA, Falcons, Braves
🎓	91.9	WVGS	‖			Georgia Southern College

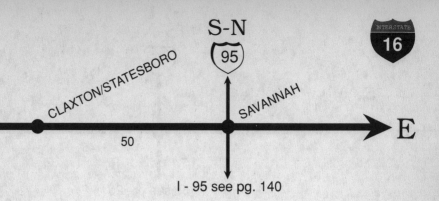

CLAXTON/STATESBORO

SAVANNAH

E

50

I - 95 see pg. 140

FORMAT / TUNE TO		STATION	SIGNAL POWER	TRAFFIC REPORT	NEWS	SPECIAL PROGRAMMING
SAVANNAH AREA						
Adult Cor	97.3	WAEV	|||	🚗	AM DRIVE	Morn. Humor
Adult Cor	98.7	WYKZ	|||	🚗	AM DRIVE	Morn. Humor; Jobline 7:05am
Adult Cor	106.1	WHHR	||	🚗	🕐	News also on the 1/2 hr; Morn. Humor; Stk. Mkt. 9:30am; Italian Su 10–11am
Adult Cor	107.9	WIJY	|||	⚡	AM & PM DRIVE	**LITE HITS;** Jazz Trax Su 6pm
Top40	99.7	WHTK	|||	⚡	SEE S.P.	News 11am, 5pm; D. Sholin's Insider Sa 6–10am; Rick Dee's Top 40 Su 7–10am
Top40	102.1	WZAT	|||	🚗	AM DRIVE	Morn. Humor
🎸	95.5	WIXV	|||	🚗	AM DRIVE	Morn. Humor; 5:00 Traffic Jam M–F 5pm; Electric Lunch (Classic Rock) M–F 12N
🤠	92.1	WSKX	||			**LITE ROCK;** Morn. Humor; Stk. Mkt. AM Drive
🤠	94.1	WCHY	|||	⚡	AM DRIVE	American Ctry. Ctdwn. Sa 6pm; Weekly Ctry. Music Ctdwn. Su 9pm
☀OLDIES	106.9	WLOW	|||	🚗	🕐	**BIG BAND; EASY LISTENING;** L. King Su–F 11pm–5am; America in the Morning 5–6am
R&B	93.1	WEAS	|||		SEE S.P.	News 6:50am, 4:50pm; Spts. News 6:30, 7:30am; On the Move/T. Joyner Sa 6–9am
Lite Hits	96.5	WJCL	|||	🚗	🕐	Jazz Sa 7–10pm; Breeze Special Sa 10pm–12M; Breakfast with Burl Su 6–9am
🎹	89.9	WJWJ	||	⚡	MORE	**NPR;** News 12N, W.E. Sa 10am–12N; Prairie Home Compan. Sa 6pm; Car Talk Sa 9am
🎹	91.1	WSVH	|||	⚡	MORE	**NPR; APR;** News: W.E. Sa & Su 10–11am, ATC 5–6pm; Symph./Orch. M–Thu 8–10pm
✝✝✝	89.5	WYFS	|||			
✝✝✝	103.9	WGEC	||	⚡	🕐	Morn. Lite M–F 6–8am; Focus on Fam. M–F 10am, 7pm; Inst. for Liv. M–F 8am, 7:30pm

NORTH OR SOUTH ON I-95 SEE PAGE 140

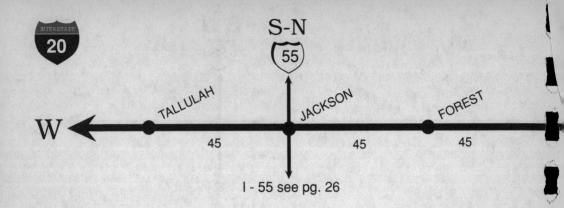

I - 55 see pg. 26

FORMAT ♪ TUNE TO		STATION	SIGNAL POWER	TRAFFIC REPORT	NEWS	SPECIAL PROGRAMMING
FARTHER WEST SEE WESTERN EDITION						
TALLULAH/VICKSBURG AREA						
🎸	106.7	WSTZ	|||	🚗	A.M. DRIVE	Up Close Th 10pm; Desert Island Discs Tu 10pm; Flashback Su 8–9pm
👢	95.1	WQNZ	|||	◇	🕐	Farm Report 10:30am; Paul Harvey 12N; Stk. Mkt. 5pm
👢	98.7	WIIN	|||			
👢	101.1	WBBV	||	◇	🕐	News on 1/2 hr; Agri. Rpts. 6:30am, 12:15, 2:36pm; Spts.News 7:05am, 12:05, 3:15pm
👢	104.9	KBYO	||			
JACKSON AREA						
AdultPop	96.3	WSLI	|||	🚗		
Top40	95.5	WOHT	|||	🚗	A.M. DRIVE	**R & B;** Morn. Humor; Public Affairs Su 6–8am
👢	102.9	WMSI	|||	🚗	🕐	Farm Report 5:30am; Paul Harvey 7:30am, 12N, 6pm
☼OLDIES	94.7	WTYX	|||	🚗	A.M. DRIVE	Morn. Humor
R&B	99.7	WJMI	|||	🚗	AM & PM DRIVE	The Ctdwn. Su 10am–12N; On the Move Sa 6–9pm; Power Jam Sa 9pm–12M
E ✿ Z	101.7	WLIN	||	◇	🕐	
🐟	91.3	WMPN	|||		MORE	**NPR; APR;** News: W.E. Sa & Su 8–11am; Mktplace M–F 6:30–7pm; Jazz M–F 10pm
ek-lek-tik	90.1	WMPR	|||	🚗	🕐	**NPR;** Top 40; Religious; R & B; Rap; Oldies; Jazz; Community Affairs programs
🎓	88.5	WJSU	||			**JAZZ; R & B;** Jackson State U.
✝✝✝	93.5	WHJT	||		🕐	**CHRISTIAN CONTEMPORARY**

S-N
(59)

↑
MERIDIAN ———— YORK ———— EUTAW ————————→ E
25   34

INTERSTATE 20

↓
I - 59 see pg. 30

FORMAT ♪ TUNE TO	STATION	SIGNAL POWER	TRAFFIC REPORT	NEWS	SPECIAL PROGRAMMING
✝✝✝ 97.7	WRJH	‖			
FOREST AREA					
🎸 92.5	WQST	‖‖	🚗	🕐	Amer. Ctry. Ctdwn. Su 12N–4pm; NASCAR Ctry. Sa 11pm–12M
🎸 95.9	WBBN	‖‖	🚗	🕐	Farm Market M–F 12:30pm; Spts. News each newscast
🎸 105.1	WBKJ	‖‖	◇	🕐	Morn. Humor
🎸 106.3	WMYQ				
(Lite Hits) 107.5	WMJW	‖‖	🚗	(SEE S.P.)	News 6, 7am; Solid Gold Sunday all oldies
MERIDIAN AREA					
TOP40 100.3	WNSL	‖‖	◇	(SEE S.P.)	News 7:26am, 12:51, 3:51pm; Paul Harvey 7:30am, 12:15, 5pm
TOP40 101.3	WJDQ	‖‖		(MORE)	News 12N; Lunchtime at the Oldies M–F 12:05pm; Casey Kasem Sa 6pm
🎸 95.1	WZMP	‖‖			
🎸 97.1	WOKK	‖‖	◇	(MORE)	News 12N, Paul Harvey
🎸 102.5	WJKX	‖‖			
🎹 88.1	WMAW	‖‖		(MORE)	**NPR; APR;** News: W.E. Sa & Su 8–11am, ATC 5–6pm, Mktpl. M–F 6:30–7pm; Jz. M–F 10pm
YORK AREA					
R&B 99.3	WSLY	‖	🚗	(SEE S.P.)	**GOSPEL** M–F 5–6am, Su All Day; News 8:55am, 12:55, 3:55pm; Public Affairs
✝✝✝ 91.9	WMBV	‖‖	◇	🕐	In Touch M–F 8am & 7pm; Focus on the Fam. M–F 6pm; Minirth-Meier Clinic M–F 12N

W ← YORK EUTAW 30 · SEE METRO BIRMINGHAM · EAST WEST · SEE METRO ATLANTA · EAST WEST 30 · 35

FORMAT ♪ TUNE TO	STATION	SIGNAL POWER	TRAFFIC REPORT	NEWS	SPECIAL PROGRAMMING
EUTAW AREA					
T°P40 106.3	WZNJ	‖		AM & PM DRIVE	
R&B 104.3	WIDO	‖	🚗	🕐	News also on the hour; Top 30 Ctdwn. Sa 11am–2pm
SEE BIRMINGHAM METRO PAGE 170					
SEE ATLANTA METRO PAGE 166					
GREENSBORO AREA					
Adult Pop 107.9	WPEZ	‖‖	◇	🕐	Lunchtime at the Oldies M–F 12N–1pm; Req. Old. M–F 7–10pm; Suprgold. Sa 7pm
T°P40 99.1	WAYS	‖‖	◇	AM & PM DRIVE	Opn. Hse. Prty. Sa 7pm–12M; C. Kasem Top 40 Su 10am–2pm; Hitline USA Su 11pm
🤠 105.3	WDEN	‖‖	◇	🕐	Inside Macon Su 2pm; American Ctry. Ctdwn. Su 10am; Top 30 Su 8pm
R&B 103.9	WGRG	‖			
WASHINGTON AREA					
T°P40 97.7	WSKS				
OLDIES 100.1	WLOV	‖	◇	🕐	Local Events 7:05am, 12:05pm; Trading Post 7:23am, 12:23pm; Agri. News 6:15am
THOMSON AREA					
🤠 101.7	WTHO	‖	🚗	🕐	Ctry. Saturday Night 9:05–10pm

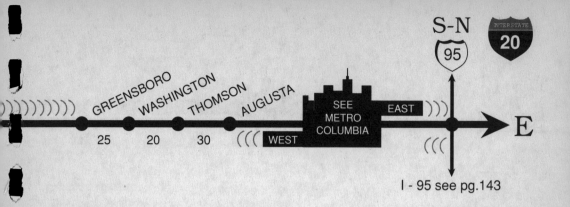

I - 95 see pg.143

FORMAT / TUNE TO		STATION	SIGNAL POWER	TRAFFIC REPORT	NEWS	SPECIAL PROGRAMMING
AUGUSTA AREA						
Adult Pop	102.7	WAJY	‖			
Adult Pop	105.7	WZNY	‖‖			
Top40	102.3	WGUS	‖			R & B
Top40	104.3	WBBQ	‖‖	🚗	🕐	Morn. Humor
🎸	96.3	WRXR	‖‖	A.M. DRIVE		CLASSIC ROCK; The Mad Music Asylum Su 8–9pm; Rockline M 11:30pm–1am
👢	99.5	WKXC	‖‖	🚗	🕐	News also on the 1/2 hr; Morn. Humor
☀OLDIES	94.3	WMTZ	‖	🚗	🕐	Morn. Humor
R&B	103.1	WFXA	‖			
E ❀ Z	98.3	WCNA	‖	◇	🕐	Business News 30 past 6, 7, 8am, 12, 4, 5pm; Spts. News 15 past 7, 8am, 6pm
🎹	89.1	WLJK	‖‖	◇	🌐MORE	NPR; News: W.E. Sa 10am–12N; Prairie Home Comp. Sa 6pm; Radio Rdr. M–F 8am
🎹	90.7	WACG	‖‖		🌐MORE	NPR; APR; News: W.E. Sa & Su 8–10am, ATC 5–6pm; Jazz Sa 9pm; Opera Sa 1:30–5pm
✝✝✝	91.7	WLPE	‖		🕐	Focus on the Fam. M–F 8am, 7pm; Minirth-Meier Clinic M–F 1pm; In Tch. M–F 9am, 8pm
SEE COLUMBIA METRO PAGE 184						
SEE I-95 PAGE 143						

W

FORMAT / TUNE TO		STATION	SIGNAL POWER	TRAFFIC REPORT	NEWS	SPECIAL PROGRAMMING
FARTHER WEST ON I-24 SEE WESTERN EDITION						
PADUCAH AREA						
Adult Pop	100.7	KGMO	|||	◇	AM DRIVE	Morn. Humor
Top 40	96.9	WDDJ	|||	🚗	AM & PM DRIVE	Morn. Humor
Top 40	103.7	WBLN	|||			**ALBUM ROCK**
🎸	98.3	WRIK	||			**TOP 40**
🎸☮	102.3	WCBL	||	◇	🕐	**OLDIES;** Spts.: U. of KY, Cardinals, Local; Reelin' in the Years
👢	93.3	WKYQ	|||			
👢	94.7	WXID	|||	◇	🕐	Morn. Humor; Stk. Mkt. 5:15pm; Spts.: High School, U. of Kentucky
👢	102.9	KEZS	|||	◇	AM DRIVE	Paul Harvey 5:30, 7:30, 11:30am; Spts.: Cardinals, S.E. MO Basketball
E ❄ Z	105.5	WREZ	||			
🎹	91.3	WKMS	|||	◇	MORE	**NPR; APR;** News: W.E. Sa 7–8am, Su 11am–1pm; Jazz M–Th 9pm–12M, F 9–11pm
PRINCETON AREA						
Adult Pop	99.5	WKDQ	|||			
Adult Pop	104.9	WPKY			◇	MORE	News 10am, 12N, 2pm; Spts.: Local; Comm. Affairs M–Sa 4pm; Farm M–F 11:45am
Top 40	93.9	WKTG	|||	◇	MORE	News 12N; Spts.: U. of KY, High School; Church programming Su 6pm–12M
👢	97.7	WHRZ	||	◇	🕐	Back 40 Su 1pm; Overdrive Truckers Top 10 Su 9:05pm; Agri-Net M–Sa 5:20am
👢	101.9	WKYA	|||		🕐	Spts.: U. of Kentucky, CBS Baseball

14

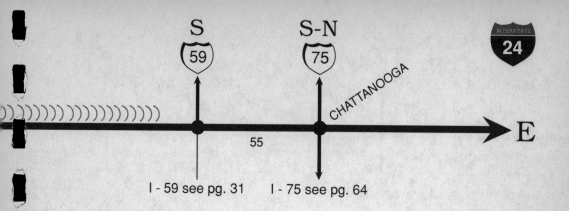

🛡️ 59

🛡️ 75

CHATTANOOGA

🛡️ INTERSTATE 24

55

E

I - 59 see pg. 31
I - 75 see pg. 64

FORMAT ♪ TUNE TO		STATION	SIGNAL POWER	TRAFFIC REPORT	NEWS	SPECIAL PROGRAMMING
Lite Hits	106.3	WBZD	‖			
✝✝✝	89.9	WSOF	‖‖			
SEE NASHVILLE METRO PAGE 202						
CHATTANOOGA AREA						
Adult Pop	97.3	WKXJ	‖‖	🚗	🕐	**TOP 40;** Morn. Humor
Top40	106.5	WSKZ	‖‖			
🎸	102.3	WFXS	‖			
🤠	96.5	WDOD	‖‖	🚗	SEE S.P.	News 7am; Morn. Humor
🤠	100.7	WUSY	‖‖	🚗	🕐	Morn. Humor
☀OLDIES	101.9	WSGC	‖	🚗	AM & PM DRIVE	Morn. Humor
R&B	94.3	WJTT	‖			
Lite Hits	102.7	WBDX	‖	🚗	AM & PM DRIVE	Dick Clark Sa 6–10am; Special of the Week Su 6–9am; Love Songs M–Su 7pm–12M
E ❄ Z	92.3	WDEF	‖‖	🚗	🕐	Stk. Mkt. 4:05, 5:05pm; Spts. News 4:30pm
🎹	90.5	WSMC	‖‖	🚗	MORE	**NPR;** Stk. Mkt. M–F 7:50am, 4:45pm; Classics by Request Su 8pm
🎺	88.1	WUTC	‖‖	◇	SEE S.P.	**NPR; APR;** News 8, 9, 10am, 12N; MonitoRadio M–F 6–7am, 6:30–7pm
✝✝✝	88.9	WMBW	‖‖	🚗	AM & PM DRIVE	Clockwatcher M–F 6:30–8:30am; Minirth-Meier Clinic M–F 1–2pm
✝✝✝	89.7	WDYN	‖‖	◇	🕐	News 12N; How to Manage Your Money M–F 4:45pm; Child. Programs M–F 4:05pm
TALK	1150	WGOW	‖			

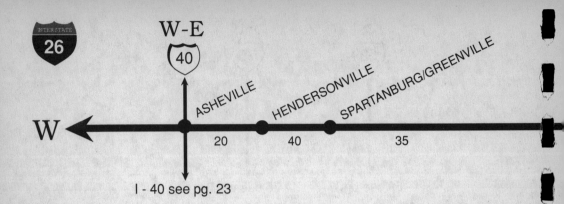

I - 40 see pg. 23

FORMAT ♪ TUNE TO		STATION	SIGNAL POWER	TRAFFIC REPORT	NEWS	SPECIAL PROGRAMMING
WEST OR EAST ON I-40 SEE PAGE 23						
ASHEVILLE AREA						
T°P40	99.9	WKSF	‖‖‖	🚗	SPOT NEWS	Morn. Humor
👢	104.9	WQNS	‖‖‖			
🎹	88.1	WCQS	‖‖	⚡	MORE	**NPR;** News 12N; Stk. Mkt. M–F 12N & 4:30pm; Stardate 7:30am & 6:30pm
✝✝✝	91.3	WKDB	‖‖	⚡	🕐	**BLACK GOSPEL**
✝✝✝	106.9	WMIT	‖‖‖	⚡	🕐	
HENDERSONVILLE AREA						
A♪dult Cor	102.5	WMYI	‖‖‖			
🎺	93.3	WBBO	‖‖‖	⚡	MORE	News 12:45pm; Stk. Mkt. 7:15pm; Spts. Minute 7:15, 8:15am, 4:15, 5:15pm
ek-lek´-tik	88.7	WNCW	‖‖‖	⚡	MORE	**NPR;** News: W.E. Sa & Su 6–10am; Crossroads M–F 9am–5pm; Car Talk Sa 12N
SPARTANBURG/GREENVILLE AREA						
T°P40	101.9	WCKZ	‖‖‖	🚗	AM DRIVE	Morn. Humor; Thunderstorm (Mix) Sa 10pm–12M
T°P40	107.3	WANS	‖‖‖	🚗	AM DRIVE	Morn. Humor
🎸	101.1	WCKN	‖‖‖			**OLDIES**
🎸	96.5	WPLS	‖		SEE SP	News 8, 10am, 4, 6pm; Top 35 W 7pm; Jazz Su 5–7pm; Dance 9–11pm; Class. Su 1–3pm
👢	92.5	WESC	‖‖‖	🚗	AM DRIVE	Spts.: U. of South Carolina Football
👢	100.5	WSSL	‖‖‖			

CLINTON 20 — SEE METRO COLUMBIA — WEST — E

FORMAT 🎵 TUNE TO		STATION	SIGNAL POWER	TRAFFIC REPORT	NEWS	SPECIAL PROGRAMMING
🥾	105.3	WAGI	|||	⚡	🕐	Gospel Evenings
☀️ OLDIES	93.7	WFBC	|||	🚗	AM DRIVE	Oldies Cafe M–F 12N–1pm; Five o'clock Freeway Freebees M–F 5–6pm
☀️ OLDIES	96.1	WWMG	|||	🚗	AM DRIVE	Morn. Humor; Sunday Nite at the Beach 7pm–12M
R&B	103.9	WLWZ	||			
E ❄ Z	94.5	WMUU	|||	🚗	🕐	CLASSICAL M–F 2–3, 7:30–10pm; Su 2–3pm; RELIGIOUS M–F 12M-5am; Stk. Mkt. hourly
E ❄ Z	98.1	WBFM	|||	⚡	🕐	Spts.: Clemson; Wax Works (Nostalgia) M–F 10am, Sa 7–10pm
E ❄ Z	98.9	WSPA	|||	⚡	MORE	News 11am, 1, 3pm; Stk. Mkt. 12:15, 5:15pm; Health Tips 10:15am; Weekly Spec. Sa 7pm
🛋	90.1	WEPR	|||	⚡	MORE	NPR; News: W.E. Sa 10am–12N; Prairie Home Comp. Sa 6pm; Radio Rdr. M–F 8am
✝✝✝	89.3	WLFJ	|||	⚡	MORE	News 12N, 3pm; Morn. Humor
✝✝✝	91.1	WYFG	|||		🕐	
✝✝✝	91.7	WTBI	||			
🎸	910	WORD	||	🚗	🕐	News also on the 1/2 hr, 6–7pm; Spts.: Clemson U; Sportsline M–F 5–6pm
CLINTON AREA						
🥾	96.7	WSCZ	||	🚗	🕐	News also five after hr; Spts.: Clemson U., NASCAR; Amer. Ctry. Ctdwn. Sa 8am
R&B	103.5	WMTY	||	⚡	🕐	On the Move with Tom Joyner Sa 9pm–12M
SEE COLUMBIA METRO PAGE 184						

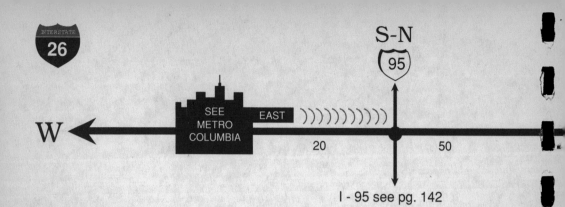

I - 95 see pg. 142

FORMAT ♪ TUNE TO		STATION	SIGNAL POWER	TRAFFIC REPORT	NEWS	SPECIAL PROGRAMMING
SEE COLUMBIA METRO PAGE 184						
CHARLESTON AREA						
Adult Cor	96.9	WXTC	|||	🚗	A M DRIVE	**LITE HITS**; Morn. Humor
Adult Cor	100.7	WSUY	||	🚗	A M DRIVE	News Updates thru day; Morn. Humor; Public Affairs Su 6–7am
Top40	95.1	WSSX	|||	🚗	AM & PM DRIVE	Morn. Humor; Rick Dee's Wkly. Top 40 Sa 6–10am; Amer. Top 40 Su 8am–12N
Top40	107.5	WKQB	|||	🚗	MORE	News 10am, 4pm; Morn. Humor
🎸	96.1	WAVF	|||	🚗		Morn. Humor
🎸☮	98.1	WYBB	|||			
👢🤠	103.5	WEZL	|||	🚗	MORE	News 12N; Morn. Humor; Spts. News 7:15, 8:15, 9:15am, 4:15, 5:15, 6:15pm
☀OLDIES	102.5	WXLY	|||	🚗	A M DRIVE	Morn. Humor; Spts.: Citadel Coll.; Live from 60's Su 6–9am; Beach Show Su 2–5pm
R&B	93.5	WWWZ	||			

N

17

CHARLESTON

E

SHORE RTE. see pg.156

FORMAT ♪ TUNE TO	STATION	SIGNAL POWER	TRAFFIC REPORT	NEWS	SPECIAL PROGRAMMING
R&B 94.3	WUJM	‖	🚗	AM & PM DRIVE	Morn. Humor; Public Affairs Su 5:30–6am
R&B 104.5	WDXZ	‖‖			
🎹 89.3	WSCI	‖‖	◇	MORE	**NPR;** News: W.E. Sa 10am–12N; Prairie Home Comp. Sa 6pm; Radio Rdr. M–F 8am
🎹 105.5	WJYQ	‖			
🎺 101.7	WMGL	‖	🚗	AM & PM DRIVE	**ADULT POPULAR**
✝✝✝ 88.5	WFCH	‖‖			
✝✝✝ 90.7	WYFH	‖‖		🕐	
✝✝✝ 91.5	WKCL	‖‖			Holy Spirit Bible College
TALK 1250	WTMA	‖	🚗	🕐	Extended News 6–9am, 5–7pm; Stk. Mkt. drive times; Spts.: NASCAR Races
SOUTH ON US 17 SEE I-95 PAGE 141					
NORTH ON US 17 (SHORE ROUTE) SEE PAGE 156					

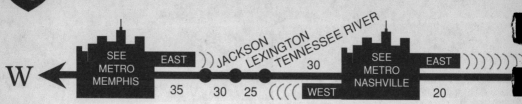

FORMAT ♪ TUNE TO		STATION	SIGNAL POWER	TRAFFIC REPORT	NEWS	SPECIAL PROGRAMMING
SEE MEMPHIS METRO PAGE 196						
JACKSON AREA						
Adult Con	93.1	WNBE	‖			
Adult Con	97.7	WLOT	‖	◇	MORE	News 12N; Morn. Humor
Adult Con	103.1	WMXX	‖	🚗	🕐	**OLDIES;** Lunchtime at the Oldies M–F 12N–1pm; 60's at Six; Dick Clark Su Morn.
Top 40	92.3	WYNU	‖‖	◇	AM & PM DRIVE	**CLASSIC ROCK;** Morn. Humor
Top 40	102.3	WZDQ	‖			
Top 40	105.3	WLSZ	‖			
🤠	104.1	WTNV	‖‖	◇	AM DRIVE	Paul Harvey 7:30, 8:30am, 12N, 5:30pm; Nashville Live Su 7:30pm
R&B	95.9	WFKX	‖			
🎺	91.5	WFHC	‖	◇	🕐	**CLASSICAL** Su 1–5pm; Blues W 7–10pm; Sa 6–10pm; Fresh Air M–F 8–10am
LEXINGTON AREA						
Adult Con	99.3	WZLT	‖	◇	SEE S.P.	News: 7am, 12N, 4pm; Spts.: Cardinals, College; All Request Sa 7–10pm
🎻	100.9	WHZZ	‖			**TOP 40**
🤠	106.9	WWYN	‖‖			
TENNESSEE RIVER AREA						
Adult Con	98.3	WRJB	‖			
🤠	94.3	WIST	‖	◇	🕐	**OLDIES; GOSPEL;** News on the hour in the evenings; Farm News M–F mornings

CARTHAGE — 25 — COOKEVILLE — 30 — CROSSVILLE — 30 — HARRIMAN — 20 — OAK RIDGE → E

FORMAT / TUNE TO	STATION	SIGNAL POWER	TRAFFIC REPORT	NEWS	SPECIAL PROGRAMMING
SEE NASHVILLE METRO PAGE 202					
CARTHAGE AREA					
(country) 101.7	WJLE	‖			
(country) 102.3	WUCZ	‖	⚡	(MORE)	News 12N
COOKEVILLE AREA					
Adult Pop 98.3	WHUB	‖	⚡	🕐	News also on the 1/2 hour
Top 40 107.1	WRJT	‖		(AM DRIVE)	Rick Dees Sa 6–10am; Hot Mix Sa 8pm–12M; Future Hits Su 7–8am; S. Shannon Su 6pm
(rock) 105.5	WSMT	‖	🚗	🕐	Morn. Humor; Don Steel (Oldies) Su 9am–12N
(country) 94.7	WGSQ	‖‖‖			
E ❀ Z 95.9	WXKG	‖			
ek-lek'-tik 88.5	WTTU	‖		(SEE S.P.)	**DANCE/RAP; JAZZ; NEW METAL; CHRISTIAN CONTEMPORARY;** News 11am, 4pm
CROSSVILLE AREA					
Adult Pop 99.3	WXVL	‖			
(country) 102.5	WEGE	‖	⚡	🕐	P. Harvey 7:30, 11:30am, 5:10pm; Nostalgia/Big Band Sa 7pm–12M; Oldies F 7–9pm
HARRIMAN AREA					
Adult Pop 93.9	WAYA	‖		🕐	Morning Interview 7:30am
(country) 92.7	WLIQ	‖	⚡	(SEE S.P.)	News 7, 9, 10am, 12N, 5pm; Ctry. Top 30 Su 1–5pm; Farm News M–F 9:30am
(country) 101.3	WECO	‖	⚡	🕐	Spts.: U. of Tennessee; American Ctry. Ctdwn. Su 5–9pm

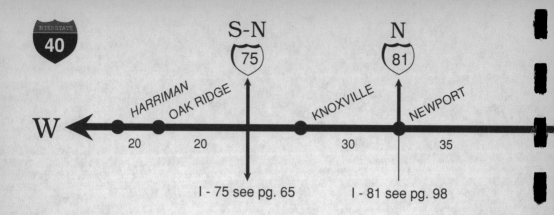

S-N 🛡75

N 🛡81

I - 75 see pg. 65   I - 81 see pg. 98

FORMAT 🎵 TUNE TO		STATION	SIGNAL POWER	TRAFFIC REPORT	NEWS	SPECIAL PROGRAMMING
OAK RIDGE AREA						
TOP 40	100.3	WOKI	‖‖	⬦	A M DRIVE	
🤠	93.5	WLIL	‖	⬦	🕐	**RELIG.;** News also on the 1/2 hr; Stk. Mkt. 40 past hr; Spts. News 20 after & 10 to hr.
🤠	98.3	WDEH	‖	⬦	🕐	**SOUTHERN GOSPEL;** Mull's Singing Convention M–F 4–6pm, Sa 6:30–8:30pm
🤠	98.7	WXVO	‖	⬦	🕐	American Ctry. Ctdwn. Sa 6–10pm; Ctry. Classics Su 6–9pm
🤠	99.1	WLOD	‖	🚗	AM & PM DRIVE	Farm Market Reports 5am; Agri. Weather 12N; Tobacco Talk Program F 12:05pm
☀OLDIES	94.3	WKNF	‖	🚗	A M DRIVE	
KNOXVILLE AREA						
Adult Pop	102.1	WMYU	‖‖	🚗	🕐	Morn. Humor
🎸	93.1	WWZZ	‖			Classic CD Su 12M
🎸	103.5	WIMZ	‖‖	🚗	A M DRIVE	Morn. Humor; Probe Su 7:30–8am; Pirate Radio Sa 7pm–12M; Z Rock Su 7–11pm
🤠	95.7	WGAP	‖			
🤠	107.7	WIVK	‖‖	🚗	MORE	News 12N; Morn. Humor
Lite Hits	97.5	WEZK	‖‖			
🎹	91.9	WUOT	‖‖	⬦	MORE	**NPR; APR;** ATC Sa & Su 5–6pm; Frsh. Air M–F 4–5pm; Opera Sa 1:30–4pm; Jazz Sa 9pm
✝✝✝	95.3	WYFC	‖			
TALK	850	WUTK	‖‖			U. of Tennessee

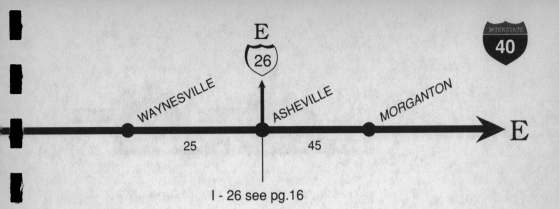

E

26

WAYNESVILLE   ASHEVILLE   MORGANTON

25   45

INTERSTATE
40

E

I - 26 see pg.16

FORMAT / TUNE TO	STATION	SIGNAL POWER	TRAFFIC REPORT	NEWS	SPECIAL PROGRAMMING
NEWPORT AREA					
Adult Pop	94.9 WIKQ	‖‖	◇	🕐	Spts.: U. of Tennessee
Adult Pop	95.9 WAZI	‖	◇	🕐	**TOP 40**
Top40	101.5 WQUT	‖‖	◇	MORE	News 12N; Morn. Humor; Casey Kasem Su 9am–1pm
👢	99.3 WNOX	‖	🚗	🕐	News also on the 1/2 hr; Business Reports hourly; Spts. News
👢	105.5 WSEV	‖			
🎹	89.5 WETS	‖‖	MORE		**NPR; APR;** News: W.E. Sa & Su 8–10am; Jazz M–Thu 10pm–1am, F, Sa, Su 12M–1am
WAYNESVILLE					
👢	104.9 WQNS	‖‖	🚗	🕐	Morn. Humor; Spts.: NASCAR, Local High School; Ctry. Ctdwn. Sa 9am–12N
ASHEVILLE AREA					
Adult Pop	93.7 WFBC	‖‖	🚗	AM DRIVE	Oldies Cafe M–F 12N–1pm; Five o'clock Freeway Freebees M–F 5–6pm
Adult Pop	102.5 WMYI	‖‖			
Top40	99.9 WKSF	‖‖	🚗	SPOT NEWS	Morn. Humor
👢	92.5 WESC	‖‖	🚗	AM DRIVE	Spts.: U. of South Carolina Football
🎹	88.1 WCQS	‖	◇	MORE	**NPR;** News 12N; Stk. Mkt. M–F 12N & 4:30pm; Stardate 7:30am & 6:30pm
✝✝✝	91.3 WKDB	‖	◇	🕐	**BLACK GOSPEL**
✝✝✝	106.9 WMIT	‖‖	◇	🕐	

W ← ASHEVILLE MORGANTON 20 NORTH SEE METRO CHARLOTTE NORTH WEST SEE METRO WINSTON SALEM ETC. EAST 25 45

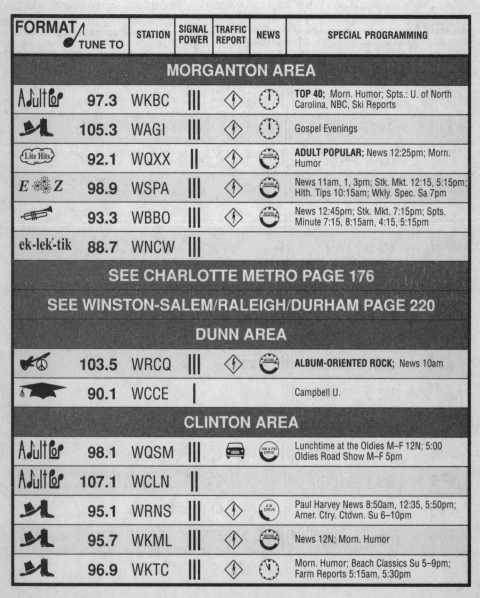

FORMAT ♪ TUNE TO	STATION	SIGNAL POWER	TRAFFIC REPORT	NEWS	SPECIAL PROGRAMMING
MORGANTON AREA					
Adult Pop	97.3 WKBC	|||	◇	🕐	**TOP 40;** Morn. Humor; Spts.: U. of North Carolina, NBC, Ski Reports
👢	105.3 WAGI	|||	◇	🕐	Gospel Evenings
Lite Hits	92.1 WQXX	||	◇	MORE	**ADULT POPULAR;** News 12:25pm; Morn. Humor
E ❄ Z	98.9 WSPA	|||	◇	MORE	News 11am, 1, 3pm; Stk. Mkt. 12:15, 5:15pm; Hlth. Tips 10:15am; Wkly. Spec. Sa 7pm
🎺	93.3 WBBO	|||	◇	MORE	News 12:45pm; Stk. Mkt. 7:15pm; Spts. Minute 7:15, 8:15am, 4:15, 5:15pm
ek-lek´-tik	88.7 WNCW	|||			
SEE CHARLOTTE METRO PAGE 176					
SEE WINSTON-SALEM/RALEIGH/DURHAM PAGE 220					
DUNN AREA					
🎸	103.5 WRCQ	|||	◇	MORE	**ALBUM-ORIENTED ROCK;** News 10am
🎓	90.1 WCCE					Campbell U.
CLINTON AREA					
Adult Pop	98.1 WQSM	|||	🚐	AM & PM DRIVE	Lunchtime at the Oldies M–F 12N; 5:00 Oldies Road Show M–F 5pm
Adult Pop	107.1 WCLN	||			
👢	95.1 WRNS	|||	◇	AM DRIVE	Paul Harvey News 8:50am, 12:35, 5:50pm; Amer. Ctry. Ctdwn. Su 6–10pm
👢	95.7 WKML	|||	◇	MORE	News 12N; Morn. Humor
👢	96.9 WKTC	|||	◇	🕐	Morn. Humor; Beach Classics Su 5–9pm; Farm Reports 5:15am, 5:30pm

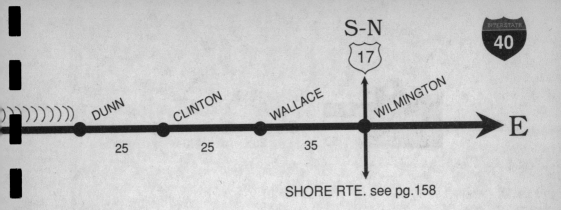

S-N
17

INTERSTATE 40

DUNN — CLINTON — WALLACE — WILMINGTON — E

25   25   35

SHORE RTE. see pg.158

FORMAT / TUNE TO	STATION	SIGNAL POWER	TRAFFIC REPORT	NEWS	SPECIAL PROGRAMMING
R & B 102.3	WOKN	‖			
E Z 107.9	WNCT	‖‖	◇	MORE	News 10, 11am, 3pm; Stk. Mkt. 10:15am, 2:15, 4:15pm; Frank Sinatra Sa 8–10pm
🎹 89.1	WFSS	‖‖	◇	MORE	**NPR;** Contemporary Gospel Su 6am–12N; Latin Mus. Sa 10am–12N; Reggae Sa 12N
WALLACE AREA					
Adult Pop 94.3	WZKB	‖	◇	MORE	News 12N; Beach Music Sa 5–7pm; Christian Rock Su 7–8am & 7–8pm
Top 40 99.1	WZFX	‖‖	🚗	◷	**R & B;** Jazz Styles Su 7pm–12M; Fox Rock F & Sa 7pm–12M
Top 40 99.9	WVBS	‖‖	🚗	AM & PM DRIVE	Office Request Lunch Hour M–F 12N–1pm; Breakfast Club M–F 7–9am
OLDIES 98.7	WKOO	‖‖			
R & B 101.9	WIKS	‖‖			
🎓 89.3	WTEB	‖‖			Craven Community College
WILMINGTON AREA					
Adult Pop 97.3	WMFD	‖‖	◇	◷	**JAZZ;** Morn. Humor
Adult Pop 102.7	WGNI	‖‖	🚗	◷	Morn. Humor
🎸 107.5	WSFM	‖‖	◇	AM & PM DRIVE	**ALBUM ROCK;** Flashback Su 8pm; Westwood One Presents (Concert) Su 10am
👢 101.3	WWQQ	‖‖	🚗	◷	Talk Shows; American Ctry. Ctdwn.; Countryline USA
🎹 91.3	WHQR	‖‖	◇	MORE	**NPR; APR; JAZZ** Sa 10:30am–12N, 10pm–12M, Su 10pm–1am; News: W.E. Sa 8–10am
NORTH OR SOUTH ON US 17 SEE PAGE 158					

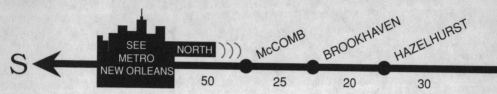

FORMAT ♪ TUNE TO		STATION	SIGNAL POWER	TRAFFIC REPORT	NEWS	SPECIAL PROGRAMMING
SEE NEW ORLEANS METRO PAGE 204						
McCOMB AREA						
Adult Pop	94.1	WXLT	‖‖			
Top40	105.7	WAKH	‖‖	◇	MORE	**ADULT POPULAR;** News 12:30, 1:30pm
Top40	107.9	WZKX	‖	◇	A.M. DRIVE	Morn. Humor
BROOKHAVEN AREA						
🥾	92.1	WBKN	‖	◇	🕐	Paul Harvey; Morn. Humor
🥾	95.1	WQNZ	‖‖	◇	🕐	Farm Report 10:30am; Paul Harvey 12N; Stk. Mkt. 5pm
🎹	88.9	WMAU	‖‖		MORE	News: W.E. Sa & Su 8–11am; ATC 5–6pm; Mktpl. M–F 6:30–7pm; Jazz M–F 10pm
HAZELHURST AREA						
🥾	100.9	WMDC	‖	◇	🕐	News also on the 1/2 hour
Lite Hits	107.5	WMJW	‖‖	🚗	SEE S.P.	News 6, 7am; Solid Gold Sunday all oldies
JACKSON AREA						
Adult Pop	96.3	WSLI	‖‖	🚗		
Top40	95.5	WOHT	‖‖	🚗	A.M. DRIVE	R & B; Morn. Humor; Public Affairs Su 6–8am
🎸	106.7	WSTZ	‖‖	🚗	A.M. DRIVE	Up Close Th 10pm; Desert Island Discs Tu 10pm; Flashback Su 8–9pm
🥾	92.5	WQST	‖‖	🚗	🕐	Amer. Ctry. Ctdwn. Su 12N–4pm; NASCAR Ctry. Sa 11pm–12M
🥾	98.7	WIIN	‖‖			

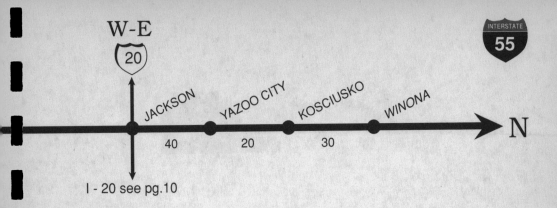

W-E
20
JACKSON　YAZOO CITY　KOSCIUSKO　WINONA
40　20　30
N

I - 20 see pg.10

FORMAT TUNE TO		STATION	SIGNAL POWER	TRAFFIC REPORT	NEWS	SPECIAL PROGRAMMING
🥾	102.9	WMSI	|||	🚗	🕐	Farm Reports 5:30am; Paul Harvey 7:30am, 12N, 6pm
OLDIES	94.7	WTYX	|||	🚗	AM DRIVE	Morn. Humor
R&B	99.7	WJMI	|||	🚗	AM & PM DRIVE	The Ctdwn. Su 10am–12N; On the Move Sa 6–9pm; Power Jam Sa 9pm–12M
E Z	101.7	WLIN	||	⚡	🕐	
🎹	91.3	WMPN	|||		MORE	NPR; APR; News: W.E. Sa & Su 8–11am, ATC 5–6pm; Mktplace M–F 6:30–7pm
ek-lek-tik	90.1	WMPR	|||	🚗	🕐	NPR; Top 40; Religious; R & B; Rap; Oldies; Jazz; Community Affairs programming
🎓	88.5	WJSU	||			JAZZ; R & B; Jackson State U.
†††	97.7	WRJH	||			
†††	93.5	WHJT	||		🕐	CHRISTIAN CONTEMPORARY
YAZOO CITY						
TOP40	92.1	WJNS	||			
KOSCIUSKO AREA						
🥾	102.5	WAGR	||	⚡	🕐	OLDIES 1/2 TIME; Agri. Info. Station 5:30, 6:40, 9:45, 10:15, 11:45am, 12:15, 4:15pm
🥾	105.1	WBKJ	|||	⚡	🕐	Morn. Humor
R&B	106.3	WLTD	||			R & B OLDIES
Lite Hits	89.5	WVTH	|||		🕐	Holmes Jr. College

INTERSTATE 55

FORMAT ♪ TUNE TO		STATION	SIGNAL POWER	TRAFFIC REPORT	NEWS	SPECIAL PROGRAMMING
WINONA AREA						
Adult Pop	93.9	WGRM	‖	◇	🕐	Casey Kasem Sa 2–6pm
Adult Pop	96.1	WLZA	‖‖	🚗	🕐	Requests Friday All Day; Special Programs on weekends
Adult Pop	99.1	WYMX	‖‖		MORE	News 12N
🤠👢	96.7	WONA	‖	◇	🕐	Stk. Mkt. 10:36am, 2:36pm; Spts. Local; Amer. Ctry. Ctdwn. Su 1–5pm
R&B	104.3	WGNL	‖‖			
🎹	90.9	WMAO	‖‖		MORE	**NPR; APR;** News: W.E. Sa & Su 8–11am, ATC 5–6pm; Marketplace M–F 6:30–7pm
✝✝✝	107.9	WFCA	‖‖			
GRENADA AREA						
Adult Pop	98.5	WZLQ	‖‖	◇	🕐	Stk. Mkt. 5:20pm; Supergold Sa 7pm–12M
🤠👢	95.7	WTGY	‖	◇	🕐	Black Music in the Evening
OLDIES	100.1	WQXB	‖		🕐	
SEE MEMPHIS METRO PAGE 196						
NORTH OF MEMPHIS SEE WESTERN EDITION						

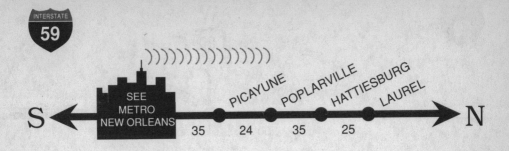

INTERSTATE 59

S ← SEE METRO NEW ORLEANS — 35 — PICAYUNE — 24 — POPLARVILLE — 35 — HATTIESBURG — 25 — LAUREL → N

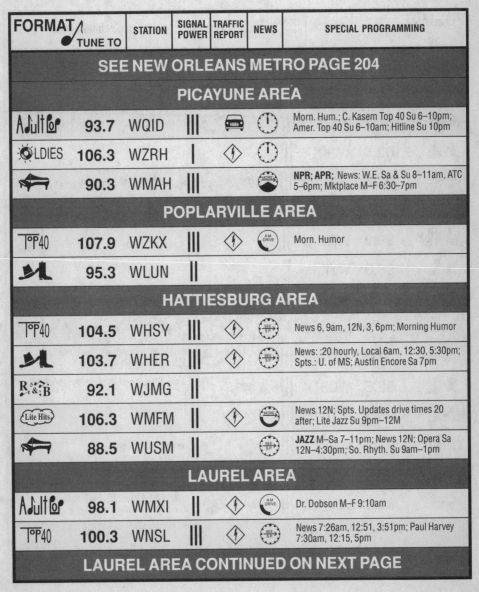

FORMAT ♪ TUNE TO		STATION	SIGNAL POWER	TRAFFIC REPORT	NEWS	SPECIAL PROGRAMMING
SEE NEW ORLEANS METRO PAGE 204						
PICAYUNE AREA						
Adult Pop	93.7	WQID	‖‖	🚗	🕐	Morn. Hum.; C. Kasem Top 40 Su 6–10pm; Amer. Top 40 Su 6–10am; Hitline Su 10pm
Oldies	106.3	WZRH	‖	◇	🕐	
(jazz)	90.3	WMAH	‖‖		MORE	**NPR; APR;** News: W.E. Sa & Su 8–11am, ATC 5–6pm; Mktplace M–F 6:30–7pm
POPLARVILLE AREA						
Top 40	107.9	WZKX	‖‖	◇	AM DRIVE	Morn. Humor
(country)	95.3	WLUN	‖			
HATTIESBURG AREA						
Top 40	104.5	WHSY	‖‖	◇	SEE SP	News 6, 9am, 12N, 3, 6pm; Morning Humor
(country)	103.7	WHER	‖‖	◇	SEE SP	News: :20 hourly, Local 6am, 12:30, 5:30pm; Spts.: U. of MS; Austin Encore Sa 7pm
R & B	92.1	WJMG	‖			
Lite Hits	106.3	WMFM	‖	◇	MORE	News 12N; Spts. Updates drive times 20 after; Lite Jazz Su 9pm–12M
(jazz)	88.5	WUSM	‖		SEE SP	**JAZZ** M–Sa 7–11pm; News 12N; Opera Sa 12N–4:30pm; So. Rhyth. Su 9am–1pm
LAUREL AREA						
Adult Pop	98.1	WMXI	‖	◇	AM DRIVE	Dr. Dobson M–F 9:10am
Top 40	100.3	WNSL	‖‖	◇	SEE SP	News 7:26am, 12:51, 3:51pm; Paul Harvey 7:30am, 12:15, 5pm
LAUREL AREA CONTINUED ON NEXT PAGE						

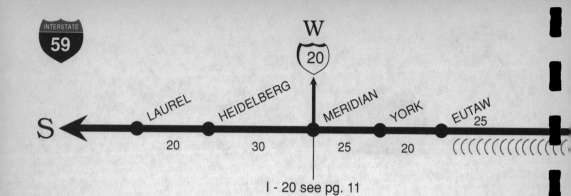

S ← LAUREL · HEIDELBERG · MERIDIAN · YORK · EUTAW 25

W / 20 (Interstate 59)

20 · 30 · 25 · 20

I - 20 see pg. 11

FORMAT ♪ TUNE TO		STATION	SIGNAL POWER	TRAFFIC REPORT	NEWS	SPECIAL PROGRAMMING
CONTINUATION OF LAUREL AREA						
🥾	95.9	WBBN	‖‖	🚗	🕐	Farm Markets M–F 12:30pm; Spts. News each newscast
🥾	101.7	WKNZ	‖	⬦	MORE	News 12N; Spts. News; Listener Contests
🥾	102.5	WJKX	‖‖			
Lite Hits	107.5	WMJW	‖‖	🚗	SEE ▶	News 6, 7am; Solid Gold Sunday all oldies
HEIDELBERG AREA						
Adult Pop	99.3	WEEZ	‖			
🥾	98.3	WYKK	‖			
☼ OLDIES	93.5	WIZK	‖	⬦	🕐	Spts. News; Morn. Humor
MERIDIAN AREA						
TOP40	101.3	WJDQ	‖‖		MORE	News 12N; Lunchtime at the Oldies M–F 12N; C. Kasem Sa 6pm
🥾	92.5	WQST	‖‖	🚗	🕐	Amer. Ctry. Ctdwn. Su 12N-4pm; NASCAR Ctry. Sa 11pm–12M
🥾	95.1	WZMP	‖‖			
🥾	97.1	WOKK	‖‖	⬦	MORE	News 12N; Paul Harvey
🥾	106.3	WMYQ	‖			
🎹	88.1	WMAW	‖‖		MORE	**NPR; APR;** News: W.E. Sa & Su 8–11am, ATC 5–6pm; Marketplace M–F 6:30–7pm

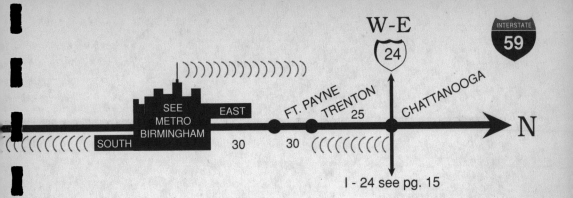

I - 24 see pg. 15

FORMAT ♪ TUNE TO		STATION	SIGNAL POWER	TRAFFIC REPORT	NEWS	SPECIAL PROGRAMMING
YORK AREA						
R&B	99.3	WSLY	‖	🚗	SEE S.P.	**GOSPEL** M–F 5–6am, Su All Day; News 8:55am, 12:55, 3:55pm; Public Affairs
✝✝✝	91.9	WMBV	‖‖	⚡	🕐	In Touch M–F 8am & 7pm; Focus on the Fam. M–F 6pm; Minirth-Meier Clinic M–F 12N
EUTAW AREA						
Top40	106.3	WZNJ	‖		AM & PM DRIVE	
R&B	104.3	WIDO	‖	🚗	🕐	News also on the hour; Top 30 Ctdwn. Sa 11am–2pm
SEE BIRMINGHAM METRO PAGE 170						
FT. PAYNE AREA						
Adult Pop	99.1	WAHR	‖‖	🚗	🕐	**LITE HITS;** Oldies Cafe Show 12N–1pm
👢	98.3	WKEA	‖	⚡	SEE S.P.	News 7 past hour; Spts.: U. of AL; Amer. Ctry. Ctdwn. Su 12N; On a Ctry. Rd. Su 7pm
🛋	89.3	WLRH	‖‖	⚡	MORE	**NPR; APR;** News: W.E. Sa & Su 7–9am, ATC 4–5pm; Mktpl. M–F 5:30–6pm
TRENTON AREA						
👢	101.7	WVSV	‖			
Lite Hits	102.7	WBDX	‖	🚗	AM & PM DRIVE	Dick Clark Sa 6–10am; Special of the Week Su 6–9am; Love Songs M–Su 7pm–12M
FARTHER NORTH ON I-59 SEE I-24 PAGE 15						

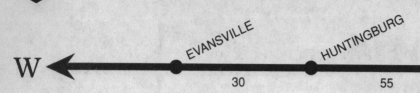

W ←

EVANSVILLE 30

HUNTINGBURG 55

FORMAT ♪ TUNE TO	STATION	SIGNAL POWER	TRAFFIC REPORT	NEWS	SPECIAL PROGRAMMING
FARTHER WEST ON I-64 SEE WESTERN EDITION					
EVANSVILLE AREA					
Adult ♫ 98.1	WRAY	|||	◇⚡	🕐	Stk. Mkt. 9:30am, 2pm; Farm Reports 6:45am; Spts. News 4:15pm, Cardinals
Adult ♫ 99.5	WKDQ	|||			
Adult ♫ 104.1	WIKY	|||			**EASY LISTENING**
Adult ♫ 107.1	WBNL						
🎸 89.1	WVJC	|||	◇	🕐	Illinois Eastern Community College
🎸 103.1	WGBF	||		🕐	Morn. Humor
🎸☮ 94.9	WRBT	|||		A M DRIVE	
👢 97.3	WRUL	|||	◇⚡	🕐	News also on the 1/2 hour; Spts.
👢 105.3	WYNG	|||	🚗	MORE	News 12N, 3pm; Spts. News 7:45am, 5:30pm, John Madden 3:30pm
E ❄ Z 91.1	WVUB	|||	◇⚡	SEE S.P.	**APR;** News 7am, 12N, 4pm; MonitoRadio M–F 6–7am, 4:30–5:30pm, Sa & Su 6–7am
🎹 88.3	WNIN	|||	◇⚡	MORE	**NPR; JAZZ** News 12N, 3pm
🎺 91.5	WUEV	||			**R & B** M–F 7–10pm, Sa 6–11pm; Heav. Met. M–W 11pm; Odys. New Age M, W, F 10am
ek-lek'-tik 89.5	WKPB	|||	◇⚡	MORE	**NPR; APR;** News: Midday Ed. 12N, W.E. Sa 7–8am; Radio Reader M–F 5:30pm
ek-lek'-tik 90.7	WPSR	|||	◇⚡	🕔	**EDUCATION** Programming for Schoolchildren in Grades K–9; News 1, 2pm
✝✝✝ 101.5	WBGW	||		🕔	
HUNTINGBURG AREA					

32

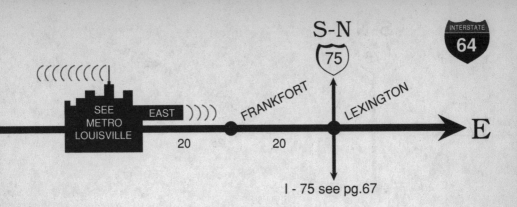

S-N
(75)

INTERSTATE
64

FRANKFORT   LEXINGTON

SEE METRO LOUISVILLE   EAST

20   20

E

I - 75 see pg.67

FORMAT / TUNE TO		STATION	SIGNAL POWER	TRAFFIC REPORT	NEWS	SPECIAL PROGRAMMING
Top40	96.1	WSTO	|||	◇	🕐	Morn. Humor
Top40	104.7	WITZ	|||	🚗	🕐	**ADULT POPULAR**; Amer. Top 40 Su 6pm; NASCAR Racing Su; C. Kasem Sa 3pm
Top40	106.5	WRTB	|||	◇	AM & PM DRIVE	Morning Humor
🤠👢	92.5	WBKR	|||	◇	MORE	News 12N; Morning Humor; Agri. Markets; NASCAR Racing
🤠👢	100.9	WBDC	||	🚗	🕐	Spts. News 8:30am; Farm Reports 6:05, 11:30am, 12:20pm
SEE LOUISVILLE METRO PAGE 194						
FRANKFORT						
Adult Pop	104.9	WKYW	||	◇	🕐	Ctdwn. USA Su 1–4pm; Thur Nite Mus. Special 8pm–12M; Live Dedications F 8pm
🎓	89.9	WVBA	||			Kentucky State U.
LEXINGTON AREA						
Adult Pop	96.7	WCOZ	||			
Adult Pop	100.1	WLFX	||	🚗	SPOT NEWS	Morn. Humor
Top40	94.5	WLAP	|||	◇	AM DRIVE	**ADULT POPULAR**; Morn. Humor
🎸	98.1	WKQQ	|||		MORE	News 11am; Classic Cafe M–F 12N; Block Prty. Sa 7pm–12M
🤠👢	92.9	WVLK	|||	🚗	🕐	Spts.: U. of KY; R. Emery Show 8:55pm; Amer. Ctry. Ctdwn. Sa 8pm–12M, Su 12N
☀️OLDIES	103.1	WTKT	||	🚗	SEE SP'L	News 7:20, 11:20am, 5:20pm; Live from the 60's Su 6pm; Psychic Call-In Su 7:30pm
R&B	102.5	WCKU	||	◇		
LEXINGTON AREA CONTINUED ON NEXT PAGE						

33

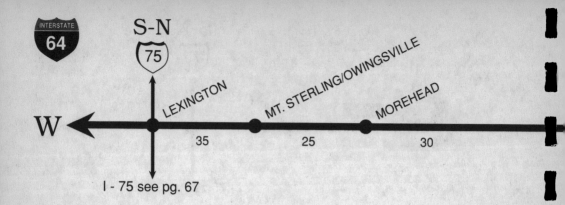

I - 75 see pg. 67

FORMAT ♪ TUNE TO		STATION	SIGNAL POWER	TRAFFIC REPORT	NEWS	SPECIAL PROGRAMMING
	**CONTINUATION OF LEXINGTON AREA**
🛋	88.9	WEKU	‖‖		MORE	**NPR; APR;** News: W.E. Sa & Su 8–10am; Mountain Stage Sa 7–9pm; Car Talk Sa 6pm
✝✝✝	106.3	WJMM	‖	⚡	SEE S.P.	News 6am, 2, 3, 4pm; Blk. Gospel Sa 6pm–12M; Focus on the Family M–F 9:30am, 5pm
=NEWS=	91.3	WUKY	‖‖		MORE	**INFORMATION** 5am–9:30pm; **CLASSICAL** 9:30pm–5am; News: W.E. Sa 8–9am, Su 8am
🎓	88.1	WRFL	‖		SEE S.P.	Pacifica News 7:45–8:15pm; Spts. News 3:20, 11:10pm
	**MT. STERLING/OWINGSVILLE**
👢	105.5	WMST	‖			
👢	107.1	WKCA	‖	⚡	MORE	News 12N, 5pm; Ctry. Ctdwn. Su 1–4pm; Gosp. Su 6am–12N; Farm 5:45am, 12:20pm
	**MOREHEAD**
T0P40	92.1	WMOR	‖			
🎺	90.3	WMKY	‖‖	⚡	🕐	**NPR; FOLK;** ATC M–F 4:30–6pm ; Stk. Mkt. 4:15pm; Spts.: Morehead State U.
	**GRAYSON AREA**
Adult Pop	95.5	WQHY	‖‖	⚡	🕐	Morn. Humor; Spts.: U. of KY Wildcats; Amer. Top 40 Sa 8pm–12M
Adult Pop	102.3	WUGO	‖			
👢	98.9	WSIP	‖‖			
👢	104.1	WPAY	‖‖			**TALK**
	**HUNTINGTON AREA**
Adult Pop	92.7	WCMI	‖	⚡	🕐	Spts.: U. of KY, Cin. Reds, Local Spts. News 20 before & 20 after the hour 10am–7pm

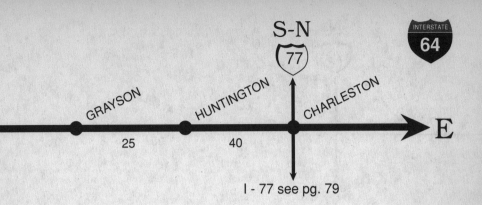

I - 77 see pg. 79

FORMAT ♪ TUNE TO		STATION	SIGNAL POWER	TRAFFIC REPORT	NEWS	SPECIAL PROGRAMMING
A♪ult Pop	93.7	WRVC	|||	🚗	MORE	LITE ROCK; News 12N; Supergold Sa & Su 7pm–12M; Crulsin' Amer. Csn. Brucie Su 7am
TOP40	100.5	WKEE	|||	◇	AM DRIVE	Morn. Humor
🎸☮	101.5	WGTR	|||			
👢🎵	103.3	WTCR	|||	◇	AM DRIVE	Morn. Humor; Stk. Mkt. 4:45pm; Spts. News 6:20, 7:20, 8:20am
👢🎵	105.5	WLGC	||	◇	AM & PM DRIVE	Morn. Humor; Stk. Mkt. 5:10pm; Spts.: U. of KY
E ❀ Z	106.3	WAEZ	||			TALK
E ❀ Z	107.1	WMLV	||			
🎹	89.9	WVWV	||		MORE	NPR; APR; News: W.E. Sa 8–11am, Su 11am-1pm; Mtn. Stage Sa 6–8pm, Su 3–5pm
ek-lek′-tik	88.1	WMUL			◇	MORE	News 12N, 1, 2pm; Prgsv. Rock, AOR, Jazz, Oldies, R & B; Spts. View Call-In W 7pm
🎓	89.1	WOUL	|||			Ohio U.
†††	91.9	WMEJ	||	◇		EZ; Dr. C. Stanley 10–10:30am; Dr. C. Swindall 9–9:30am; Dr. J. Dobson 8–8:30am
†††	107.9	WEMM	|||	◇	SEE S.P.	News 6am, 4, 5pm; Stk. Mkt. 5:06, 10:06pm
TALK TALK	930	WRVC	||			
CHARLESTON AREA						
A♪ult Pop	99.9	WVAF	|||	🚗	AM DRIVE	Morn. Humor
A♪ult Pop	107.3	WLZT	|||	🚗	AM DRIVE	
TOP40	102.7	WVSR	|||			
CHARLESTON AREA CONTINUED ON NEXT PAGE						

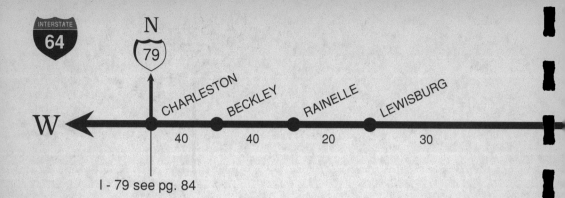

I - 79 see pg. 84

FORMAT ♪ TUNE TO		STATION	SIGNAL POWER	TRAFFIC REPORT	NEWS	SPECIAL PROGRAMMING
CONTINUATION OF CHARLESTON AREA						
🎸	105.1	WKLC	‖‖	🚗		**ADULT POPULAR;** Morn. Humor
🤠	97.5	WQBE	‖‖	🚗	AM & PM DRIVE	Morn. Humor
Lite Hits	96.1	WVNS	‖‖	🚗	AM & PM DRIVE	Morn. Humor; Stk. Mkt. 8:55am, 4:55, 5:55pm; Church Services Su 11am
E ❄ Z	94.5	WBES	‖	⚡	MORE	News 12N; Mkt. Reports on the 1/2 hr; Spotlight Sa 10am; Symphony Su 9pm
🎹	88.5	WVPN	‖‖	⚡	MORE	**NPR; APR;** News: W.E. Sa 8–11am, Su 11am–1pm; Mtn. Stg. Sa 6–8pm, Su 3–5pm
✝✝✝	100.9	WJYP	‖	⚡	SEE SP	**EASY LISTENING;** News 6, 7, 11am, 3, 4pm
BECKLEY AREA						
T⊙P40	103.7	WCIR	‖‖	🚗	AM & PM DRIVE	Stk. Mkt. 4:50pm; Am. Top 40 Su 6–10am; Old. M–F 9–10:20am; R. Dee Su 2–6pm
T⊙P40	104.5	WHAJ	‖‖	⚡	AM & PM DRIVE	Morn. Hum.; Spts. News 20 after the hour 5–9am; 104 Min. with ... M–F 1:20pm
🎸☮	94.1	WAXS	‖‖	⚡	🕐	**OLDIES;** Morn. Hum.; J. Zippo In the Morning M–F 6:10am, Sa & Su 7–11am
🤠	99.5	WJLS	‖‖			
🤠	102.3	WMTD	‖			
🤠	105.9	WTNJ	‖‖	🚗	🕐	Spts. News 6:35, 7:35, 8:35am, Sptsline M–F 6:10–7pm; P Harvey 8:30am, 1, 4, 5pm
🎹	91.7	WVPB	‖‖	⚡	MORE	**NPR; APR;** News: W.E. Sa 8–11am, Su 11am–1pm; Mtn. Stg. Sa 6–8pm, Su 3–5pm
RAINELLE						
Adult Pop	96.7	WRRL	‖			
LEWISBURG AREA						

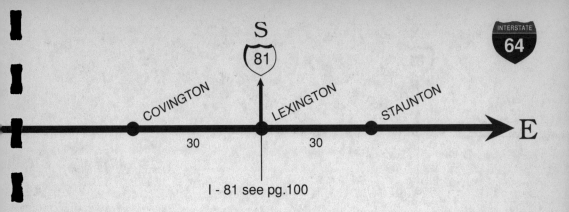

I - 81 see pg.100

FORMAT ♪ TUNE TO		STATION	SIGNAL POWER	TRAFFIC REPORT	NEWS	SPECIAL PROGRAMMING
🎩👢	105.5	WKCJ	‖	⬧⚡	SEE SP	News at 15 after the hour; Amer. Ctry. Ctdwn. Su 2–6pm
E ❀ Z	97.7	WRON	‖			
COVINGTON AREA						
A♪ult Pop	99.1	WSLQ	‖‖			OLDIES; The Breakfast Club M–F 5–9am; Car Tunes M–F 3–7pm; Weekend oldies
A♪ult Pop	100.9	WIQO	‖	⬧⚡	SEE SP	TOP 40; CLASSIC ROCK; News :45; Commonwealth Conversations Su 12N
T♀P40	92.3	WXLK	‖‖	⬧⚡	AM DRIVE	Morn. Humor
🎩👢	103.9	WXCF	‖	⬧⚡	🕐	Morn. humor; Spts. News; Farm News; Religious
E ❀ Z	94.9	WPVR	‖‖	🚗	🕔	Stk. Mkt. hourly; Special of the Week Su 12N; Big Band Sa 8pm
🎹	89.1	WVTF	‖‖	⬧⚡	MORE	NPR; All That Jazz Sa 10pm; Bluegrass Su 7pm; Jazz Club Sa 8pm
LEXINGTON AREA						
☮	96.7	WREL	‖			
🎩👢	107.9	WYYD	‖‖		AM & PM DRIVE	House Prty. Sa 8–10pm; Amer. Ctry. Ctdwn. Su 8pm–12M; NASCAR Live Tu 7pm
✝✝✝	88.3	WRVL	‖‖	⬧⚡	AM & PM DRIVE	Insight for Living 10am; Focus on the Family 1:30pm
STAUNTON AREA						
T♀P40	93.5	WSGM	‖	⬧⚡	MORE	ADULT POP; Stk. Mkt. 5:30pm; Spts. News 8:15am, 5:15pm; Consumer Rpt. 11am
T♀P40	100.7	WQPO	‖‖	⬧⚡	MORE	News 12N; Morn. Humor
🎸☮	105.1	WRDJ	‖	⬧⚡	🕐	
STAUNTON AREA CONTINUED ON NEXT PAGE						

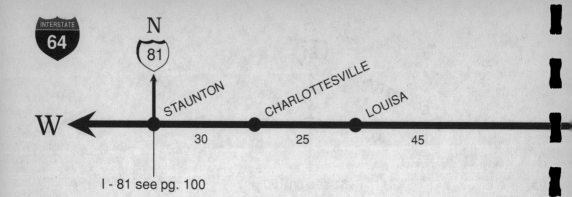

I - 81 see pg. 100

FORMAT ♪ TUNE TO	STATION	SIGNAL POWER	TRAFFIC REPORT	NEWS	SPECIAL PROGRAMMING
CONTINUATION OF STAUNTON AREA					
🤠	104.3	WKCY	|||	⚡	MORE◔	News 12N; Morn. Humor; Spts. News 7:40am, 5:40pm
🤠	105.5	WSKO	||	⚡	🕐	News also on the 1/2 hr; Spts. News M–F 7:45, 8:45am; Bus. Rpt. M–F 5:45pm
☀OLDIES	99.7	WANV	|||	⚡	🕐	Solid Gold Scrapbook Sa 7pm–12M; Lite Jazz Su 9pm–2am
E ❀ Z	94.3	WTON	|||	⚡	AM & PM DRIVE	
🎹	90.7	WMRA	|||	⚡	MORE◔	**NPR;** News 12N; Blues Valley Sa 10pm–1am; Public Affairs M–F 6:30pm; Bluegrass
CHARLOTTESVILLE AREA					
T○P40	92.7	WUVA	||		AM & PM DRIVE	Spts.; News Features
T○P40	96.7	WJMA	||	⚡	AM & PM DRIVE	**ADULT POPULAR; R & B;** Spts. News 45 past hour drive times
🎸	97.5	WWWV	|||	⚡	AM DRIVE	**ALBUM-ORIENTED ROCK;** Flashback Su 7pm; Live Show Su 8pm; Rock Today Su 10pm
🎸	91.3	WTJU					U. of Virginia
🤠	102.3	WCYK	||	⚡	🕐	Amer. Ctry. Ctdwn. Su 12N–4pm; Westwood One Presents... F Nite
Lite Hits	95.1	WQMZ	||			
🎹	89.3	WVTU	|||	⚡	🕐	**NPR;** All That Jazz Sa 10pm; Jazz Club Sa 8pm; Bluegrass Su 7pm
LOUISA AREA					
AdultPop	101.5	WBQB	|||	⚡	AM & PM DRIVE	R & R Oldies Sa 7pm; Supergold Su 7pm; Rock, Roll & Remember Su 11am
🤠	93.3	WFLS	|||	🚐	🕐	Morn. Humor; NASCAR Races Su afternoon; Weekly Ctry. Ctdwn. Sa 9pm
🤠	105.5	WLSA	||	⚡	🕐	Spts. News 7:45am, 4:45pm; Amer. Ctry. Ctdwn. Sa 1–5pm

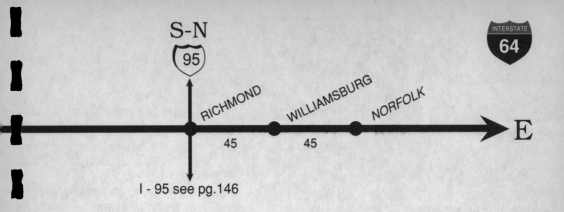

FORMAT ♪ TUNE TO		STATION	SIGNAL POWER	TRAFFIC REPORT	NEWS	SPECIAL PROGRAMMING
†‖†	90.5	WJYJ	‖‖	⬦⚡	AM & PM DRIVE	**CHRISTIAN CONTEMPORARY;** Focus on Fam. 12N & 9pm; Insight for Living 12:30pm
RICHMOND AREA						
Adult Pop	103.7	WMXB	‖‖	🚗	AM DRIVE	Morn. Humor
Top 40	94.5	WRVQ	‖‖	🚗	AM & PM DRIVE	Morn. Humor; Spts. News 7:35am, 5:25pm
🎸	102.1	WRXL	‖‖	🚗	AM DRIVE	**CLASSIC ROCK;** Morn. Humor
🤠🎵	95.3	WKHK	‖‖	🚗	AM DRIVE	Morn. Humor
☀OLDIES	106.5	WVGO	‖‖	🚗		Morn. Humor
R&B	92.7	WCDX	‖			
E ❁ Z	98.1	WTVR	‖‖	🚗	🕐	Stk. Mkt. 1, 2, 3pm; Sinatra, His Music Sa 7–9pm
🎹	88.9	WCVE	‖‖	⬦⚡	MORE	**JAZZ** M–F 11pm–1am, Sa 8pm–12M, Su 12M–2am; **NPR; APR;** News: W.E. 8–10am
†‖†	92.1	WDYL	‖	🚗	MORE	**CHRISTIAN CONTEMPORARY;** News 1, 2, 3pm
†‖†	100.1	WYFJ	‖	⬦⚡	🕐	Public Affairs Tu 2:05pm
🤠🎵	1140	WRVA	"C"	🚗	🕐	News also 12–1pm; Stk. Mkt. hourly; Spts.: U. of VA, C. Noe (Spts.) Su 7–10pm
WILLIAMSBURG						
☀OLDIES	96.5	WDCK	‖‖	🚗	AM DRIVE	Public Affairs Su 5:30–6am
ek-lek-tik	90.7	WCMW	‖		SEE S.P.	News 9am, 4pm; Spts.: Wm. & M. College; Quiz Kid Su 10pm–12M; Talk Su 7–8pm

WILLIAMSBURG

W ← ● 45

FORMAT / TUNE TO		STATION	SIGNAL POWER	TRAFFIC REPORT	NEWS	SPECIAL PROGRAMMING
NORFOLK AREA						
Adult Cop	94.9	WJQI	|||	🚗	🕐	Morn. Humor; Love Songs 7pm–12M
Adult Cop	101.3	WWDE	|||	🚗	AM & PM DRIVE	Morn. Humor
Top 40	91.5	WYCS	|||	◇	🕐	Public Affairs; General Education, Health
Top 40	104.5	WNVZ	|||			
Top 40	105.3	WMXN	|||	🚗		**ADULT POPULAR**; Morn. Humor
🎸	92.1	WTZR	||		SEE STP	News 6:30, 8:30am; New Metal Su 5–7pm; Dr. Dem. Su 11pm–1am; Prgsv. Rock Su 9am
🎸	98.7	WNOR	|||			**CLASSIC ROCK**
🎸☮	106.9	WAFX	|||	🚗	🕐	News also on the 1/2 hour; Morn. Humor
👢	90.3	WHRO	|||	🚗		**NPR; APR;** Opera Sa 1:30–5pm; W/Hearts & Voices Su 12N–1pm; Pipedreams Su 7pm
👢	94.1	WKEZ	|||			
👢	97.3	WGH	|||	🚗	🕐	Morn. Humor; Ctry. Ctdwn. Su 9pm–12M
👢	100.5	WCMS	|||	🚗	MORE	News 12N, 3pm, Paul Harvey 9am, 12:30, 6pm; Bluegrass Su 7am & 11pm
☀OLDIES	95.7	WLTY	|||	🚗	AM DRIVE	Morn. Humor

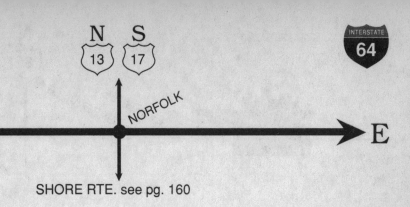

SHORE RTE. see pg. 160

FORMAT ♪ TUNE TO	STATION	SIGNAL POWER	TRAFFIC REPORT	NEWS	SPECIAL PROGRAMMING
R&B 93.7	WMYK	‖‖			**ADULT R & B**
R&B 102.9	WOWI	‖‖			
E❄Z 92.9	WFOG	‖‖	🚗	🕐	Morn. Hum.; Sunday Morn. Mag. 7–8am; Big Band Jump Sa 8–10pm
🎹 88.7	WFOS	‖‖	◇⚡	AM & PM DRIVE	**JAZZ;** Stk .Mkt. 12N; Detroit Symph. W 7pm; World's Greatest Orchestras Sa 7pm
🎺 88.3	WHOV	‖	🚗	🕐	**R & B;** Hispanic Sa 8am–1pm; Reggae Su 6–10pm; Talk M–F 4pm; Gospel Su 11am–1pm
🎺 91.1	WNSB	‖	🚗	🕐	UPI Roundtable; Blues; Misty Mornings; Reggae Jamboree
🎓 89.9	WRVS	‖‖			Elizabeth State U.
✝✝✝ 96.1	WKSV	‖‖	🚗		**CHRISTIAN CONTEMPORARY**
✝✝✝ 99.7	WYFI	‖‖	◇⚡	🕐	Turning Point 8:30pm; Insight for Living 10:30pm; Back to the Bible 9:30am
✝✝✝ 107.7	WXRI	‖‖	🚗	🕐	**CHRISTIAN CONTEMPORARY;** On the Line M–F 12N–2pm
NEWS 1310	WGH	‖‖	🚗	ALL NEWS	**SPTS.:** U. of VA, NBA, High School, Orioles; Sports Talk M–F 5–8pm
TALK 850	WNIS	‖‖	🚗	🕐	Ext. News 6–9am; News also on the 1/2 hour; Stk. Mkt. :55 Hrly.; Spts.: Orioles, Redskins

NORTH OR SOUTH ON SHORE ROUTE SEE PAGE 160

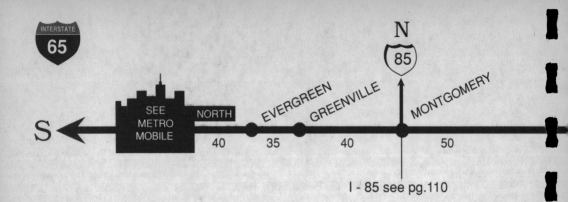

I - 85 see pg.110

FORMAT ♪ TUNE TO		STATION	SIGNAL POWER	TRAFFIC REPORT	NEWS	SPECIAL PROGRAMMING
SEE MOBILE METRO PAGE 200						
EVERGREEN AREA						
T♥P40	98.1	WWSF	‖‖			
👢	99.3	WMFC	‖	◇	🕐	Paul Harvey 7:30am, 12N, 5:10pm
Lite Hits	93.3	WIJK	‖‖	◇	🕐	Morn. Humor; Stk. Mkt. Reports; Spts.; Farm News
GREENVILLE AREA						
A♪ult♥	95.9	WKXN	‖	◇	🕐	Morn. Hum.; P. Harvey News; Spts.: U. of AL Football & Local H.S.; Solid Gold Sa Night
👢	94.3	WQZX	‖			
R&B	105.7	WZHT	‖‖			
🎹	89.9	WTSU	‖‖		MORE	**NPR; EZ; JAZZ;** News: W.E. Sa 7–8am, ATC Sa & Su 4–5pm; Opera Sa 12N–3pm
MONTGOMERY AREA						
A♪ult♥	103.3	WSYA	‖‖	🚗	SEE S.P.	**OLDIES;** News 10:50am, 4:20pm; Spts.: U. of AL; Supergold Sa 6pm–12M; Oldies F 7pm
T♥P40	100.9	WALX	‖‖			
T♥P40	101.9	WHHY	‖‖	🚗	🕐	Morn. Humor
🎸	95.1	WXFX	‖‖	◇	AM DRIVE	70's at 7pm; Guide to New Music Su 8pm; The Nevada Smith Affair Su 6–10am
👢	92.3	WLWI	‖‖	🚗	MORE	News 12N; Spts. News 7:10, 8:10am, 4:40, 5:40pm; Ctry. Ctdwn. Su 9am
☼LDIES	98.9	WBAM	‖‖	◇	AM DRIVE	Morn. Humor
🎺	90.7	WVAS	‖‖	◇	MORE	News 11am, 3pm; Spts.: Alabama State U.

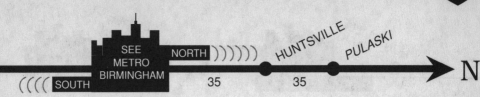

INTERSTATE 65

SEE METRO BIRMINGHAM · NORTH)))))) · HUNTSVILLE · PULASKI · SOUTH ((((· 35 · 35 · N

FORMAT ♪ TUNE TO		STATION	SIGNAL POWER	TRAFFIC REPORT	NEWS	SPECIAL PROGRAMMING
✝✝✝	89.1	WLBF	|||	◇	🕐	Spts. News 6:30am; Minirth-Meier Clinic 12N; Bus. Rpts. 7:30am, 5:28pm; Open Line 8pm
SEE BIRMINGHAM METRO PAGE 170						
HUNTSVILLE AREA						
Adult Cfr	99.1	WAHR	|||	🚗	🕐	**LITE HITS;** Oldies Cafe Show 12N–1pm
Adult Cfr	107.3	WQLT	|||	◇	🕐	Morn. Humor
Top40	100.3	WVNA	|||	◇	AM & PM DRIVE	Spts.: Crimson Tide Football; C. Kasem Su 10am–2pm; S. Shannon Top 30 Su 8–11pm
Top40	104.3	WZYP	|||	🚗	🕐	Morn. Humor; Spts.: Alabama Crimson Tide Football
🤠	102.1	WDRM	|||			
E ❀ Z	96.9	WRSA	|||	🚗	🕐	Business Reports; Health News; Spts.
🛋	89.3	WLRH	|||	◇	MORE	**NPR; APR;** News: W.E. Sa & Su 7–9am, ATC 4–5pm; Mktpl. M–F 5:30–6pm; Folk F 10pm
🛋	91.3	WBHL	|||	◇	🕐	**RELIGIOUS;** Stk. Mkt.; ABC Spts.
🎓	90.9	WJAB	|||			Alabama A & M
✝✝✝	90.1	WOCG	|||	◇	MORE	News 12N; Morn. Humor
✝✝✝	91.7	WBQM	||		🕐	
✝✝✝	95.1	WNDA	|||	◇	🕐	Met Opera Sa; Symphony Music Su 1pm
TALK	770	WVNN	||	🚗	🕐	**NEWS INTENSIVE;** Spts.: CBS Baseball, Auburn U.; Mkts. :20 & :50 6, 7am, 4, 5pm

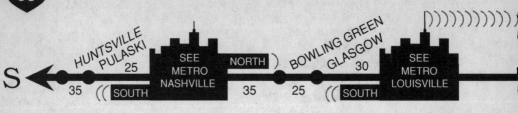

FORMAT ♪ TUNE TO		STATION	SIGNAL POWER	TRAFFIC REPORT	NEWS	SPECIAL PROGRAMMING
PULASKI AREA						
Adult Pop	95.9	WDXE	‖	⚡	🕐	Spts.: U. of Tennessee, Local High School
Adult Pop	98.3	WINJ	‖	⚡	🕐	
🤠	92.1	WLLX	‖		MORE	News 12N; Spts.: High School; Amer. Ctry. Ctdwn. Sa 6pm, Su 1pm
🤠	105.5	WYTM	‖	⚡	SEE S.P.	News 6am, 12N, 5:50pm; Spts.: U. of TN, Local; Newsmakers (local) M–F 9am
SEE NASHVILLE METRO PAGE 202						
BOWLING GREEN AREA						
Adult Pop	96.7	WCBZ	‖	⚡	SEE	News 12N; Community Reports 6:05am, 10:05pm
Adult Pop	99.3	WVLE	‖			**COUNTRY**
Adult Pop	107.1	WBLG	‖			
🎸	98.3	WDNS	‖	⚡	🕐	Home Cookin (Spotlight on Local Music); High Voltage; Silver Bullet Midnight Munch
🎹	88.9	WKYU	‖‖		MORE	**NPR;** News: W.E. Sa 7–8am; ATC Sa & Su 4–5pm; Big Band & Jazz Sa 6pm–5am
✝✝✝	90.7	WCVK	‖‖	⚡	🕐	Morn. Humor
GLASGOW AREA						
Top40	105.5	WOVO	‖	🚗	🕐	**CLASSIC HITS;** Farm Reports; Spts.: Local, U. of KY; Classic Cafe 12N
Top40	106.7	WHHT	‖	⚡	MORE	News 12N; Rick Dee Top 40 Su 4–8pm; C. Kasem Top 40 Su 8am–12N
🤠	95.1	WPRX	‖‖‖			
ek-lek-tik	102.3	WLOC	‖	⚡	🕐	Su at the Dockery (Blues); That Tall Lonesome Sound (Bluegrass) 10pm

FORMAT ♪ TUNE TO		STATION	SIGNAL POWER	TRAFFIC REPORT	NEWS	SPECIAL PROGRAMMING
SEE LOUISVILLE METRO PAGE 194						
SEE INDIANAPOLIS METRO PAGE 192						
LAFAYETTE AREA						
Adult Pop	99.7	WSHW	‖‖	◇	SEE S.P.	News 20 after the hour; Stk. Mkt. 5:35pm; Oldies on CD all day
Top40	96.5	WAZY	‖‖	◇	AM DRIVE	Morn. Humor; Casey Kasem Su 10am–2pm
🤠	100.5	WWKI	‖‖	◇	🕐	Morn. Humor
🤠	105.3	WASK	‖‖	◇	🕐	
☀OLDIES	93.5	WKHY	‖			
E ❀ Z	102.9	WNJY	‖	◇	🕐	Stk. Mkt. 8am, 5pm; Sol. Gold Sa 7pm–12M; D. Sanborn Su 9–11am; Big Band Su 7–9am
MONTICELLO/KENTLAND						
Adult Pop	94.1	WGFA	‖‖	◇	🕐	**COUNTRY; CLASSIC ROCK; OLDIES**
Adult Pop	95.3	WKJM	‖			
Adult Pop	98.3	WIBN	‖			
ek-lek´-tik	107.7	WMRS	‖	◇	🕐	News also on the 1/2 hr; Stk. Mkt. :40 hourly; Trading Post M–Sa 9–10am; Class. Su 12N
RENSSELAER						
Top40	99.9	WBUS	‖‖	◇	AM DRIVE	Casey Kasem Top 40 Su 8am–12N
Lite Hits	97.7	WLQI	‖	◇	MORE	News 12N, Paul Harvey; Spts.: White Sox
SEE CHICAGO METRO PAGE 178						

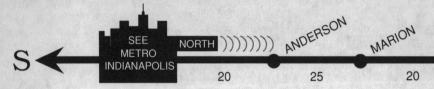

S ← SEE METRO INDIANAPOLIS — NORTH))))))) ANDERSON • MARION •
20   25   20

FORMAT ♪ TUNE TO		STATION	SIGNAL POWER	TRAFFIC REPORT	NEWS	SPECIAL PROGRAMMING
SEE INDIANAPOLIS METRO PAGE 192						
ANDERSON AREA						
Adult Pop	97.9	WLHN	|||	◇	🕐	Morn. Humor; Spts.: High School; Oldies Su Night; 70's Sa Morning
Adult Pop	101.7	WEWZ	||	◇	🕐	Spts.: Colts, IN U, Pacers, High School
Adult Pop	104.1	WLBC	|||	◇	🕐	**CLASSIC ROCK;** Morn. Humor; Stk. Mkt.; Spts.
Adult Pop	104.9	WOKZ	||	◇	AM & PM DRIVE	**CLASSIC ROCK;** Lunchtime at the Oldies M–F 12N; Top 8 at 8pm M–F; Oldies Request Sa
🤠	96.7	WAXT	||			
🤠	102.5	WMDH	|||	◇	MORE	News 12N, 3pm
☀OLDIES	91.7	WEEM			◇	🕐	News also on the 1/2 hour, Ext. News M–F 12:30–1pm, 3:30–4pm; Spts.: H.S.
🎹	92.1	WBST	||			**NPR; APR; NEWS; INFORMATION**
🎵	1240	WHBU			🚗	🕐	News also on the 1/2 hr; Spts.: Reds, White Sox, Colts, Pacers; R. Limbaugh M–F 11am
MARION AREA						
🤠	99.3	WCJC	||			
🤠	100.5	WWKI	|||	◇	🕐	Morn. Humor
E ❄ Z	106.9	WMRI	|||			
HUNTINGTON/WABASH						
Adult Pop	95.9	WKUZ					
Adult Pop	100.1	WNUY	||	◇	MORE	**OLDIES;** News 12N; Spts. News :15 & :45 6–9am; Farm Reports M–F 5:30–6am

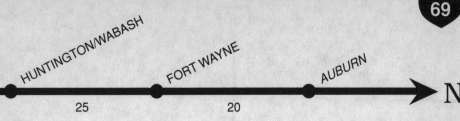

FORMAT ♪ TUNE TO		STATION	SIGNAL POWER	TRAFFIC REPORT	NEWS	SPECIAL PROGRAMMING
T○P40	92.7	WQTZ	‖			
☼LDIES	103.1	WOWO	‖	🚗	🕐	Spts.; Farm Reports
TALK TALK	105.1	WQTX	‖	🚗	🕐	Stk. Mkt. M–W 11am, 8pm; Spts.: Purdue, Notre Dame; Sports Talk Sa 11am–12N
FORT WAYNE AREA						
Adult Pop	95.1	WAJI	‖‖	◇	AM DRIVE	Morn. Humor; Lunchtime Oldies M–F 12N–1pm; Car Tunes M–F 5–6pm
Adult Pop	107.3	WRSW	‖‖	🚗	🕐	Morn. Humor
T○P40	97.3	WMEE	‖‖	🚗	AM DRIVE	R. Dee Top 40 Su 9am; American Top 40 Su 6pm; Cola Cola Hot 9 M–Sa 7pm
T○P40	106.3	WBBE	‖			
🎸	103.9	WXKE	‖	🚗	🕐	Morn. Humor
🎸	98.9	WBYR	‖‖	🚗	AM DRIVE	Morn. Humor
R&B	107.9	WJFX	‖	◇	AM DRIVE	**ADULT ORIENTED;** Oldies Sa 8–11am; Blues Sa 11am–2pm; Hot Mix Sa 7–11pm
Lite Hits	101.7	WEZV	‖	◇	MORE	**ADULT POPULAR;** News 12N, 3pm
🎹	89.1	WBNI	‖‖		MORE	**NPR; APR;** News: W.E. Sa 6–8am, ATC Sa & Su 6–7pm; Jazz M–Su 10pm–2am, Sa 8–11am
✝✝✝	88.3	WLAB	‖	🚗	🕐	**CHRISTIAN CONTEMPORARY;** Black Gospel Sa 7pm–12M, Su 9pm–12M
✝✝✝	90.3	WBCL	‖‖	◇	🕐	Stk. Mkt. 12N, 5pm; Farm Report 6:45am, 12N, 2:30pm; Spts. News drive times
TALK TALK	1250	WGL	|	🚗	🕐	Stk. Mkt. M–W 11am, 8pm; Spts.: Purdue, Notre Dame

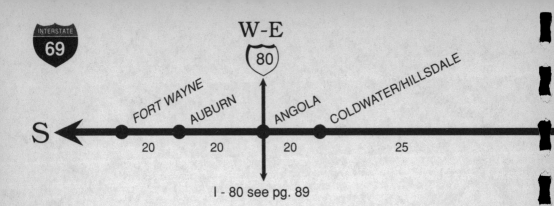

W-E

80

FORT WAYNE AUBURN ANGOLA COLDWATER/HILLSDALE

S

20   20   20   25

I - 80 see pg. 89

FORMAT TUNE TO		STATION	SIGNAL POWER	TRAFFIC REPORT	NEWS	SPECIAL PROGRAMMING
AUBURN AREA						
AdultPop	98.1	WDFM	|||	◇	◷	
🤠	93.3	WBTU	|||	🚗	A.M. DRIVE	Morn. Humor
🎺	105.5	WIFF	||	◇	SPOT. NEWS	**CONTEMPORARY JAZZ;** Spts.: Local
☀LDIES	1190	WOWO	"C"			
ANGOLA						
AdultPop	100.1	WLKI	||	◇	MORE	**TOP 40;** News 12N, 3pm
🎸☮	88.3	WEAX					**PROGRESSIVE ROCK; RELIGIOUS**
COLDWATER/HILLSDALE						
🤠	98.5	WNWN	|||	◇	◷	P. Harvey 8:30am, 12N, 5:30pm; Spts. News AM Drive, 4pm; Ctry. Ctdwn. Su 11am
E ❄ Z	92.1	WCSR	||	◇	◷	Farm News; Spts.
BATTLE CREEK AREA						
AdultPop	106.5	WQLR	|||		◷	Stk. Mkt. 10:55am, 2:55, 4:55pm; Special/ Week Su 7am; Portraits in Sound Su 8pm
Top40	95.3	WBXX	||	◇	A.M. DRIVE	C. Kasem Sa 6–10am; Future Hits Su 6am; Scott Shannon Su 7–10am
Top40	103.3	WKFR	|||		AM & PM DRIVE	R. Dee's Top 40 Su 9am–1pm; Hitline USA Su 11pm; Hometown Ctdwn. Sa 6–9pm
🎸	106.1	WJXQ	|||	◇	A.M. DRIVE	In the Studio Su 6pm; King Biscuit Flower Hr. Su 11pm; Blues Cruise Su 7–11pm
🎸☮	107.7	WRKR	|||		A.M. DRIVE	Reelin' in Years Su 9am–12N; King Biscuit Flower Hour Su 9pm; Pub. Affairs Su 8am
☀LDIES	94.1	WIBM	|||	◇	MORE	News 12N; Morn. Humor; Dick Bartley Sa 7–10am

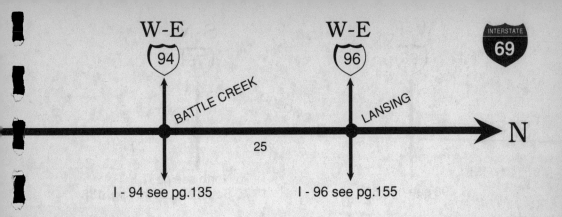

I - 94 see pg.135

I - 96 see pg.155

FORMAT ♪ TUNE TO		STATION	SIGNAL POWER	TRAFFIC REPORT	NEWS	SPECIAL PROGRAMMING
E ❄ Z	104.9	WELL	‖	◇	🕛	**BIG BAND**
🎹	102.1	WMUK	‖‖			**NPR;** Public Affairs; Western Michigan U.
†‡†	89.3	WSAE	‖	◇	🕐	**CHRISTIAN CONTEMPORARY;** Spts. News M–F 40 after hr. 7, 8am, 2, 5pm
†‡†	96.7	WUFN	‖	◇	🕐	Call-In M–F 1pm & 9pm
LANSING AREA						
A♪ult Cop	99.1	WFMK	‖‖	🚗		Morn. Humor
T°P40	92.1	WGOR	‖			**ALBUM-ORIENTED ROCK**
T°P40	94.9	WVIC	‖‖	◇	🕐	Morn. Humor
T°P40	101.7	WKKP	‖	◇	MORE	**ADULT POPULAR;** News 11:15am, 3:15pm; Spts.: MI State
🎸☮	92.7	WMMQ	‖	◇	AM DRIVE	All-Request Lunch 12N–1pm; Blues Cruise Su 8pm–12M; All-Request Sa 7pm–12M
🎸☮	93.7	WJFM	‖‖	🚗	AM DRIVE	Morn. Humor; Jazz Show/David Sanborn Su 8–10am
👢	100.7	WITL	‖‖		AM & PM DRIVE	Stk. Mkt.; Ctry. Ctdwn. Su 2–6pm
Lite Hits	97.5	WJIM	‖‖	🚗	🕛	Morn. Humor
E ❄ Z	105.7	WOOD	‖‖	🚗	🕐	Morn. Humor
🎹	90.5	WKAR	‖‖	◇	MORE	**NPR;** News 12N; Jazz F 6:30–10pm; Whad'Ya Know Sa 8–10pm; Folk Su 8–9pm
🎹	104.1	WVGR	‖‖		MORE	**NPR;** News: W.E. Sa & Su 10am–12N; Mktpl. M–F 6:30–7pm; Swing Sa 8–10pm
ek-lek-tik	88.9	WDBM	‖	◇	MORE	News 10am, 2pm; Spts. News; New Feature Show W 7pm; Rock Over London Su 9pm
LANSING AREA CONTINUED ON NEXT PAGE						

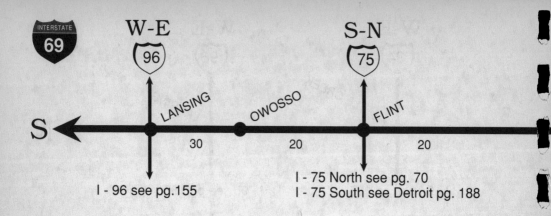

W-E 96

S-N 75

LANSING   OWOSSO   FLINT

S ◀——————

30   20   20

I - 96 see pg.155

I - 75 North see pg. 70
I - 75 South see Detroit pg. 188

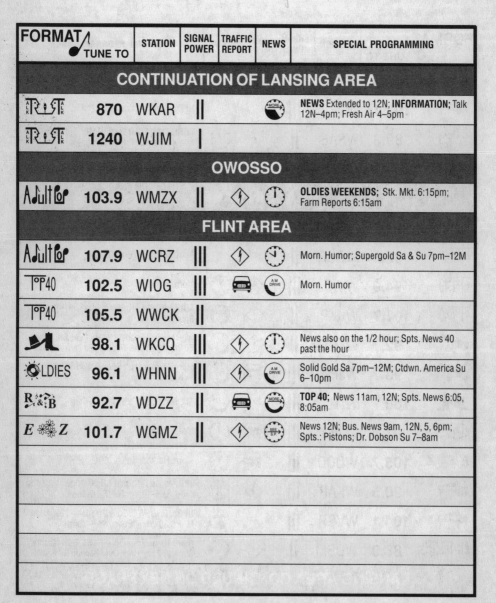

FORMAT ♪ TUNE TO		STATION	SIGNAL POWER	TRAFFIC REPORT	NEWS	SPECIAL PROGRAMMING
CONTINUATION OF LANSING AREA						
TRUST	870	WKAR	‖		MORE	NEWS Extended to 12N; **INFORMATION**; Talk 12N–4pm; Fresh Air 4–5pm
TRUST	1240	WJIM	⎮			
OWOSSO						
Adult Pop	103.9	WMZX	‖	◇	○	**OLDIES WEEKENDS**; Stk. Mkt. 6:15pm; Farm Reports 6:15am
FLINT AREA						
Adult Pop	107.9	WCRZ	‖‖	◇	○	Morn. Humor; Supergold Sa & Su 7pm–12M
Top40	102.5	WIOG	‖‖	🚗	AM DRIVE	Morn. Humor
Top40	105.5	WWCK	‖			
👢	98.1	WKCQ	‖‖	◇	○	News also on the 1/2 hour; Spts. News 40 past the hour
☀OLDIES	96.1	WHNN	‖‖‖	◇	AM DRIVE	Solid Gold Sa 7pm–12M; Ctdwn. America Su 6–10pm
R&B	92.7	WDZZ	‖	🚗	MORE	**TOP 40**; News 11am, 12N; Spts. News 6:05, 8:05am
E✿Z	101.7	WGMZ	‖	◇	SEE EP	News 12N; Bus. News 9am, 12N, 5, 6pm; Spts.: Pistons; Dr. Dobson Su 7–8am

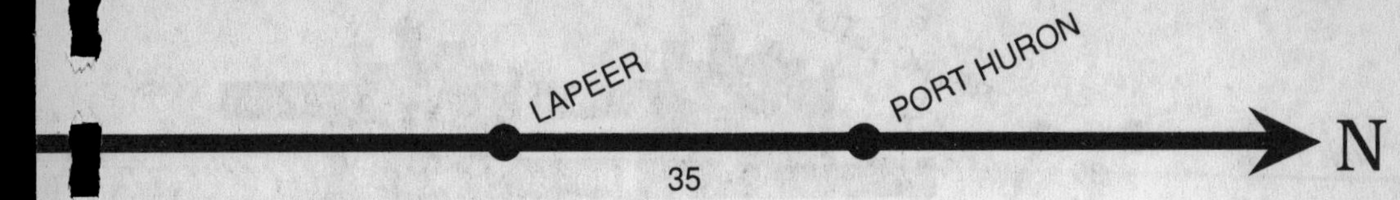

LAPEER   PORT HURON

35   N

FORMAT TUNE TO	STATION	SIGNAL POWER	TRAFFIC REPORT	NEWS	SPECIAL PROGRAMMING
🎹 91.1	WFUM	‖‖	◇⚡	MORE	NPR; News: W.E. Sa & Su 10am–12N; Mktpl. M–F 6:30–7pm; Swing Sa 8–10pm
ek-lek´-tik 90.1	WUCX	‖‖		SEE S.P.	NPR; News: ATC M–F 5–6:30pm, W.E. Sa 8–10am, ATC 5–6pm; Mktpl. M–F 6:30–7pm
ek-lek´-tik 95.1	WFBE	‖‖			NPR; APR
✝✝✝ 89.1	WBYF	‖‖			
✝✝✝ 99.7	WUGN	‖‖	◇⚡	🕐	News 11am, 12N, 2, 3pm; Morn. Hum.; Farm Rpt. 4:50am; Focus on the Family 9:30am
♪RиSτ 790	WSGW	‖	🚗	🕐	News every 10 min. AM Drive; Stk. Mkt. :50 6am–6pm; Spts.: Tigers, Spartans, Lions
LAPEER					
Adult ♩♫♪ 103.1	WDEY	‖			
PORT HURON					
Adult ♩♫♪ 99.9	CFGX	‖			
🤠👢 107.1	WSAQ	‖	🚗	🕐	Startracks Sa 7pm; On A Ctry. Road Su 3–6pm; On Track Sa 6–6:30am
ek-lek´-tik 90.3	CBEG	‖			
✝✝✝ 88.3	WNFA	⎸		🕐	CHRISTIAN CONTEMPORARY; Insight for Living M–F 9am; In Touch M–F 8:25pm
FARTHER EAST SCAN FOR CANADIAN STATIONS					

W ← TERRE HAUTE GREENCASTLE 25 30))))) WEST SEE METRO INDIANAPOLIS EAST NORTH SEE METRO CINCINNATI NORTH)))))))

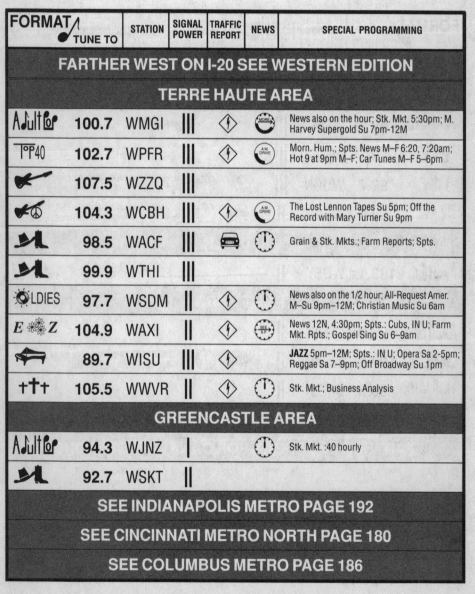

FORMAT ♪ TUNE TO	STATION	SIGNAL POWER	TRAFFIC REPORT	NEWS	SPECIAL PROGRAMMING
FARTHER WEST ON I-20 SEE WESTERN EDITION					
TERRE HAUTE AREA					
AdultPop	100.7	WMGI ‖‖	◇	MORE	News also on the hour; Stk. Mkt. 5:30pm; M. Harvey Supergold Su 7pm–12M
Top40	102.7	WPFR ‖‖	◇	AM DRIVE	Morn. Hum.; Spts. News M–F 6:20, 7:20am; Hot 9 at 9pm M–F; Car Tunes M–F 5–6pm
🎸	107.5	WZZQ ‖‖			
🎸☮	104.3	WCBH ‖‖	◇	AM DRIVE	The Lost Lennon Tapes Su 5pm; Off the Record with Mary Turner Su 9pm
👢	98.5	WACF ‖‖	🚗	⏱	Grain & Stk. Mkts.; Farm Reports; Spts.
👢	99.9	WTHI ‖‖			
OLDIES	97.7	WSDM ‖	◇	⏱	News also on the 1/2 hour; All-Request Amer. M–Su 9pm–12M; Christian Music Su 6am
E Z	104.9	WAXI ‖	◇	SEE SP	News 12N, 4:30pm; Spts.: Cubs, IN U; Farm Mkt. Rpts.; Gospel Sing Su 6–9am
🛋	89.7	WISU ‖‖	◇		**JAZZ** 5pm–12M; Spts.: IN U; Opera Sa 2–5pm; Reggae Sa 7–9pm; Off Broadway Su 1pm
✝✝✝	105.5	WWVR ‖	◇	⏱	Stk. Mkt.; Business Analysis
GREENCASTLE AREA					
AdultPop	94.3	WJNZ ‖		⏱	Stk. Mkt. :40 hourly
👢	92.7	WSKT ‖			
SEE INDIANAPOLIS METRO PAGE 192					
SEE CINCINNATI METRO NORTH PAGE 180					
SEE COLUMBUS METRO PAGE 186					

FORMAT ♪ TUNE TO		STATION	SIGNAL POWER	TRAFFIC REPORT	NEWS	SPECIAL PROGRAMMING
CAMBRIDGE AREA						
Adult Cor	96.7	WCMJ	‖	◇	🕐	Stock Market; Sports
Adult Cor	99.3	WTNS	‖	◇	🕐	**CLASSIC ROCK; OLDIES;** News also on the 1/2 hr; Spts.: Local H.S., OH State, Browns
🎸	90.7	WMCO	‖	◇	MORE	**JAZZ; CLASSIC ROCK; COUNTRY;** News also on the 1/2 hour
🎹	89.1	WOUC	‖‖	◇		**NPR;** Ohio State U.
WHEELING AREA						
Adult Cor	97.3	WKWK	‖‖	◇	AM & PM DRIVE	**LITE HITS;** Paul Harvey M–F 8:30am, 5:35pm; Solid Gold Sa 7pm–12M
T⊕P40	100.5	WOMP	‖‖	◇	🕐	Morn. Hum.; R. Dee Top 40 Su 6–10am; Hot Mix Sa 6–10pm; Metal Shop Sa 10pm–2am
T⊕P40	103.5	WRKY	‖‖	◇	AM & PM DRIVE	News 11:40am, 2:40pm; R. Dee Top 40 Sa 9am; Hit Msc. USA Su 7pm; C. Kasem Su 9am
🎸	107.5	WEGW	‖‖			
🎿	98.7	WOVK	‖‖	◇	AM & PM DRIVE	Morn. Humor; American Ctry. Ctdwn. Su 10am; Solid Gold Ctry. M–F 12M–1am
E ❀ Z	105.5	WHLX	‖	◇	A M DRIVE	
🎹	89.9	WVNP	‖‖	◇	MORE	**NPR; APR;** News: W.E. Sa 8–11am, Su 11am–1pm; Mtn. Stge. Sa 6–8pm, Su 3–5pm
✝✝✝	96.5	WRKP	‖	◇	🕐	**TALK;** Doctor on Call M–F 12N; On the Line M–F 1–2pm; Christian Ctdwn. USA Sa 1pm
♫R♪S♫	1290	WOMP	‖	◇	🕐	Ext. News 6–9am; Stk.Mkt. 4:50pm; Spts.: LSU, Indians, Steelers; Polka Su 9am–1pm
SEE PITTSBURG METRO PAGE 214						

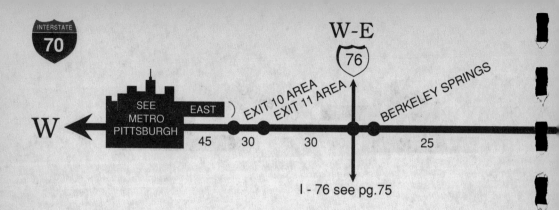

INTERSTATE 70

W ← SEE METRO PITTSBURGH — EAST — 45 — 30 — 30 — 25

W-E 76

EXIT 10 AREA
EXIT 11 AREA
BERKELEY SPRINGS

I-76 see pg.75

FORMAT / TUNE TO	STATION	SIGNAL POWER	TRAFFIC REPORT	NEWS	SPECIAL PROGRAMMING
SEE PITTSBURGH METRO PAGE 214					
EXIT 10 AREA					
Adult Pop — 95.5	WKYE	|||	⚡	🕐	**CLASSIC ROCK;** Morn. Humor; News 12N; Flashback F 10pm; Solid Gold Sa 7pm
Adult Pop — 96.5	WKQS	|||			**OLDIES**
Adult Pop — 97.7	WVSC	||	⚡	MORE	**TOP 40;** News 12N; Morn. Humor
E ❄ Z — 101.7	WYSN	||	⚡	🕐	Morn. Humor; Stk. Mkt. 4:50, 5:50pm
EXIT 11 AREA					
Adult Pop — 107.5	WAYC	||	⚡	MORE	News 3:57, 4:57pm
Top40 — 106.1	WKGO	|||			
🤠 — 100.9	WRAX	||	⚡	🕐	Spts.: High School, Pirates, NASCAR Races; Route 101 Bluegrass daily
🤠 — 104.3	WSKE	||	⚡	🕐	Paul Harvey M–Sa 8:30am, 12N, M–F 4:35pm; Howard Cosell 8:20am, 5:20pm
🤠 — 105.3	WFRB	|||			
E ❄ Z — 98.1	WFBG	|||	⚡	🕐	
BERKELEY SPRINGS					
🤠 — 93.5	WCST			⚡	🕐	Spts.: Redskins, W. VA U., Maryland Football Sa, High School Football Friday PM
WILLIAMSPORT/HAGERSTOWN AREA					
Adult Pop — 92.1	WGLL	||	⚡	MORE	News 12N, 3pm; Supergold F & Sa 7pm–12M; Live ... 60's Su 9am–12N; Big Band Su 6pm
Adult Pop — 92.5	WINC	|||	⚡		Morn. Humor; Spts.: U. of VA Football/Basketball

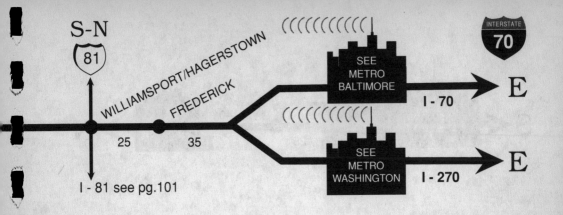

S-N
81
WILLIAMSPORT/HAGERSTOWN
FREDERICK
25   35

I - 81 see pg.101

SEE METRO BALTIMORE   I - 70   E
SEE METRO WASHINGTON   I - 270   E

INTERSTATE 70

FORMAT / TUNE TO		STATION	SIGNAL POWER	TRAFFIC REPORT	NEWS	SPECIAL PROGRAMMING
Adult Pop	106.9	WARX	|||	⚡		Jazz Brunch Su 9am–12N; Magic After Dark M–Sa 9pm–12M; Ski Rpts. Thu–Sa 7:45 am
Top40	95.1	WIKZ	|||	⚡	MORE	News 11:53am; Christian Contemporary Music Su 7–9am
Top40	96.7	WQCM					
Top40	97.5	WKMZ	|||	⚡	🕐	Morn. Humor; Open House Party Sa & Su 7pm–12M
🤠	95.9	WYII	||	⚡	🕐	NBC Morningline Spts. 6:15am, Updates 7:45am; Farm Mkt. Reports 12:50pm
🤠	101.5	WAYZ	|||			
🤠	102.5	WUSQ	|||	⚡	MORE	News 12N; Amer. Ctry. Ctdwn. Sa 5–9pm; NASCAR Sa 9–11pm; Midnight CD M–F
E Z	94.3	WKSL	||			**RELIGIOUS**
E Z	104.7	WWMD	|||	🚗	🕐	Stock Market 4:45pm
🛋	88.9	WVEP	|||		MORE	**NPR; APR;** News: W.E. Sa 8–11am, Su 11am–1pm; Mtn. Stge. Sa 6–8pm, Su 3–5pm
✝✝✝	90.5	WCRH	|||	⚡	🕐	**CHRISTIAN CONTEMPORARY;** Insight for Living; Focus on the Family
Rock	1410	WHAG			⚡	🕐	News also on the 1/2 hour
FREDERICK AREA						
Adult Pop	103.1	WAFY	||	⚡	🕐	
Top40	103.9	WZYQ	||	🚗	AM & PM DRIVE	Morn. Humor; Rick Dee's Top 40 Ctdwn. Su 8am–12N
E Z	99.9	WFRE	|||	🚗	🕐	**BIG BAND; LITE HITS;** News also on 1/2 hr; Swing Sa 8pm; Special of the Week Su 9am

EAST ON I-70 SEE BALTIMORE METRO PAGE 168

SOUTHEAST ON I-270 SEE WASHINGTON METRO PAGE 218

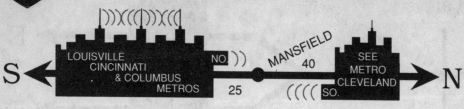

FORMAT ♪ TUNE TO		STATION	SIGNAL POWER	TRAFFIC REPORT	NEWS	SPECIAL PROGRAMMING
SEE LOUISVILLE METRO PAGE 194						
SEE CINCINNATI METRO PAGE 180						
SEE COLUMBUS METRO PAGE 186						
MANSFIELD AREA						
Adult Cont.	102.3	WQLX	||			
Top 40	105.3	WYHT	|||	◇		Morn. Humor
(guitar)	88.9	WRDL	|			Spts. Rap (Talk) Su 8–9pm; Oldies Sa 6–10am; Jazz W 3–3:30pm; Blues Su 1pm
(boots)	101.3	WNCO	|||	◇	◷	Morn. Humor; Farm Reports 5:45am
(boots)	104.5	WQKT	|||	◇	◷	Stk. Mkt.; Spts.; Farm Reports
Lite Hits	106.1	WVNO	|||	◇	SPOT NEWS	
(piano)	91.7	WOSV	||	🚗	◷	
(clarinet)	107.7	WBZW	||		◷	Stk. Mkt. 7:25am
✝✝✝	90.7	WVMC	|			
SEE CLEVELAND METRO PAGE 182						

FORMAT ♪ TUNE TO		STATION	SIGNAL POWER	TRAFFIC REPORT	NEWS	SPECIAL PROGRAMMING
FARTHER WEST ON I-74 SEE WESTERN EDITION						
COVINGTON AREA						
ᴛᴏᴘ40	102.1	WDNL	‖‖	◇	AM & PM DRIVE	Solid Gold Sa 6–11pm; Ctdwn. USA Su 4–8pm; D. Bartley Oldies Su 7am–12N
	103.1	WCDV	‖	◇	MORE	News 12N; Morn. Humor
	98.5	WACF	‖‖	🚗	🕐	Grain & Stk. Mkts.; Farm Reports; Spts.
	99.1	WIAI	‖‖	◇	AM & PM DRIVE	
✝✝✝	90.3	WFOF	‖‖			
CRAWFORDSVILLE AREA						
Adult Cont	99.7	WSHW	‖‖			
Adult Cont	103.9	WIMC	‖	◇	MORE	News 12N, 5pm; Stk. Mkt. 6:50, 7:45am, Update 11am; Comm. Focus Tu–F 8:05am
ᴛᴏᴘ40	96.5	WAZY	‖‖	◇	AM DRIVE	Morn. Humor; Casey Kasem Su 10am–2pm
	106.3	WNDY	‖		🕐	**CLASSIC ROCK**; Spts.; Ethnic Programs
	105.3	WASK	‖‖	◇	🕐	
OLDIES	93.5	WKHY	‖			
SEE INDIANAPOLIS METRO PAGE 192						
SEE CINCINNATI METRO PAGE 180						

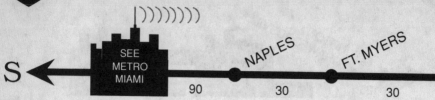

FORMAT ♪ TUNE TO		STATION	SIGNAL POWER	TRAFFIC REPORT	NEWS	SPECIAL PROGRAMMING
SEE MIAMI METRO PAGE 198						
NAPLES AREA						
Adult Pop	101.1	WAVV	‖‖			
Adult Pop	103.1	WSGL	‖	⚡	AM DRIVE	**OLDIES;** Spts. Live 6:35, 7:35, 8:35am
🎸	96.1	WRXK	‖‖	🚗	MORE	News 2pm; Pwrcts. Su 6–8pm; Reelin' in the Years Su 9am–12N; Request Lunch M–F 12N
OLDIES	93.5	WRGI	‖			
OLDIES	98.3	WCOO	‖	⚡		
E Z	94.5	WCVU	‖‖	🚗	🕐	Stk. Mkts. 1, 4, 6pm
E Z	105.5	WIXI	‖			**ADULT STANDARDS**
✝✝✝	90.9	WSOR	‖‖		MORE	News 12N, 1, 2, 3pm
CHRISTIAN TALK	1270	WNOG	‖	⚡	🕐	News also on the 1/2 hr; Stk. Mkt. :54 5, 6, 7, 8, 11am, 4, 5pm; Spts.: Dolphins
FT. MYERS AREA						
TOP40	91.5	WSRX	‖			
TOP40	96.9	WINK	‖‖	🚗	SEE EP	News every quarter hour; Morn. Humor; Stk. Mkt.; Rick Dee Top 40 Su 6pm
🎸	103.7	WAKS	‖‖	🚗	AM DRIVE	Morn. Humor
🎸☮	99.3	WZCR	‖	🚗	🕐	
👢	101.9	WHEW	‖‖	⚡	MORE	News 12N
👢	107.1	WCKT	‖‖	🚗	SEE EP	News 9am; Morn. Humor; American Ctry. Ctdwn. Su 9–11am

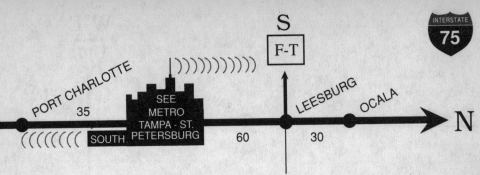

Florida Turnpike South see Orlando pg. 210

FORMAT ♪ TUNE TO		STATION	SIGNAL POWER	TRAFFIC REPORT	NEWS	SPECIAL PROGRAMMING
☀OLDIES	95.3	WOLZ	‖			
🛋	90.1	WSFP	‖‖		MORE ▸	**NPR;** Morn. Humor; Jazz M–F 12M–5am; Florida Report 4:30–5pm
✝✝✝	88.7	WAYJ	‖‖	◇	🕐	**CHRISTIAN CONTEMPORARY;** Christian Ctdwn. Amer. Su 9–10am
TᴀʟᴋR♪ST	1240	WINK	|	🚗	🕐	News also on the 1/2 hr; Stk. Mkt. AM Drive, 12N, 5:30pm; Spts.: Dolphins, Gators
PORT CHARLOTTE AREA						
Aᴊultᴘᴏᴩ	92.9	WQLM	‖‖	◇	🕐	Stk. Mkt. 4:30pm
Aᴊultᴘᴏᴩ	100.1	WEEJ	|	◇	🕐	Morn. Humor
👢	98.3	WOKD	‖			
✝✝✝	91.3	WSEB	‖‖	◇	SPOT NEWS	
SEE TAMPA/ST. PETERSBURG METRO PAGE 216						
SOUTHEAST ON FLA. TPK. TO ORLANDO SEE PAGE 210						
LEESBURG AREA						
Aᴊultᴘᴏᴩ	98.5	WKTK	‖‖			
Aᴊultᴘᴏᴩ	107.7	WMGF	‖‖	🚗	A.M. DRIVE	Morn. Humor
Tᴏᴘ40	106.7	WXXL	‖‖	🚗	A.M. DRIVE	Morn. Humor
OCALA AREA						
Tᴏᴘ40	93.7	WMMZ	‖‖			
OCALA AREA CONTINUED ON THE NEXT PAGE						

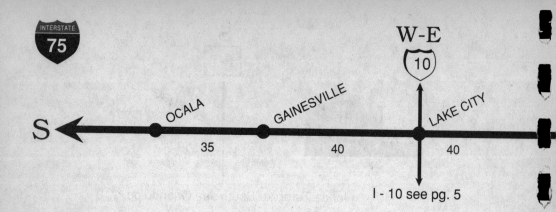

I-10 see pg. 5

FORMAT ♪ TUNE TO		STATION	SIGNAL POWER	TRAFFIC REPORT	NEWS	SPECIAL PROGRAMMING
CONTINUATION OF OCALA AREA						
🤠	102.3	WTRS	‖‖‖			
E ❋ Z	92.9	WMFQ	‖‖‖	◇	🕐	Spts.: U. of Florida, Buccaneers
✝✝✝	88.1	WHIJ	‖‖	◇	🕐	**CHRISTIAN CONTEMPORARY**; Focus on the Family 9am; Money Matters 6pm
TALK	1370	WOCA	‖‖	◇	🕐	News also on the 1/2 hr; Stk. Mkt. 12:22pm; Spts.: Gators, Game of the week
GAINESVILLE AREA						
Adult Pop	97.7	WLCL	‖‖	◇	AM & PM DRIVE	Morn. Humor
Top 40	92.1	WFEZ	‖‖			
Top 40	99.9	WNFI	‖‖‖	◇	AM DRIVE	Amer. Top 40 Su 8am–12N; Direct Hits Su 9–11pm; UK Chart Attack Su 11pm–12M
Top 40	105.5	WYKS	‖‖	◇	MORE	News 10am, 4pm; Morn. Humor
🎸	103.7	WRUF	‖‖‖			
🤠	100.9	WYGC	‖‖	◇	MORE	News 12N; Amer. Ctry. Ctdwn. Su 10am–2pm; Gospel Greats Su 8–10am
☀ OLDIES	104.9	WYOC	‖‖			
🛋	89.1	WUFT	‖‖‖	◇	MORE	**NPR; APR**; News: W.E. Sa & Su 8–10am; ATC Sa 5:15–6pm; Jazz M–F 9–11pm, Sa 5–8pm
✝✝✝	90.5	WYFB	‖‖‖			
TALK	1230	WGGG	‖			
LAKE CITY AREA						
Adult Pop	94.3	WNFB	‖‖‖	🚗	🕐	

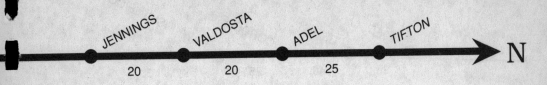

INTERSTATE 75

JENNINGS — 20 — VALDOSTA — 20 — ADEL — 25 — TIFTON → N

FORMAT ♪ TUNE TO		STATION	SIGNAL POWER	TRAFFIC REPORT	NEWS	SPECIAL PROGRAMMING
👢	98.1	WQHL	|||	⚡	🕐	Spts.; Christian Program
👢	102.1	WQLC	||		AM & PM DRIVE	
JENNINGS						
R&B	104.9	WIMV	||			
VALDOSTA						
Adult Pop	95.7	WQPW	|||	⚡	AM & PM DRIVE	Morn. Humor; Public Affairs Su 7–8am
Adult Pop	96.7	WZLS	||			
Adult Pop	105.3	WSTI	||			
👢	92.9	WAAC	|||	⚡	🕐	P. Harvey M–F 8:30am, 12:06, 5:30pm; Spts. News 7:30am, 4:30pm, Racing 7:30pm
🎹	91.7	WWET	||		MORE	**NPR; APR;** News: W.E. 8–10am, ATC 5–6pm; Jazz Sa 9pm; Opera Sa 1:30–5pm
ek-lek´-tik	90.9	WVVS			⚡		Alternative; Live Concerts; Comedy; Urban Contemporary
✝✝✝	101.1	WAFT	|||	⚡	MORE	News :55 11am, 12, 2, 3pm; Facts & Fellowship M–F 5:30pm; Thru the Bible 12:12pm
ADEL AREA						
👢	92.1	WDDQ	||	⚡	🕐	News also on the 1/2 hr; Spts.; Ctry. Ctdwn.; Ctry. Quiz Giveaway
👢	93.9	WMTM	|||	⚡	🕐	News also on 1/2 hr; Farm :20 6, 7am, 12, 4pm; P. Harvey 8:30, 9:30am, 12:05pm
E Z	95.3	WJYF	||			

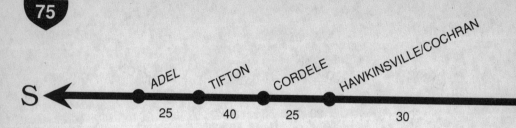

INTERSTATE 75

S ← ADEL · TIFTON · CORDELE · HAWKINSVILLE/COCHRAN
25 · 40 · 25 · 30

FORMAT ♪ TUNE TO		STATION	SIGNAL POWER	TRAFFIC REPORT	NEWS	SPECIAL PROGRAMMING
TIFTON AREA						
Adult Pop	99.5	WDMG	‖‖			**TOP 40**
Adult Pop	100.3	WSGY	‖‖	◇		Lost Lennon Tapes Su 10–11am; D. Bartley Oldies Sa 7pm–12M; Dr. Demento Su 10pm
🤠	97.7	WKAA	‖			
🤠	106.7	WOKA	‖‖	◇	🕐	**OLDIES;** Farm Report 6:20am; Coffee Break (Call-In) Talk 10am
R&B	96.3	WJIZ	‖‖	◇	🕐	Rappin' with Mary Sa 10am; Ministers' Wives Sa 9am
E❄Z	104.5	WGPC	‖‖	◇	🕐	News also on the 1/2 hour; Spts.: U. of GA, Braves, GA Tech
🎹	91.1	WABR	‖‖			
CORDELE						
🤠	98.3	WFAV	‖	◇	SEE S.P.	News 12N; Morn. Humor; Farm Reports
HAWKINSVILLE/COCHRAN AREA						
🤠	96.7	WVMG	‖		SEE S.P.	News 7am, 12N, 5pm; Stk. Mkt. 6:45am, 12:15, 5:15pm; Ctry. Today Su 6pm
🤠	103.9	WCEH	‖	◇	🕐	News also on 1/2 hr; P. Harvey M–F 8:30am, M–Sa 12:06pm; Sprgld. Sa & Su 6pm–12M
R&B	100.9	WPGA	‖	◇	🕐	Pillow Talk M–F 9pm–12M; All-Night Theatre M–F 12M
🎹	89.7	WDCO	‖‖	◇	MORE	**NPR; APR; JAZZ** Sa 9am–12N; News: W.E. Sa & Su 8–10am; Thistle & Shamrock Sa 8pm
MACON AREA						
Adult Pop	107.9	WPEZ	‖‖	◇	🕐	Lunchtime Oldies M–F 12N–1pm; Request Oldies M–F 7–10pm; Supergold Sa 7pm
Top40	99.1	WAYS	‖‖	◇	AM & PM DRIVE	Open Hse. Prty. Sa 7pm–12M; C. Kasem Top 40 Su 10am–2pm; Hitline USA Su 11pm

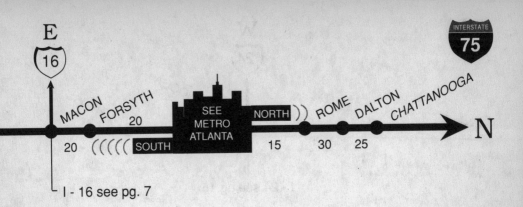

I - 16 see pg. 7

FORMAT ♪ TUNE TO		STATION	SIGNAL POWER	TRAFFIC REPORT	NEWS	SPECIAL PROGRAMMING
T°P40	101.7	WPPR	‖	◇		R. Dee's Top 40 Su 10am; S. Shannon Ctdwn. Sa 9pm; J. Landers Ctdwn. Su 8pm
🎸	106.3	WQBZ	‖		A M DRIVE	Elec. Lunch M–F 12N; Psychedelic Psupper M–F 6pm; Concert Calendar M–F 4:35pm
🤠	97.9	WKXK	‖	◇	🕐	Morn. Humor; Spts.: U. of GA
🤠	105.3	WDEN	‖‖	◇	🕐	Inside Macon Su 2pm; American Ctry. Ctdwn. Su 10am; Top 30 Su 8pm
☼LDIES	107.1	WQXM	‖	◇	AM & PM DRIVE	Morn. Humor; Solid Gold Sa 7pm–12M; US Hall of Fame Su 5–10pm
†††	91.5	WPWB	‖‖		🕐	Focus on the Family 8am, 7pm; Minirth-Meier Clinic 1pm; In Touch 9am, 8pm
†††	91.3	WJTG	‖‖		🕐	Unshackled M–F 6:30pm; Focus on the Family M–F 8pm, Sa 6pm; Su Sounds 4:05pm
FORSYTH AREA						
🤠	104.1	WYAI	‖‖	🚗	A M DRIVE	Local Ctry. Ctdwn. Sa 7–10am; NASCAR Ctry. Su 8–11am
R&B	100.1	WFXM	‖	◇	A M DRIVE	Morn. Humor; On the Phone with Tyrone M–F 7:45am; Inside Middle Georgia Su 6am
🚤	88.1	WJSP	‖‖	◇	MORE	**NPR; APR; JAZZ** Sa 9am–12N; News: W.E. Sa & Su 8–10am; Thistle & Shmrck. Sa 8pm
†††	93.3	WVFJ	‖‖	◇	🕐	Focus on the Fam. M–F 10:30am; Point of View M–F 2pm; In Touch M–F 9:05am, 9pm
SEE ATLANTA METRO PAGE 166						
ROME AREA						
Adult Cor	97.7	WKCX	‖	◇	AM & PM DRIVE	Morn. Humor; Spts.; Entertainment News
☼LDIES	102.3	WQTU	‖	🚗	🕐	Morn. Humor; Spts.: U. of AL; Dick Bartley Sa 7–11
DALTON						
🤠	98.9	WQMT	‖	◇	SEE REP	News 11:55am; Spts. News 6:45, 7:45am, 5:15, 6:15pm

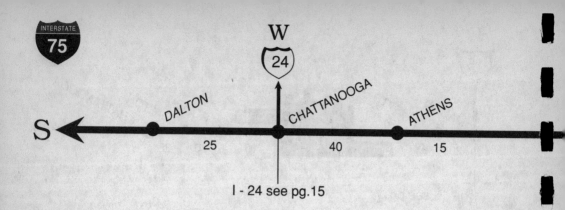

I - 24 see pg.15

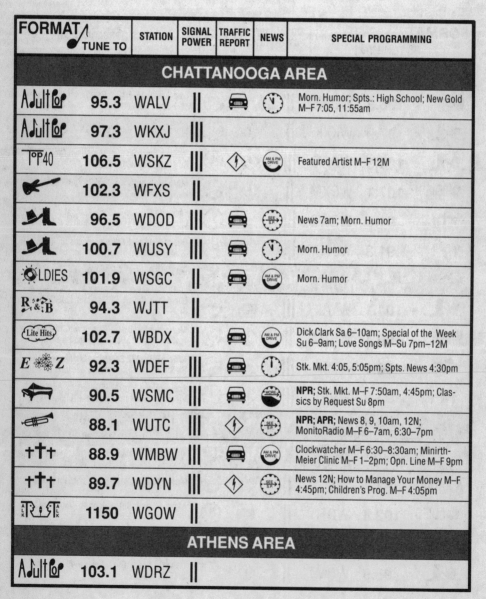

FORMAT / TUNE TO		STATION	SIGNAL POWER	TRAFFIC REPORT	NEWS	SPECIAL PROGRAMMING
CHATTANOOGA AREA						
Adult Pop	95.3	WALV	||	🚗	🕐	Morn. Humor; Spts.: High School; New Gold M–F 7:05, 11:55am
Adult Pop	97.3	WKXJ	|||			
Top40	106.5	WSKZ	|||	⚡	AM & PM DRIVE	Featured Artist M–F 12M
🎸	102.3	WFXS	||			
🤠	96.5	WDOD	|||	🚗	SEE S.P.	News 7am; Morn. Humor
🤠	100.7	WUSY	|||	🚗	🕐	Morn. Humor
OLDIES	101.9	WSGC	||	🚗	AM & PM DRIVE	Morn. Humor
R&B	94.3	WJTT	||			
Lite Hits	102.7	WBDX	||	🚗	AM & PM DRIVE	Dick Clark Sa 6–10am; Special of the Week Su 6–9am; Love Songs M–Su 7pm–12M
E ❄ Z	92.3	WDEF	|||	🚗	🕐	Stk. Mkt. 4:05, 5:05pm; Spts. News 4:30pm
🎹	90.5	WSMC	|||	🚗	MORE	**NPR;** Stk. Mkt. M–F 7:50am, 4:45pm; Classics by Request Su 8pm
🎺	88.1	WUTC	|||	⚡	SEE S.P.	**NPR; APR;** News 8, 9, 10am, 12N; MonitoRadio M–F 6–7am, 6:30–7pm
✝✝✝	88.9	WMBW	|||	🚗	AM & PM DRIVE	Clockwatcher M–F 6:30–8:30am; Minirth-Meier Clinic M–F 1–2pm; Opn. Line M–F 9pm
✝✝✝	89.7	WDYN	|||	⚡	SEE S.P.	News 12N; How to Manage Your Money M–F 4:45pm; Children's Prog. M–F 4:05pm
ROCK	1150	WGOW	||			
ATHENS AREA						
Adult Pop	103.1	WDRZ	||			

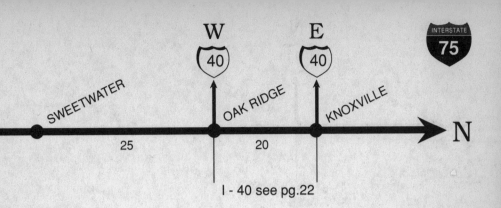

I - 40 see pg.22

FORMAT ♪ TUNE TO		STATION	SIGNAL POWER	TRAFFIC REPORT	NEWS	SPECIAL PROGRAMMING
🐄	101.7	WJSQ	‖			
🐄	104.9	WTCX	‖	🚗	🕐	Morn. Humor; Spts.: U. of TN; Wildlife/Fishing/Hunting Report 6:10am
SWEETWATER AREA						
Adult Pop	93.9	WAYA	‖		🕐	Morning Interview 7:30am
🐄	98.3	WDEH	‖	⚡	🕐	**SOUTHERN GOSPEL;** Mull's Singing Convention M–F 4–6pm, Sa 6:30–8:30pm
OAK RIDGE						
Top40	100.3	WOKI	‖‖	⚡	🌙 A M DRIVE	
🐄	93.5	WLIL	‖	⚡	🕐	**RELIGIOUS;** News also on 1/2 hr; Stk.Mkt. :40 hourly; Spts. News :20 & :50 hourly
🐄	98.7	WXVO	‖	⚡	🌙	American Ctry. Ctdwn. Sa 6–10pm; Ctry. Classics Su 6–9pm
🐄	99.1	WLOD	‖	🚗	AM & PM DRIVE	Farm Mkt. Report 5am; Agri. Weather Report 12N; Tobacco Talk Program F 12:05pm
☀OLDIES	94.3	WKNF	‖	🚗	A M DRIVE	
KNOXVILLE AREA						
Adult Pop	94.9	WIKQ	‖‖‖	⚡	🕐	Spts.: U. of Tennessee
Adult Pop	102.1	WMYU	‖‖‖	🚗	🕐	Morn. Humor
🎸	93.1	WWZZ	‖			Classic CD Su 12M
🎸	103.5	WIMZ	‖‖‖	🚗	🌙 A M DRIVE	Morn. Humor; Probe Su 7:30–8am; Pirate Radio Sa 7pm–12M; Z Rock Su 7–11pm
🐄	95.7	WGAP	‖			

KNOXVILLE AREA CONTINUED ON NEXT PAGE

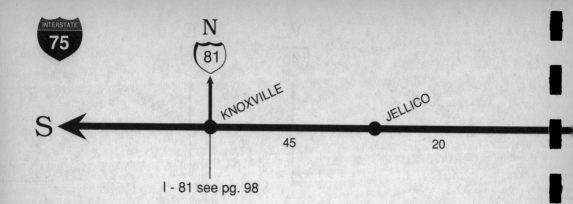

I - 81 see pg. 98

FORMAT ♪ TUNE TO		STATION	SIGNAL POWER	TRAFFIC REPORT	NEWS	SPECIAL PROGRAMMING
🤠	99.3	WNOX	‖	🚗	🕐	News also on the 1/2 hr; Business Reports hourly; Spts. News
🤠	105.5	WSEV	‖			
🤠	107.7	WIVK	‖‖	🚗	MORE	News 12N; Morn. Humor
Lite Hits	97.5	WEZK	‖‖			
🎹	91.9	WUOT	‖‖	◇	MORE	**NPR; APR;** ATC Sa & Su 5–6pm; Frsh. Air M–F 4–5pm; Opera Sa 1:30–4pm; Jazz Sa 9pm
✝✝✝	95.3	WYFC	‖			
TALK	850	WUTK	‖‖			U. of Tennessee

CONTINUATION OF KNOXVILLE AREA

JELLICO AREA

FORMAT ♪ TUNE TO		STATION	SIGNAL POWER	TRAFFIC REPORT	NEWS	SPECIAL PROGRAMMING
TOP40	104.9	WQLA	‖	◇	🕐	**COUNTRY;** Spts. News 4:30, 5:30pm; Solid Gold Oldies Su 12N–6pm
🎸☮	92.7	WMIK	‖	◇	🕐	Spts.: U. of Kentucky

CORBIN/BARBOURVILLE

FORMAT ♪ TUNE TO		STATION	SIGNAL POWER	TRAFFIC REPORT	NEWS	SPECIAL PROGRAMMING
Adult Pop	105.7	WTBK	‖		🕐	**CLASSIC HITS;** AM Talk Show M–F 10–11:30am
Adult Pop	107.3	WCTT	‖‖			
TOP40	103.1	WWXL	‖			
🎸	93.9	WJDJ	‖‖	◇	🕐	Powercuts Sa 10pm; Live Concerts at various times
🤠	93.5	WYWY	‖			
🤠	99.5	WKDP	‖‖	◇	🕐	Ctry. Ctdwn. Sa 8am–12N, Su 1–5pm; All Request M–F 11:30am–1pm

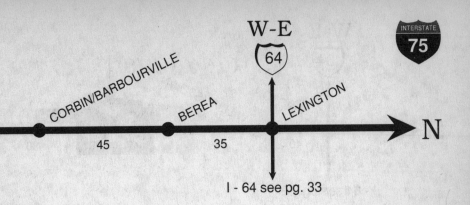

I - 64 see pg. 33

FORMAT / TUNE TO		STATION	SIGNAL POWER	TRAFFIC REPORT	NEWS	SPECIAL PROGRAMMING
🤠	101.1	WSGS	|||			
🤠	103.9	WWEL	||	⬦	🕐	Morn. Humor
🎹	89.7	WDCL	|||	⬦	MORE	NPR; APR; ECLECTIC; News 1–1:30pm; Radio Reader M–F 6:30pm; Car Talk Sa 6pm
✝✝✝	90.5	WTHL	|||	⬦	🕐	Southern Gospel Sa 8pm–12M
BEREA AREA						
Adult Pop	101.7	WMCQ	||	⬦	🕐	Morn. Humor; Stk. Mkt. AM & PM; Spts.: Reds, U. of Kentucky
Adult Pop	105.1	WRNZ	||			
🤠	95.9	WRSL					
LEXINGTON AREA						
Adult Pop	96.7	WCOZ	||			
Adult Pop	100.1	WLFX	||	🚗	SPOT NEWS	Morn. Humor
Adult Pop	104.9	WKYW	¦¦	⬦	🕐	Ctdwn. USA Su 1–4pm; Thur Nite Music Special 8pm–12M; Live Dedications F 8pm
TOP40	94.5	WLAP	|||	⬦	A.M. DRIVE	ADULT POPULAR; Morn. Humor
🎸	98.1	WKQQ	|||		MORE	News 11am; Classic Cafe M–F 12N; Block Party Sa 7pm–12M
OLDIES	103.1	WTKT	||	🚗	SEE S.P.	News 7:20, 11:20am, 5:20pm; Live ... 60's Su 6pm; Psychic Call-In Su 7:30pm
🤠	92.9	WVLK	|||	🚗	🕐	Spts.: U. of KY; Ralph Emery Show 8:55pm; Amer. Ctry. Ctdwn. Sa 8pm–12M, Su 12N
R&B	102.5	WCKU	||	⬦		
LEXINGTON AREA CONTINUED ON NEXT PAGE						

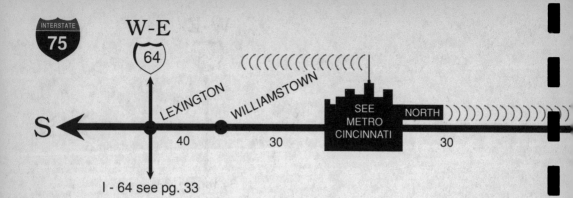

I - 64 see pg. 33

FORMAT ♪ TUNE TO		STATION	SIGNAL POWER	TRAFFIC REPORT	NEWS	SPECIAL PROGRAMMING
CONTINUATION OF LEXINGTON AREA						
🎹	88.9	WEKU	‖‖		MORE	**NPR; APR;** News: W.E. Sa & Su 8–10am; Mountain Stage Sa 7–9pm; Car Talk Sa 6pm
🎓	88.1	WRFL	‖		SEE S.P.	Pacifica News 7:45–8:15pm; Spts. News 3:20, 11:10pm
🎓	89.9	WVBA	‖			Kentucky State U.
🎓	91.3	WUKY	‖‖		MORE	**INFORM.** 5am–9:30pm; **CLASS.** 9:30pm–5am; News: W.E. Sa 8–9am, Su 8–11am
✝✝✝	106.3	WJMM	‖	◇	SEE	News 6am, 2, 3, 4pm; Black Gospel Sa 6pm–12M; Focus on the Fam. M–F 9:30am, 5pm
WILLIAMSTOWN AREA						
👢	95.3	WIOK	‖			
👢	102.3	WCYN	‖			
SEE CINCINNATI METRO PAGE 180						
SIDNEY						
Lite Hits	105.5	WMVR	‖	◇	🕐	News also on the 1/2 hr; Stk. Mkt. 12:15, 5:15pm; Farm M–F 6:05, 6:30am, 12:35, 1pm
LIMA AREA						
Adult Cor	104.9	WLSR	‖			
TOP40	92.1	WZOQ	‖	◇	AM & PM DRIVE	Morn. Humor
👢	102.1	WIMT	‖‖			
👢	107.1	WDOH	‖	◇	🕐	Morn. Humor; Stk. Mkt. 5:30pm; Focus on the Community Su 10:30am
🎹	90.7	WGLE	‖‖	◇	MORE	**NPR; APR;** MonitoRadio M–F 4:30–5pm, Sa & Su 12N–1pm; Opera Sa 1:30–5pm

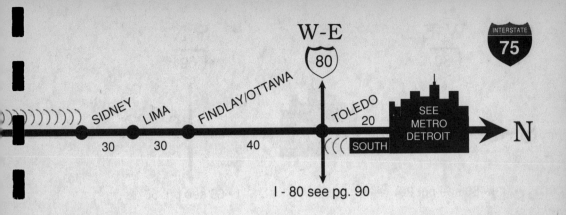

I - 80 see pg. 90

FORMAT ♪ TUNE TO		STATION	SIGNAL POWER	TRAFFIC REPORT	NEWS	SPECIAL PROGRAMMING
✝✝✝	97.7	WTGN	‖			
FINDLAY/OTTAWA						
Adult Pop	100.5	WKXA	‖‖			
Adult Pop	103.7	WTTF	‖‖	🚗	🕐	**OLDIES;** News also on the 1/2 hour; Farm Reports; Spts.
🎸	106.3	WQTL	‖	◇	MORE	**OLDIES;** News 10, 11am, 12N, 6pm; Supergold Sa & Su 7pm–12M; Reelin' in the Yrs. Su 9am
Lite Hits	96.7	WBVI	‖	◇	AM DRIVE	Dick Clark Top 40; Solid Gold Sa 7pm–12M
TOLEDO AREA						
Adult Pop	105.5	WWWM	‖		AM DRIVE	**OLDIES;** Stk. Mkt.
TOP 40	92.5	WVKS	‖‖	◇	AM DRIVE	Morn. Humor; Rick Dee Top 40 Sa 6–9am; Open House Party Sa 7–11pm
TOP 40	93.5	WRQN	‖			
🎸	104.7	WIOT	‖‖	🚗	SPOT NEWS	Morn. Humor
🎸	94.5	WXKR	‖‖	🚗	AM & PM DRIVE	Morn. Humor; Mexican Program Su 6–7am
🤠	99.9	WKKO	‖‖	🚗	MORE	News 12N; Morn. Humor
Lite Hits	101.5	WLQR	‖‖	🚗	🕐	Morn. Humor; Spts. News drive times; Jazz/New Age weekend evenings
🎹	91.3	WGTE	‖‖	◇	MORE	**NPR; APR;** Stk. Mkt. 12N, 4pm; News: ATC Sa & Su 5–6pm, MonitoRadio M–F 4:30–5pm
✝✝✝	102.3	WPOS	‖	◇	🕐	
SEE DETROIT METRO PAGE 188						

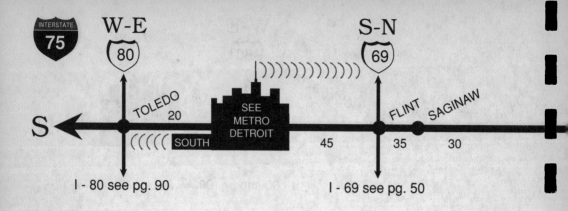

I - 80 see pg. 90

I - 69 see pg. 50

FORMAT ♪ TUNE TO		STATION	SIGNAL POWER	TRAFFIC REPORT	NEWS	SPECIAL PROGRAMMING
SEE DETROIT METRO PAGE 188						
FLINT AREA						
A♪dult Pop	107.9	WCRZ	‖‖	◇	🕐	Morn. Humor; Supergold Sa & Su 7pm–12M
Top40	105.5	WWCK	‖			
R&B	92.7	WDZZ	‖	🚗	MORE	**TOP 40;** News 11am, 12N; Spts. News 6:05, 8:05am
🎹	91.1	WFUM	‖‖	◇	MORE	**NPR;** News: W.E. Sa & Su 10am–12N; Mktpl. M–F 6:30–7pm; Swing Sa 8–10pm
ek-lek-tik	95.1	WFBE	‖‖			**NPR; APR**
SAGINAW AREA						
A♪dult Pop	98.9	WOWE	‖			
A♪dult Pop	102.1	WLEW	‖‖	🚗	🕐	Fishing Reports 5:15, 6:15, 7:15, 8:15, 9:15am
Top40	102.5	WIOG	‖‖	🚗	AM DRIVE	Morn. Humor
🎸	93.3	WKQZ	‖‖			
🤠	94.5	WCEN	‖‖	◇	🕐	America in the Morning 5–6am; Amer. Ctry. Ctdwn. Su 6–10pm; Ctry. Calendar 12:20pm
🤠	98.1	WKCQ	‖‖	◇	🕐	News also on the 1/2 hour; Spts. News 40 past the hour
☀LDIES	92.1	WIDL	‖	◇	SEE EP	**CLASSIC HITS;** News 4pm; R & R Oldies Sa 7pm–12M; Lost Lennon Tapes Su 5pm
☀LDIES	96.1	WHNN	‖‖	◇	AM DRIVE	Solid Gold Sa 7pm–12M; Ctdwn. America Su 6–10pm
R&B	107.1	WTLZ	‖			
Lite Hits	106.3	WGER	‖	🚗	MORE	**EZ;** News 12N; Jazz M–S 7pm–12M; Scoring at the Movies Sa 6–7pm

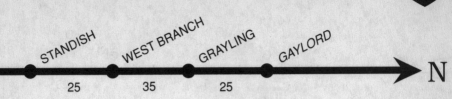

STANDISH 25 WEST BRANCH 35 GRAYLING 25 GAYLORD N

FORMAT ♪ TUNE TO		STATION	SIGNAL POWER	TRAFFIC REPORT	NEWS	SPECIAL PROGRAMMING
ek-lek´-tik	90.1	WUCX	|||		SEE SP.	**NPR;** News: ATC M–F 5–6:30pm, W.E. Sa 8–10am, ATC 5–6pm; Mktpl. M–F 6:30–7pm
††††	99.7	WUGN	|||	◇	◔	News 11am, 12N, 2, 3pm; Morn. Hum.; Farm Rprt. 4:50am; Focus on the Fam. 9:30am
ᴿᴷ ᴸ ˢᵀ ᴷ	790	WSGW	||	🚗	◔	News every 10 minutes AM Drive; Stk.Mkt. :50 6am–6pm; Spts.: Tigers, Spartans, Lions
STANDISH AREA						
A dult Pop	97.7	WMRX	||	🚗	◔	Spts.: U. of MI, H.S.; Community Updates every hr; Sounds of Sinatra Su 8–10pm
☀OLDIES	96.9	WSTD	||	◇	◔	
E ❄ Z	103.1	WGDN	||	◇	◔	**BIG BAND;** Spts.: Tigers; Farm Reports
WEST BRANCH AREA						
A dult Pop	92.9	WKJF	|||			
A dult Pop	98.5	WUPS	|||			
🤠	104.7	WKJC	|||	🚗	◔	P. Harvey 8:30am, 12:06, 4:30pm; On a Ctry. Road Sa 7–11am; Star Tracks Sa 6pm
GRAYLING AREA						
A dult Pop	101.9	WLDR	|||	◇	MORE	News 12N; Morn. Humor; Dick Clark Ctdwn. Su 12N–4pm
🎻	97.5	WKLT	|||			
🤠	101.1	WGRY	||			
🤠	103.5	WTCM	|||	◇	◔	P. Harvey M–F 8:30am, 12:05, 5:30pm, Sa 8:30am, 12:10pm; Ctry. Gold Sa 7pm–12M
🎷	88.7	WIAA	|||	◇	MORE	**NPR; APR;** MonitoRadio Su 8am; National Press Club W 1pm; Garrison Keillor Sa 6pm
ᴿᴷ ᴸ ˢᵀ ᴷ	580	WTCM	||	◇	◔	Ext. News 6–9am; Stk. Mkt. AM Drive 12:35, 5:10, 5:24pm; Spts.: Tgrs., Lions, Cen., MI U.

S ← GRAYLING 25 GAYLORD 25

FORMAT TUNE TO	STATION	SIGNAL POWER	TRAFFIC REPORT	NEWS	SPECIAL PROGRAMMING
GAYLORD AREA					
TOP40 **106.7**	WKPK	|||	⚡	(SEE S.P.)	News 40 past the hr; Rick Dee Su 9am–1pm; Amer. Dance Trax Su 9pm
TOP40 **107.7**	WHSB	|||	🚗	(MORE)	**OLDIES;** News 11am, 12N; Supergold Sa 7pm–12M; Amer. Top 40 Su 12N–4pm
🤠 **93.5**	WCLX	||	⚡	🕐	P. Harvey M–F 8:30am, 12:05, 5:30pm, Sa 8:30am, 12:10pm; Ctry. Gold Sa 7pm–12M
🤠 **99.3**	WATZ	|||	⚡	🕐	Farm Report M–F 5:30am; Spts. News 7:10am, 5:40pm; Ctry. Gold Sa 7pm
☀️OLDIES **95.3**	WMJZ	||			
Lite Hits **92.5**	WAIR	|||	⚡	🕐	Pillow Talk 9pm–12M
🎹 **91.7**	WCML	|||		(MORE)	**NPR;** News: W.E. Sa 8–9am, Su 8–10am; Mktplace M–F 6:30–7pm; Piano Jazz Sa 3pm
🎹 **100.9**	WIZY	||			
✝✝✝ **89.9**	WLJN	|||			
✝✝✝ **90.5**	WPHN	|||	⚡	🕐	Focus ... Fam. M–F 11am, 7pm; Minirth-Meier Clinic M–F 1pm; Prime Time Am. M–F 4:30pm
PETOSKEY AREA					
Adult Pop **103.9**	WLTO	|||	⚡	(MORE)	**COUNTRY OLDIES;** News 1am, 12N, 3pm; Stk. Mkt. 5:40pm; Back 40 Folk Rev. Su 9am
TOP40 **105.9**	WKHQ	|||	⚡	(AM & PM DRIVE)	C. Kasem Top 40 Su 9am–1pm; Amer. Top 40 Su 6–10pm; Supergold Sa 7pm–12M
Lite Hits **98.9**	WJML	|||	⚡	(MORE)	**ADULT POPULAR;** News 12N; Spts. News 6:45, 7:45, 8:45am; Jazz Su 9am–12N
E❄Z **96.3**	WMBN	|||	⚡	(MORE)	News 12N; Stk. Mkt. 5:15pm
E❄Z **96.7**	WMLQ	|||			**ADULT STANDARDS**
CHEBOYGAN/ST. IGNACE AREA					

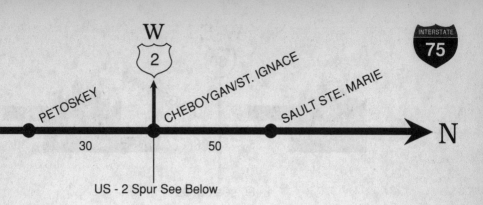

FORMAT / TUNE TO	STATION	SIGNAL POWER	TRAFFIC REPORT	NEWS	SPECIAL PROGRAMMING
🎻 105.1	WGFM	‖‖	◇	MORE	News 12N; Morn. Humor
👢 102.9	WMKC	‖‖		🕐	
US 2 SPUR WEST					
NEWBERRY AREA					
Adult Cor 93.5	WNBY	‖	◇	🕐	**TOP 40;** Paul Harvey 8:30am, 12N, 3pm; Spts: Tigers; Oldies Sa & Su PM
Adult Cor 97.9	WUPQ	‖‖	◇	🕐	Some Ctry. Music; Snow Mobile Rprt. M–Sa 8:45am; AAA Road Rprt. 7:35, 8:35am
ESCANABA AREA					
Top40 97.1	WGLQ	‖‖	◇	AM & PM DRIVE	Amer. Top 40 Sa 9am–1pm; Supergold Sa 7pm–12M; Hangin' with Hollywood Su 7pm
👢 104.7	WYKX	‖‖	◇	🕐	Morn. Humor; Farm Reports
☀OLDIES 103.3	WFXD	‖‖	◇	🕐	News also on the 1/2 hour; Morn. Humor
🎹 90.1	WNMU	‖‖	◇	MORE	**NPR; APR;** News: W.E. Sa & Su 8–10am; MntRadio. M–Su 5–6am; Med. Meet Sa 10am
FATHER WEST ON US 2 SEE WESTERN EDITION					
SAULT STE. MARIE AREA					
Adult Cor 101.3	WSUE	‖‖			
Top40 99.5	WYSS	‖‖	🚗	MORE	News 12:20pm; C. Kasem Top 40 Su 12N–4pm; Amer. Top 40 Su 6–10am
👢 104.3	CJQM	‖‖			
Lite Hits 100.5	CHAS	‖‖			
🎹 98.3	WCMZ	‖		MORE	**NPR;** News: W.E. Sa 8–9am, Su 8–10am; Mktplace M–F 6:30–7pm; Piano Jazz Sa 3pm

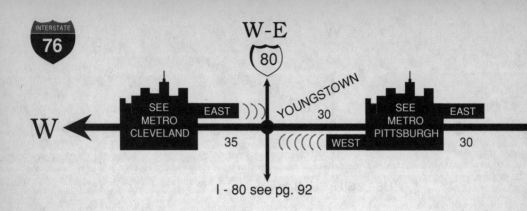

W-E
80

W

INTERSTATE **76**

YOUNGSTOWN

SEE METRO CLEVELAND — EAST — 35

30

WEST — 30

SEE METRO PITTSBURGH — EAST

I - 80 see pg. 92

FORMAT ♪ TUNE TO		STATION	SIGNAL POWER	TRAFFIC REPORT	NEWS	SPECIAL PROGRAMMING
SEE CLEVELAND METRO PAGE 182						
YOUNGSTOWN AREA						
A♪ult Pop	98.9	WKBN	‖‖			
A♪ult Pop	102.9	WYFM	‖‖	🚗	🕐	Morn. Humor
TOP40	101.1	WHOT	‖‖			
🎸	95.1	WRKU	‖‖	◇	AM DRIVE	**CLASSIC ROCK;** Morn. Humor
🎸	106.1	WNCD	‖	◇	🕐	**CLASSIC ROCK;** Morn. Humor; New Age Su 6–8am
🤠	105.1	WQXK	‖‖	◇	AM DRIVE	Morn. Humor; Top 9 at 9pm M–F
☀OLDIES	93.3	WBBG	‖‖		AM DRIVE	
E ❄ Z	95.9	WOJY	‖			
🎹	88.5	WYSU	‖‖	◇	MORE	**NPR; APR; JAZZ;** News: W.E. Sa & Su 8–10am, ATC 5–6pm; Mktpl. M–F 6:30–7pm
TALK	570	WKBN	‖	◇	🕐	News also on the 1/2 hr; Stk. Mkt. :27 after AM Drive, 12N, 5pm; Spts.: CBS, Steelers
TALK	1240	WBBW	‖	◇	🕐	**NEWS; SPTS.:** Cavaliers, Browns, Indians, 49ers, Penguins; Mkts. AM Dr. :24 12N, 5pm
SEE PITTSBURGH METRO PAGE 214						
EXIT 10 AREA						
A♪ult Pop	95.5	WKYE	‖‖	◇	🕐	**CLASSIC ROCK;** Morn. Humor; News 12N; Flashback F 10pm; Solid Gold Sa 7pm
A♪ult Pop	96.5	WKQS	‖‖			**OLDIES**
A♪ult Pop	97.7	WVSC	‖	◇	MORE	**TOP 40;** News 12N; Morn. Humor

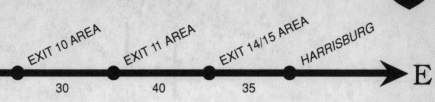

EXIT 10 AREA   EXIT 11 AREA   EXIT 14/15 AREA   HARRISBURG   E

30   40   35

FORMAT ♪ TUNE TO		STATION	SIGNAL POWER	TRAFFIC REPORT	NEWS	SPECIAL PROGRAMMING
E❄Z	101.7	WYSN	‖	◇	🕐	Morn. Humor; Stk. Mkt. 4:50, 5:50pm
✝✝✝	90.3	WAIJ	‖‖			
EXIT 11 AREA						
AdultPop	107.5	WAYC	‖	◇	🕐MORE	News 3:57, 4:57pm
TOP40	106.1	WKGO	‖‖			
👢	100.9	WRAX	‖	◇	🕐	Spts.: High School, Pirates, NASCAR Races; Route 101 Bluegrass daily
👢	102.9	WROG	‖‖			
👢	104.3	WSKE	‖	◇	🕐	Paul Harvey M–Sa 8:30am, 12N, M–F 4:35pm; Howard Cosell 8:20am, 5:20pm
👢	105.3	WFRB	‖‖			
E❄Z	98.1	WFBG	‖‖	◇	🕐	
EXIT 14/15 AREA						
AdultPop	92.1	WGLL	‖	◇	🕐MORE	News 12N, 3pm; Supergold F & Sa 7pm–12M; Live from the 60's Su 9am–12N
AdultPop	106.9	WARX	‖‖			
TOP40	95.1	WIKZ	‖‖	◇	🕐MORE	News 11:53am, Christian Contemporary Music Su 7–9am
TOP40	97.5	WKMZ	‖	◇	🕐	Morn. Humor; Open House Party Sa & Su 7pm–12M
👢	101.5	WAYZ	‖‖			
E❄Z	104.7	WWMD	‖‖	🚗	🕐	Stk. Mkt. 4:45pm

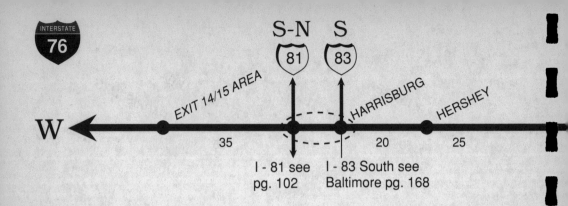

FORMAT ♪ TUNE TO		STATION	SIGNAL POWER	TRAFFIC REPORT	NEWS	SPECIAL PROGRAMMING
HARRISBURG AREA						
Adult Cont	99.3	WIMX	‖	🚗	MORE	OLDIES; News 2:55pm; Friday Night Live at Wanda's; Lunchtime at the Oldies M–F 12N
Top 40	104.1	WNNK	‖‖	🚗	🕐	Morn. Humor; Stk. Mkt.; Spts. News AM Drive
🎸	93.5	WTPA	‖			
👢	102.3	WHYL	‖	🚗	MORE	News 12N
👢	107.7	WGTY	‖‖	🚗	MORE	News 12N; Morn. Humor
OLDIES	94.9	WWKL	‖‖			
E ❀ Z	97.3	WHP	‖‖	🚗	AM DRIVE	
🛋	89.5	WITF	‖‖	🚗	MORE	NPR; News on the hour; Folk Sa 8–10pm; Classical Requests W 6:30–9pm
NEWS	1230	WKBO	‖	🚗	ALL NEWS	International News on hr. & 1/2 hr; Local Anchors & Field Reporters Live on Scene
TALK	580	WHP	‖			
HERSHEY AREA						
Adult Cont	100.1	WUFM	‖			
Adult Cont	103.3	WARM	‖‖	🚗	🕐	OLDIES; Noontime at the Oldies 12N–1pm; Love Sounds 9pm–12M
Top 40	92.1	WCTX	‖	🚗	🕐	OLDIES
Top 40	98.5	WYCR	‖‖			
🎸	92.7	WHTF	‖			OLDIES
👢	106.7	WRKZ	‖‖			

FORMAT 🎵 TUNE TO		STATION	SIGNAL POWER	TRAFFIC REPORT	NEWS	SPECIAL PROGRAMMING
R&B	105.7	WQXA	|||	🚗		Morn. Humor
✝✝✝	96.1	WGCB	|||			
EPHRATA AREA						
Adult Pop	107.5	WYCL	|||			OLDIES
Top40	96.9	WLAN	|||	🚗	A.M. DRIVE	Morn. Humor
Top40	102.5	WRFY	|||	🚗	A.M. DRIVE	**ADULT POPULAR;** Morn. Humor
👢	105.1	WIOV	|||			
E❄Z	101.3	WNCE	|||	🚗	🕐	Stk. Mkt. 12:15, 5:45pm; Spectrum 10am, 7, 11pm; Jazz Show Su 10am–12N
✝✝✝	90.3	WJTL	||		AM & PM DRIVE	
✝✝✝	94.5	WDAC	|||	⬦	SPOT. NEWS	Farm News 5–6am; Christ. Music Daily 4:30, 8:30am; Financial Advice 7:30am, 3:30pm
SEE PHILADELPHIA METRO PAGE 212						

FORMAT / TUNE TO		STATION	SIGNAL POWER	TRAFFIC REPORT	NEWS	SPECIAL PROGRAMMING
SEE COLUMBIA METRO PAGE 184						
SEE CHARLOTTE METRO PAGE 176						
ELKIN AREA						
Adult Pop	97.3	WKBC	|||	⚡	🕐	TOP 40; Morn. Humor; Spts.: U. of NC, NBC; Ski Reports daily in winter
OLDIES	100.9	WIFM	||	⚡	🕐	Spts. News 7:20am, 5:25, 10:10pm, Sa 7:20am
BLUE RIDGE PARKWAY AREA						
🎸	96.3	WROV	|||	⚡	AM DRIVE	CLASSIC ROCK; Classic Nine 9–9:45am; Short Order Lunch 12N; Vintage Block 6pm
🤠	98.1	WBRF	|||	⚡	🕐	Farm Reports 12:25pm; Spts.: College; Community Focus M 6:30pm
WYTHEVILLE AREA						
TOP40	92.3	WXLK	|||	⚡	AM DRIVE	Morn. Humor
🤠	93.9	WMEV	|||			
🤠	107.1	WPSK	||	⚡	MORE	News 12N, 3pm; Spts. News 7:45am; World of Racing 11:30am; House Party Sa 8–11pm
E Z	94.9	WPVR	|||	🚗	🕐	Stk. Mkt. hourly; Special of the Week Su 12N; Big Band Sa 8pm
🎹	89.1	WVTF	|||	⚡	MORE	NPR; All That Jazz Sa 10pm; Bluegrass Su 7pm; Jazz Club Sa 8pm
BLUEFIELD AREA						
Adult Pop	100.9	WKMY	||			
TOP40	104.5	WHAJ	|||	⚡	AM & PM DRIVE	Morn. Humor; Spts. News 10 after the hr. 5–9am; 104 Minutes with ... M–F 1:20pm
🤠	95.9	WAEY	||	⚡	🕐	Morn. Humor; NASCAR Racing

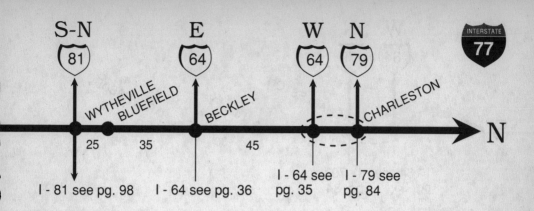

I - 81 see pg. 98   I - 64 see pg. 36   I - 64 see pg. 35   I - 79 see pg. 84

FORMAT ♪ TUNE TO		STATION	SIGNAL POWER	TRAFFIC REPORT	NEWS	SPECIAL PROGRAMMING
	106.3	WBDY	‖	◇	🕐	Morn. Humor; Stk. Mkt. 5:50pm; Spts. News 7:30am
BECKLEY AREA						
TOP40	103.7	WCIR	‖‖	🚗	AM & PM DRIVE	Stk.Mkt. 4:50pm; Amer. Top 40 Su 6–10am; Oldies M–F 9–10:20am; R. Dee Su 2–6pm
	99.5	WJLS	‖‖			
	102.3	WMTD	‖			
	105.9	WTNJ	‖‖	🚗	🕐	Spts. News 6:35, 7:35, 8:35am, Sportsline M–F 6:10–7pm; P. Harvey 8:30am, 1, 4, 5pm
	94.1	WAXS	‖‖	◇	🕐	**OLDIES;** Morn. Humor; J. Zippo In the Morning M–F 6–10am, Sa & Su 7–11am
	91.7	WVPB	‖‖	◇	MORE	**NPR; APR;** News: W.E. Sa 8–11am, Su 11am–1pm; Mtn. Stg. Sa 6–8pm, Su 3–5pm
CHARLESTON AREA						
Adult Pop	93.7	WRVC	‖‖	🚗	MORE	**LITE ROCK;** News 12N; Supergold Sa & Su 7pm–12M; Cousin Brucie Su 7am
Adult Pop	99.9	WVAF	‖‖	🚗	AM DRIVE	Morn. Humor.
Adult Pop	107.3	WLZT	‖‖	🚗	AM DRIVE	
TOP40	100.5	WKEE	‖‖	◇	AM DRIVE	Morn. Humor
TOP40	102.7	WVSR	‖‖	🚗		
	105.1	WKLC	‖‖	🚗		**ADULT POPULAR;** Morn. Humor
	97.5	WQBE	‖‖	🚗	AM & PM DRIVE	Morn. Humor
	103.3	WTCR	‖‖	◇	AM DRIVE	Morn. Humor; Stk. Mkt. 4:45pm; Spts. News 6:20, 7:20, 8:20am
CHARLESTON AREA CONTINUED ON THE NEXT PAGE						

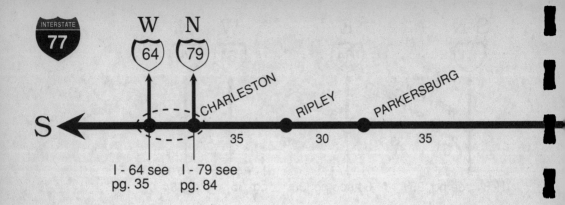

I-64 see pg. 35   I-79 see pg. 84

FORMAT ♪ TUNE TO		STATION	SIGNAL POWER	TRAFFIC REPORT	NEWS	SPECIAL PROGRAMMING
CONTINUATION OF CHARLESTON AREA						
E ❄ Z	94.5	WBES	‖	⬦⚡	MORE	News 12N; Mkt. Reports on the 1/2 hr; Spotlight Sa 10am; Symphony Su 9pm
Lite Hits	96.1	WVNS	‖‖	🚗	AM & PM DRIVE	Morn. Humor; Stk. Mkt. 8:55am, 4:55, 5:55pm; Church Services Su 11am
🎹	88.5	WVPN	‖‖	⬦⚡	MORE	**NPR; APR;** News: W.E. Sa 8–11am, Su 11am–1pm; Mtn. Stg. Sa 6–8pm, Su 3–5pm
✝✝✝	100.9	WJYP	‖	⬦⚡	SEE 9-5	**EASY LISTENING;** News 6, 7, 11am, 3, 4pm
✝✝✝	107.9	WEMM	‖‖	⬦⚡	SEE 9-5	News 6am, 4, 5pm; Stk. Mkt. 5:06, 10:06am
RIPLEY AREA						
🎸	106.1	WRZZ	‖	⬦⚡	AM DRIVE	**CLASSIC HITS;** King Biscuit; Lost Lennon Tapes; R & R Never Forgets; In Concert
🎸☮	101.5	WGTR	‖‖	⬦⚡	AM DRIVE	BBC Classics Tracks M–F 8pm; Off the Record with Mary Turner Su 6–7pm
👢	98.3	WCEF	‖			
PARKERSBURG AREA						
A♪ult Pop	93.9	WRRR	‖‖	⬦⚡	🕐	
A♪ult Pop	102.1	WEYQ	‖‖			
Top40	95.1	WXIL	‖‖		MORE	News 12N
👢	99.1	WHCM	‖			
👢	103.1	WXKX	‖	⬦⚡	AM DRIVE	E. Pitts M–F 7:20am, 3:20pm, Sa :20 after 6, 7, 8, 9, 10am; J.B. Briggs M, W, F 6:20am
👢	107.1	WNUS	‖	⬦⚡	MORE	News 12N; Morn. Humor; Spts.: WV U. Football, Basketball
☀LDIES	100.1	WDMX	‖	🚗	AM & PM DRIVE	Morn. Humor

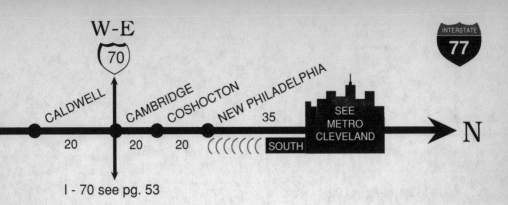

W-E
70

INTERSTATE 77

CALDWELL • CAMBRIDGE • COSHOCTON • NEW PHILADELPHIA — 35 — SEE METRO CLEVELAND

20   20   20   (((((((SOUTH

N

I - 70 see pg. 53

FORMAT ♪ TUNE TO		STATION	SIGNAL POWER	TRAFFIC REPORT	NEWS	SPECIAL PROGRAMMING
🎹	88.3	WMRT	‖	⚡	🕐 SEE	**NPR; JAZZ;** News 6:55, 8:55am, 12:55, 4:55pm
🎹	90.3	WVPG	‖‖		MORE	**NPR; APR;** News: W.E. Sa 8–11am, Su 11am–1pm; Mtn. Stg. Sa 6–8pm, Su 3–5pm
🎓	91.3	WOUB	‖‖			Ohio U.
✝✝✝	89.5	WCVV	‖‖		🕐	
CALDWELL AREA						
🤠	104.9	WWKC	‖			
CAMBRIDGE AREA						
A♪ult Pop	96.7	WCMJ	‖	⚡	🕐	Spts. News; Stk. Mkt.
🎹	89.1	WOUC	‖‖	⚡		**NPR;** Ohio U.
COSHOCTON						
A♪ult Pop	99.3	WTNS	‖	⚡	🕐	**CLASSIC ROCK; OLDIES;** News also on the 1/2 hour
NEW PHILADELPHIA AREA						
T⁰P40	95.9	WNPQ	‖			
🤠	99.9	WTUZ	‖	⚡	🕐	Morn. Humor
Lite Hits	101.7	WJER	‖	⚡	🕐	Morn. Humor; Stk. Mkt. 12N & 5pm; Agri. Reports 5:45am
SEE CLEVELAND METRO PAGE 182						

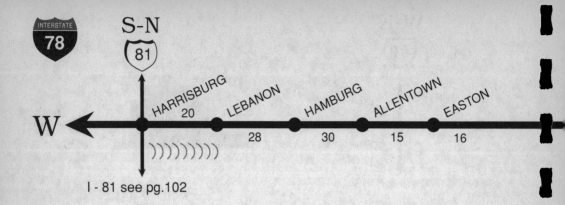

I - 81 see pg.102

FORMAT ♪ TUNE TO		STATION	SIGNAL POWER	TRAFFIC REPORT	NEWS	SPECIAL PROGRAMMING
FARTHER WEST SEE I-81 PAGE 102						
LEBANON AREA						
Adult Pop	100.1	WUFM	‖			
Top40	96.9	WLAN	‖‖	🚗	AM DRIVE	Morn. Humor
🤠	105.1	WIOV	‖‖			
E ❀ Z	101.3	WNCE	‖‖	🚗	🕐	Stk. Mkt. 12:15, 5:45pm; Spectrum 10am, 7, 11pm; Jazz Show Su 10am–12N
✝✝✝	94.5	WDAC	‖‖	◇	SPOT NEWS	Farm News 5–6am; Christ. Music daily 4:30, 8:30am; Financial Advice 7:30am, 3:30pm
HAMBURG AREA						
Adult Pop	107.5	WYCL	‖‖			**OLDIES**
Top40	101.9	WAVT	‖‖	◇	AM DRIVE	Morn. Humor
Top40	102.5	WRFY	‖‖	🚗	AM DRIVE	**ADULT POPULAR;** Morn. Humor
ALLENTOWN AREA						
Top40	104.1	WAEB	‖‖	🚗	SEE S.P.	News 25 after the hr.; AM Dance Traxx Sa 11pm–2am; C. Kasem Top 40 Su 8am–12N
🎸☮	95.1	WZZO	‖‖	🚗	AM DRIVE	**ALBUM ROCK;** Morn. Humor
E ❀ Z	100.7	WFMZ	‖‖	🚗	🕐	
ek-lek´-tik	91.3	WLVR	‖			Spts.; Classical Su Evenings; Jazz M–F 5–7pm; Heavy Metal Sa
ek-lek´-tik	91.7	WMUH	‖	◇	SEE S.P.	**NPR;** Pacifica News M–F 4:30–5pm; La Voz Caribe Su 9am–12N; Mus. of India Sa 6–9am

CLINTON

INTERSTATE 287 AREA

15

WEST

SEE METRO NEW YORK CITY

E

FORMAT / TUNE TO		STATION	SIGNAL POWER	TRAFFIC REPORT	NEWS	SPECIAL PROGRAMMING
EASTON						
Adult Pop	96.1	WLEV	|||			
Top40	99.9	WHXT	|||	🚗	SPOT NEWS	Morn. Humor
CLINTON AREA						
Top40	97.5	WPST	|||	🚗	MORE	**ALBUM ROCK; CLASSIC HITS;** News 12N; American Top 40 Su 9am–1pm
🎸	91.9	WNTI	|||			Centenary College
☀OLDIES	101.5	WKXW	|||	🚗	🕐	**Talk;** Passion Phone M–F 8pm–12M
ek-lek-tik	103.3	WPRB	|||	⚡	SEE S.P.	**PROGRESSIVE ROCK; JAZZ; CLASSICAL;** News 6, 8, 10am, 12N, 2, 4, 6pm
††††	94.5	WCHR	|||	⚡	MORE	News 12N, 12:30, 1, 1:30, 2, 3:30
I-287 AREA						
Adult Pop	98.3	WMGQ	||	🚗	MORE	News 12N, 3pm; Oldies Sa 7pm–12M; Folk/Acous. Su 8–10am; Jazz Su 7–8pm
🎸	88.7	WRSU				SEE	News 10am, 12N; Special/Ethnic Prog. M–F 9–10am, 6–10pm, Su 6am–10pm
††††	99.1	WAWZ	|||			
SEE NEW YORK CITY METRO PAGE 206						

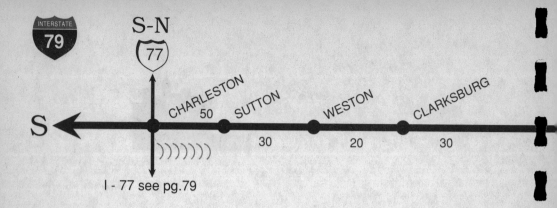

I - 77 see pg.79

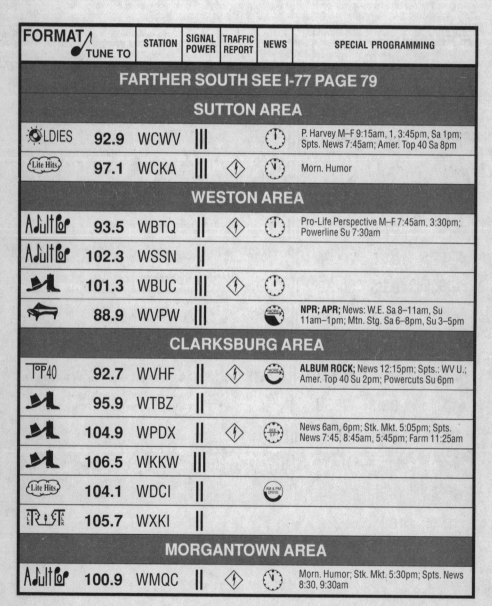

FORMAT ♪ TUNE TO		STATION	SIGNAL POWER	TRAFFIC REPORT	NEWS	SPECIAL PROGRAMMING
FARTHER SOUTH SEE I-77 PAGE 79						
SUTTON AREA						
OLDIES	92.9	WCWV	‖‖		⏱	P. Harvey M–F 9:15am, 1, 3:45pm, Sa 1pm; Spts. News 7:45am; Amer. Top 40 Sa 8pm
Lite Hits	97.1	WCKA	‖‖	⚡	⏱	Morn. Humor
WESTON AREA						
Adult Pop	93.5	WBTQ	‖	⚡	⏱	Pro-Life Perspective M–F 7:45am, 3:30pm; Powerline Su 7:30am
Adult Pop	102.3	WSSN	‖			
🤠	101.3	WBUC	‖‖	⚡	⏱	
🎹	88.9	WVPW	‖‖		MORE	**NPR; APR;** News: W.E. Sa 8–11am, Su 11am–1pm; Mtn. Stg. Sa 6–8pm, Su 3–5pm
CLARKSBURG AREA						
TOP40	92.7	WVHF	‖	⚡	MORE	**ALBUM ROCK;** News 12:15pm; Spts.: WV U.; Amer. Top 40 Su 2pm; Powercuts Su 6pm
🤠	95.9	WTBZ	‖			
🤠	104.9	WPDX	‖	⚡	SEE S.P.	News 6am, 6pm; Stk. Mkt. 5:05pm; Spts. News 7:45, 8:45am, 5:45pm; Farm 11:25am
🤠	106.5	WKKW	‖‖			
Lite Hits	104.1	WDCI	‖		AM & PM DRIVE	
TALK	105.7	WXKI	‖			
MORGANTOWN AREA						
Adult Pop	100.9	WMQC	‖	⚡	⏱	Morn. Humor; Stk. Mkt. 5:30pm; Spts. News 8:30, 9:30am

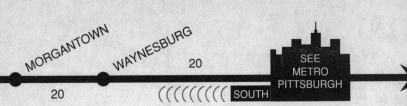

MORGANTOWN   WAYNESBURG   20   SEE METRO PITTSBURGH

20   SOUTH   N

FORMAT ♪ TUNE TO		STATION	SIGNAL POWER	TRAFFIC REPORT	NEWS	SPECIAL PROGRAMMING
T○P40	97.9	WFGM	|||	⚡	🕐	Stk. Mkt. 5:40pm; Spts. News :20 after 6, 7, 8am, 5, 6pm; Ski Reports 9:40am, 4:40pm
T○P40	101.9	WVAQ	|||			
🎸	94.3	WRLF	||	⚡	🕐	**CLASSIC ROCK;** Stk. Mkt. 4:55pm; Spts. News 7:25, 8:25am, 5:45pm; Spts.: WV U.
🎸☮	100.1	WCLG	||	⚡	AM & PM DRIVE	
🎸	91.7	WWVU					West Virginia U.
👢	96.7	WKMM	||	🚗	🕐	Spts.; Senior Citizens Report; Farm Reports; Truckers News
🎹	90.9	WVPM	|||	⚡	MORE	**NPR; APR;** News: W.E. Sa 8–11am, Su 11am–1pm; Mtn. Stg. Sa 6–8pm, Su 3–5pm
WAYNESBURG AREA						
A♪ult Pop	97.3	WKWK	|||	⚡	AM & PM DRIVE	**LITE HITS;** Paul Harvey M–F 8:30am, 5:35pm; Solid Gold Sa 7pm–12M
A♪ult Pop	99.3	WPQR	||	⚡	🕐	Morn. Humor; Spts.: Penn State, High School; Oldies Fri PM; Polka Su
T○P40	100.5	WOMP	|||	⚡	🕐	Morn. Hum.; R. Dee Top 40 Su 6–10am; Hot Mix Sa 6–10pm; Metal Shop Sa 10pm–2am
🎸☮	107.5	WEGW	|||			
👢	98.7	WOVK	|||	⚡	AM & PM DRIVE	Morn. Humor; American Ctry. Ctdwn. Su 10am; Solid Gold Ctry. M–F 12M–1am
👢	103.1	WANB	||	🚗	🕐	Stk. Mkt. 5, 6pm; Spts.: Pirates, Steelers
🎹	89.9	WVNP	|||	⚡	MORE	**NPR; APR;** News: W.E. Sa 8–11am, Su 11am–1pm; Mtn. Stg. Sa 6–8pm, Su 3–5pm
✝✝✝	106.9	WRIJ	||	⚡	🕐	Southern Gospel mornings; Contemporary Christian afternoons; USA Spts.
SEE PITTSBURGH METRO PAGE 214						

SEE PITTSBURGH METRO PAGE 214

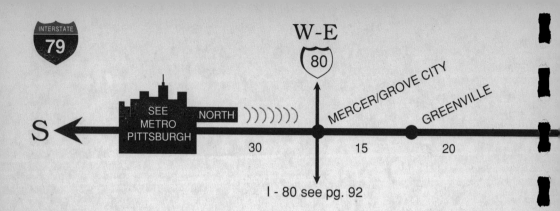

I - 80 see pg. 92

FORMAT ♪ TUNE TO		STATION	SIGNAL POWER	TRAFFIC REPORT	NEWS	SPECIAL PROGRAMMING
SEE PITTSBURGH METRO PAGE 214						
MERCER/GROVE CITY AREA						
AdultPop	98.9	WKBN	|||			
AdultPop	102.9	WYFM	|||	🚗	🕐	Morn. Humor
Top40	101.1	WHOT	|||			
🎸	95.1	WRKU	|||	⚡	AM DRIVE	**CLASSIC ROCK;** Morn.Humor
🤠👢	103.9	WWIZ	||	⚡	🕐	Spts.: Steelers, Panthers, High School; Ctry. Oldies Sa 6pm–1am; Ctry. Top 10 Sa 10am
🤠👢	105.1	WQXK	|||	⚡	AM DRIVE	Morn. Humor; Top 9 at 9pm M–F
☀OLDIES	93.3	WBBG	|||		AM DRIVE	
E ❀ Z	95.9	WOJY	||			
🎹	88.5	WYSU	|||	⚡	MORE	**NPR; APR; JAZZ;** News: W.E. Sa & Su 8–10am, ATC 5–6pm; Mktpl. M–F 6:30–7pm
†††	96.7	WKTX						**CHRISTIAN CONTEMPORARY**
𝓡𝓲𝓼𝓔	570	WKBN	||	⚡	🕐	News also on the 1/2 hr; Stk.Mkt. :27 after AM Drive, 12N, 5pm; Spts.: CBS, Steelers
GREENVILLE AREA						
AdultPop	99.3	WFRA	||	⚡	MORE	**OLDIES;** News 12N, 3pm; Morn. Humor; Stk. Mkt.; Spts.
AdultPop	107.1	WEXC	||			OLDIES
🤠👢	98.5	WRJS	|||	⚡	MORE	News 12N, 3pm; Farm Show
🎓	88.1	WTGP			⚡		**TOP 40; PROGRESSIVE ROCK; ALBUM-ORIENTED ROCK; CLASSIC ROCK**

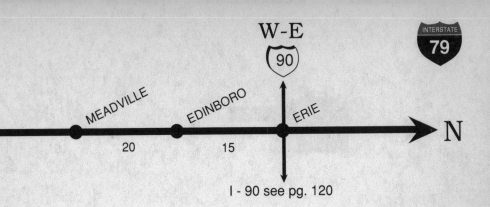

I - 90 see pg. 120

FORMAT ♪ TUNE TO		STATION	SIGNAL POWER	TRAFFIC REPORT	NEWS	SPECIAL PROGRAMMING
MEADVILLE AREA						
Adult Pop	94.3	WEOZ	‖			OLDIES
🎸	101.7	WVCC	‖			
🤠	100.3	WZPR	‖‖	◇⚡	SPOT NEWS	Stk. Mkt.; Farm Reports; Spts.
EDINBORO AREA						
🤠	97.9	WXTA	‖	◇⚡	AM DRIVE	Morn. Humor; Ctry. Ctdwn. Sa 7–10pm
Lite Hits	97.1	WREO	‖‖	◇⚡		
✝✝✝	105.5	WGOJ	‖			
✝✝✝	106.3	WCTL	‖	◇⚡	⏲	Stk. Mkt.; Talk Shows; Farm Reports; Spts.
ERIE AREA						
Adult Pop	99.9	WXKC	‖‖	◇⚡	AM DRIVE	Morn. Humor; Solid Gold Sa 7pm–12M; Supergold Su 7pm–12M
Top40	102.3	WJET	‖	🚗	⏲	Morn. Humor
Top40	103.7	WCCK	‖‖	◇⚡	AM DRIVE	Morn. Humor
🎸	100.9	WRKT	‖	◇⚡	AM DRIVE	Blaz. Trntble. Su 10–11pm; Homegrown 101 Su 11pm; Rock & Roll Never Forgets Su 8pm
🎸	89.9	WERG	‖	◇⚡	MORE	News 3, 3:30pm; R & B Sa; Italian Su 9am; Spanish Su 12N; Polka Su 3pm
🎹	91.3	WQLN	‖‖	◇⚡	SEE SP	**NPR; APR;** Ext. News: 10am–12N, 5–6:30pm, W.E. Sa 12N–1:30pm, Su 10am–12N
✝✝✝	88.1	WEFR	‖‖			
TALK	1450	WPSE	‖			Pennsylvania State U.

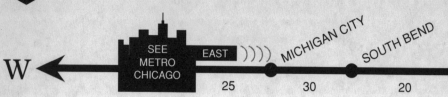

INTERSTATE 80

W ← SEE METRO CHICAGO | EAST)))) MICHIGAN CITY | SOUTH BEND

25   30   20

FORMAT ♪ TUNE TO		STATION	SIGNAL POWER	TRAFFIC REPORT	NEWS	SPECIAL PROGRAMMING
	**SEE CHICAGO METRO PAGE 178**
	**MICHIGAN CITY AREA**
👢	96.7	WCOE	‖			
E ❀ Z	95.9	WEFM	‖	🚗	MORE	**ADULT POPULAR;** News 9:55, 11:55am, 1:55pm
	**SOUTH BEND AREA**
Adult Pop	99.9	WHFB	‖‖	◇⚡	AM & PM DRIVE	New Adult Popular 8pm–1am; P. Harvey M–F 8:30am; All-Request Lunchtime 12N
Adult Pop	101.5	WNSN	‖‖		AM DRIVE	Supergold Sa & Su 7pm–1am; Live from the 60's Su 9am–12N; Gold Lunch M–F 12N
Top 40	92.9	WNDU	‖‖	◇⚡	MORE	News 12:33pm; Amer. Top 40 Su 8am–12N; R. Dee Sa 6–10am; Open Hse. Party Su 7pm
Top 40	103.9	WZZP	‖	🚗	SPOT NEWS	Morn. Humor
🎸	95.3	WAOR	‖	◇⚡	AM & PM DRIVE	Morn. Humor; Rockline M Evening
👢	102.3	WGTC	‖‖		AM DRIVE	American Ctry. Ctdwn. Su 10am–2pm
🎓	88.9	WSND	‖			Notre Dame U.
🎓	90.7	WAUS	‖‖			Andrews U.
†✝†	103.1	WHME	‖	◇⚡	AM DRIVE	Morn. Humor; Spts.: White Sox
TALK	1580	WAMJ	‖	◇⚡	🕐	News also on the 1/2 hr; Spts.: Purdue; S. J. Raphael M–F 6–9pm; R. Limbaugh M–F 12N
	**ELKHART AREA**
Adult Pop	107.3	WRSW	‖‖	🚗	🕐	Morn. Humor
Lite Hits	97.7	WZOW	‖			

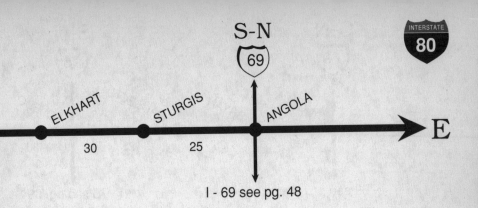

I - 69 see pg. 48

FORMAT ♪ TUNE TO		STATION	SIGNAL POWER	TRAFFIC REPORT	NEWS	SPECIAL PROGRAMMING
E ❀ Z	92.1	WDOW	‖	◇	MORE	**RELIGIOUS GOSPEL** 6–11pm; News 12N; Stk.Mkt. 4:20pm; Religious Music all day Su
E ❀ Z	100.7	WYEZ	‖‖			
🎹	91.1	WGCS	‖	◇	MORE	**RELIGIOUS;** News 4pm; Adventures in Good Music/Karl Haas; Spanish Program
🎺	88.1	WVPE	‖‖	◇		**APR;** News: BBC 7, 11:37am; Prairie Home Companion Sa 6–8pm; Marketplace 5pm
✝✝✝	104.7	WFRN	‖‖	◇	🕐	**CHRISTIAN CONTEMPORARY;** Focus on the Family 11:30am; Insight for Living 9am

STURGIS AREA

FORMAT		STATION	SIGNAL POWER	TRAFFIC REPORT	NEWS	SPECIAL PROGRAMMING
Adult Con	95.9	WLKM	‖	◇	🕐	**TALK** 7pm–12M; Farm Report 6:15am, 12:30pm; C. Kasem Sa 1:10pm
Adult Con	99.3	WMSH	‖	◇	AM DRIVE	Morn. Humor; Spts.: High School
Adult Con	106.5	WQLR	‖‖		🕐	Stk. Mkt. :55 10am, 2, 4pm; Special of the Week Su 7–10am; Portraits in Sound Su 8pm
🎸☮	107.7	WRKR	‖‖		AM DRIVE	Reelin' in the Years Su 9am–12N; King Biscuit Flower Hr. Su 9–10pm; Pub. Affairs Su 8am
🎓	102.1	WMUK	‖‖			**NPR;** Public Affairs; Western Michigan U.

ANGOLA AREA

FORMAT		STATION	SIGNAL POWER	TRAFFIC REPORT	NEWS	SPECIAL PROGRAMMING
Adult Con	95.1	WAJI	‖‖	◇	AM DRIVE	Morn. Humor; Lunchtime at the Oldies M–F 12N–1pm; Car Tunes M–F 5–6pm
Adult Con	100.1	WLKI	‖	◇	MORE	**TOP 40;** News 12N, 3pm
Top40	97.3	WMEE	‖‖	🚗	AM DRIVE	Rick Dee Top 40 Su 9am; American Top 40 Su 6pm; Cola Cola Hot 9 M–Sa 7pm
Top40	103.3	WKFR	‖‖		AM & PM DRIVE	Rick Dee's Top 40 Su 9am–1pm; Hitline USA Su 11pm; Hometown Ctdwn. Sa 6–9pm
👢	93.3	WBTU	‖‖	🚗	AM DRIVE	Morn. Humor

ANGOLA AREA CONTINUED ON THE NEXT PAGE

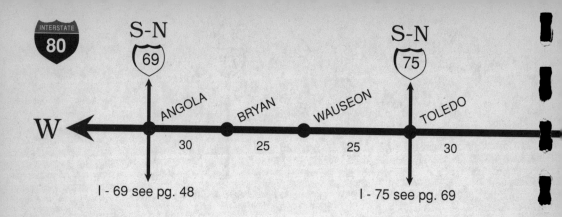

I - 69 see pg. 48

I - 75 see pg. 69

FORMAT ♪ TUNE TO	STATION	SIGNAL POWER	TRAFFIC REPORT	NEWS	SPECIAL PROGRAMMING
CONTINUATION OF ANGOLA AREA					
👢 98.5	WNWN	‖‖	◇	🕐	P. Harvey 8:30am, 12N, 5:30pm; Spts. News AM Drive, 4pm; Ctry. Ctdwn. Su 11am
🎹 89.1	WBNI	‖‖		MORE	NPR; APR; News: W.E. Sa 6–8am; ATC Sa & Su 6–7pm; Jazz M–Su 10pm–2am, Sa 8am
✝✝✝ 90.3	WBCL	‖‖	◇	🕐	Stk.Mkt. 12N, 5pm; Farm Report 6:45am, 12N, 2:30pm; Spts. News drive times
BRYAN AREA					
Adult Pop 98.1	WDFM	‖‖	◇	🕐	
Adult Pop 100.9	WBNO	‖	◇	🕐	**TOP 40;** News also :55 hourly; Stk. Mkt.; Spts.; Farm Reports
☀OLDIES 105.9	WZOM	‖	◇	🕐	**CLASSIC HITS; CLASSIC ROCK;** Spts.: High School; Superstar Concerts Sa 9:30pm
WAUSEON AREA					
Adult Pop 103.1	WNDH	‖	◇	🕐	OLDIES
Adult Pop 103.9	WLEN	‖	◇	MORE	**CTRY.;** News 11am, 12N, 3pm; Farm M–Sa 5:15am, 12:40pm; Hispanic Su 1–4:30pm
👢 95.3	WQTE	‖			
☀OLDIES 96.1	WMTR	‖			
TOLEDO AREA					
Adult Pop 105.5	WWWM	‖		AM DRIVE	OLDIES; Stk. Mkt.
TOP40 92.5	WVKS	‖‖	◇	AM DRIVE	Morn. Humor; Rick Dee Top 40 Sa 6–9am; Open House Party Sa 7–11pm
TOP40 93.5	WRQN	‖			
🎸 104.7	WIOT	‖‖	🚗	SPOT NEWS	Morn. Humor

FREMONT — SANDUSKY — 30 — 25 — WEST — SEE METRO CLEVELAND — E

FORMAT ♪ TUNE TO		STATION	SIGNAL POWER	TRAFFIC REPORT	NEWS	SPECIAL PROGRAMMING
🥾	99.9	WKKO	|||	🚗	⏱	News 12N; Morn. Humor
Lite Hits	101.5	WLQR	|||	🚗	🕐	Morn. Humor; Spts. News drive times; Jazz/New Age weekend evenings
🎹	91.3	WGTE	|||	◇	⏱	**NPR; APR;** News: ATC Sa & Su 5–6pm; Stk. Mkt. 12N, 4pm; MonitoRadio M–F 4:30–5pm
†✝†	90.3	WOTL	||			
†✝†	102.3	WPOS	||	◇	🕐	
FREMONT AREA						
A♪ult Pop	99.1	WFRO	|||			
A♪ult Pop	103.7	WTTF	|||	🚗	🕐	**OLDIES;** News also on the 1/2 hour; Farm Reports; Spts.
TOP40	92.1	WNRR	||	◇	⏱	News 12N; Morn. Humor; Spts.: Notre Dame Football
🎸☮	94.5	WXKR	|||	🚗	AM & PM DRIVE	Morn. Humor; Mexican Program Su 7–8am
🥾	100.9	WLCO	||	◇	SEE SP	News 9am, 12N, 3, 5:50pm; Farm Reports; Overdrive Trucking News
☀OLDIES	95.7	WRED	||	◇		**JAZZ** Sa evening
†✝†	97.7	WGGN	||		⏱	**CHRISTIAN CONTEMPORARY;** News 2, 3pm; Christian Ctdwn. Sa 6–8pm
SANDUSKY AREA						
A♪ult Pop	95.3	WLKR	||			**TOP 40**
A♪ult Pop	102.7	WCPZ	|||		⏱	**JAZZ** Su morning & evening; News 11am; Fishing Reports
SEE CLEVELAND METRO PAGE 182						

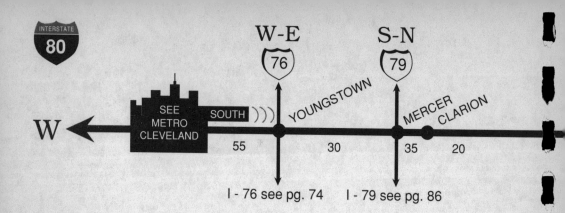

I - 76 see pg. 74   I - 79 see pg. 86

FORMAT ♪ TUNE TO		STATION	SIGNAL POWER	TRAFFIC REPORT	NEWS	SPECIAL PROGRAMMING
SEE CLEVELAND METRO PAGE 182						
YOUNGSTOWN AREA						
Adult Pop	98.9	WKBN	|||			
Adult Pop	102.9	WYFM	|||	🚗	🕐	Morn. Humor
Top 40	101.1	WHOT	|||			
🎸	95.1	WRKU	|||	⚡	AM DRIVE	CLASSIC ROCK; Morn. Humor
🎸	106.1	WNCD	||	⚡	🕐	CLASSIC ROCK; Morn. Humor; New Age Su 6–8am
👢	105.1	WQXK	|||	⚡	AM DRIVE	Morn. Humor; Top 9 at 9pm M–F
☀OLDIES	93.3	WBBG	|||		AM DRIVE	
E ❄ Z	95.9	WOJY	||			
🎹	88.5	WYSU	|||	⚡	MORE	NPR; APR; JAZZ; News: W.E. Sa & Su 8–10am, ATC 5–6pm; Mktpl. M–F 6:30–7pm
📻🎙📻	570	WKBN	||	⚡	🕐	News also on the 1/2 hr; Stk. Mkt. :27 during AM Drive, 12N, 5pm; Spts.: CBS, Steelers
📻🎙📻	1240	WBBW			⚡	🕐	NEWS; SPTS.: Cavaliers, Browns, Indians, 49ers, Pengns.; Mkts. AM Drive, :24 12N, 5pm
MERCER AREA						
Adult Pop	99.3	WFRA	||	⚡	MORE	OLDIES; News 12N, 3pm; Morn. Humor; Stk. Mkt.; Spts.
Adult Pop	106.7	WWKS	|||	⚡	AM & PM DRIVE	Morn. Humor; Legendary Lunch M–F 12N–1pm
Adult Pop	107.1	WEXC	||			OLDIES
👢	98.5	WRJS	|||	⚡	MORE	News 12N, 3pm; Farm Show

92

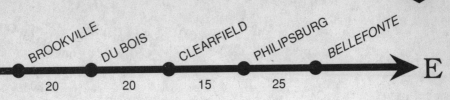

BROOKVILLE — DU BOIS — CLEARFIELD — PHILIPSBURG — BELLEFONTE

20 · 20 · 15 · 25 · E

FORMAT ♪ TUNE TO		STATION	SIGNAL POWER	TRAFFIC REPORT	NEWS	SPECIAL PROGRAMMING
🥾	100.3	WZPR	|||	⚡	SPOT NEWS	Stk. Mkt.; Farm Reports; Spts.
🥾	103.9	WWIZ	||	⚡	🕐	Spts: Steelers, Panthers, High School; Ctry. Oldies Sa 6pm–1am; Ctry. Top 10 Sa 10am
✝✝✝	96.7	WKTX	||			**CHRISTIAN CONTEMPORARY**
CLARION						
T♥P40	92.7	WCCR	||	⚡	SEE S.P.	News 7, 8am, 12N, 5pm; Stk. Mkt.; Spts.; Ethnic Programs; Farm Reports
🎓	91.7	WCUC	||	⚡		**TOP 40; ALBUM ROCK; ADULT POPULAR**
BROOKVILLE						
A♪dult Pop	95.9	WMKX	||			
DU BOIS AREA						
A♪dult Pop	99.5	WDSN	||	⚡	MORE	News 12N; Stk. Mkt. 12:15, 5:15pm; Spts.: Panthers; Supergold Sa 7pm–12M
A♪dult Pop	105.5	WPXZ	||	⚡	🕐	**TOP 40;** News also on the 1/2 hour; Stk. Mkt.
T♥P40	97.5	WKYN	|||			
🥾	102.1	WOWQ	|||	⚡		
E❀Z	107.3	WDBA	|||	⚡	MORE	**RELIGIOUS;** News 12N, 2, 3pm; Spts.; Agriculture
CLEARFIELD						
T♥P40	93.5	WQYX			⚡	SPOT NEWS	Morn. Humor; American Top 40 Sa 9am–1pm; Rick Dee Top 30 CD Su 8am
PHILIPSBURG						
🥾	105.9	WPHB	||	🚗	🕐	Morn. Humor; Spts. News AM & PM; Polish Polka Party Sa & Su

FORMAT ♪ TUNE TO		STATION	SIGNAL POWER	TRAFFIC REPORT	NEWS	SPECIAL PROGRAMMING
BELLEFONTE AREA						
Adult Pop	95.3	WZWW	‖			
Top 40	103.1	WBHV	│	◇		Morn. Humor
🎸	97.1	WQWK	‖	◇	AM DRIVE	Pwrcts. Su 6–8pm; On Stg. M–Su 3:30, 5:30, 8:30pm; In Concert M–Sa 4:20, 6:20pm
🤠	101.1	WGMR	‖‖	◇	🕐	
E ❀ Z	98.1	WFBG	‖‖	◇	🕐	
ek-lek′-tik	91.1	WPSU	│	◇	MORE	**NPR;** News 11:50am, 4:50pm; Stk. Mkt. 4:50pm; Spts. Rap F 6:30pm
†✝†	89.9	WTLR	‖‖			
LOCK HAVEN						
Adult Pop	92.1	WSNU	‖			
WILLIAMSPORT AREA						
Adult Pop	102.7	WKSB	‖‖	◇	MORE	**OLDIES;** News 4:50pm; Spts.: Penn State; All- Request Weekends
Adult Pop	107.9	WGBE	‖	◇	🕐	Spts: Local; Blues Su 9pm–12M; Oldies Sa 10am–12N; Sounds of Sinatra Su 10am–12N
Top 40	99.3	WFXX	‖	◇	SEE S.P.	News 9:50am, 3:50pm; Rick Dee's Top 40 Sa 6–10am; Casey Kasem Su 6–10am
🎸☮	97.7	WRKK	‖	◇		
🤠	99.9	WHUM	‖			
🤠	105.1	WILQ	‖‖	◇	MORE	News 12N, 3pm; Farm Reports; Spts.; Paul Harvey
☀ OLDIES	95.5	WKHL	‖	🚗	AM DRIVE	Kool Cafe M–F 6–7pm; Kool Cruisin' & Park- ology Sa 8pm–1am; Su Morn. Live 8am–12N

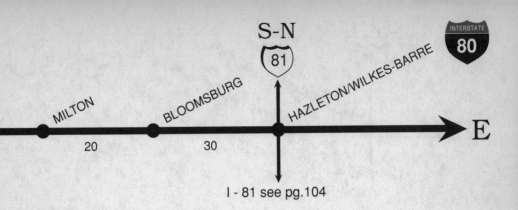

S-N 81

INTERSTATE 80

MILTON

BLOOMSBURG

HAZLETON/WILKES-BARRE

20   30

E

I - 81 see pg.104

FORMAT ♪ TUNE TO		STATION	SIGNAL POWER	TRAFFIC REPORT	NEWS	SPECIAL PROGRAMMING
✝✝✝	93.5	WJSA	‖	◇	◷	Stk. Mkt. :27 6am, 6pm; Adven. in Odyssey Sa 6:30pm; Focus on the Fam. M–Sa 3:30pm
MILTON AREA						
Top40	94.1	WQKX	‖‖	◇	◷	
Top40	103.9	WHTO	‖			
🎸	88.9	WQSU	‖‖	◇	◷	Morn. Humor; Special Programs daily 12N–1:30pm
🤠	98.3	WWBE			MORE	News 12N; Amer. Ctry. Ctdwn. Sa 8pm, Su 9am; Amer. Farmer M–F 5:30am
Lite Hits	96.3	WUNS	‖	◇	◷	
E ✿ Z	100.9	WOEZ	‖	◇	MORE	News on the 1/2 hr. on the odd hrs; Special of the Week Su 9am; Portraits in Sound Su 7pm
✝✝✝	91.3	WGRC	‖	◇	◷	**CHRISTIAN CONTEMPORARY;** Spts. News drive times
BLOOMSBURG AREA						
Top40	106.5	WHLM	‖‖	🚗	◷	Rock Roots Su 10am–1pm; C. Kasem Top 40 Su 5–9pm; Future Hits Su 9pm
🤠	95.9	WBNE	‖	◇	◷	Sportsbeat 8:50am; Automotive Digest 5:30pm; Healthwatch 10:30am
🎓	91.1	WBUQ			SPOT NEWS	Bloomsburg U.
✝✝✝	96.7	WPGM	‖	🚗	◷	
HAZLETON/WILKES-BARRE AREA						
Adult Pop	92.9	WMGS	‖‖	◇	AM & PM DRIVE	LITE HITS; Morn. Humor; Oldies 12N; Love Songs 9pm–12M
Adult Pop	101.3	WGBI	‖‖			
HAZLETON AREA CONTINUED ON THE NEXT PAGE						

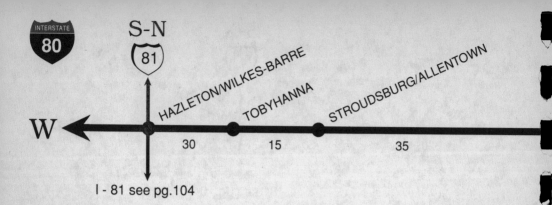

I-81 see pg.104

FORMAT ♪ TUNE TO		STATION	SIGNAL POWER	TRAFFIC REPORT	NEWS	SPECIAL PROGRAMMING
CONTINUATION OF HAZLETON AREA						
T°P40	98.5	WKRZ	‖‖			
T°P40	101.9	WAVT	‖‖	◇⚡	A.M. DRIVE	Morn. Humor
👢	93.7	WDLS	‖	◇⚡	MORE	News 11:50am; Ctry. Ctdwn. Su 12N–3pm; Overdrive Truckers Ctdwn. Su 11pm
☀OLDIES	92.1	WEAY	‖	◇⚡	🕐	Stk. Mkt. :15 AM Drive; Jimmy Dee Oldies F–Sa 7–9pm; Dick Clark Oldies Su 12N
E ❀ Z	97.9	WWSH	‖‖	◇⚡	🕐	Wall Street Report M–F 7, 9am, 12N, 1, 4, 6pm, Sa & Su 10, 11am, 12N
🎹	89.9	WVIA	‖‖		MORE	**NPR; APR;** News: W.E. Sa & Su 8–10am, ATC 5–6pm; Swing Street Jazz Su 7–11pm
ek-lek´-tik	90.7	WCLH	‖	◇⚡	SEE S.P.	News 12N, 6pm; Wilkes College
TⱢⱢ⸆TⱢ	980	WILK	‖			
TOBYHANNA						
🎸	107.9	WPMR	‖	🚗	A.M. DRIVE	**CLASSIC ROCK;** Morn. Humor
STROUDSBURG/ALLENTOWN AREA						
A♪dult Pop	96.1	WLEV	‖‖			
A♪dult Pop	106.3	WFMV	‖			

DOVER 30   SEE METRO NEW YORK CITY   E

WEST

FORMAT ♪ TUNE TO		STATION	SIGNAL POWER	TRAFFIC REPORT	NEWS	SPECIAL PROGRAMMING
T○P40	93.5	WSBG	‖	🚗	MORE	News 12N; Morn. Humor; Saturday Night Dance Party; Alternative Music Su evening
T○P40	99.9	WHXT	‖‖	🚗	SPOT NEWS	Morn. Humor
T○P40	104.1	WAEB	‖‖	🚗	SEE S.P.	News 25 after the hour; AM Dance Traxx Sa 11pm–2am; C. Kasem Top 40 Su 8am–12N
E ❀ Z	100.7	WFMZ	‖‖	🚗	🕐	
ek-lek′-tik	89.7	WDVR	‖	◇		Church Services Su 6am–12N; Amer. Indian Music Sa 6–8am; Traditional Ctry. F 7pm
🎓	90.3	WESS	‖	◇	SEE S.P.	News 11:50am, 5:50pm; Morn. Humor; Spts.
DOVER AREA						
A♪ult Pop	102.3	WSUS	‖			
T○P40	103.7	WNNJ	‖	🚗	SEE S.P.	News 10am, 4pm; Morn. Humor
🎸	105.5	WDHA	‖	🚗	AM DRIVE	Morn. Humor; Ski Reports 9:05am, 5:05pm
🎓	91.9	WNTI	‖‖			**ADULT POPULAR; OLDIES;** Centenary College
†††	99.1	WAWZ	‖‖	◇	🕐	**INSPIRATIONAL MUSIC;** Insight for Living 11:30am; Focus on the Family 9am, 4:30pm
SEE NEW YORK CITY METRO PAGE 206						

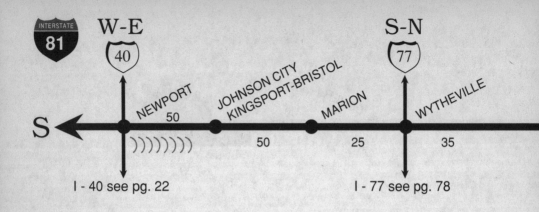

I - 40 see pg. 22

I - 77 see pg. 78

FORMAT ♪ TUNE TO		STATION	SIGNAL POWER	TRAFFIC REPORT	NEWS	SPECIAL PROGRAMMING
FARTHER SOUTH SEE I-40 PAGE 23						
JOHNSON CITY/KINGSPORT-BRISTOL AREA						
Adult Pop	98.5	WTFM	‖‖			Solid Gold Lunch 12:30–1pm; Live from the 60's Sa 12M–3am, Su 9am–12N
Top40	101.5	WQUT	‖‖	◇	MORE	News 12N; Morn. Humor; Casey Kasem Su 9am–1pm
Top40	104.9	WZXY	‖			
🎸	103.9	WXIS	‖‖	◇	MORE	News 12N; Spts.; American Top 40 Sa 9am; King Biscuit Flower Hour Su 9pm
🎸☮	92.7	WABN	‖	◇	MORE	News 12N, 3pm; Morn. Humor; Spts.
🤠👢	96.9	WXBQ	‖‖	🚗	🕐	
🤠👢	99.3	WUSJ	‖	◇	A.M. DRIVE	Morn. Humor
☀LDIES	104.3	WEYE	‖	◇	🕐	Morn. Humor
🎹	89.5	WETS	‖‖		MORE	**NPR; APR;** News: W.E. Sa & Su 8–10am; Jazz M–Thu 10pm–1am, F, Sa, Su 12M–1am
✝✝✝	91.5	WHCB	‖‖	◇	🕐	**EDUCATIONAL;** Outdoor Report Sa 7am; Living in Today's World M–F 9:25am
MARION AREA						
Adult Pop	97.3	WKBC	‖‖	◇	🕐	**TOP 40;** Morn. Humor; Spts.: U. of North Carolina, NBC; Ski Reports
Top40	102.5	WOLD	‖			**ADULT POPULAR**
🤠👢	93.9	WMEV	‖‖			
WYTHEVILLE AREA						
Top40	104.5	WHAJ	‖‖	◇	AM & PM DRIVE	Morn. Humor; Spts. News 20 after the hr. 5–9am; 104 Minutes with…M–F 1:20pm

INTERSTATE **81**

CHRISTIANSBURG   ROANOKE   LYNCHBURG/BUENA VISTA

25   40   **N**

FORMAT ♪ TUNE TO		STATION	SIGNAL POWER	TRAFFIC REPORT	NEWS	SPECIAL PROGRAMMING
🥾	98.1	WBRF	‖‖	◇	🕐	Farm Reports 12:25pm; Spts.: College; Community Focus M 6:30pm
🥾	107.1	WPSK	‖	◇	MORE	News 12N, 3pm; Spts. News 7:45am; World of Racing 11:30am; House Party Sa 8–11pm
CHRISTIANSBURG AREA						
🎸	104.9	WVVV	‖	◇	🕐	**CLASSIC ROCK;** Spts.: Virginia Tech
🥾	101.7	WRIQ	‖	◇	🕐	Stk. Mkt. 6:30pm
ek-lek'-tik	89.9	WVRU	‖	◇	🕐	Old Radio Comedy & Drama Su 6–7pm; Children's Programming Su 5–6pm, 7–7:30pm
ek-lek'-tik	90.7	WUVT	‖			Jazz M–F 9am–12N, Su 6–9am; New Music M–F 3–9pm; Local Zone (Live) Su 7pm
✝✝✝	100.7	WFNR	‖	◇	🕐	**BLUEGRASS; SOUTH. GOSPEL;** News also on the 1/2 hour; It's Your Time 12N–1pm
ROANOKE AREA						
A♪ultPop	99.1	WSLQ	‖‖			**OLDIES;** The Breakfast Club M–F 5–9am; Car Tunes (Oldies) M–F 3–7pm; Wknds.: Oldies
Top40	92.3	WXLK	‖‖	◇	AM DRIVE	Morn. Humor
🎸	96.3	WROV	‖‖	◇	AM DRIVE	**CLASSIC ROCK;** Classic Nine 9–9:45am; Short Order Lunch 12N; Vintage Block 6pm
🥾	93.5	WJLM	‖	🚐	SPOT NEWS	Ski Reports
🥾	103.3	WAKG	‖‖	◇	MORE	News 12:30, 1:30pm; NASCAR Racing
E ❄ Z	94.9	WPVR	‖‖	🚐	🕐	Stk. Mkt. hourly; Special of the Week Su 12N; Big Band Sa 8pm
🛋	89.1	WVTF	‖‖	◇	MORE	**NPR;** All That Jazz Sa 10pm; Bluegrass Su 7pm; Jazz Club Sa 8pm
🎶	960	WFIR	‖			

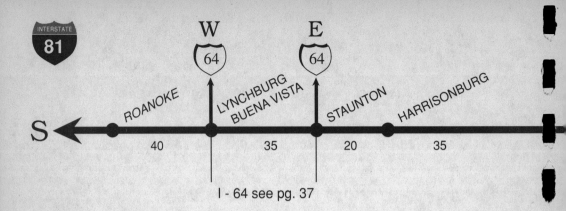

INTERSTATE 81

W 64   E 64

S ← ROANOKE   LYNCHBURG BUENA VISTA   STAUNTON   HARRISONBURG

40   35   20   35

I - 64 see pg. 37

FORMAT ♪ TUNE TO	STATION	SIGNAL POWER	TRAFFIC REPORT	NEWS	SPECIAL PROGRAMMING
LYNCHBURG/BUENA VISTA AREA					
96.7	WREL	‖			
107.9	WYYD	‖‖		AM & PM DRIVE	House Party Sa 8–10pm; Amer. Ctry. Ctdwn. Su 8pm–12M; NASCAR Live Tu 7pm
88.3	WRVL	‖‖	◇	AM & PM DRIVE	Insight for Living 10am; Focus on the Family 1:30pm
STAUNTON AREA					
TOP40 93.5	WSGM	‖	◇	MORE	**ADULT POPULAR;** Stk.Mkt. 5:30pm; Spts. News 8:15am, 5:15pm; Consum. Rprt. 11am
105.5	WSKO	‖	◇		News also on the 1/2 hr.; Spts. News M–F 7:45, 8:45am; Business Report M–F 5:45pm
OLDIES 99.7	WANV	‖‖	◇		Solid Gold Scrapbook Sa 7pm–12M; Lite Jazz Su 9pm–2am
E Z 94.3	WTON	‖‖	◇	AM & PM DRIVE	
HARRISONBURG AREA					
Adult Pop 98.5	WPKZ	‖‖	◇	AM & PM DRIVE	
TOP40 100.7	WQPO	‖‖	◇	MORE	News 12N, 3pm; Morn. Humor
105.1	WRDJ	‖	◇		
104.3	WKCY	‖‖	◇	MORE	News 12N; Morn. Humor; Spts. News 7:40am, 5:40pm
90.7	WMRA	‖‖	◇	MORE	**NPR;** News 12N; Blues Valley Sa 10pm–1am; Public Affairs M–F 6:30pm; Bluegrass
WOODSTOCK AREA					
Adult Pop 106.3	WLCC	‖	◇		**OLDIES; NEWS;** Spts.: Redskins; Live from the 60's Sa PM; Farm News 6:05am
96.9	WSIG	‖			

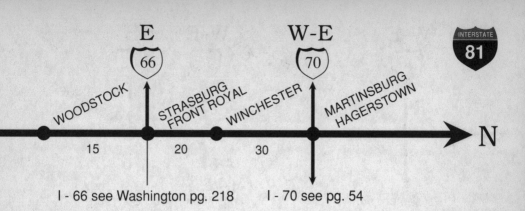

I - 66 see Washington pg. 218   I - 70 see pg. 54

FORMAT ♪ TUNE TO	STATION	SIGNAL POWER	TRAFFIC REPORT	NEWS	SPECIAL PROGRAMMING
E ❄ Z	95.9 WAZR	‖			RELIGIOUS
†††	103.9 WYFT	‖	⚡	🕐	Insight for Living M–F 10:30am; Questions and Answers Sa 12:30pm
STRASBURG/FRONT ROYAL AREA					
Adult Pop	95.3 WFTR	‖	⚡	🕐	Talknet Su–F 7pm–1am; Radio Kandy Sa 5–7pm; Rock & Roll Oldies Sa 7pm–12M
Adult Pop	104.9 WESI	‖	⚡	🕐	Ctdwn. America Su 10am–2pm; National Mus. Survey Sa 9am–12N; Oldies Su 6–11pm
Top40	99.3 WFQX	‖			
☀ OLDIES	107.7 WMJR	‖‖	🚗	MORE	News 12N; Solid Gold Sa 7pm–12M; Req. Su 7pm–12M; Solid Gold Scrapbook Su 9am
WINCHESTER AREA					
Adult Pop	92.5 WINC	‖‖	⚡		Morn. Humor; Spts.: U. of VA Football/Basketball
Adult Pop	98.3 WXVA	‖	🚗	🕐	
Adult Pop	105.5 WAPP	‖			
🤠	102.5 WUSQ	‖‖	⚡	MORE	News 12N; Amer. Ctry. Ctdwn. Sa 5–9pm; Nascar Ctry. Sa 9–11pm; Midnight CD M–F
†††	91.3 WTRM	‖‖	⚡	AM & PM DRIVE	
MARTINSBURG/HAGERSTOWN AREA					
Adult Pop	106.9 WARX	‖‖	⚡		Jazz Brunch Su 9am–12N; Magic After Dark M–Sa 9pm–12M; Ski Rprts. Thu–Sa 7:45am
Top40	96.7 WQCM	‖			
Top40	97.5 WKMZ	‖‖	⚡	🕐	Morn. Humor; Open House Party Sa & Su 7pm–12M
MARTINSBURG/HAGERSTOWN CONTINUED NEXT PAGE					

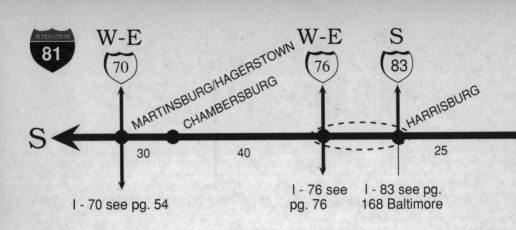

I - 70 see pg. 54

I - 76 see pg. 76

I - 83 see pg. 168 Baltimore

FORMAT / TUNE TO	STATION	SIGNAL POWER	TRAFFIC REPORT	NEWS	SPECIAL PROGRAMMING
CONTINUATION OF MARTINSBURG/HAGERSTOWN AREA					
95.9	WYII	‖	◇	🕐	NBC Morningline Sports 6:15am, Updates 7:45am; Farm Mkt. Reports 12:50pm
E✿Z 99.9	WFRE	‖‖	🚗	🕐	**BIG BAND; LITE HITS;** News also on 1/2 hr; Swing Sa 8pm; Spec. of the Week Su 9am
E✿Z 104.7	WWMD	‖‖	🚗	🕐	Stk. Mkt. 4:45pm
88.9	WVEP	‖‖		MORE	**NPR; APR;** News: W.E. Sa 8–11am, Su 11am–1pm; Mtn. Stg. Sa 6–8pm, Su 3–5pm
✝✝✝ 90.5	WCRH	‖‖	◇	🕐	**CHRISTIAN CONTEMPORARY;** Insight for Living; Focus on the Family
1410	WHAG	‖	◇	🕐	News also on the 1/2 hour
CHAMBERSBURG AREA					
Adult Pop 92.1	WGLL	‖	◇	MORE	News 12N, 3pm; Sprgld. F & Sa 7pm–12M; Live ... 60's Su 9am; Big Band Su 6pm
Top40 95.1	WIKZ	‖‖	◇	MORE	News 11:53am; Christian Contemporary Music Su 7–9am
101.5	WAYZ	‖‖			
107.7	WGTY	‖‖	🚗	MORE	News 12N; Morn. Humor
E✿Z 94.3	WKSL	‖			**RELIGIOUS**
HARRISBURG AREA					
Adult Pop 99.3	WIMX	‖	🚗	MORE	**OLDIES;** News 2:55pm; Fri. Night Live at Wanda's; Lunchtime at the Oldies M–F 12N
Adult Pop 103.3	WARM	‖‖	🚗	🕐	**OLDIES;** Morn. Humor; Noontime at the Oldies 12N–1pm; Love Sounds 9pm–12M
Top40 104.1	WNNK	‖‖	🚗	🕐	Morn. Humor; Stk. Mkt.; Spts. News AM Drive
93.5	WTPA	‖			

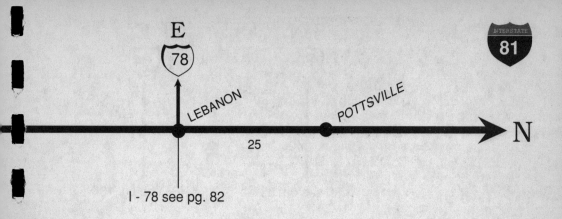

E
🛡️78

LEBANON   POTTSVILLE

25   N

INTERSTATE 81

I - 78 see pg. 82

FORMAT 🎵 TUNE TO		STATION	SIGNAL POWER	TRAFFIC REPORT	NEWS	SPECIAL PROGRAMMING
👢	102.3	WHYL	‖	🚗	MORE	News 12N
👢	106.7	WRKZ	‖‖	🚗	A M DRIVE	Morn. Humor
☀️OLDIES	94.9	WWKL	‖‖			
R&B	105.7	WQXA	‖‖	🚗		Morn. Humor
E 🌼 Z	97.3	WHP	‖‖	🚗	A M DRIVE	
🎹	89.5	WITF	‖‖	🚗	MORE	**NPR;** News on the hr; Folk Sa 8–10pm; Classical Requests W 6:30–9pm
NEWS	1230	WKBO	‖	🚗	ALL NEWS	International News on the hr. & 1/2 hr.; Local Anchors & Field Reporters Live on Scene
T🗣️LK	580	WHP	‖			
LEBANON AREA						
Adult Pop	100.1	WUFM	‖			
T⁰P40	92.1	WCTX	‖	🚗	🕐	**OLDIES**
T⁰P40	96.9	WLAN	‖‖	🚗	A M DRIVE	Morn. Humor
T⁰P40	102.5	WRFY	‖‖	🚗	A M DRIVE	**ADULT POPULAR;** Morn. Humor
👢	105.1	WIOV	‖‖			
E 🌼 Z	101.3	WNCE	‖‖	🚗	🕐	Stk. Mkt. 12:15, 5:45pm; Spectrum 10am, 7, 11pm; Jazz Show Su 10am–12N
✝✝✝	94.5	WDAC	‖‖	◇	SPOT NEWS	Farm News 5–6am; Christ. Music daily 4:30, 8:30am; Financial Advice 7:30am, 3:30pm

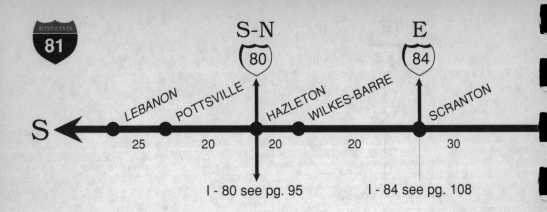

I - 80 see pg. 95   I - 84 see pg. 108

FORMAT / TUNE TO		STATION	SIGNAL POWER	TRAFFIC REPORT	NEWS	SPECIAL PROGRAMMING
	**POTTSVILLE AREA**
Adult Cor	105.5	WMGH	||			
Top40	94.1	WQKX	|||	◇	🕐	
Top40	101.9	WAVT	|||	◇	AM DRIVE	Morn. Humor
	**HAZLETON AREA**
Adult Cor	103.1	WQEQ	||	◇	🕐	Morn. Humor
Top40	106.5	WHLM	|||	🚗	🕐	Rock Roots Su 10am–1pm; C. Kasem Top 40 Su 5–9pm; Future Hits Su 9pm
E ❀ Z	97.9	WWSH	|||	◇	🕐	Wall Street Report M–F 7, 9am, 12N, 1, 4, 6pm, Sa & Su 10, 11am, 12N
	**WILKES-BARRE AREA**
Adult Cor	92.9	WMGS	|||	◇	AM & PM DRIVE	**LITE HITS;** Morn. Humor; Oldies 12N; Love Songs 9pm–12M
Top40	98.5	WKRZ	|||			
👢	93.7	WDLS	||	◇	MORE	News 11:50am; Ctry. Ctdwn. Su 12N–3pm; Overdrive Truckers Ctdwn. Su 11pm
☀OLDIES	92.1	WEAY	||	◇	🕐	Stk. Mkt. :15 AM Drive; Jimmy Dee Oldies F–Sa 7–9pm; Dick Clark Oldies Su 12N
ek-lek-tik	90.7	WCLH	||	◇	SEE BELOW	News 12N, 6pm; Wilkes College
✝✝✝	88.1	WRGN	||	◇	🕐	Minirth–Meier Clinic 1pm; Primetime Amer. 4:30pm; Bible Quiz 7:15am; Call-In 10:30am
📻ᴿᴷ 🎷	980	WILK	||			
	**SCRANTON AREA**
Adult Cor	101.3	WGBI	|||			

E
88

MONTROSE · BINGHAMTON · CORTLAND · N

20   45

INTERSTATE 81

I - 88 SPUR SEE NEXT PAGE

FORMAT / TUNE TO		STATION	SIGNAL POWER	TRAFFIC REPORT	NEWS	SPECIAL PROGRAMMING
Adult Cont	104.9	WWDL	‖	◇	SPOT NEWS	Breeze Special Su 10am–12N; Lite Gold Sa 7pm–12M; Community Forum Su 7:30–8am
Top 40	102.3	WWRB	‖	◇	AM DRIVE	Open House Party Sa, Su 7pm; Amer. Top 40 Su 10am–2pm; Comedy Hour Su 7am
	107.1	WEZX	‖	◇	MORE	News 1pm; Morn. Humor
Oldies	94.3	WSGD	‖	🚗	AM DRIVE	Morn. Humor
	89.9	WVIA	‖‖		MORE	NPR; APR; News: W.E. Sa & Su 8–10am, ATC 5–6pm; Swing Street Jazz Su 7–11pm
Talk	1550	WARD	‖			
MONTROSE AREA						
	92.5	WKGB	‖	◇	SEE S.P.	News 4pm; Morn. Humor; Classic Rock Cafe 12N; Powercuts Su PM; Rockline M PM
✝✝✝	96.5	WPEL	‖‖	◇	🕐	
BINGHAMTON AREA						
Adult Cont	103.3	WMXW	‖			
Adult Cont	105.7	WMRV	‖‖	🚗	SPOT NEWS	Morn. Humor
Top 40	99.1	WAAL	‖‖	🚗	🕐	Morn. Humor; Casey Kasem Su 8am–12N
	90.5	WHRW	‖		SPOT NEWS	State U. of New York; Ethnic Programs
	98.1	WHWK	‖‖	◇	SPOT NEWS	Ctry. Today Sa 6–7pm; Amer. Ctry. Ctdwn. Su 12N–4pm
Oldies	101.7	WQXT	‖			
	89.3	WSKG	‖‖		MORE	NPR; APR; News: W.E. Sa 10am–12N, Su 11am–1pm, ATC 5–6pm; Jazz F 8pm

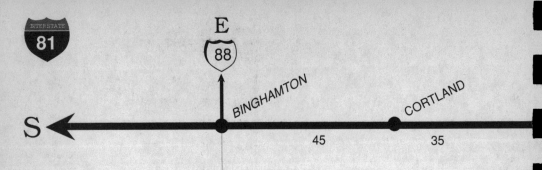

S ← BINGHAMTON ---- 45 ---- CORTLAND ---- 35 ----

E 88 I-81

I - 88 SPUR SEE BELOW

FORMAT / TUNE TO		STATION	SIGNAL POWER	TRAFFIC REPORT	NEWS	SPECIAL PROGRAMMING
	**I-88 SPUR (SIDNEY/ONEONTA)**					
TOP40	100.9	WCDO	‖	◇⚡	🕐	News also on the 1/2 hr; Stk. Mkt. 5:10, 6:10pm; Star Tracks F 6:10pm
🎸☮	103.1	WZOZ	‖	◇⚡	AM & PM DRIVE	Juke Box Sa Nite 6–9pm; Live from the 60's Sa 9pm–12M; Jazz Cafe Su 8–11am
E ❄ Z	103.9	WSRK	‖	◇⚡	🕐	Stk. Mkt. 8am, 1, 5:30pm; Feature Time (Community Affairs) Su 10am
	**FARTHER NORTHEAST ON I-88 SEE I-90 PAGE 126**					
	**CORTLAND AREA**					
A dult Pop	97.3	WYXL	‖‖	◇⚡	AM & PM DRIVE	
A dult Pop	103.7	WQNY	‖‖	◇⚡	A M DRIVE	Morn. Humor; Solid Gold Sa 7pm–12M; Reelin' in the Years Su 12N–3pm
TOP40	99.9	WNYP	‖‖	◇⚡	A M DRIVE	Morn. Humor
🎸	93.5	WVBR	‖	◇⚡	🕐	This Sunday 7pm; Being Ourselves (Feminist Radio) Su 10:30am
🎸	91.7	WICB	‖	◇⚡	SEE S.P.	**JAZZ** M 11am–4pm, Thu & F 12N–4pm; News M, Tu, W, F 6:30pm, Thu 6pm; Blues W 10am
Lite Hits	93.9	WKXZ	‖‖		AM & PM DRIVE	Stk. Mkt. 12:10, 5:50pm; Light Jazz Mix 9pm–1am; Jazz Show Su 9pm
🎹	90.9	WSQG	‖		MORE	NPR; APR; News: W.E. Sa 10am–12N, Su 11am–1pm; Jazz F 8pm; Opera Sa 1:30pm
	**SYRACUSE AREA**					
A dult Pop	94.5	WYYY	‖‖	🚗	A M DRIVE	**TOP 40;** Morn. Humor; Oldies Sa 7pm–12M; C. Kasem Top 40 Su 6–10pm
TOP40	93.1	WNTQ	‖‖	🚐	AM & PM DRIVE	Morn. Humor; Shadoe Stevens American Top 40 Su 6am
🎸	95.7	WAQX	‖‖	◇⚡	A M DRIVE	Morn. Humor; Street Talk Su AM
Lite Hits	100.9	WEZG	‖	🚗	MORE	News 4:40pm, News & Views M–F 1:52pm; Morn. Humor; Syracuse Spectrum Su 6am

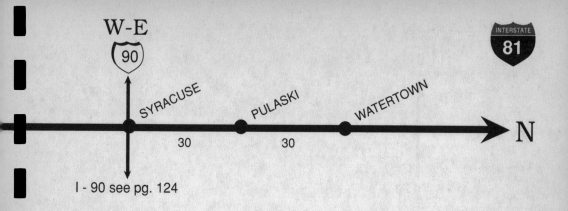

W-E 90

I - 90 see pg. 124

INTERSTATE 81

SYRACUSE — 30 — PULASKI — 30 — WATERTOWN — N

FORMAT ♪ TUNE TO		STATION	SIGNAL POWER	TRAFFIC REPORT	NEWS	SPECIAL PROGRAMMING
☮	104.7	WKFM	|||	🚗	⊙MORE	News 10am; Comedy Break M–F 5pm; Kix Classics Sa 10am–12N; 6-Pack Su 6pm
🤠	106.9	WPCX	|||		⊙MORE	News 10am, 12N; Farm Reports 5am; Spts. News 5:30, 10am
☀OLDIES	92.1	WSEN	|||			
E ❀ Z	107.9	WRHP	|||			
🎹	91.3	WCNY	|||		⊙SEE S.P.	**NPR;** News: ATC M–F 5–6:30pm, 10am, 7:30pm; Opera Sa 1:30pm; Jazz M–F 6:30pm
🎹	105.1	WVOA	|||	◇	⊙	Voices of the Arts M–F 7:20am, 4:20, 6:20pm; Video Review Tu–F 5:20pm
🎺	88.3	WAER	||	◇	⊙MORE	**NPR;** News also on the 1/2 hr; Afropop Worldwide Su 10–11pm
✝✝✝	102.9	WMHR	|||			
PULASKI AREA						
A♪ult Pop	105.5	WGES	||	🚗	⊙	MRN Races Su 12N; NASCAR Live Tu 7–8pm
🤠	101.7	WSCP	||			
ek-lek′-tik	89.9	WRVO	|||			**NPR;** State U. of New York
WATERTOWN AREA						
ᴛᴼᴾ40	93.5	WTNY	||	◇	⊙AM DRIVE	American Top 40 Su 9am–1pm; Hitline USA Su 11pm–12M
🎸	97.5	WCIZ	|||	◇	⊙AM DRIVE	Morn. Humor
Lite Hits	103.1	WTOJ	||	◇	⊙MORE	News 12N; Morn. Humor
🎹	90.9	WJNY	|||		⊙SEE S.P.	**NPR;** Nws. ATC M–F 5-6:30pm, 10am, 7:30pm; Opera Sa 1:30–5pm; Jazz M–F 6:30–7:30pm
NORTH OF WATERTOWN SCAN FOR CANADIAN STATIONS						

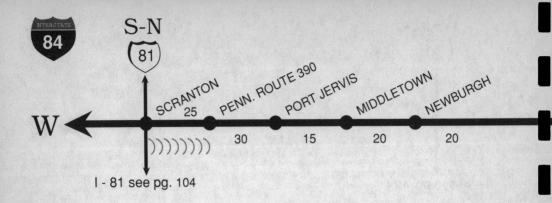

S-N
(81)

SCRANTON 25   PENN. ROUTE 390   PORT JERVIS   MIDDLETOWN   NEWBURGH
30   15   20   20

W

I - 81 see pg. 104

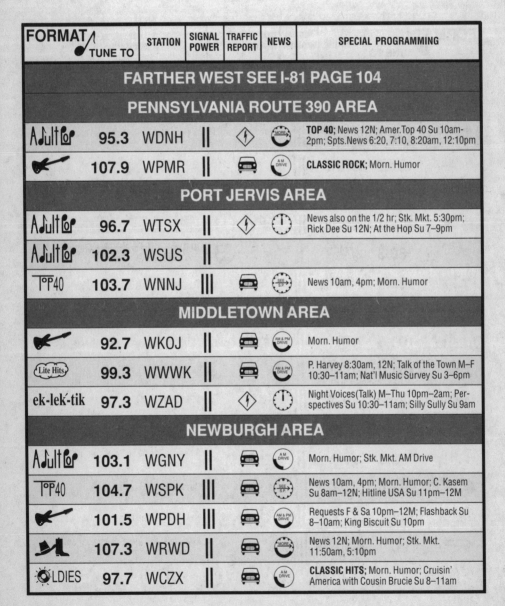

FORMAT / TUNE TO		STATION	SIGNAL POWER	TRAFFIC REPORT	NEWS	SPECIAL PROGRAMMING
FARTHER WEST SEE I-81 PAGE 104						
PENNSYLVANIA ROUTE 390 AREA						
Adult Pop	95.3	WDNH	‖	◇	MORE	**TOP 40;** News 12N; Amer.Top 40 Su 10am–2pm; Spts.News 6:20, 7:10, 8:20am, 12:10pm
🎸	107.9	WPMR	‖	🚗	A M DRIVE	**CLASSIC ROCK;** Morn. Humor
PORT JERVIS AREA						
Adult Pop	96.7	WTSX	‖	◇	🕐	News also on the 1/2 hr; Stk. Mkt. 5:30pm; Rick Dee Su 12N; At the Hop Su 7–9pm
Adult Pop	102.3	WSUS	‖			
TOP40	103.7	WNNJ	‖‖	🚗	SEE SP	News 10am, 4pm; Morn. Humor
MIDDLETOWN AREA						
🎸	92.7	WKOJ	‖	🚗	AM & PM DRIVE	Morn. Humor
Lite Hits	99.3	WWWK	‖	🚗	AM & PM DRIVE	P. Harvey 8:30am, 12N; Talk of the Town M–F 10:30–11am; Nat'l Music Survey Su 3–6pm
ek-lek′-tik	97.3	WZAD	‖	◇	🕐	Night Voices(Talk) M–Thu 10pm–2am; Perspectives Su 10:30–11am; Silly Sully Su 9am
NEWBURGH AREA						
Adult Pop	103.1	WGNY	‖	🚗	A M DRIVE	Morn. Humor; Stk. Mkt. AM Drive
TOP40	104.7	WSPK	‖‖	🚗	SEE SP	News 10am, 4pm; Morn. Humor; C. Kasem Su 8am–12N; Hitline USA Su 11pm–12M
🎸	101.5	WPDH	‖‖	🚗	AM & PM DRIVE	Requests F & Sa 10pm–12M; Flashback Su 8–10am; King Biscuit Su 10pm
🤠	107.3	WRWD	‖	🚗	MORE	News 12N; Morn. Humor; Stk. Mkt. 11:50am, 5:10pm
☀OLDIES	97.7	WCZX	‖	🚗	A M DRIVE	**CLASSIC HITS;** Morn. Humor; Cruisin' America with Cousin Brucie Su 8–11am

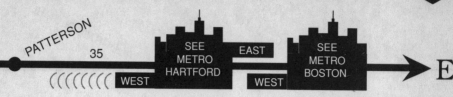

PATTERSON 35 WEST SEE METRO HARTFORD EAST WEST SEE METRO BOSTON E

INTERSTATE 84

FORMAT ♪ TUNE TO	STATION	SIGNAL POWER	TRAFFIC REPORT	NEWS	SPECIAL PROGRAMMING
Lite Hits 92.1	WRNQ	‖			
E ❋ Z 100.7	WHUD	‖‖	🚗	AM DRIVE	Morn. Humor; Stk. Mkt.
88.7	WRHV	‖	◇	MORE	**APR;** News 10am, 12N, 2pm; Music for a Late Afternoon 4–6pm; Morn. Prog. 6–9am
90.9	WAMK	‖‖	◇	MORE	**NPR; APR; ECLECTIC;** News: M–F 12N–1pm, W.E. Sa & Su 12N–2pm
96.9	WEXT	‖			
†✝† 89.7	WFGB	‖‖		🕐	**CHRISTIAN ADULT POPULAR MUSIC**
PATTERSON AREA					
Adult Cor 105.5	WMJV	‖			
Top40 106.3	WVIP	‖	🚗	SEE P.	News at :15 and :45; Morn. Humor
SEE HARTFORD METRO PAGE 190					
SEE BOSTON METRO PAGE 172					

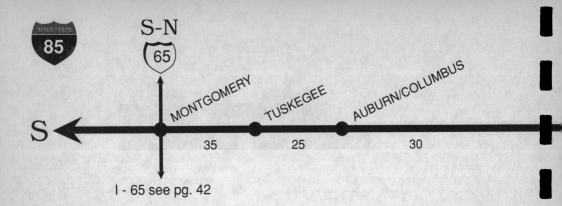

I - 65 see pg. 42

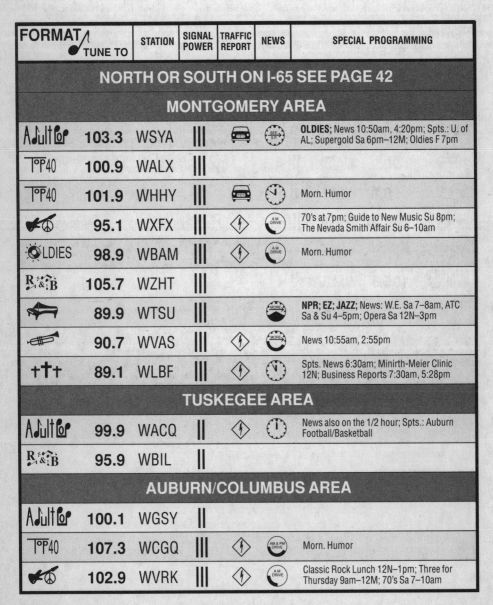

FORMAT ♪ TUNE TO		STATION	SIGNAL POWER	TRAFFIC REPORT	NEWS	SPECIAL PROGRAMMING
NORTH OR SOUTH ON I-65 SEE PAGE 42						
MONTGOMERY AREA						
A♪ult Pop	103.3	WSYA	‖‖	🚗	SEE S.P.	**OLDIES;** News 10:50am, 4:20pm; Spts.: U. of AL; Supergold Sa 6pm–12M; Oldies F 7pm
Top40	100.9	WALX	‖‖			
Top40	101.9	WHHY	‖‖	🚗	🕐	Morn. Humor
🎸☮	95.1	WXFX	‖‖	◇	AM DRIVE	70's at 7pm; Guide to New Music Su 8pm; The Nevada Smith Affair Su 6–10am
☀OLDIES	98.9	WBAM	‖‖	◇	AM DRIVE	Morn. Humor
R&B	105.7	WZHT	‖‖			
🎹	89.9	WTSU	‖‖		MORE	**NPR; EZ; JAZZ;** News: W.E. Sa 7–8am, ATC Sa & Su 4–5pm; Opera Sa 12N–3pm
🎺	90.7	WVAS	‖‖	◇	MORE	News 10:55am, 2:55pm
✝✝✝	89.1	WLBF	‖‖	◇	🕐	Spts. News 6:30am; Minirth-Meier Clinic 12N; Business Reports 7:30am, 5:28pm
TUSKEGEE AREA						
A♪ult Pop	99.9	WACQ	‖	◇	🕐	News also on the 1/2 hour; Spts.: Auburn Football/Basketball
R&B	95.9	WBIL	‖			
AUBURN/COLUMBUS AREA						
A♪ult Pop	100.1	WGSY	‖			
Top40	107.3	WCGQ	‖‖	◇	AM & PM DRIVE	Morn. Humor
🎸☮	102.9	WVRK	‖‖	◇	AM DRIVE	Classic Rock Lunch 12N–1pm; Three for Thursday 9am–12M; 70's Sa 7–10am

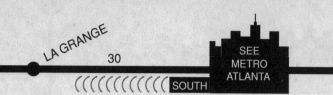

LA GRANGE 30

SEE METRO ATLANTA

SOUTH

N

FORMAT / TUNE TO		STATION	SIGNAL POWER	TRAFFIC REPORT	NEWS	SPECIAL PROGRAMMING
🎵	97.7	WKKR	‖			
🎵	106.1	WSTH	‖‖	⚡	SEE S.P.	News 11am, 5pm; Paul Harvey; Morn. Humor; Spts.; Larry King
R&B	98.3	WAGH	‖			
R&B	104.9	WFXE	‖	⚡	AM & PM DRIVE	Love Ballads/Jazz Format; Inspirations Across Amer. Su 9am
🎹	91.7	WTJB	‖	⚡	MORE	**NPR; EZ; JAZZ;** News: W.E. Sa 7–8am, ATC Sa & Su 4–5pm; Opera Sa 12N–3pm
ek-lek´-tik	91.1	WEGL	‖	⚡	SEE S.P.	News 6:50am, 5:50pm; Stardate 6pm & 10pm; Specialty Programs
✝✝✝	89.5	WYFK	‖‖			
✝✝✝	90.5	WFRC	‖	⚡	MORE	News 2:55pm; Open Forum 10–11:30pm; For Your Information 5:35am, 12:40pm
LA GRANGE AREA						
🎵	100.9	WCJM	‖	⚡	SEE S.P.	**COUNTRY GOSPEL;** News 7, 10, 11am, 3pm
🎵	102.3	WELR	‖	⚡	🕐	News also on the 1/2 hour; Farm Reports; Spts.
🎵	104.1	WYAI	‖‖	🚗	AM DRIVE	Local Ctry. Ctdwn. Sa 7–10am; NASCAR Ctry. Su 8–11am; Public Affairs Su 5–8am
🎹	88.1	WJSP	‖‖			
✝✝✝	90.9	WOAK	‖	⚡	MORE	News 12N, 1pm; Old-Time Quarter Hour M 9:30pm; Gospel Favorite Requests F 9:30am
✝✝✝	93.3	WVFJ	‖‖	⚡	🕐	Focus on the Fam. M–F 10:30am; Point of View M–F 2pm; In Touch M–F 9:05am, 9pm
SEE ATLANTA METRO PAGE 166						

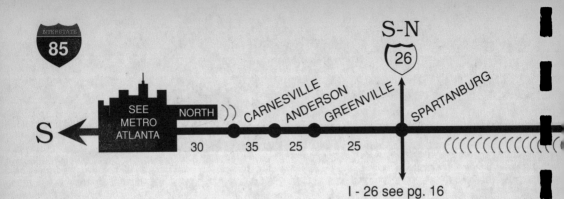

I - 26 see pg. 16

FORMAT / TUNE TO		STATION	SIGNAL POWER	TRAFFIC REPORT	NEWS	SPECIAL PROGRAMMING
	**SEE ATLANTA METRO PAGE 166**						
	**CARNESVILLE AREA**						
👢	99.3	WCON	‖‖‖	⬦	🕐	News also on the 1/2 hour; Morn. Humor
👢	106.1	WZLI	‖‖‖	⬦	🕐	Spts.: Georgia College Football
☀OLDIES	103.7	WPUP	‖‖	⬦	SEE S.P.	**ADULT POP; EZ; LITE HITS;** News 8:30am, 5:30pm; Spts. News 7:40am, 5:40pm
✝✝✝	90.9	WRAF	‖‖‖	⬦	🕐	Toccoa Falls College
	**ANDERSON AREA**						
TOP40	107.3	WANS	‖‖‖	🚗	A M DRIVE	Morn. Humor
🎸	101.1	WCKN	‖‖‖			**OLDIES**
🎸	88.1	WSBF	‖	🚗	🕐	Talk Show M–F 6:30pm; Jazz M–F 4–7pm; Class. Su 10am–1pm; Folk Su 1–4pm
👢	103.1	WRIX	‖	⬦	🕐	**TALK;** News also on the 1/2 hour; Spts.; Oldies Show
E❀Z	98.1	WBFM	‖‖‖	⬦	🕐	Spts.: Clemson; Wax Works (Nostalgia) M–F 10am, Sa 7–10pm
	**GREENVILLE AREA**						
🎸	96.5	WPLS	‖		SEE S.P.	News 8, 10am, 4, 6pm; Top 35 W 7pm; Jazz Su 5–7pm; Dance 9–11pm; Class. Su 1–3pm
👢	92.5	WESC	‖‖‖	🚗	A M DRIVE	Spts.: U. of South Carolina Football
👢	100.5	WSSL	‖‖‖			
☀OLDIES	93.7	WFBC	‖‖‖	🚗	A M DRIVE	Oldies Cafe M–F 12N–1pm; Five o'clock Freeway Freebees M–F 5–6pm
R&B	103.9	WLWZ	‖			

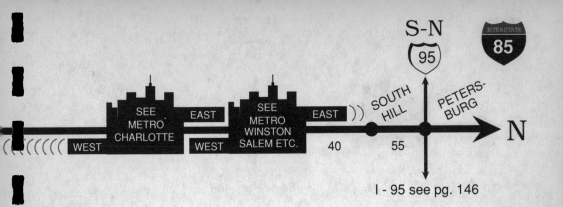

I - 95 see pg. 146

FORMAT ♪ TUNE TO		STATION	SIGNAL POWER	TRAFFIC REPORT	NEWS	SPECIAL PROGRAMMING
E❄Z	94.5	WMUU	|||	🚗	🕐	**CLASSICAL** M–F 2–3, 7:30–10pm; Su 2–3pm; **RELIGIOUS** M–F 12M–5am; Stk. Mkt. hrly.
🎹	90.1	WEPR	|||	◇	MORE	**NPR;** News: W.E. Sa 10am–12N; Prairie Home Comp. Sa 6pm; Radio Read. M–F 8am
†††	89.3	WLFJ	|||	◇	MORE	News 12N, 3pm; Morn. Humor
🆃🅰🅻🅺	1330	WFBC	||	🚗	🕐	News also on the 1/2 hr, 6–7pm; Spts.: Clemson U; Sportsline M–F 5–6pm
SPARTANBURG AREA						
Adult ♥	102.5	WMYI	|||			
🤠	105.3	WAGI	|||	◇	🕐	Gospel Evenings
E❄Z	98.9	WSPA	|||	◇	MORE	News 11am, 1, 3pm; Stk.Mkt. 12:15, 5:15pm; Health Tips 10:15am; Weekly Special Sa 7pm
🎺	93.3	WBBO	|||	◇	MORE	News 12:45pm; Stk.Mkt. 7:15pm; Spts. Minute 7:15, 8:15am, 4:15, 5:15pm
†††	91.1	WYFG	|||		🕐	
†††	106.9	WMIT	|||	◇	🕐	
🆃🅰🅻🅺	910	WORD	||	🚗	🕐	News also on the 1/2 hr, 6–7pm; Spts.: Clemson U.; Sportsline M–F 5–6pm
SEE CHARLOTTE METRO PAGE 176						
SEE WINSTON-SALEM/RALEIGH/DURHAM PAGE 220						
SOUTH HILL AREA						
🤠	104.7	WSVS	|||	◇	🕐	Stk.Mkt. 12N, 6pm; Spts.News AM Drive; Farm Mkt. Reports 6am, 12N; Gospel Su AM
🤠	105.5	WSHV	||			
FARTHER NORTH SEE I-95 PAGE 146						

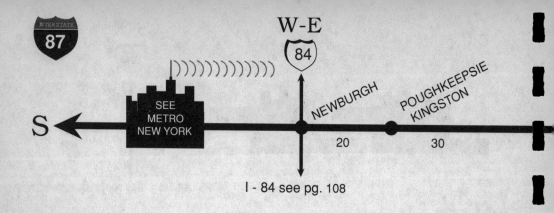

I - 84 see pg. 108

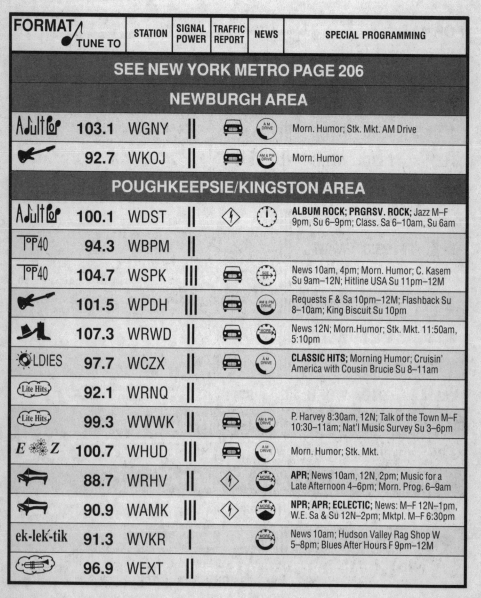

FORMAT ♪ TUNE TO		STATION	SIGNAL POWER	TRAFFIC REPORT	NEWS	SPECIAL PROGRAMMING
SEE NEW YORK METRO PAGE 206						
NEWBURGH AREA						
Adult Pop	103.1	WGNY	‖	🚗	AM DRIVE	Morn. Humor; Stk. Mkt. AM Drive
🎸	92.7	WKOJ	‖	🚗	AM & PM DRIVE	Morn. Humor
POUGHKEEPSIE/KINGSTON AREA						
Adult Pop	100.1	WDST	‖	◇	🕐	ALBUM ROCK; PRGRSV. ROCK; Jazz M–F 9pm, Su 6–9pm; Class. Sa 6–10am, Su 6am
Top40	94.3	WBPM	‖			
Top40	104.7	WSPK	‖‖	🚗	SEE S.P.	News 10am, 4pm; Morn. Humor; C. Kasem Su 9am–12N; Hitline USA Su 11pm–12M
🎸	101.5	WPDH	‖‖	🚗	AM & PM DRIVE	Requests F & Sa 10pm–12M; Flashback Su 8–10am; King Biscuit Su 10pm
🤠	107.3	WRWD	‖	🚗	MORE	News 12N; Morn.Humor; Stk. Mkt. 11:50am, 5:10pm
OLDIES	97.7	WCZX	‖	🚗	AM DRIVE	CLASSIC HITS; Morning Humor; Cruisin' America with Cousin Brucie Su 8–11am
Lite Hits	92.1	WRNQ	‖			
Lite Hits	99.3	WWWK	‖	🚗	AM & PM DRIVE	P. Harvey 8:30am, 12N; Talk of the Town M–F 10:30–11am; Nat'l Music Survey Su 3–6pm
E❄Z	100.7	WHUD	‖‖	🚗	AM DRIVE	Morn. Humor; Stk. Mkt.
🎹	88.7	WRHV	‖	◇	MORE	APR; News 10am, 12N, 2pm; Music for a Late Afternoon 4–6pm; Morn. Prog. 6–9am
🎹	90.9	WAMK	‖‖	◇	MORE	NPR; APR; ECLECTIC; News: M–F 12N–1pm; W.E. Sa & Su 12N–2pm; Mktpl. M–F 6:30pm
ek-lek-tik	91.3	WVKR	‖		MORE	News 10am; Hudson Valley Rag Shop W 5–8pm; Blues After Hours F 9pm–12M
🎵	96.9	WEXT	‖			

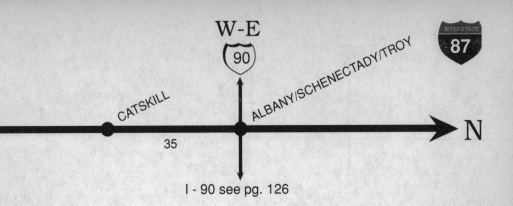

CATSKILL

ALBANY/SCHENECTADY/TROY

INTERSTATE 87

N

35

I - 90 see pg. 126

FORMAT / TUNE TO		STATION	SIGNAL POWER	TRAFFIC REPORT	NEWS	SPECIAL PROGRAMMING
✝✝✝	89.7	WFGB	‖‖		🕐	CHRISTIAN ADULT POPULAR MUSIC
CATSKILL AREA						
TᵒP40	98.5	WQKZ	‖	🚗	AM & PM DRIVE	C. Kasem Su 2–6pm; Big Run on the Radio Su 9–10am; Local Top 40 Sa 11am–3pm
E ❀ Z	93.5	WRVW	‖			
ALBANY/SCHENECTADY/TROY AREA						
A𝒹ult 𝒸oℓ	97.7	WKOL	‖	◇	AM & PM DRIVE	Morn. Humor
A𝒹ult 𝒸oℓ	100.9	WKLI	‖	🚗	AM & PM DRIVE	Morn. Humor; Stk. Mkt. 5:20pm; R & R Oldies Sa 7pm–12M; Love Songs M–F 9pm
TᵒP40	92.3	WFLY	‖‖	🚗	AM & PM DRIVE	Morn. Hum.; C. Kasem Su 11am–3pm; Rock. Amer. Su 6–9am; Amer. Top 40 Sa 6–10pm
TᵒP40	96.7	WVKZ	‖			
🎸	88.3	WVCR	‖‖	◇		Urban 6–9am, 6–9pm; Heavy Mtl. 12M–3am; Polka Su 9pm–12M; Span. Su 12N–6pm
🎸	106.5	WPYX	‖‖	🚗	AM DRIVE	Electric Lunch M–F 12N; 70's at 7pm M–F; Jazz Brunch Su 9am–12N
🎸	103.9	WQBK	‖	🚗	AM DRIVE	
👢	107.7	WGNA	‖‖	🚗	AM DRIVE	Morn. Humor
☀️LDIES	98.3	WSHZ	‖	🚗	MORE	News 11am; Blue Plate Special 12N; 9 o'clock Req. Hour; Back Seat Req. 11pm
☀️LDIES	99.5	WGY	‖‖	🚗	AM DRIVE	Morn. Humor; All-Request Oldies Sa 7pm–12M
E ❀ Z	95.5	WROW	‖‖	🚗	🕐	Special of the Week Su 9am–12N
🎹	89.1	WMHT	‖‖		🕐	News also on the 1/2 hour; Adven. in Good Music M–F 11am; N.E. Showcase Thu 8pm
ALBANY/SCHENECTADY CONTINUED ON NEXT PAGE						

115

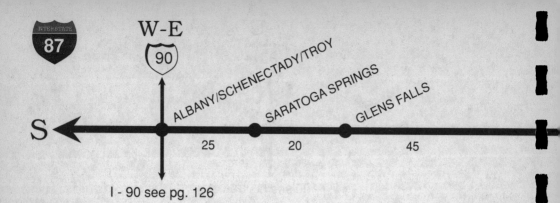

I - 90 see pg. 126

FORMAT / TUNE TO		STATION	SIGNAL POWER	TRAFFIC REPORT	NEWS	SPECIAL PROGRAMMING
CONTINUATION OF ALBANY/SCHENECTADY AREA						
🎹	90.3	WAMC	‖‖	⬙⚡	MORE	**NPR; APR; ECLECTIC;** News M–F 12N–1pm; W.E. Sa & Su 12N–2pm; Mktpl. 6:30–7pm
🎷	103.1	WHRL	‖	⬙⚡	🕐	Stk. Mkt. 12:05, 5:05pm; Business Beat 12:35, 4:35pm; D. Sanborn/Jazz Su 2pm
ek-lek´-tik	91.5	WRPI	‖‖		SEE S.P.	Pacifica News 6:30pm; Spts.: RPI; Public Folk Su 6–8pm; Ethnic Programs Su 9am
═NEWS═	1540	WPTR	"C"	🚗	ALL NEWS	**TALK; SPTS.:** Mets, Patriots, Siena College; Business News :20 & :50
TR¹⊙ST	1300	WQBK	‖	⬙⚡	🕐	Stk. Mkt. 10 before hour Drives; Jim Horne 6:30–10am; John Greaney 6:30–8pm
A♪ult Pop	810	WGY	"C"	🚗	🕐	**TALK** 8pm–5am; News also on the 1/2 hour; Morn. Humor; R. Limbaugh 12N–3pm
SARATOGA SPRINGS AREA						
A♪ult Pop	101.3	WSSV	‖			
A♪ult Pop	102.3	WQQY	|	⬙⚡	🕐	News also on the 1/2 hour; Morn. Humor; Horse Racing Results in Season
🎸	102.7	WEQX	‖‖	⬙⚡	MORE	**ALBUM-ORIENTED ROCK;** News 10:50am; Rock Over London Su 7pm; Jazz Su 8pm
GLENS FALLS AREA						
A♪ult Pop	101.7	WENU	‖	⬙⚡	🕐	R & R Oldies Sa 7pm–12M; Romancing the Oldies Su 6pm–12M; Class Reunion M–F 9am
T°P40	97.1	WZRT	‖‖	⬙⚡	MORE	**ADULT POPULAR;** News 12N; Spts News :50 6, 7, 8am, 3, 4, 5pm; Oldies Sa 7pm
T°P40	107.1	WAYI	‖			
🎸☮	95.9	WYLR	‖	⬙⚡	AM & PM DRIVE	Almost Live from Sweetfish(Local Bands) Su 6pm; Concert Series (Live) Sa 11pm
👢	93.5	WSCG	‖	⬙⚡	🕐	News also on the 1/2 hr; Bite of the Barkeater Sa 7:50am; Infisherman Show M–S 6:45am
Lite Hits	98.1	WJJR	‖‖	⬙⚡	🕐	**EASY LISTENING**

TICONDEROGA/PORT HENRY — PLATTSBURGH — ST. ALBANS

55   20

N

FORMAT ♪ TUNE TO		STATION	SIGNAL POWER	TRAFFIC REPORT	NEWS	SPECIAL PROGRAMMING
🎹	88.7	WRVT	|||	⬦	MORE	**NPR; APR; JAZZ** M–F 6:30–9pm; News: W.E. Sa & Su 8–10am; Opera Sa 1–5pm
TICONDEROGA/PORT HENRY						
🎸	106.7	WIZN	|||			
☀️LDIES	92.1	WMNM			⬦	AM & PM DRIVE	**CLASSIC HITS; ADULT POPULAR;** Trivia 8:30am, 4:30pm; Astrologer 7:30am
🎹	103.9	WANC	||	⬦	MORE	**NPR; APR; ECLECTIC;** News M–F 12N–1pm; W.E. Sa & Su 12N–2pm; Mktpl. M–F 6:30pm
PLATTSBURGH AREA						
A♪ult Pop	99.9	WGFB	|||			
T♪P40	95.3	WXXX	||	⬦	AM & PM DRIVE	Open House Party Sa & Su 7pm–12M; Rick Dee Sa 6–10am; C. Kasem Su 6–10am
👢	98.9	WOKO	|||	⬦	MORE	News 12N, 3pm; Morn. Humor; American Ctry. Ctdwn. Su 8am–12N
Lite Hits	92.9	WEZF	|||		AM & PM DRIVE	Stk.Mkt. 4:40, 5:40pm; Prognosis (Health) Su 6:30–6:45am; Religious Su 6:45–7am
🎹	107.9	WVPS	|||		MORE	**NPR; APR; JAZZ** M–F 6:30–9pm; News: W.E. Sa & Su 8–10am; Opera Sa 1–5pm
ek-lek´-tik	91.9	WCFE	||		SEE S.P.	**NPR; APR; CLASS;** MonitoRadio 8–9am, 4–5pm; Drama, Local Music & Public Affairs
NEWS	1230	WJOY			⬦	ALL NEWS	Stk.Mkt. :15 & :45 thru day; Spts.: Red Sox, Celtics, Bruins; Spts. Final 12M–5am
TALK	1070	WKDR	||			
ST. ALBANS						
👢	102.3	WLFE	||	⬦	🕐	Ctry. Ctdwn. Sa 9am–12N; Ctry. Gold Sa (Live) 7pm–12M; On a Ctry. Road Su 9pm
NORTH OF PLATTSBURGH SCAN FOR CANADIAN STATIONS						

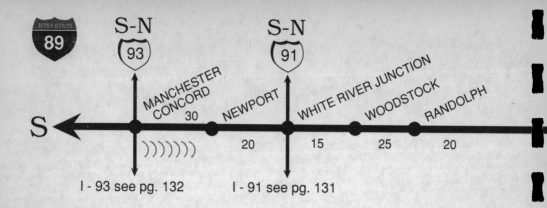

I - 93 see pg. 132   I - 91 see pg. 131

FORMAT ♪ TUNE TO	STATION	SIGNAL POWER	TRAFFIC REPORT	NEWS	SPECIAL PROGRAMMING
FARTHER SOUTHEAST SEE I-93 PAGE 132					
NEWPORT AREA					
TOP40 106.1	WHDQ	‖‖	◇	MORE	News 2:50pm; C. Kasem Sa 6–10am; Live ... 60's Su 9am–12N; Rick Dee Su 7–11pm
101.7	WXXK	‖	◇	AM & PM DRIVE	Spts. News 20 past drives times; Business News AM & PM
ARTISTS 1020	WNTK	‖	🚗	🕐	Morn. Humor; Spts.: Yankees, Patriots, Colby, Sawyer College; AM Mag. M–F 6–9am
WHITE RIVER JUNCTION AREA					
95.3	WKXE	‖			
99.3	WFRD	‖	◇	MORE	**ALBUM-ORIENTED ROCK;** News 3pm; Religious music Su 6–10am
Lite Hits 92.3	WTSL	‖	◇	🕐	Stk. Mkt. 5:30pm; D. Clark Sa 8am–12N; Solid Gold Sa 7pm–12M; Ski Rpts. 7:30, 8:30am
89.5	WVPR	‖‖		MORE	**NPR; APR; JAZZ** M–F 6:30-9pm; Nws.: W.E. Sa & Su 8–10am, ATC 5–6pm; Opera Sa 1–5pm
WOODSTOCK					
☀OLDIES 93.9	WMXR	‖			**TOP 40**
RANDOLPH					
102.3	WCVR	‖	◇	🕐	Morn. Humor; Stk. Mkt. 5:30pm
MONTPELIER AREA					
Adult Cor 107.1	WORK	‖	◇	🕐	Stk.Mkt. 5:03pm; Spts.: Norwich U.; Cousin Brucie Su 9am–12N; D. Bartley Sa 7pm–12M
104.7	WNCS	‖‖	◇	MORE	News 11:50am, Hot Lunch M–F 12:20–1pm; Licorice Pizza Tu–Thu 10:30pm
ek-lek-tik 91.1	WGDR	‖	◇	SEE STR	Pacif. Nws. 7, 12N, 6pm; Shrtwv. Nws. 8am; Agri. Rprts. 7:15am; V. of Sandino Thu 7pm

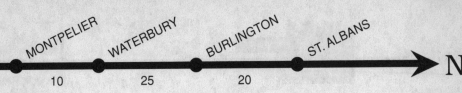

MONTPELIER   WATERBURY   BURLINGTON   ST. ALBANS

10   25   20   N

FORMAT / TUNE TO		STATION	SIGNAL POWER	TRAFFIC REPORT	NEWS	SPECIAL PROGRAMMING
WATERBURY						
OLDIES	101.7	WVMX	‖‖	🚗	MORE	CLASSIC HITS; ADULT POPULAR; TOP 40; News 12N; Ski Reports :40 6, 7, 8am
✝✝✝	103.1	WGLY	‖			
BURLINGTON AREA						
Adult Con	99.9	WGFB	‖‖			
Top40	95.3	WXXX	‖	⚡	AM & PM DRIVE	Open House Party Sa & Su 7pm–12M; Rick Dee Sa 6–10am; Casey Kasem Su 6–10am
🎸	106.7	WIZN	‖‖			
🎸	90.1	WRUV	‖			U. of Vermont
ek-lek´-tik	91.9	WCFE	‖		SEE S.P.	NPR; APR; CLASS; MonitoRadio 8–9am, 4–5pm; Drama, Local Music & Public Affairs
👢	98.9	WOKO	‖‖	⚡	MORE	News 12N, 3pm; Morn. Humor; American Ctry. Ctdwn. Su 8am–12N
Lite Hits	92.9	WEZF	‖‖		AM & PM DRIVE	Stk. Mkt. 4:40, 5:40pm; Prognosis (Health) Su 6:30–6:45am; Religious Su 6:45–7am
🎹	107.9	WVPS	‖‖		MORE	NPR; APR; JAZZ M–F 6:30–9pm; News: W.E. Sa & Su 8–10am; Opera Sa 1–5pm
NEWS	1230	WJOY	‖	⚡	ALL NEWS	Stk. Mkt. :15 & :45 thru day; Spts.: Red Sox, Celtics, Bruins; Spts. Final 12M–5am
TALK	1070	WKDR	‖			
ST. ALBANS						
👢	102.3	WLFE	‖	⚡	🕐	Ctry. Ctdwn. Sa 9am–12N; Ctry. Gold Sa (Live) 7pm–12M; On a Ctry. Road Su 9pm
NORTH OF ST. ALBANS SCAN FOR CANADIAN STATIONS						

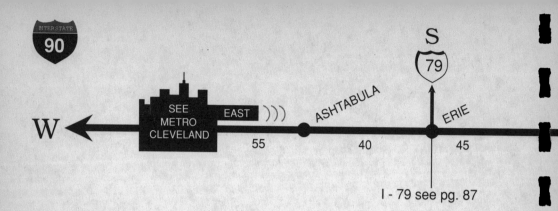

FORMAT ♪ TUNE TO		STATION	SIGNAL POWER	TRAFFIC REPORT	NEWS	SPECIAL PROGRAMMING
WEST OF CLEVELAND SEE I-80 PAGE 91						
SEE CLEVELAND METRO PAGE 182						
ASHTABULA AREA						
Adult Pop	104.9	WDON	‖	⚡	AM & PM DRIVE	LITE HITS; J. Madden Spts. Quiz daily 8:10am, 4pm; Oldies Sa 7pm–12M
Lite Hits	97.1	WREO	‖‖	⚡		
✝✝✝	105.5	WGOJ	‖			
ERIE AREA						
Adult Pop	99.9	WXKC	‖‖	⚡	A M DRIVE	Morn. Humor; Solid Gold Sa 7pm–12M; Supergold Su 7pm–12M
Top40	102.3	WJET	‖	🚗	🕐	Morn. Humor
Top40	103.7	WCCK	‖‖	⚡	A M DRIVE	Morn. Humor
🎸	95.9	CFPL	‖‖			
🎸	100.9	WRKT	‖	⚡	A M DRIVE	Blaz. Turntable Tu 10–11pm; Homegrown 101 Su 11pm; R & R Never Forgets Su 8pm
🎸	89.9	WERG	‖	⚡	MORE	News 3, 3:30pm; Rhythm & Blues Sa; Spanish Su 12N–3pm; Italian Su 9am–12N
👢	97.9	WXTA	‖	⚡	A M DRIVE	Morn. Humor; Ctry. Ctdwn. Sa 7–10am
👢	100.3	WZPR	‖‖	⚡	SPOT NEWS	Stk. Mkt.; Farm Reports; Spts.
E ❀ Z	92.3	WRRN	‖	⚡		Morn. Humor; Stk. Mkt. 6pm; Big Band Jump Su 5pm; Memories Su 3pm
🎹	91.3	WQLN	‖‖	⚡	SEE 11TH	NPR; APR; Ext. News 10am–12N, 5–6:30pm; W.E. Sa 12N–1:30pm, Su 10am–12N
🎓	88.9	WFSE	‖			Edinboro U.

DUNKIRK   BUFFALO   E

35

FORMAT / TUNE TO		STATION	SIGNAL POWER	TRAFFIC REPORT	NEWS	SPECIAL PROGRAMMING
✝✝✝	106.3	WCTL	‖	◇⚡	🕐	Stk. Mkt.; Talk Shows; Farm Reports; Spts.
─NEWS─	1530	WEHN	ǀ	◇⚡	ALL NEWS	OFF AIR AT SUNSET; Stk. Mkt. every 1/2 hr; Spts.: Buffalo Bills, Updates thru day
ROCK	1450	WPSE	ǀ			Pennsylvania State U.
DUNKIRK AREA						
A♪dult Cop	93.3	WWSE	‖‖	◇⚡	🕐	News also on the 1/2 hour; Solid Gold Sa 7pm–12M
A♪dult Cop	96.5	WCQA	‖			
BUFFALO AREA						
A♪dult Cop	92.9	WBUF	‖‖	🚗	🕐	
T°P40	97.7	CHTZ	‖‖			
T°P40	98.5	WKSE	‖‖	🚗	🕐	News also 20 after the hour; Morn. Humor
T°P40	102.5	WMJQ	‖‖	🚗	AM DRIVE	Morn. Humor
🎸	96.9	WGR	‖‖	🚗	AM DRIVE	Morn. Humor; Classic Rock & New Releases
🎸	103.3	WUFX	‖‖	🚗	AM & PM DRIVE	Morn. Humor
👢	106.5	WYRK	‖‖	🚗	AM & PM DRIVE	Amer. Ctry. Ctdwn. Su 9am–1pm; Ctry. Classics Sa & Su 6–7pm; Requests M–F 12N
☀OLDIES	104.1	WHTT	‖‖	🚗	AM DRIVE	Morn. Humor
R & B	93.7	WBLK	‖‖			
Lite Hits	96.1	WJYE	‖‖	🚗	AM & PM DRIVE	
BUFFALO AREA CONTINUED ON THE NEXT PAGE						

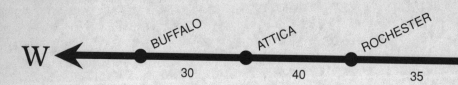

W ← BUFFALO 30 ATTICA 40 ROCHESTER 35

FORMAT ♪ TUNE TO		STATION	SIGNAL POWER	TRAFFIC REPORT	NEWS	SPECIAL PROGRAMMING
CONTINUATION OF BUFFALO AREA						
E❄Z	105.7	CHRE	‖‖	⬦	🕐	Jazz Inspiration Su 10pm–12M; Nightcap M–F 10pm–12M
E❄Z	107.7	WEZQ	‖‖	🚗	SPOT NEWS	Stk. Mkt. 11:57am, 4:57pm; Public Service Su 6–8am
🎹	94.5	WNED	‖‖	⬦	MORE	**APR;** News 3:30, 3:57pm; Garrison Keillor Sa 6pm; Karl Haas M–F 11am; CD Sa 10am
🎺	88.7	WBFO	‖‖		MORE	**NPR;** News: W.E. Sa & Su 8–10am, ATC 5–6pm; Blues Su 9pm–12M; Swing Su 10am–12N
✝✝✝	89.9	WFBF	‖‖		MORE	News 12:35pm; Unshackled 7:30–8pm; Family Bible Study 9:26–10am, 8:30–9pm
✝✝✝	99.5	WDCX	‖‖			
𝕋𝕒𝕝𝕜	550	WGR	‖	🚗	🕐	Stk. Mkt. AM & PM Drives; Spts.: Bills, Bisons, Sabres
𝕋𝕒𝕝𝕜	1520	WWKB	"C"	🚗	🕐	News also on the 1/2 hr; B. Williams M–F 7–10pm; N. Myers M–F 10pm–1am
ATTICA AREA						
AdultPop	101.7	WBTF	‖			
🎸	90.7	WGCC	‖	⬦	MORE	News 12N
ROCHESTER AREA						
AdultPop	100.5	WVOR	‖‖	🚗	AM & PM DRIVE	Rock & Roll Oldies Sa 7pm–12M; Jazz Su 7–9am; Top 30 Ctdwn. Su 9am–1pm
AdultPop	101.3	WRMM	‖‖	🚗	A M DRIVE	
Top40	97.9	WPXY	‖‖			
🎸	96.5	WCMF	‖‖	🚗	MORE	News 10am; Morn. Humor; Rockline M 12M; Time Out for Rochester Su 7:30–8am
🎸	90.5	WBER	‖			La Voz Latina (Hispanic) M–F 10:30am–12:30pm; Metal. Overdrive Sa 11pm–3am

GENEVA   SYRACUSE

40

E

FORMAT 🎵 TUNE TO	STATION	SIGNAL POWER	TRAFFIC REPORT	NEWS	SPECIAL PROGRAMMING
🎩 92.5	WBEE	|||	🚗	AM & PM DRIVE	Amer. Ctry. Ctdwn. Su 8am–12N; Ctry. Gold Sa 7pm–12M; WBEE Top 9 at 9pm M–F
☀️OLDIES 98.9	WKLX	|||			
R&B 103.9	WDKX	||	🚗	AM & PM DRIVE	Weekly Top 10 Ctdwn. Sa 7–8pm; On the Move Sa 5–8am; Club 104 Sa 8pm–3am
Lite Hits 95.1	WZSH	|||	🚗	MORE	News 12N
🎹 91.5	WXXI	|||	🚗	AM & PM DRIVE	APR; Fascinatin' Rhythm Sa 12N; With Heart & Voice Su 8am & 6pm; Karl Haas M–F 10am
ek-lek´-tik 88.5	WRUR				MORE	**PRGSV. ROCK; CLASS; JAZZ; R & B; FOLK; SPANISH;** News12N, 2, 5pm
ek-lek´-tik 89.1	WBSU			⚡	MORE	News 12N; Educational Programs M–F 10am–4pm; Symphony M–Su 12N–2pm
ek-lek´-tik 89.7	WITR	||	⚡	SEE S.P.	News 7:45, 8:45am, 1:45, 5:45pm; Rochester Sessions Tu 10–11pm; Reggae Sa 5–8pm
🎷🎸🎺 1180	WHAM	"C"	🚗	🕐	News also on the 1/2 hr, Extended 4–6pm; R. Limbaugh M–F 2–4pm; Dr.D. Edell M–F 1pm
GENEVA AREA					
A🎵dult Pop 97.3	WYXL	|||	⚡	AM & PM DRIVE	
A🎵dult Pop 98.5	WNYR	||	⚡	AM & PM DRIVE	Dick Clark Sa 2–6pm; New Horizons (Jazz) Su 10am–12N; Fraze at the Flicks M–F 6:10am
A🎵dult Pop 99.3	WSFW	||	⚡	MORE	News 12N, 3pm; Ital. Mus. Su 12N–2pm; Big Band Su 7–9am; Agri. Bus. M–F 5:30, 6am
A🎵dult Pop 101.7	WECQ			⚡	MORE	News 12N, 3pm; American Top 40 Sa 8am; Casey Kasem Top 40 Su 12N
🎺 102.3	WLKA	||			
✝✝✝ 88.1	WFRW	|||		MORE	News 12:55, 2:55pm; Unshackled M–Su 7:30pm; Radio Reading Circle M–F 1pm

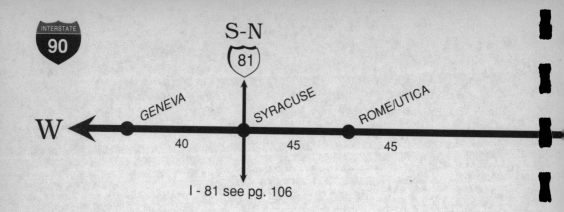

I - 81 see pg. 106

FORMAT ♪ TUNE TO		STATION	SIGNAL POWER	TRAFFIC REPORT	NEWS	SPECIAL PROGRAMMING
SYRACUSE AREA						
Adult Pop	94.5	WYYY	‖‖	🚗	AM DRIVE	TOP 40; Morn. Humor; Oldies Sa 7pm–12M; C. Kasem Top 40 Su 6–10pm
Adult Pop	105.5	WGES	‖	🚗	🕐	Stk. Mkt. 7, 10am, 12N, 4pm; Interview with Psychic Tu 12N–1pm; Blues Thu 9pm–2am
Adult Pop	106.3	WMCR	‖			
Top40	93.1	WNTQ	‖‖	🚗	AM & PM DRIVE	Morn. Humor; Shadoe Stevens American Top 40 Su 6am
🎸	95.7	WAQX	‖‖	◇	AM DRIVE	Morn. Humor; Street Talk Su AM
🎸☮	104.7	WKFM	‖‖	🚗	MORE	News 10am; Comedy Break M–F 5pm; Kix Classics Sa 10am–12N; 6-Pack Su 6pm
🤠	106.9	WPCX	‖‖		MORE	News 10am, 12N; Farm Reports 5am; Spts. News 5:30, 10am
☀️OLDIES	92.1	WSEN	‖‖			
E ✿ Z	107.9	WRHP	‖‖			
Lite Hits	100.9	WEZG	‖	🚗	MORE	News 4:40pm, News & Views M–F 1:52pm; Morn. Humor; Syracuse Spectrum Su 6am
🎷	91.3	WCNY	‖‖		SEE S.P.	NPR; News: ATC M–F 5-6:30pm, 10am, 7:30pm; Oper. Sa 1:30–5pm; Jz. M–F 6:30pm
🎷	105.1	WVOA	‖	◇	🕐	Voices of the Arts M–F 7:20am, 4:20, 6:20pm; Video Review Tu–F 5:20pm
🎺	88.3	WAER	‖	◇	MORE	NPR; News also on the 1/2 hr; Afropop Worldwide Su 10–11pm
ek-lek´-tik	89.9	WRVO	‖‖			NPR; State U. of New York
✝✝✝	102.9	WMHR	‖‖			
ROME/UTICA AREA						
Adult Pop	93.5	WIBQ	‖	◇	MORE	News 10am, 3pm; CC Bickins Rock & Roll Revival Sa 6pm–12M

CANAJOHARIE   JOHNSTOWN AMSTERDAM   ALBANY SCHENECTADY   E

15   30

FORMAT / TUNE TO		STATION	SIGNAL POWER	TRAFFIC REPORT	NEWS	SPECIAL PROGRAMMING
Adult Pop	98.7	WLZW	III	⬦	MORE	**LITE HITS;** News 10:55am, 4:55pm
Adult Pop	104.3	WKGW	III	⬦	AM DRIVE	Morn. Humor; Solid Gold Sa PM
Top 40	107.3	WRCK	III			Dance Trax Sa 7pm–12M; Future Hits Su 7am; C. Kasem Top 40 Su 8am–12N
🎸	94.9	WKLL	III	⬦	AM DRIVE	Beatle Break M–F 10:15am; Classic Cafe M–F 12N; Desert Island Classics M–F 9:10pm
🎸	90.1	WRCU	II			Colgate U.
🤠	96.1	WFRG	III	⬦	AM DRIVE	Bog Party (Southern Rock) F 7pm–12M; Amer. Mus. Mkrs. Su 9am–1pm & 8pm–12M
OLDIES	92.7	WYUT	II			**ADULT STANDARDS**
OLDIES	102.5	WUUU	III	⬦	AM DRIVE	Request Party F 7pm–12M; Supergold Sa 7pm–12M; U.S. Hall of Fame Su 7pm–12M
🎹	89.5	WUNY	III		SEE S.P.	**NPR;** News 10am, 7:30pm, ATC Sa & Su 5–6pm; Opr. Sa 1:30–5pm; Jazz M–F 6:30pm
TALK	950	WIBX	II	⬦	🕐	**NEWS; SPTS.;** News also on 1/2 hr; Spts.: Mets, Giants, Syracuse U., Knicks, Rangers
CANAJOHARIE AREA						
🎹	93.3	WCAN	II	⬦	MORE	**NPR; APR; ECLECTIC;** News M–F 12N–1pm, W.E. Sa & Su 12N–2pm; Mktpl. M–F 6:30pm
✝✝✝	101.9	WJIV	III	⬦	🕐	
JOHNSTOWN/AMSTERDAM AREA						
🎸	97.7	WKOL	II	⬦	AM & PM DRIVE	Morn. Humor; Beatle Mania Su 10am–2pm
OLDIES	103.5	WSHQ	III	🚗	MORE	News 10:50am; Blue Plate Special 12N; 9 o'clock Request Hour; Back Seat Req. 11pm
OLDIES	104.9	WSRD	II			

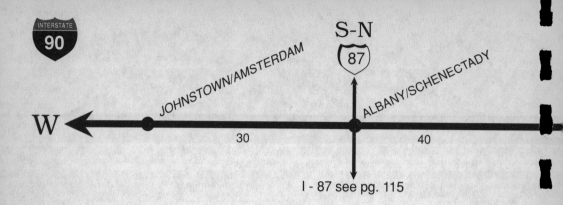

I - 87 see pg. 115

FORMAT / TUNE TO		STATION	SIGNAL POWER	TRAFFIC REPORT	NEWS	SPECIAL PROGRAMMING
ALBANY/SCHENECTADY/TROY AREA						
Adult Cor	100.9	WKLI	‖	🚗	AM & PM DRIVE	Stk. Mkt. 5:20pm; Rock & Roll Oldies Sa 7pm–12M; Love Songs M–F 9pm–2am
Top 40	92.3	WFLY	‖‖	🚗	AM & PM DRIVE	Morn. Hum.; C. Kasem Su 11am–3pm; Rckn. Amer. Su 6–9am; Amer. Top 40 Sa 6–10pm
Top 40	96.7	WVKZ	‖			
🎸	88.3	WVCR	‖‖	⚡		Urban 6–9am, 6–9pm; Heavy Mtl. 12M–3am; Polka Su 9pm–12M; Spanish Su 12N–6pm
🎸	106.5	WPYX	‖‖	🚗	A M DRIVE	Elec. Lunch M–F 12N; 70's at 7pm M–F; Jazz Brunch Su 9am–12N; House Party Sa 7pm
🎸	103.9	WQBK	‖	🚗	A M DRIVE	
🎸	102.7	WEQX	‖	⚡	MORE	**ALBUM-ORIENT. ROCK;** News 10:50am; Rck. Ov. Lond. Su 7pm–12M; Jazz Tracks Su 8pm
🎩	107.7	WGNA	‖‖	🚗	A M DRIVE	Morn. Humor
OLDIES	98.3	WSHZ	‖	🚗	MORE	News 10:50am; Blue Plate Special 12N; 9 o'clock Request Hr; Back Seat Req. 11pm
OLDIES	99.5	WGY	‖‖	🚗	A M DRIVE	Morn. Humor; All-Request Oldies Sa 7pm–12M
E ❄ Z	95.5	WROW	‖‖	🚗	🕐	Special of the Week Su 9am–12N
🎹	89.1	WMHT	‖‖		🕐	News also on the 1/2 hour; Adven. in Good Mus. M–F 11am; N.E.Showcase Thu 8pm
🎹	90.3	WAMC	‖‖	⚡	MORE	**NPR; APR; ECLECTIC;** News M–F 12N–1pm; W.E. Sa & Su 12N–2pm; Mktpl. 6:30–7pm
🎺	103.1	WHRL	‖	⚡	🕐	Stk. Mkt. 12:05, 5:05pm; Business Beat 12:35, 4:35pm; D. Sanborn/Jazz Su 2pm
ek-lek-tik	91.5	WRPI	‖‖		SEE LP	Pacifica News 6:30pm; Spts.: RPI; Public Folk Su 6–8pm; Ethnic Programs Su 9am
NEWS	1540	WPTR	"C"	🚗	ALL NEWS	**TALK; SPORTS:** Mets, Patriots, Siena College; Business News :20 & :50
🎻🎸	1300	WQBK	‖	⚡	🕐	Stk. Mkt. 10 before hr. drive times; Jim Horne 6:30–10am; John Greaney 6:30–8pm

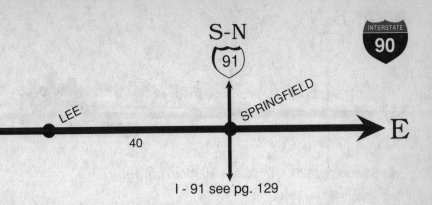

I - 91 see pg. 129

FORMAT ♪ TUNE TO		STATION	SIGNAL POWER	TRAFFIC REPORT	NEWS	SPECIAL PROGRAMMING
Adult Pop	810	WGY	"C"	🚗	🕐	**TALK** 8pm–5am; News also on the 1/2 hour; Morn. Humor; R. Limbaugh 12N–3pm
LEE AREA						
Top40	101.7	WRCZ	I	⬦	AM DRIVE	C. Kasem Su 8am–12N; Scott Shannon Su 9–11pm
Top40	105.5	WBEC	II	⬦	MORE	News 12N; American Top 40 Su 8am–12N; Rick Dee's Top 40 Su 6–10pm
Lite Hits	95.9	WUPE	II	⬦	AM DRIVE	Spts.: Red Sox, Patriots; Press Conference (Public Affairs) Su 8:30am
Lite Hits	105.1	WBBS	II	⬦	🕐	**LITE JAZZ;** Folk Sa 4–6pm; Jazz F 8–10pm; Berkshires by Candlelight Su–Thu 9pm–12M
SPRINGFIELD AREA						
Adult Pop	93.1	WHYN	III	🚗	AM DRIVE	Morn. Humor; Dick Bartley Oldies Sa 7pm–12M
Adult Pop	94.7	WMAS	III	⬦	MORE	News 12N; Stk. Mkt. news times; Beatles Su 11am–12N
Top40	96.5	WTIC	III	🚗	MORE	News 12N; Top 10 Tu 8pm; Public Affairs Su AM
Top40	99.3	WHMP	II			
🎸	102.1	WAQY	III	🚗	AM DRIVE	**CLASSIC ROCK;** Ethnic Program Su 6am; Public Service
🎸	106.9	WCCC	III	🚗	AM DRIVE	Morn. Humor; Pirate Radio Sa 7pm–12M
🎸☮	100.9	WRNX	II	⬦	AM & PM DRIVE	**ALBUM-ORIENTED ROCK; PRGSV. ROCK; ADULT POPULAR;** Morn. Humor
Lite Hits	100.5	WRCH	III	🚗	AM & PM DRIVE	Pillow Talk nightly 10pm–1am
🎹	88.5	WFCR	III	⬦	MORE	**NPR; APR;** News: W.E. Sa 8–11am; Jazz M–F 6:30–7:30pm; Opera Sa 1:30pm
ek-lek'-tik	90.7	WTCC	II	⬦	AM DRIVE	Morn. Humor; Black Spectrum M–F 4–8pm; Midmorning Jazz M–F 10am–12N
SPRINGFIELD AREA CONTINUED ON THE NEXT PAGE						

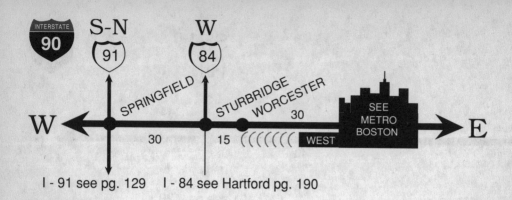

I - 91 see pg. 129   I - 84 see Hartford pg. 190

FORMAT ♪ TUNE TO		STATION	SIGNAL POWER	TRAFFIC REPORT	NEWS	SPECIAL PROGRAMMING
CONTINUATION OF SPRINGFIELD AREA						
ᴋRᴋSᴋ	1080	WTIC	"C"	🚗	🕐	**LITE HITS** 5:30–6pm; Stk. Mkt. every hr. 9:30am–6pm; Spts.: Red Sox, Whalers
ᴋRᴋSᴋ	1270	WSPR	‖	🚗	🕐	Stk. Mkt. AM Drive, Business 5pm; Spts.: Bruins, Patriots, U. of MA, Knicks, Yukons
STURBRIDGE						
👢	100.1	WQVR	‖	⚡	🕐	Spts.: Red Sox, Celtics; Ctry. Music Hall of Fame Sa 10am; Ctry. Ctdwn. Sa 8am
WORCESTER						
AJultPop	104.5	WXLO	‖‖	⚡	AM & PM DRIVE	Morn. Humor; Supergold Sa 7pm–12M; Ctdwn. America Su 8am–12N
🎸	107.3	WAAF	‖‖	🚗	AM DRIVE	Su Night Special 9pm; Noontime Work Force M–F 12N; Electric Brunch Su 10am
Lite Hits	96.1	WSRS	‖‖	⚡	AM & PM DRIVE	
ek-lek´-tik	90.5	WICN	‖	⚡	MORE	**NPR; APR;** News: ATC 5–6:30pm, Mktpl. 6:30–7pm; Acoustic M–F 8–10pm
ek-lek´-tik	91.3	WCUW	∣	⚡	SPOT NEWS	Scottish Sa 10:30am–12N; Pol. Sa 2–3:30pm; Blues F & Sa 6–9pm; Folk M–Thu 5pm
🎓	88.1	WCHC	∣			College of the Holy Cross
SEE BOSTON METRO PAGE 172						

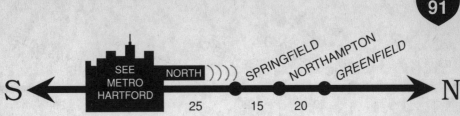

FORMAT ♪ TUNE TO		STATION	SIGNAL POWER	TRAFFIC REPORT	NEWS	SPECIAL PROGRAMMING
SEE HARTFORD METRO PAGE 190						
SPRINGFIELD AREA						
Adult Pop	93.1	WHYN	‖‖	🚗	AM DRIVE	Morn. Humor; Dick Bartley Oldies Sa PM; Cousin Brucie's Cruisin' America
Adult Pop	94.7	WMAS	‖‖	◇	MORE	News 12N; Stk. Mkt. news times; Beatles Su 11am–12N
Top40	96.5	WTIC	‖‖	🚗	MORE	News 12N; Top 10 Tu 8pm; Public Affairs Su AM
🎸	102.1	WAQY	‖‖	🚗	AM DRIVE	**CLASSIC ROCK;** Ethnic Program Su 6am; Public Service
Lite Hits	100.5	WRCH	‖‖	🚗	AM & PM DRIVE	Pillow Talk nightly 10pm–1am
TALK	930	WREB	‖	🚗	🕐	Stk. Mkt. 12:15pm; Spts.: Local; K. Lynn 6–10am; B. Hiesler 10am–3pm; J. Cashman 3pm
TALK	1080	WTIC	"C"	🚗	🕐	**LITE HITS** 5:30–6pm; Stk. Mkt. every hr. 9:30am–6pm; Spts.: Red Sox, Whalers
TALK	1270	WSPR	‖	🚗	🕐	Stk. Mkt. AM Drive, Business 5pm; Spts.: Bruins, Patriots, U. of MA, Knicks, Yukons
NORTHAMPTON AREA						
Top40	99.3	WHMP	‖			
🎸	107.3	WAAF	‖‖	🚗	AM DRIVE	Su Night Special 9pm; Noontime Work Force M–F 12N; Electric Brunch Su 10am
🎸☮	100.9	WRNX	‖	◇	AM & PM DRIVE	**ALBUM-ORIENTED ROCK; PROGRESSIVE ROCK; ADULT POPULAR;** Morn. Humor
🎸	89.3	WAMH	‖		🕐	Jazz M 6pm–2am; Rap F 6–8pm; Class. Su 12N–4pm; Reggae Su 5–8pm
Lite Hits	96.1	WSRS	‖‖	◇	AM & PM DRIVE	
🎹	88.5	WFCR	‖‖	◇	MORE	**NPR; APR;** News: W.E. Sa 8–11am; Jazz M–F 6:30–7:30pm; Opera Sa 1:30pm
NORTHAMPTON AREA CONTINUED ON NEXT PAGE						

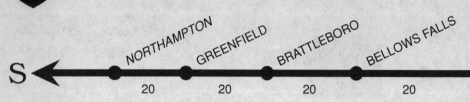

S ← NORTHAMPTON — 20 — GREENFIELD — 20 — BRATTLEBORO — 20 — BELLOWS FALLS — 20

FORMAT / TUNE TO	STATION	SIGNAL POWER	TRAFFIC REPORT	NEWS	SPECIAL PROGRAMMING
CONTINUATION OF NORTHAMPTON AREA					
ek-lek-tik 91.1	WMUA	I		(SEE S.P.)	News 9am, 12N, 5pm; Public Affairs Sa & Su 6–7pm; Ctry., Blues & Bluegrass Su 1–6pm
GREENFIELD AREA					
Adult Pop 98.3	WHAI	I	⚡	AM & PM DRIVE	R & R Mem. Time Su 6–10pm; D. Clark Sa 8pm–12M; Pulse of Franklin Cty. Su 9:30am
Top 40 99.9	WCAT	II	⚡	AM DRIVE	Morn. Humor
BRATTLEBORO AREA					
Adult Pop 96.7	WTSA	I	⚡	MORE	Stk. Mkt. 5:20pm; Supergold Sa 7pm; C. Kasem Su 12N; Live from the 60's Su 4pm
Adult Pop 104.9	WYRY	II	🚗	MORE	**CLASSIC ROCK;** News 12N–1pm; Morn. Humor; Dick Clark Sa & Su 3–7pm
Top 40 103.7	WKNE	III	⚡	🕐	Jukebox Sa Nite Oldies 7pm–12M; The Lighter Side, Lite Rock/Folk Su 6–10am
🎸 92.7	WKVT	II	⚡	🕐	Morn. Humor; Oldies F 7pm–12M, Sa 7pm–12M; Album Rock Feature Su 8–10pm
TALK 1220	WKBK	I	🚗	🕐	News also five to the hr; Pat Desmarais M–F 5–9:30am
BELLOWS FALLS					
🎸☮ 107.1	WBFL	II	⚡	AM & PM DRIVE	Morn. Humor; Dr. Demento Su 8pm; American Top 40 Su 10am; Classic LP M–F 11pm
CLAREMONT AREA					
Adult Pop 93.5	WMKS	II	⚡	🕐	Morn. Humor; Oldies Party Sa 7pm–12M; "Arlo Mudge It" M–F 7:40am
Top 40 106.1	WHDQ	III	⚡	MORE	News 2:50pm; C. Kasem Sa 6–10am; Live ... 60's Su 9am-12N; R. Dee Su 7–11pm
👢 101.7	WXXK	II	⚡	AM & PM DRIVE	Spts. News 20 past drive times; Business News AM & PM
🎹 89.5	WVPR	III		MORE	**NPR; APR; JAZZ** M–F 6:30–9pm; News: W.E. Sa & Su 8–10am; Opera Sa 1–5pm

INTERSTATE 91

CLAREMONT — WHITE RIVER JUNCTION — HAVERHILL — ST. JOHNSBURY → N

20 35 25

FORMAT / TUNE TO		STATION	SIGNAL POWER	TRAFFIC REPORT	NEWS	SPECIAL PROGRAMMING
TALK	1020	WNTK	‖	🚗	🕐	Morn. Humor; Spts.: Yankees, Patriots, Colby, Sawyer Colleges; AM Mag. M–F 6–9am
WHITE RIVER JUNCTION AREA						
🎸	95.3	WKXE	‖			
🎸	99.3	WFRD	‖	⚡	MORE	ALBUM-ORIENTED ROCK; News 3pm; Religious music Su 6–10am
OLDIES	93.9	WMXR	‖			TOP 40
Lite Hits	92.3	WTSL	‖	⚡	🕐	Stk. Mkt. 5:30pm; D. Clark Sa 8am–12N; Sol. Gold Sa 7pm–12M; Ski Rpts. 7:30, 8:30
HAVERHILL						
👢	101.3	WYKR	‖	⚡	MORE	News 12N, 2pm; Farm Prog. 6:30am; Spts. News 9:45am; Trivia 7:35, 8:30, 9:30am
ST. JOHNSBURY AREA						
Adult Cor	98.3	WGMT	‖	🚗	🕐	Health Watch M–F 7:45am; Dick Clark Oldies Sa 8pm–12M; C. Kasem Su 9am–1pm
TOP 40	103.7	WZPK	‖‖‖	⚡	AM DRIVE	Morn. Humor
🎸	91.5	WWLR	‖	⚡	SEE S.F.	CLASSIC ROCK; News 12N, 5pm; Spts.: Lyndon Vikings; Jazz Su 9pm–12M
👢	105.5	WNKV	‖			
👢	106.3	WMTK	‖	⚡	🕐	News also on the 1/2 hour; Morn. Humor; American Ctry. Ctdwn. Su 10am–2pm
E Z	94.9	WHOM	‖‖‖		MORE	News 12N; Stk. Mkt. 4:30pm
FARTHER NORTH SCAN FOR CANADIAN STATIONS						

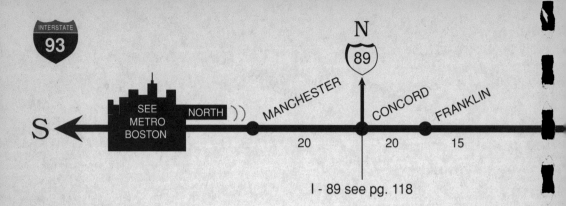

INTERSTATE 93

N
89

SEE METRO BOSTON — NORTH))) — MANCHESTER — CONCORD — FRANKLIN

S

20   20   15

I - 89 see pg. 118

FORMAT ♪ TUNE TO		STATION	SIGNAL POWER	TRAFFIC REPORT	NEWS	SPECIAL PROGRAMMING
	SEE BOSTON METRO PAGE 172					
	MANCHESTER AREA					
Adult Cor	95.7	WZID	|||	🚗	🕐	Stk. Mkt. 7:30am, 12N, 5pm; Spts. News :15 & :45 AM Drive; Eye on NH Su 6:45am
Top40	106.3	WHOB	||			
Top40	107.1	WERZ	||	🚗	MORE	News 2:50pm; Morn. Humor
🎸	100.3	WHEB	|||	⚡	AM & PM DRIVE	Rockline M 11:30pm–1am; In the Studio Su 8–9pm; Concert Series Su 9pm
🎸	101.1	WGIR	|||	🚗	AM DRIVE	Block Prty. F 6pm–Su 7pm; In Concert Sa 10:30pm; Wax Mus. (Oldies) Su 8am–12N
👢	97.5	WOKQ	|||	⚡	SEE S.P.	News 6–7am, 12N–1pm; Morn. Humor
TALK	610	WGIR	||	⚡	MORE	**NEWS;** Stk. Mkt. :15 6, 7, 8:40am, 4:50, 5:23pm; Spts.: Patriots, Celtics
	CONCORD AREA					
Adult Cor	102.3	WKXL	||	⚡	AM & PM DRIVE	Stk. Mkt. 5:23pm; Spts.: Bruins, Red Sox, U. of NH, Local; Coffee Chat M–F 8:40–9am
Adult Cor	105.5	WJYY	||	⚡	MORE	News 12N; Stk. Mkt. 12N, 5:30pm; Dateline People Su 8:30am; Undercurrents Su 7:30am
OLDIES	99.1	WNNH	||	🚗		Morn. Humor; Cruisin' America with Cousin Brucie Su 9pm
🎹	89.1	WEVO	|||	⚡	MORE	**NPR; APR; NEWS;** Jazz 7–11pm; Fresh Air M–F 4–5pm; Af. Pop Sa 6–7pm; Folk Sa 7pm
	FRANKLIN AREA					
Adult Cor	94.1	WFTN	||	⚡	🕐	P. Harvey 8:35am, 12:06, 5:20pm; Nat'l Mus. Surv. Sa 9am–12N; Oldies Sa 7pm–2am
Adult Cor	98.3	WLNH	||	🚗	MORE	News 12N; Morn. Humor; Ski Reports; Summer Recreation Reports
Adult Cor	104.9	WLKZ	||	🚗	AM & PM DRIVE	Morn. Humor

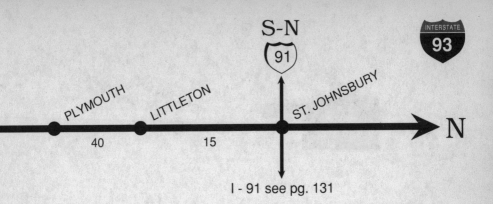

S-N
91

INTERSTATE
93

PLYMOUTH   LITTLETON   ST. JOHNSBURY   N

40   15

I - 91 see pg. 131

FORMAT ♪ TUNE TO	STATION	SIGNAL POWER	TRAFFIC REPORT	NEWS	SPECIAL PROGRAMMING
PLYMOUTH AREA					
T○P40 100.1	WPNH	‖	⬦⚡	MORE	**ADULT POPULAR;** News 12N; C. Kasem Su 1pm; Dr. Demento Su 8pm; Big Band Su 6am
T○P40 103.7	WZPK	‖‖	⬦⚡	AM DRIVE	Morn. Humor
Lite Hits 101.5	WWSS	‖	⬦⚡	AM & PM DRIVE	Morn. Humor; Stk. Mkt. 7:30am, 5pm; Lakes Region Close–up Su 7:30am
E ❀ Z 94.9	WHOM	‖‖		MORE	News 12N; Stk. Mkt. 4:30pm
LITTLETON					
🥾 106.3	WMTK	‖	⬦⚡	🕐	News also on the 1/2 hour; Morn. Humor; American Ctry. Ctdwn. Su 10am–2pm
ST. JOHNSBURY AREA					
AdultPop 98.3	WGMT	‖	🚗	🕐	Health Watch M–F 7:45am; Dick Clark Oldies Sa 8pm–12M; C. Kasem Su 9am–1pm
🎸 91.5	WWLR	‖	⬦⚡	SEE S.P.	**CLASSIC ROCK;** News 12N, 5pm; Spts.: Lyndon Vikings; Jazz Su 9pm–12M
🥾 105.5	WNKV	‖			
NORTH OR SOUTH ON I-91 SEE PAGE 131					

133

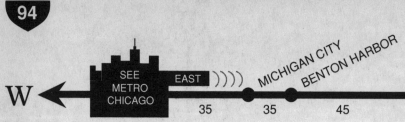

FORMAT ♪ TUNE TO		STATION	SIGNAL POWER	TRAFFIC REPORT	NEWS	SPECIAL PROGRAMMING
	**SEE CHICAGO METRO PAGE 178**					
	**MICHIGAN CITY AREA**					
👢	96.7	WCOE	‖			
E ❄ *Z*	95.9	WEFM	‖	🚗	MORE	**ADULT POPULAR;** News 9:55, 11:55am, 1:55pm
	**BENTON HARBOR AREA**					
A♪ult Pop	99.9	WHFB	‖‖	⚡	AM & PM DRIVE	New Adult Popular 8pm–1am; Paul Harvey M–F 8:30am; All-Request Lunchtime 12N
A♪ult Pop	101.5	WNSN	‖‖		AM DRIVE	Sprgld. Sa & Su 7pm–1am; Live from the 60's Su 9am–12N; Lunchtime Gold M–F 12N
Top40	92.9	WNDU	‖‖	⚡	MORE	News 12:33pm; Amer. Top 40 Su 8am–12N; R. Dee Sa 6–10am; Opn. House Prty. Su 7pm
Top40	103.9	WZZP	‖	🚗	SPOT NEWS	Morn. Humor
Top40	107.1	WIRX	‖			
🎸	95.3	WAOR	‖	⚡	AM & PM DRIVE	Morn. Humor; Flashback Su 8am; Rockline M 11:30pm; Live Show Su 8pm
👢	102.3	WGTC	‖‖		AM DRIVE	American Ctry. Ctdwn. Su 10am–2pm
Lite Hits	98.3	WCSY	‖	⚡	🕐	Stk. Mkt. 5:30pm; Morn. Humor; P. Harvey 8:30am, 12:30, 5pm; Solid Gold Sa 4pm
E ❄ *Z*	92.1	WDOW	‖	⚡	MORE	**RELIGIOUS GOSPEL** 6–11pm; News 12N; Stk. Mkt. 4:20pm; Religious Music Su all day
E ❄ *Z*	100.7	WYEZ	‖‖			
🎹	90.7	WAUS	‖‖			Andrews U.
🎺	88.1	WVPE	‖‖	⚡		**APR;** News: BBC 7, 11:37am; Prairie Home Companion Sa 6–8pm; Marketplace 5pm
✝✝✝	104.7	WFRN	‖‖	⚡	🕐	**CHRISTIAN CONTEMPORARY;** Focus on the Family 11:30am; Insight for Living 9am

KALAMAZOO   BATTLE CREEK   JACKSON

20   40   E

FORMAT ♪ TUNE TO	STATION	SIGNAL POWER	TRAFFIC REPORT	NEWS	SPECIAL PROGRAMMING
KALAMAZOO AREA					
Adult ♪♫	95.9	WLKM	‖	⬧	🕐	**TALK** 7pm–12M; Farm Report 6:15am, 12:30pm; C. Kasem Sa 1:10pm
Adult ♪♫	96.1	WYXX	‖			
Adult ♪♫	100.9	WQXC	‖		MORE	News 12N; Morn. Humor; Jazz/Soft R & B Su 12M; Public Service Sa & Su 10am, 2, 6pm
Adult ♪♫	106.5	WQLR	‖‖	⬧	🕐	Stk. Mkt. :55 10am, 2, 4pm; Special of the Week Su 7–10am; Portraits in Sound Su 8pm
TOP40	97.9	WGRD	‖‖	🚗	AM DRIVE	Morn. Humor
🎸	94.5	WKLQ	‖	🚗	AM DRIVE	Morn. Humor
🎸☮	107.7	WRKR	‖‖		AM DRIVE	Reelin' in the Yrs. Su 9am–12N; King Biscuit Flower Hr. Su 9–10pm; Public Affairs Su 8am
🎓	102.1	WMUK				**NPR;** Public Affairs; Western Michigan U.
BATTLE CREEK AREA					
TOP40	95.3	WBXX	‖	⬧	AM DRIVE	C. Kasem Sa 6–10am; Future Hits Su 6–7am; S. Shannon Su 7–10am
TOP40	103.3	WKFR	‖‖		AM & PM DRIVE	Rick Dee's Top 40 Su 9am–1pm; Hitline USA Su 11pm; Hometown Ctdwn. Sa 6–9pm
🎸☮	92.7	WMMQ	‖	⬧	AM DRIVE	All-Request Lunch 12N–1pm; Blues Cruise Su 8pm–12M; All-Request Sa 7pm–12M
🎸☮	93.7	WJFM	‖‖	🚐	AM DRIVE	Morn. Humor; Jazz Show/David Sanborn Su 8–10am
👢🎩	98.5	WNWN	‖‖	⬧	🕐	P. Harvey 8:30am, 12N, 5:30pm; Spts. News AM Drive, 4pm; Ctry. Ctdwn. Su 11am
☀OLDIES	104.9	WELL	‖	⬧	🕐	**BIG BAND**
E ❋ Z	105.7	WOOD	‖‖	🚗	🕐	Morn. Humor
🎹	104.1	WVGR	‖‖		MORE	**NPR;** News: W.E. Sa & Su 10am–12N; Mktpl. M–F 6:30–7pm; Swing Sa 8–10pm

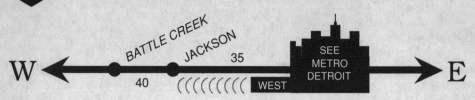

W ← BATTLE CREEK · JACKSON · 35 · 40 · WEST · SEE METRO DETROIT → E

FORMAT ♪ TUNE TO		STATION	SIGNAL POWER	TRAFFIC REPORT	NEWS	SPECIAL PROGRAMMING
JACKSON AREA						
Adult Cor	99.1	WFMK	‖‖	🚗		Morn. Humor
Top40	94.9	WVIC	‖‖	◇	🕐	Morn. Humor
🎸	106.1	WJXQ	‖‖	◇	AM DRIVE	In the Studio Su 6pm; King Biscuit Flower Hour Su 11pm; Blues Cruise Su 7–11pm
👢	100.7	WITL	‖‖		AM & PM DRIVE	Stk. Mkt.; Ctry. Ctdwn. Su 2–6pm
OLDIES	94.1	WIBM	‖‖	◇	MORE	News 12N; Morn. Humor; Dick Bartley Sa 7–10am
Lite Hits	97.5	WJIM	‖‖	🚗	🕐	Morn. Humor
🎹	90.5	WKAR	‖‖	◇	MORE	**NPR;** News 12N; Jazz F 6:30–10pm; Whad'Ya Know Sa 8–10pm; Folk Su 8–9pm
✝✝✝	89.3	WSAE	‖	◇	🕐	**CHRISTIAN CONTEMPORARY;** Spts. News M–F 40 after 7, 8am, 2, 5pm
✝✝✝	96.7	WUFN	‖	◇	🕐	Call in M–F 1pm & 9pm
TALK TALK	870	WKAR	‖		MORE	**NEWS** Extended to 12N; **INFORMATION;** Talk 12N–4pm; Fresh Air 4–5pm
SEE DETROIT METRO PAGE 188						

FORMAT ♪ TUNE TO		STATION	SIGNAL POWER	TRAFFIC REPORT	NEWS	SPECIAL PROGRAMMING
KEY WEST AREA						
A♪ult Pop	107.1	WIIS	‖	◇	🕐	Jazz Su 9am ... ...ge Su 10–11pm; Duval Stree... ...10–11pm
Top40	92.5	WEOW	‖‖	◇	MORE	News 12N; Rock Blocks M–F 2–4pm; Jazz Su 9am–2pm; American Top 40 Su 8pm
Top40	99.5	WAIL	‖‖	◇		Morn. Hum.; Lunchtime Gold 11am–1pm; R. Dee Sa 6am; C. Kasem Top 40 Su 6am & 6pm
E ❄ Z	93.5	WKRY	‖	◇	AM & PM DRIVE	**CLASS.** M–F 6–8pm, Su 9am–5pm; **JAZZ** M–F 8pm–6am, Sa 6pm–6am, Su 5pm–6am
✝✝✝	90.9	WJIR	‖	◇	🕐	**CHRISTIAN CONTEMPORARY & ROCK;** Bible Reading English & Spanish M–F 7–8am
MARATHON AREA						
A♪ult Pop	106.3	WAVK	‖	◇	MORE	News 1pm; Stk. Mkt. 5:30pm; Marine & Tide Rpts. 6:50am, 12:50pm; Spts. News 8:50am
Lite Hits	94.3	WGMX	‖	◇	🕐	News also on the 1/2 hour; Morn. Humor; Fishing Report every 15 minutes
Lite Hits	104.7	WWUS	‖‖	◇	MORE	**OLDIES; JAZZ;** News 12:30pm; Spts. News 7:15, 8:15am
PLANTATION KEY AREA						
A♪ult Pop	103.1	WFKZ	‖	◇	MORE	News 12N; Wall St. Report 12:30pm; Financial Report 5:30pm; Jazz Su 9am–12N
🤠	102.1	WKLG	‖‖	🚗	AM & PM DRIVE	Morn. Humor; Ctry. Ctdwn. Sa 9am–12N
☀OLDIES	100.3	WCTH	‖‖		🕐	**BIG BAND;** Fishing Program 8–9am; Swing Sa 9–10pm
FARTHER NORTH SEE MIAMI METRO PAGE 198						

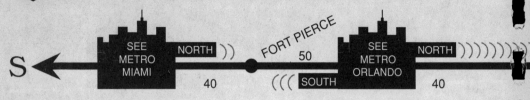

S ← | SEE METRO MIAMI | NORTH)) | FORT PIERCE | SEE METRO ORLANDO | NORTH)))))))
40 | 50 (((SOUTH | 40

FORMAT ♪ TUNE TO	STATION	SIGNAL POWER	TRAFFIC REPORT	NEWS	SPECIAL PROGRAMMING
SOUTH TO THE KEYS SEE PREVIOUS PAGE					
SEE MIAMI METRO PAGE 198					
FORT PIERCE AREA					
A♪ult Cor	103.7	WCXL	|||			
T♀P40	92.7	WZZR	|||	🚗	AM DRIVE	Morn. Humor
T♀P40	95.5	WOVV	|||	🚗	AM & PM DRIVE	Morn. Humor
🎸	98.7	WKGR	|||			
🤠	101.7	WAVW	||	◇	🕐	Top 30 Ctdwn. Su 3–7pm
E ✿ Z	93.5	WGYL	||			
E ✿ Z	102.3	WHLG	||	🚗	🕐	Bus. Report 7:40am, Bond Mkt. 11:05am; Midday Mkt. 1:05pm; Closing Mkt. 5:20pm
🎹	88.9	WQCS	|||	◇	MORE	**NPR; APR;** News on the hour; Prairie Home Companion Su 6–8pm; Opera Sa 2pm
†††	89.9	WCNO	|||			**CHRISTIAN CONTEMPORARY;** In Touch M–F 8am; Haitian Sa & Su 8–10pm
†††	91.7	WWFR	|||			
SEE ORLANDO METRO PAGE 210					
ST. AUGUSTINE AREA					
A♪ult Cor	97.7	WUVU	||	◇	🕐	Morn. Humor
A♪ult Cor	105.5	WSOS	||	◇	🕐	News also on the 1/2 hour; Morn. Humor; Spts.: FL State U. Football Sa 1pm
T♀P40	99.9	WNFI	|||	◇	AM DRIVE	Morn. Hum.; Amer. Top 40 Su 8am–12N; Dir. Hits Su 9–11pm; UK Chart Su 11pm–12M

S ← KEY WEST — MARATHON — PLANTATION KEY — 35 — SEE METRO MIAMI → N

40   45   SOUTH

FORMAT TUNE TO		STATION	SIGNAL POWER	TRAFFIC REPORT	NEWS	SPECIAL PROGRAMMING
KEY WEST AREA						
Adult Pop	107.1	WIIS	II	⚡	🕐	Jazz Su 9am–2pm; Outer Fringe Su 10–11pm; Duval Street Shuffle F 10–11pm
Top 40	92.5	WEOW	III	⚡	MORE	News 12N; Rock Blocks M–F 2–4pm; Jazz Su 9am–2pm; American Top 40 Su 8pm
Top 40	99.5	WAIL	III	⚡		Morn. Hum.; Lunchtime Gold 11am–1pm; R. Dee Sa 6am; C. Kasem Top 40 Su 6am & 6pm
E ❄ Z	93.5	WKRY	I	⚡	AM & PM DRIVE	**CLASS.** M–F 6–8pm, Su 9am–5pm; **JAZZ** M–F 8pm–6am, Sa 6pm–6am, Su 5pm–6am
✝✝✝	90.9	WJIR	I	⚡	🕐	**CHRISTIAN CONTEMPORARY & ROCK;** Bible Reading English & Spanish M–F 7–8am
MARATHON AREA						
Adult Pop	106.3	WAVK	I	⚡	MORE	News 1pm; Stk. Mkt. 5:30pm; Marine & Tide Rpts. 6:50am, 12:50pm; Spts. News 8:50am
Lite Hits	94.3	WGMX	I	⚡	🕐	News also on the 1/2 hour; Morn. Humor; Fishing Report every 15 minutes
Lite Hits	104.7	WWUS	III	⚡	MORE	**OLDIES; JAZZ;** News 12:30pm; Spts. News 7:15, 8:15am
PLANTATION KEY AREA						
Adult Pop	103.1	WFKZ	II	⚡	MORE	News 12N; Wall St. Report 12:30pm; Financial Report 5:30pm; Jazz Su 9am–12N
🤠	102.1	WKLG	III	🚗	AM & PM DRIVE	Morn. Humor; Ctry. Ctdwn. Sa 9am–12N
☀ OLDIES	100.3	WCTH	III		🕐	**BIG BAND;** Fishing Program 8–9am; Swing Sa 9–10pm
FARTHER NORTH SEE MIAMI METRO PAGE 198						

FORMAT ♪ TUNE TO		STATION	SIGNAL POWER	TRAFFIC REPORT	NEWS	SPECIAL PROGRAMMING
SOUTH TO THE KEYS SEE PREVIOUS PAGE						
SEE MIAMI METRO PAGE 198						
FORT PIERCE AREA						
Adult Pop	103.7	WCXL	|||			
Top40	92.7	WZZR	|||	🚗	AM DRIVE	Morn. Humor
Top40	95.5	WOVV	|||	🚗	AM & PM DRIVE	Morn. Humor
🎸	98.7	WKGR	|||			
🎩👢	101.7	WAVW	||	◇	🕐	Top 30 Ctdwn. Su 3–7pm
E Z	93.5	WGYL	||			
E Z	102.3	WHLG	||	🚗	🕐	Bus. Report 7:40am, Bond Mkt. 11:05am; Midday Mkt. 1:05pm; Closing Mkt. 5:20pm
🎹	88.9	WQCS	|||	◇	MORE	**NPR; APR;** News on the hour; Prairie Home Companion Su 6–8pm; Opera Sa 2pm
✝✝✝	89.9	WCNO	|||			**CHRISTIAN CONTEMPORARY;** In Touch M–F 8am; Haitian Sa & Su 8–10pm
✝✝✝	91.7	WWFR	|||			
SEE ORLANDO METRO PAGE 210						
ST. AUGUSTINE AREA						
Adult Pop	97.7	WUVU	||	◇	🕐	Morn. Humor
Adult Pop	105.5	WSOS	||	◇	🕐	News also on the 1/2 hour; Morn. Humor; Spts.: FL State U. Football Sa 1pm
Top40	99.9	WNFI	|||	◇	AM DRIVE	Morn. Hum.; Amer. Top 40 Su 8am–12N; Dir. Hits Su 9–11pm; UK Chart Su 11pm–12M

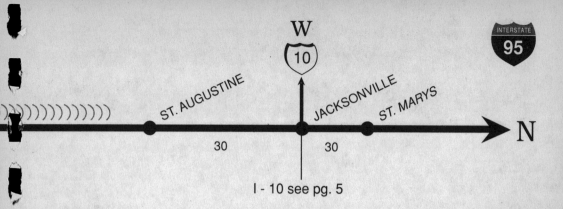

I - 10 see pg. 5

FORMAT ♪ TUNE TO	STATION	SIGNAL POWER	TRAFFIC REPORT	NEWS	SPECIAL PROGRAMMING
R&B	92.7	WZAZ	‖	🚗	AM DRIVE	Morn. Humor; Mark Little (Talk) Su 4pm

JACKSONVILLE AREA

FORMAT	TUNE TO	STATION	SIGNAL POWER	TRAFFIC REPORT	NEWS	SPECIAL PROGRAMMING
Adult Pop	96.1	WEJZ	‖‖	🚗	AM DRIVE	
Adult Pop	102.9	WIVY	‖‖	🚗		Morn. Humor; After Dark (Jazz/Urban) Su–F 9pm–1am; JAXX Jazz, Su 8am–12N
Top40	95.1	WAPE	‖‖			
🎸	104.5	WFYV	‖‖	🚗	AM DRIVE	Morn. Humor; Dangerous Exposure Su 11pm
👢	92.1	WJXR	‖	🚗	🕐	Morn. Humor; Sports; Swap Shop & Auction Sa AM; Farm Reports M–F 5:30am
👢	99.1	WQIK	‖‖	🚗	MORE	News 3:50, 4:50pm; Morn. Humor; Hit Kicker Sunday Magazine 6:30–7am
👢	107.3	WCRJ	‖‖	🚗	AM DRIVE	Top 30 Sa 6–9am; Su Sunrise 7:30am; Ctry. Top 10 Su 10pm; Nashville Live Su 8:30pm
☀OLDIES	96.9	WKQL	‖‖	🚗	AM DRIVE	Dick Clark Su 8pm–12M; Daily Nooner M–F 12N; 60's at 6pm M–F; 70's at 7pm M–F
E ❋ Z	90.9	WKTZ	‖‖	◇	🕐	
🛋	89.9	WJCT	‖‖		MORE	**NPR; APR; JAZZ; BIG BAND;** The Metro/Interview/Variety M–F 4am
✝✝✝	88.1	WNCM	‖	◇	🕐	**CHRISTIAN CONTEMPORARY**
✝✝✝	88.7	WJFR	‖		AM & PM DRIVE	
✝✝✝	91.7	WNLE	‖‖	◇	🕐	**SOUTHERN GOSP.; SACRED;** Minirth-Meier Clinic 1pm; Bible Conference Time 11am
TALK	600	WOKV	‖	🚗	MORE	**NEWS;** Stk. Mkt. 6:50, 7:50, 8:50am, 5:50pm; Spts.: U. of FL, Dolphins, Magic

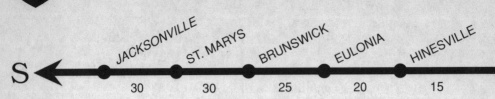

S ← ... JACKSONVILLE · ST. MARYS · BRUNSWICK · EULONIA · HINESVILLE

| 30 | 30 | 25 | 20 | 15 |

FORMAT♪ TUNE TO		STATION	SIGNAL POWER	TRAFFIC REPORT	NEWS	SPECIAL PROGRAMMING
ST. MARYS AREA						
Adult Pop	106.3	WKBX	‖	◇	🕐	HOT ADULT POPULAR; TOP 40; Spts.: U. of GA; Timewarp (Oldies) M–F 12N–2pm
🤠	93.5	WLKC	‖		🕐	Fishing Rpts. 7:30am, 4:45pm; P. Harvey 12:45, 8:45pm; Spts. News 6:30, 9:30am
☀OLDIES	100.7	WIOI	‖‖	🚗	AM DRIVE	Morn. Humor
BRUNSWICK AREA						
Adult Pop	102.5	WBGA	‖‖	🚗	MORE	OLDIES; LITE HITS; CLASSIC ROCK; News 12N; Supergold Sa 7pm–2am, Su 6pm–1am
TOP40	101.5	WHJX	‖‖			R & B
TOP40	103.3	WHFX	‖‖	◇	AM & PM DRIVE	
🎹	90.1	WXVS	‖‖		MORE	NPR; APR; News: W.E. Sa & Su 8–10am; ATC 5–6pm; Jazz Sa 9pm; Opera Sa 1:30–5pm
EULONIA AREA						
Adult Pop	105.5	WIFO	‖			
🤠	94.5	WBYZ	‖‖	🚗	🕐	Ctry. Ctdwn. Su 2–6pm
☀OLDIES	98.3	WGCO	‖‖	◇	AM DRIVE	Morn. Humor; Live from the 60's Su 12N–3pm; Sa Nite at the Oldies 7pm–12M
✝✝✝	88.3	WLPT	‖‖		🕐	Focus on the Family 8am, 7pm; Minirth-Meier Clinic 1pm; In Touch 9am, 8pm
HINESVILLE						
🤠	92.1	WSKX	‖			LITE ROCK; Morn. Humor; Stk. Mkt. AM Drive
SAVANNAH AREA						
Adult Pop	97.3	WAEV	‖‖	🚗	AM DRIVE	Morn. Humor

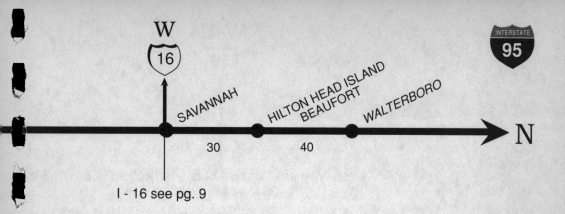

W
16

SAVANNAH   HILTON HEAD ISLAND   WALTERBORO
            BEAUFORT

30   40   N

INTERSTATE 95

I - 16 see pg. 9

FORMAT / TUNE TO		STATION	SIGNAL POWER	TRAFFIC REPORT	NEWS	SPECIAL PROGRAMMING
Top 40	102.1	WZAT	|||	🚗	AM DRIVE	Morn. Humor
🎸	95.5	WIXV	|||	🚗	AM DRIVE	Morn. Humor; 5 o'clock Traffic Jam M–F 5pm; Electric Lunch (Classic Rock) M–F 12N
👢	94.1	WCHY	|||	◇	AM DRIVE	American Ctry. Ctdwn. Sa 6pm; Weekly Ctry. Music Ctdwn. Su 9pm
R&B	93.1	WEAS	|||		SEE S.P.	News 6:50am, 4:50pm; Spts. News 6:30, 7:30am; On the Move/Tom Joyner Sa 6–9am
Lite Hits	96.5	WJCL	|||	🚗	🕐	Jazz Sa 7–10pm; Breeze Special Sa 10pm–12M; Breakfast with Burl Su 6–9am
🎹	91.1	WSVH	|||	◇	MORE	NPR; APR; News: W.E. Sa & Su 10–11am, ATC 5–6pm; Sym./Orch. M–Thu 8–10pm
✝✝✝	89.5	WYFS	|||			
✝✝✝	103.9	WGEC	||	◇	🕐	Morn Lite M–F 6–8am; Focus on the Family M–F 10am, 7pm; Insight for Living M–F 8am
HILTON HEAD ISLAND/BEAUFORT AREA						
Adult Cor	98.7	WYKZ	|||	🚗	AM DRIVE	Morn. Humor; Jobline 7:05am
Adult Cor	106.1	WHHR	||	🚗	🕐	News also on the 1/2 hour; Morn. Humor; Stk. Mkt. 9:30am; Italian Su 10–11am
Adult Cor	107.9	WIJY	|||	◇	AM & PM DRIVE	**LITE HITS;** Jazz Trax Su 6pm
Top 40	99.7	WHTK	|||	◇	SEE S.P.	News 11am, 5pm; D. Sholin's Insider Sa 6–10am; Rick Dee's Top 40 Su 7–10am
👢	92.1	WBHH	||	◇	MORE	News 12N; Morn. Humor; Classics F 8pm–1am; Top 30 Ctdwn. Su 1–4pm
Oldies	104.9	WSHG	||			
Oldies	106.9	WLOW	|||	🚗	🕐	**BIG BAND; EASY LISTENING;** L. King Su–F 11pm–5am; America in the Morning 5–6am
🎹	89.9	WJWJ	|||	◇	MORE	NPR; News 12N, W.E. Sa 10am–12N; Prairie Home Companion Sa 6pm; Car Talk Sa 9am
✝✝✝	88.7	WAGP	||		🕐	**TALK; ADULT POPULAR;** Sportsfile 7:30, 9:30am; Bus. File 8:30am, 6:30, 7:30pm

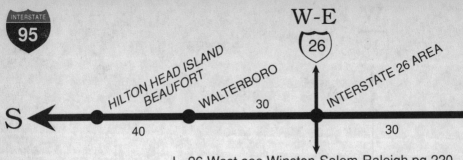

I - 26 West see Winston-Salem-Raleigh pg 220
I - 26 East see pg. 18

FORMAT / TUNE TO		STATION	SIGNAL POWER	TRAFFIC REPORT	NEWS	SPECIAL PROGRAMMING
WALTERBORO AREA						
T⁰P40	95.1	WSSX	|||	🚗	AM & PM DRIVE	Morn. Humor; Rick Dee's Weekly Top 40 Sa 6–10am; American Top 40 Su 8am–12N
🎸	96.1	WAVF	|||	🚗		Morn. Humor
🤠	100.9	WALD	||			
🤠	103.1	WBHC	||			
☀️LDIES	102.5	WXLY	|||	🚗	AM DRIVE	Morn. Hum.; Spts.: Citadel College; Live from the 60's Su 6–9am; Beach Show Su 2–5pm
R&B	104.5	WDXZ	|||			
🎹	89.3	WSCI	◇	MORE	**NPR;** News: W.E. Sa 10am–12N; Prairie Home Comp. Sa 6pm; Radio Read. M–F 8am
I-26 AREA						
AdultPop	96.9	WXTC	|||	🚗	AM DRIVE	**LITE HITS;** Morn. Humor
AdultPop	106.7	WTCB	|||	🚗	AM DRIVE	Morn. Humor; The Shag Show M–F 7–9pm; Nite-Lite M–F 10pm–12M
T⁰P40	107.5	WKQB	|||	🚗	MORE	News 10am, 4pm; Morn. Humor
🤠	102.9	WIGL	||	◇	MORE	News 10am, 12N, 2, 4pm; Carolina Comments Su 6:30am; NASCAR News daily 6pm
🤠	103.5	WEZL	|||	🚗	MORE	News 12N; Morn. Humor; Sports News 7:15, 8:15, 9:15am, 4:15, 5:15, 6:15pm
☀️LDIES	103.9	WKSO	||	◇	🕐	
R&B	90.3	WSSB	|||	🚗	🕐	Top 20 Ctdwn. Sa 7–9am; Rap Ctdwn. Sa 10–11am; Radioscope Sa 11am–12N
R&B	100.3	WMNY	||	◇	🕐	Gospel Su 6am–1pm
🎹	91.3	WLTR	|||	◇	MORE	**NPR;** News: W.E. Sa 10am–12N; Prairie Home Comp. Sa 6pm; Radio Read. M–F 8am

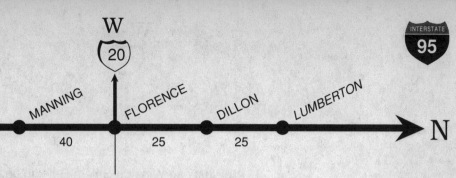

I - 20 West see Columbia pg. 184

FORMAT ♪ TUNE TO		STATION	SIGNAL POWER	TRAFFIC REPORT	NEWS	SPECIAL PROGRAMMING
MANNING AREA						
T○P40	104.7	WNOK	|||	🚗 AM DRIVE	🌙	R. Dee Sa 6–10am; Amer. Music Mag. M–F 4:30–5:30pm; Amer. Top 40 Su 6–10am
🤠	92.5	WHLZ	|||	◈	SPOT NEWS	Spts.: U. of South Carolina
🤠	97.5	WCOS	|||	◈	MORE	News 12N; P. Harvey 8:30am, 12N, 6:30pm; Top 10 at 10pm; Amer. Ctry. Ctdwn. Su 8am
🤠	100.1	WQTR	||			
R&B	101.3	WWDM	|||		AM & PM DRIVE	Kaleidoscope/Special Edit. Su 7–7:30pm; DM Connection (Request) M–F 12N–1pm
🎹	88.1	WRJA	|||	◈	MORE	**NPR;** News 12N, W.E. Sa 10am–12N; Prairie Home Comp. Sa 6pm; Radio Read. M–F 8am
ek-lek-tik	90.9	WLGI	|||	🚗		Carolina Radio Series M–Su 7pm; Jazz from the City Sa 8am; Our Jazz Heritage Sa 10am
✝✝✝	89.7	WMHK	|||	🚗	🕐	News also on the 1/2 hr, Ext. 11:45–12:55pm; Insight for Living 1:30pm; Vant. Point 6pm
FLORENCE AREA						
T○P40	104.1	WYAV	|||	◈	🕐	Morn. Humor; Rick Dee's Top 40 Ctdwn. Su 8am–12N
🎸	105.5	WDAR	||	◈	AM & PM DRIVE	Morn. Humor
R&B	106.3	WYNN	||		🕐	106 Music Mix Sa 10am–12N
DILLON AREA						
Adult Cont	94.3	WWPD	||	◈	🕐	Morn. Humor; Top 30 Su 2–5pm; Oldies Tu all day
T○P40	103.3	WJMX	|||	◈	AM & PM DRIVE	**CLASSIC ROCK;** Morn. Humor
R&B	107.1	WCIG	||	◈	🕐	**RELIGIOUS;** Gospel Music 6pm–12M; Spts.: SC State; Swap Shop 9–9:05am

I - 40 West see Winston-Salem-Raleigh pg. 220
I - 40 East see pg. 24

FORMAT / TUNE TO		STATION	SIGNAL POWER	TRAFFIC REPORT	NEWS	SPECIAL PROGRAMMING
LUMBERTON AREA						
T⁰P40	96.5	WMXF	|||	🚗	AM & PM DRIVE	Morn. Humor
♪	95.7	WKML	|||	◇	MORE→	News 12N; Morn. Humor
♪	102.3	WJSK	||	◇	🕐	Sports News 6:30am
OLDIES	105.7	WGQR	||	🚗	🕐	Morn. Humor; Spts.: High School, Carolina U.; Religious Programs Su 7am–12N
R&B	99.1	WZFX	|||	🚗	🕐	**URBAN CONTEMPORARY;** Jazz Styles Su 7pm–12M; Fox Rock F & Sa 7pm–12M
†††	100.9	WSTS	||			**SOUTHERN GOSPEL**
FAYETTEVILLE						
Adult Pop	98.1	WQSM	|||	🚗	AM & PM DRIVE	Lunchtime at the Oldies M–F 12N; 5 o'clock Oldies Road Show M–F 5pm
🐟	89.1	WFSS	|||	◇	MORE→	**NPR;** Latin Mus. Sa 10am–12N; Contemporary Gospel Su 6am–12N; Reggae Sa 12N
ROCK	640	WFNC	||			
SMITHFIELD/RALEIGH/GOLDSBORO AREA						
Adult Pop	101.5	WRAL	|||	🚗	AM & PM DRIVE	Morn. Humor; Dick Bartley's Rock & Roll Oldies Sa 7pm–12M
T⁰P40	105.1	WDCG	|||	🚗	A M DRIVE	Morn. Humor; Open House Party Sa & Su 7pm–12M; C. Kasem Top 40 Su 6–10am
🎸	103.5	WRCQ	|||	◇	MORE→	**ALBUM-ORIENTED ROCK;** Morn. Humor
♪	94.7	WQDR	|||	🚗	🕐	Morn. Humor; Farm Reports M–F 5–6am; Spts.: U. of NC
♪	96.9	WKTC	|||	◇	🕐	Morn. Humor; Beach Classics Su 5–9pm; Farm Reports 5:15am, 5:30pm
R&B	102.3	WOKN	||			

FORMAT ♪ TUNE TO		STATION	SIGNAL POWER	TRAFFIC REPORT	NEWS	SPECIAL PROGRAMMING
Lite Hits	96.1	WYLT	|||	🚗	🕐	Morn. Humor; Lite Nite Lovesongs M–F 7pm–12M
🎹	89.7	WCPE	|||		SEE S.P.	News: BBC 7, 9am, 12N, 6pm; Adven. in Good Music M–Sa 11am–12N; Opera Thu 7pm
NEWS	91.5	WUNC	|||	🚗	MORE	NPR; APR; CLASS; JAZZ; News: W.E. Sa & Su 10am–12N; Car Talk Sa 12N
TALK TALK	680	WPTF	"C"	🚗	🕐	Stk. Mkt. :50 6, 8am, 2, 3, 4, 5pm; Spts.: NC State U, Redskins, CBS
WILSON/ROCKY MOUNT AREA						
🎸	106.1	WRDU	|||	🚗	AM DRIVE	Class. 9 at 9am M–F; Vintage Block M–F 6pm; Short Order Lunch M–F 12N; Jazz Su 7am
👢	95.1	WRNS	|||	◇	AM DRIVE	Paul Harvey News 8:50am, 12:35, 5:50pm; American Ctry. Ctdwn. Su 6–10pm
OLDIES	100.7	WTRG	|||	◇	AM & PM DRIVE	Morn. Humor; Dick Clark Su AM
OLDIES	104.3	WCAS	|||	◇	AM DRIVE	ADULT POPULAR; LITE HITS; Morn. Humor; Spts.: Duke U.
R&B	92.1	WRSV	||			
Lite Hits	93.3	WDLX	|||	◇	AM DRIVE	ADULT POPULAR; Morn. Humor; Spts.: East Carolina Football & Basketball
E❋Z	107.9	WNCT	|||	◇	MORE	News 10, 11am, 3pm; Stk. Mkt. 10:15am, 2:15, 4:15pm; Frank Sinatra Sa 8–10pm
✝✝✝	92.5	WYFL	|||	◇	🕐	Stk. Mkt. 6pm
ROANOKE RAPIDS AREA						
Adult Pop	97.9	WLGQ	||	◇	SEE S.P.	News 20 after the hr; Stk. Mkt. 8:10am, 5:20pm; Jazz/David Sanborn Su 9pm
👢	102.3	WPTM	||			
✝✝✝	90.1	WPGT			◇	🕐	Money Management 8:05am; Job Opportunities 8:25am; Media Monitor 8:45am

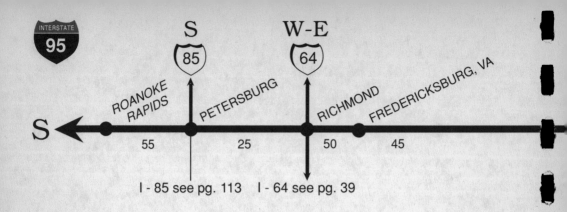

I - 85 see pg. 113   I - 64 see pg. 39

FORMAT ♪ TUNE TO		STATION	SIGNAL POWER	TRAFFIC REPORT	NEWS	SPECIAL PROGRAMMING
PETERSBURG AREA						
🔫☮	106.9	WAFX	‖‖	🚗	🕐	News also on the 1/2 hour; Morn. Humor
👢	95.3	WKHK	‖‖	🚗	AM DRIVE	Morn. Humor
R&B	99.3	WPLZ	‖		AM & PM DRIVE	
RICHMOND AREA						
Adult Pop	103.7	WMXB	‖‖	🚗	AM DRIVE	Morn. Humor
Top 40	94.5	WRVQ	‖‖	🚗	AM & PM DRIVE	Morn. Humor; Sports News 7:35am, 5:25pm
🎸	102.1	WRXL	‖‖	🚗	AM DRIVE	**CLASSIC ROCK;** Morn. Humor
☀OLDIES	96.5	WDCK	‖‖	🚗	AM DRIVE	Public Affairs Su 5:30–6am
☀OLDIES	106.5	WVGO	‖‖	🚗		Morn. Humor
R&B	92.7	WCDX	‖			
E❄Z	98.1	WTVR	‖‖	🚗	🕐	Stk. Mkt. 1, 2, 3pm; Sinatra, His Music, Sa 7–9pm
🎹	88.9	WCVE	‖‖	◇	MORE	**JAZZ** M–F 11pm–1am, Sa 8pm–12M, Su 12M–2am; **NPR; APR;** News: W.E. 8–10am
✝✝✝	92.1	WDYL	‖	🚗	MORE	**CHRISTIAN CONTEMPORARY;** News 1, 2, 3pm
✝✝✝	100.1	WYFJ	‖	◇	🕐	Public Affairs Tu 2:05pm
👢	1140	WVRA	"C"	🚗	🕐	News also 12N–1pm; Stk. Mkt. hourly; Spts.: U. of VA, Chuck Noe (Spts.) Su 7–10pm

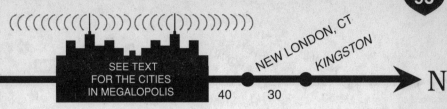

SEE TEXT
FOR THE CITIES
IN MEGALOPOLIS

NEW LONDON, CT

KINGSTON

40   30

N

FORMAT ♪ TUNE TO		STATION	SIGNAL POWER	TRAFFIC REPORT	NEWS	SPECIAL PROGRAMMING
FREDERICKSBURG AREA						
Adult Pop	101.5	WBQB	|||	◇	AM & PM DRIVE	Rock & Roll Oldies Sa 7pm; Supergold Su 7pm; Rock, Roll & Remember Su 11am
🤠	93.3	WFLS	|||	🚗	🕐	Morn. Humor; NASCAR Races Su afternoon; Weekly Ctry. Ctdwn. Sa 9pm
🎺	99.3	WYND	||			
✝✝✝	90.5	WJYJ	|||	◇	AM & PM DRIVE	**CHRISTIAN CONTEMPORARY;** Focus on the Fam. 12N & 9pm; Insight for Living 12:30pm
SEE WASHINGTON METRO PAGE 218						
SEE BALTIMORE METRO PAGE 168						
SEE PHILADELPHIA METRO PAGE 212						
SEE NEW YORK CITY METRO PAGE 206						
SEE HARTFORD METRO PAGE 190						
NEW LONDON AREA						
Top40	105.5	WQGN	||	◇		C. Kasem Top 40 Su 8am–12N; Sa Night Dance Party 9pm–12M; All-Request F 6pm
🤠	97.7	WCTY	||	◇	MORE	News 11:50am; Amer. Ctry. Ctdwn. Sa 8am, Su 5pm; On a Ctry. Road Su 7am & 10pm
OLDIES	102.3	WVVE	||	◇	MORE	News 12N; All Req. M–F 9pm–1am; D. Clark Su 8am–12N; Lost Lennon Tapes Su 9pm
Lite Hits	101.7	WBAZ	||	◇	MORE	News 12N, 1pm; Stk. Mkt. 7pm; Spts.: Mets, Giants; Boston Pops Su 10am–12N
E ❄ Z	100.9	WTYD	||	◇	MORE	News 12N; Tidehofer Dark/Love Songs M–Sa 8pm–12M; Talk Show Su 11–11:30pm
🎹	89.1	WNPR	|||	◇	MORE	**NPR; APR; NEWS:** W.E. Sa & Su 12N–1pm, ATC 5–6pm; Prairie Home Comp. Sa 6pm
ek-lek-tik	91.1	WCNI					**JAZZ; OLD ROCK; BLUES; INDUSTRIAL; FOLK; COUNTRY; DANCE; NEW ROCK**

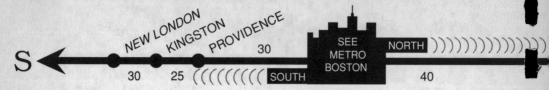

S ← NEW LONDON · KINGSTON · PROVIDENCE 30 · SEE METRO BOSTON · NORTH 40

30 · 25 · SOUTH

FORMAT ♪ TUNE TO	STATION	SIGNAL POWER	TRAFFIC REPORT	NEWS	SPECIAL PROGRAMMING
KINGSTON AREA					
🎺 103.7	WWRX	‖‖	🚗	SEE S.P.	News 7am, 1pm; Morn. Humor; Sports News 6:35, 7:35, 8:35am
🎺 100.3	WOTB	‖	🚗	🕐	Night Moods M 7–10pm; Jazz Flav. Sa & Su 9am–12N; Top 10 Jazz Show Sa 12N–1pm
ek-lek-tik 90.3	WRIU	‖		SEE S.P.	News 8:50, 11:50am, 2:50pm; Spts.: U. of RI; Meet the People F 2:30pm
PROVIDENCE AREA					
Adult Pop 93.3	WSNE	‖‖	🚗	AM DRIVE	OLDIES; Casey Kasem Su 9am–1pm, 3–7pm; Supergold Sa 7pm–2am
Top40 92.3	WPRO	‖‖	🚗	AM DRIVE	Morn. Humor; Hot Mix Sa 8pm–12M; American Top 40 Su 9am–1pm
Top40 106.3	WWKX	‖	🚗	🕐	DANCE MUSIC; Stk. Mkt.
🎸 94.1	WHJY	‖‖	🚗	AM & PM DRIVE	Morn. Humor; Rick's Hard Rock Cafe M–F 12N–1pm
🎸 95.5	WBRU	‖‖	🚗	AM & PM DRIVE	R & B; JAZZ
👢 98.1	WCTK	‖‖	🚗	AM & PM DRIVE	Amer. Ctry. Ctdwn. Su 9am–1pm; Nash. Live Su 8:30–10pm; Polish Happy Time Su 7am
☀OLDIES 101.5	WWBB	‖‖	🚗	🕐	Morn. Humor
Lite Hits 105.1	WWLI	‖‖	🚗	AM DRIVE	
TALK 630	WPRO	‖	🚗	🕐	News also on the 1/2 hr; Stk. Mkt. hrly; Spts.: Friars, Red Sox; Salty Brine M–F 5:30am
TALK 920	WHJJ	‖	🚗	🕐	Ext. News 6–9am; Stk. Mkt. hrly. 6am–9pm; Spts.: Patriots, Celtics, Bruins, U. of RI Rams
TALK 990	WALE	‖‖	🚗	🕐	Stk. Mkt. 7:52am, 5:55pm; Talk Hosts from 8am–6pm, 7pm–12M
SEE BOSTON METRO PAGE 172					

PORTSMOUTH · PORTLAND · 45 · N

FORMAT / TUNE TO		STATION	SIGNAL POWER	TRAFFIC REPORT	NEWS	SPECIAL PROGRAMMING
PORTSMOUTH AREA						
Adult Pop	95.7	WZID	|||	🚗	🕐	Stk. Mkt. 7:30am, 12N, 5pm; Spts News :15 & :45 AM Drive; Eye on NH Su 6:45am
Adult Pop	96.7	WKOS	||			
Top40	107.1	WERZ	||	🚗	MORE	News 2:50pm; Morn. Humor
🎸	100.3	WHEB	|||	⚡	AM & PM DRIVE	Morn. Humor; Rockline M 11:30pm–1am; In the Studio Su 8–9pm; Concert Ser. Su 9pm
🎸	101.1	WGIR	|||	🚗	AM DRIVE	Block Party F 6pm–Su 7pm; In Concert Sa 10:30pm; Wax Mus. (Oldies) Su 8am–12N
🎸☮	92.1	WCDQ	||	⚡	MORE	News 10:50, 11:50am; Morn. Humor; Blues M 9pm–12M
🎸	91.3	WUNH	|||			U. of New Hampshire
👢🤠	97.5	WOKQ	|||	⚡	SEE S.P.	News 6–7am, 12N–1pm; Morn. Humor
☀OLDIES	95.3	WCQL	||	🚗	MORE	News 12:30, 3:30pm
TALK TALK	610	WGIR	||	⚡	MORE	**NEWS;** Stk. Mkt. 6:15, 7:15; 8:40am, 4:50, 5:23pm; Spts.: Patriots, Celtics; Talk Hosts
PORTLAND AREA						
Top40	95.9	WHYR	||			
Top40	97.9	WWGT	|||	🚗	AM DRIVE	Morn. Humor; James St. James at 12:45 in Hollywood; C. Kasem Top 40 Su 9am
Top40	103.7	WZPK	|||	⚡	AM DRIVE	Morn. Humor
🎸	102.9	WBLM	|||	⚡	AM DRIVE	Morn. Humor
🎸☮	93.1	WMGX	|||	⚡	AM DRIVE	Morn. Humor
PORTLAND AREA CONTINUED ON THE NEXT PAGE						

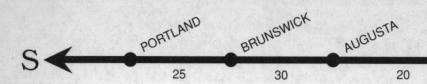

S ← · PORTLAND · BRUNSWICK · AUGUSTA
         25   30   20

FORMAT ♪ TUNE TO		STATION	SIGNAL POWER	TRAFFIC REPORT	NEWS	SPECIAL PROGRAMMING
CONTINUATION OF PORTLAND AREA						
👢	101.9	WPOR	‖‖‖	🚗	🕐	Morn. Humor
☀OLDIES	100.9	WYNZ	‖‖			
Lite Hits	94.3	WYJY	‖‖‖	🚗	MORE	News 12N, 3pm; Sunday Morning Jazz 9am–12N
E ✿ Z	94.9	WHOM	‖‖‖		MORE	News 12N; Stk. Mkt. 4:30pm
🎹	90.1	WMEA	‖‖‖	⚡	MORE	**NPR; APR;** News: W.E. Sa 12N–1pm; Music Var. M–Thu 10pm–12M; Opera Sa 1:30pm
🎹	106.3	WPKM	‖‖			Stk. Mkt. 9am, 5:40pm; Boston Pops Concert Su 8pm; Met Opera in Season
TALK	560	WGAN	‖‖	🚗	🕐	Spts.: U. of ME, Maine Mariners; Dr. Edell M, W, F 9am, Sa 11am; R. Limbaugh M–F 12N
BRUNSWICK AREA						
Adult Pop	105.9	WKRH	‖‖‖	⚡		**ADULT ROCK**
🎸	107.5	WTHT	‖‖‖			
👢	96.7	WCME	‖‖‖	⚡	MORE	News 12N; Homecooked Ctry. (Maine Music) Sa 7–8pm; Top 30 Ctry. Ctdwn. Su 1–4pm
☀OLDIES	93.9	WXGL	‖‖‖			
Lite Hits	99.9	WKZS	‖‖‖	⚡	A.M. DRIVE	Stk. Mkt. 5:45pm
🎻	98.9	WCLZ	‖‖‖	⚡	SEE S.P.	News 8, 9am; Stk. Mkt. PM; Live Acoustic Hour Sa 11am–12N
AUGUSTA AREA						
Adult Pop	104.3	WABK	‖‖‖	⚡	🕐	News also on the 1/2 hour, Paul Harvey
Top40	92.3	WMME	‖‖‖	⚡	A.M. DRIVE	Morn. Humor

WATERVILLE   BANGOR

45

N

FORMAT ♪ TUNE TO		STATION	SIGNAL POWER	TRAFFIC REPORT	NEWS	SPECIAL PROGRAMMING
🤠	101.3	WKCG	‖‖	◇⚡	MORE	News 11:56am; Gospel Su 10pm–12M; Ctry. Ctdwn. Sa 6–10pm; Su 8am–12N
Adult Pop	96.3	WWMR	‖‖	◇⚡	🕐	Playing a wide variety of music
WATERVILLE AREA						
Adult Pop	102.5	WQSS	‖‖			
Top 40	104.7	WWFX	‖‖	◇⚡	A.M. DRIVE	Morn. Humor; C. Kasem Top 40 Su 8am; On the Radio Su 7am; Eastern ME Report Su 6am
🎸	105.1	WTOS	‖‖	◇⚡	A.M. DRIVE	Morn. Humor
OLDIES	107.9	WHQO	‖			**TOP 40**
Lite Hits	98.5	WTVL	‖‖	◇⚡	SEE S.P.	News 8am, 12N, 5pm; P. Harvey 8:30am, 12N, 3:35pm; Spts.: Celtics
🎹	91.3	WMEW	‖	◇⚡	MORE	**NPR; APR;** News: W.E. Sa 12N–1pm; Music Variety M–Thu 10pm–12M; Opera Sa 1:30
BANGOR						
Adult Pop	94.5	WKSQ	‖‖	◇⚡	AM & PM DRIVE	Morn. Humor; Oldies Sa 6pm–12M
🎸	100.3	WKIT	‖‖	◇⚡	A.M. DRIVE	Morn. Humor; Request Hour M–F 12N; Traffic Jam M–F 5pm; Power Radio Sa 7pm–12M
🤠	97.1	WYOU	‖‖			
🤠	106.5	WQCB	‖‖	◇⚡	MORE	News 12N, 3pm
OLDIES	95.7	WWMJ	‖‖	🚗	A.M. DRIVE	**CLASSIC HITS;** Morn. Humor
Lite Hits	92.9	WPBC	‖‖	◇⚡	AM & PM DRIVE	Stk. Mkt. 7:30am, 12:41, 5:41pm
🎹	90.9	WMEH	‖‖	◇⚡	MORE	**NPR; APR;** News: W.E. Sa 12N–1pm; Music Variety M–Thu 10pm–12M; Opera Sa 1:30pm
BANGOR AREA CONTINUED ON THE NEXT PAGE						

S ← | BANGOR | HOWLAND | HOULTON | FORT KENT | → N
     | 30 | 70 | 90 |

FORMAT ♪ TUNE TO	STATION	SIGNAL POWER	TRAFFIC REPORT	NEWS	SPECIAL PROGRAMMING
CONTINUATION OF BANGOR AREA					
ek-lek-tik	89.9	WERU	|||			Morning Maine Magazine M–F 7–9am; On the Wing M–F 11am–2pm, Sa 11am–1pm
††† 88.5	WHCF	|||	🚗	🕐	Focus on the Family 11:30am; Insight for Living 9:30am
HOWLAND AREA					
Adult Pop	99.3	WHMX	||			**COUNTRY; ALBUM-ORIENTED ROCK**
Adult Pop	94.9	WSYY	|||	⚡	🕐	Sport News Updates hourly 5–9am; Radio Kandy Sa 10am–12N
Christik	1450	WTOX				🕐	**NEWS;** Spts.: U. of Maine Football, Hockey
HOULTON AREA					
Adult Pop	97.7	WCXU	||	⚡	MORE	News 11:30am; Solid Gold Sa 7pm–5am; D. Clark Su 7pm–12M; Hlth. News M–F 12:30pm
Adult Pop	100.1	WHOU	||			
TOP40	96.9	WDHP	|||	⚡		Morn. Humor; Farm Reports (September only) 4am
🤠	101.7	WOZI	||	⚡	🕐	Stk. Mkt. 11:30am; Talk Show 10:06–11am
Lite Hits	96.1	WTMS	|||	⚡	SEE S.P.	News 6:30am, 1:30pm; Talk Sports M–F 7:35am
🛋	106.1	WMEM	|||	⚡	MORE	**NPR; APR;** News: W.E. Sa 12N–1pm; Music Vari. M–Thu 10pm–12M; Opera Sa 1:30pm
FORT KENT AREA					
Adult Pop	102.3	WCXX	||	⚡	MORE	News 11:30am; Solid Gold Sa 7pm–5am; D. Clark Su 7pm–12M; Hlth. News M–F 12:30pm
🎓	92.1	WUFK					U. of Maine

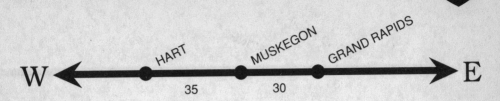

W ← HART · 35 · MUSKEGON · 30 · GRAND RAPIDS → E

INTERSTATE 96

FORMAT ♪ TUNE TO	STATION	SIGNAL POWER	TRAFFIC REPORT	NEWS	SPECIAL PROGRAMMING
HART AREA					
Adult Pop — 105.3	WCXT	‖‖	◇⚡	🕐	**LITE ROCK;** Stk. Mkt. 5:50pm; Powerline Su 8am
Adult Pop — 106.3	WKLA	‖	◇⚡	AM & PM DRIVE	**CLASSIC HITS; NEWS;** New Gold on CD 2:57pm; American Top 40 Sa 7pm
🎩👢 — 95.9	WKZC	‖			
MUSKEGON AREA					
Adult Pop — 92.1	WGHN	‖	🚗	🕐	News also on the 1/2 hour
Adult Pop — 101.7	WQFN	‖	🚗	AM DRIVE	Morn. Humor
Top 40 — 104.5	WSNX	‖‖	◇⚡	AM DRIVE	Morn. Humor
🎸☮ — 98.3	WLCS	‖	◇⚡		Flashback Su 8–10pm; Oldies Brunch Su 6am–12N; Classics to Go M–F 12N–1pm
🎩👢 — 100.1	WSHN	‖			
🎩👢 — 106.9	WMUS	‖‖	🚗	AM DRIVE	Morn. Humor; Intensive Playlist
R&B — 107.9	WMHG	‖	◇⚡	🕐	**JAZZ; RELIGIOUS;** Spts. News 8:20am, 4:20pm; On the Move/Tom Joyner Sa 10am
Lite Hits — 95.3	WKBZ	‖	◇⚡	🕐	
🎹 — 90.3	WBLV	‖‖	◇⚡	MORE	**NPR; APR; JAZZ;** News five to the hour; Garrison Keillor Sa 6pm
GRAND RAPIDS AREA					
Adult Pop — 95.7	WLHT	‖‖	🚗	AM DRIVE	**LITE HITS; OLD.;** Light Rock Cafe 12N–1pm; Lights Out 10pm–1am; Car Tunes 5–6pm
ek-lek-tik — 88.1	WYCE	‖			**COMMUNITY STATION;** World Music; Traditional, Jazz, Blues, Etc.

GRAND RAPIDS AREA CONTINUED ON NEXT PAGE

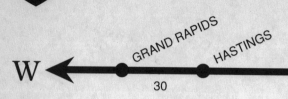

W ← GRAND RAPIDS HASTINGS

30

FORMAT ♪ TUNE TO		STATION	SIGNAL POWER	TRAFFIC REPORT	NEWS	SPECIAL PROGRAMMING
CONTINUATION OF GRAND RAPIDS AREA						
Adult Pop	96.1	WYXX	III			
Top 40	97.9	WGRD	III	🚗	AM DRIVE	Morn. Humor
🎸	94.5	WKLQ	III	🚗	AM DRIVE	Morn. Humor
🎸	96.9	WLAV	III	🚗	SPOT NEWS	Morn. Humor
🎸☮	93.7	WJFM	III	🚗	AM DRIVE	Morn. Humor; Jazz Show/David Sanborn Su 8–10am
👢	101.3	WCUZ	III	🚗	AM DRIVE	**OLDIES; LITE HITS;** P. Harvey 8:30am, 12:30pm; Spts. News 6:45, 7:45, 8:45am
👢	107.3	WODJ	III			
E ❄ Z	105.7	WOOD	III	🚗	🕐	Morn. Humor
🎹	104.1	WVGR	III		MORE	**NPR;** News: W.E. Sa & Su 10am–12N; Mktpl. M–F 6:30–7pm; Swing Sa 8–10pm
🎺	88.5	WGVU	II	🚗	AM DRIVE	**NPR**
ek-lek´-tik	89.9	WEHB	I	⚡	SPOT NEWS	**COMMUNITY STATION;** International, Ethnic; Native American W 8–10am
✝✝✝	88.9	WGNR	II	⚡	🕐	Morn. Humor
✝✝✝	89.3	WXYB	III	⚡	🕐	
✝✝✝	91.3	WCSG	III	🚗	MORE	News 12N
✝✝✝	99.3	WJQK	II	⚡	🕐	Paul Harvey 9:30am, 12:06, 4:30pm; Farm News Early AM; Sports
✝✝✝	102.9	WFUR	III	⚡	🕐	

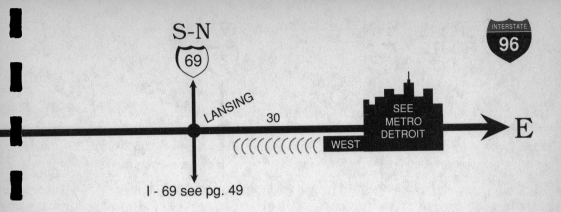

I - 69 see pg. 49

FORMAT ♪ TUNE TO		STATION	SIGNAL POWER	TRAFFIC REPORT	NEWS	SPECIAL PROGRAMMING
HASTINGS						
A♪ult Pop	100.1	WBCH	‖	🚗	🕐	**OLDIES;** Stk. Mkt.; Sports; Tourist Reports; Trivia Quiz Call-In Features
T°P40	103.3	WKFR	‖‖		AM & PM DRIVE	Rick Dee's Top 40 Su 9am–1pm; Hitline USA Su 11pm; Hometown Ctdwn. Sa 6–9pm
LANSING AREA						
A♪ult Pop	99.1	WFMK	‖‖	🚗		Morn. Humor
T°P40	92.1	WGOR	‖			**ALBUM-ORIENTED ROCK**
T°P40	94.9	WVIC	‖‖	⚡	🕐	Morn. Humor
T°P40	101.7	WKKP	‖	⚡	MORE	**ADULT POPULAR;** News 11:15am, 3:15pm; Spts.: MI State
🎸	106.1	WJXQ	‖‖	⚡	AM DRIVE	In the Studio Su 6pm; King Biscuit Flower Hour Su 11pm; Blues Cruise Su 7–11pm
🎸☮	92.7	WMMQ	‖	⚡	AM DRIVE	All-Request Lunch 12N–1pm; Blues Cruise Su 8pm–12M; All-Request Sa 7pm–12M
🎸	88.9	WDBM	‖	⚡	MORE	News 10am, 2pm; Sports News daily; New Feat. Show W 7pm; Rock Over Lond. Su 9pm
🤠	100.7	WITL	‖‖		AM & PM DRIVE	Stk. Mkt.; Ctry. Ctdwn. Su 2–6pm
☀OLDIES	94.1	WIBM	‖‖	⚡	MORE	News 12N; Morn. Humor; Dick Bartley Sa 7–10am
Lite Hits	97.5	WJIM	‖‖	⚡	🕐	Morn. Humor
🎹	90.5	WKAR	‖‖	⚡	MORE	**NPR;** News 12N; Jazz F 6:30–10pm; Whad'Ya Know Sa 8–10pm; Folk Su 8–9pm
T♪LK	870	WKAR	‖		MORE	**NEWS** Extended to 12N; **INFORMATION;** Talk 12N–4pm; Fresh Air 4–5pm
SEE DETROIT METRO PAGE 188						

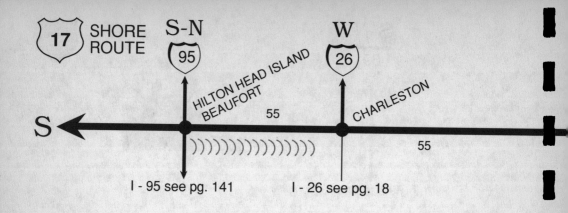

I - 95 see pg. 141   I - 26 see pg. 18

FORMAT ♪ TUNE TO	STATION	SIGNAL POWER	TRAFFIC REPORT	NEWS	SPECIAL PROGRAMMING
FARTHER SOUTH ON US 17 SEE I-95 PAGE 141					
CHARLESTON					
Adult Pop 96.9	WXTC	‖‖	🚗	A M DRIVE	**LITE HITS;** Morn. Humor
Adult Pop 100.7	WSUY	‖	🚗	A M DRIVE	News Updates thru day; Morn. Humor; Public Affairs Su 6–7am
Top40 95.1	WSSX	‖‖	🚗	AM & PM DRIVE	Morn. Humor; Rick Dee's Weekly Top 40 Sa 6–10am; American Top 40 Su 8am–12N
Top40 107.5	WKQB	‖‖	🚗	MORE	News 10am, 4pm; Morn. Humor
🎸 96.1	WAVF	‖‖	🚗		Morn. Humor
🎸 98.1	WYBB	‖‖			
👢 92.5	WHLZ	‖‖	◇	SPOT NEWS	Spts.: U. of South Carolina
👢 103.5	WEZL	‖‖	🚗	🕐	News 12N; Morn. Humor; Sports News 7:15, 8:15, 9:15am, 4:15, 5:15, 6:15pm
☀OLDIES 102.5	WXLY	‖‖			
R&B 93.5	WWWZ	‖			
R&B 94.3	WUJM	‖	🚗	AM & PM DRIVE	Morn. Humor; Public Affairs Su 5:30–6am
R&B 104.5	WDXZ	‖‖			
🎹 89.3	WSCI	‖‖	◇	MORE	**NPR;** News: W.E. Sa 10am–12N; Prairie Home Comp. Sa 6pm; Radio Reader M–F 8am
🎹 105.5	WJYQ	‖			
🎺 101.7	WMGL	‖	🚗	AM & PM DRIVE	**ADULT POPULAR**
✝✝✝ 88.5	WFCH	‖‖			

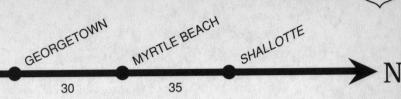

FORMAT ♪ TUNE TO		STATION	SIGNAL POWER	TRAFFIC REPORT	NEWS	SPECIAL PROGRAMMING
✝✝✝	90.7	WYFH	‖‖		🕐	
✝✝✝	91.5	WKCL	‖‖			Holy Spirit Bible College
ᴛᴀʟᴋ R S ᴛᴀʟᴋ	1250	WTMA	‖	🚗	🕐	Extended News 6–9am, 5–7pm; Stk. Mkt. Drives; Spts.: NASCAR Races
GEORGETOWN AREA						
TOP40	97.7	WBPR	‖‖		AM & PM DRIVE	C. Kasem Su 10am–2pm; Amer. Dance Traxx Su 9pm–12M; Ctdwn. USA Sa 8am–12N
👢	100.9	WQSC	‖			
☀OLDIES	106.5	WSYN	‖‖		AM DRIVE	Stk. Mkt. 12:40, 5:35pm; Su. Nite at the Beach 7–9pm; The 60's Like It Is Su 9pm–12M
E ❋ Z	93.7	WTUB	‖		AM DRIVE	Stk. Mkt. 5:30pm; Ski Reports AM Drive; Gospel Su 6am–12N
MYRTLE BEACH AREA						
Adult Pop	105.5	WNMB	‖			
TOP40	104.1	WYAV	‖‖	◇	🕐	Morn. Humor; Rick Dee's Top 40 Ctdwn. Su 8am–12N
🎸	101.7	WKZQ	‖‖	◇	MORE	News 12N; Morn. Humor; Metal Shop Sa 10pm; Rock Over London Su 9pm
👢	92.9	WZNS	‖‖	◇	🕐	Interstate Radio Network 12M–6am; Sports News M–F 4:30pm; Solid Gold Ctry Su 6am
👢	103.1	WYAK	‖	◇	AM & PM DRIVE	Morn. Humor
E ❋ Z	92.1	WJYR	‖			
🎹	90.1	WHMC	‖‖	◇	MORE	**NPR;** News W.E. Sa 10am–12N; Prairie Home Companion Sa 6pm; Radio Reader M–F 8am
ek-lek-tik	90.9	WLGI	‖‖	🚗		Carolina Radio Series M–Su 7pm; Jazz from the City Sa 8am; Our Jazz Heritage Sa 10am

FORMAT ♪ TUNE TO	STATION	SIGNAL POWER	TRAFFIC REPORT	NEWS	SPECIAL PROGRAMMING
SHALLOTTE AREA					
(Country) 93.5	WDZD	‖	⚡	AM & PM DRIVE	Sports
R&B 99.1	WZFX	‖‖			
E❄Z 106.3	WCCA	‖	⚡	🕐	**BIG BAND;** Sounds of Sinatra Sa 8–10am
WILMINGTON AREA					
Adult Pop 97.3	WMFD	‖‖	⚡	🕐	**JAZZ;** Morn. Humor
Adult Pop 102.7	WGNI	‖‖	🚗	🕐	Morn. Humor
(Rock) 107.5	WSFM	‖‖	⚡	AM & PM DRIVE	**ALBUM ROCK;** Flashback Su 8pm; Westwood One Presents (Concert) Su 10am
TOP40 99.9	WVBS	‖‖	🚗	AM & PM DRIVE	Office Request Lunch Hour M–F 12N–1pm; Breakfast Club M–F 7–9am
(Country) 101.3	WWQQ	‖‖	🚗	🕐	Amer. Ctry. Ctdwn. Sa 8pm–12M; Hard Core Ctry. Su 10pm–12M; Ctry. Today F 8pm
(Piano) 91.3	WHQR	‖‖	⚡	MORE	**NPR; APR; JAZZ** Sa 10:30am–12N, 10pm–12M, Su 10pm–1am; News: W.E. Sa 8–10am
JACKSONVILLE/NEW BERN AREA					
Adult Pop 96.3	WRHT	‖‖	⚡	AM & PM DRIVE	Sports News 6:50, 7:50am; Rick Dee's Top 40 Sa 6–10am; C. Kasem Su 10am–2pm
Adult Pop 99.5	WVVY	‖‖			
Adult Pop 106.5	WSFL	‖‖	⚡	MORE	**LITE HITS; OLD.;** Stk. Mkt. 8:50am, 5:50pm; Sld. Gold Sa 7pm–3am; D.Clark Su 8am–12N
(Rock) 103.3	WZYC	‖‖		AM DRIVE	Morn. Humor; Classic Rock Cafe M–F 12N; Oldies Sa 7–10am; Powercuts Su 6–8pm
(Rock) 105.5	WXQR	‖			
(Country) 95.1	WRNS	‖‖	⚡	AM DRIVE	Paul Harvey News 8:50am, 12:35, 5:50pm; American Ctry. Ctdwn. Su 6–10pm

JACKSONVILLE / NEW BERN — WASHINGTON — WILLIAMSTON → N

50   20

FORMAT ♪ TUNE TO		STATION	SIGNAL POWER	TRAFFIC REPORT	NEWS	SPECIAL PROGRAMMING
🥾	97.7	WKCP	‖			
☀️OLDIES	98.7	WKOO	‖‖	◇	🕐	Ski Reports W, Thu 9am, 4pm; D. Bartley Sa 7pm–12M; Sunday Nite at the Beach 6–8pm
R&B	101.9	WIKS	‖‖			
🎹	89.3	WTEB	‖‖			Craven Community College
ek-lek´-tik	104.9	WMSQ	‖	◇	🕐	American Top 40 Su 8am–12N; Paul Harvey News
✝✝✝	90.7	WOTJ	‖‖	◇	MORE	News 12N, 2pm; Selected Preaching 9:05pm; Christian View of the News 5:05, 11pm
WASHINGTON AREA						
A♪ult Pop	98.3	WCZI	‖			**OLDIES**
🎸	106.1	WRDU	‖‖	🚗	AM DRIVE	Classic 9 at 9am M–F; Vintage Block M–F 6pm; Shrt. Ord. Lnch. M–F 12N; Jazz Su 7am
Lite Hits	93.3	WDLX	‖‖	◇	AM DRIVE	**ADULT POPULAR;** Morn. Humor; Spts.: East Carolina Football & Basketball
E ❀ Z	107.9	WNCT	‖‖	◇	MORE	News 10, 11am, 3pm; Stk. Mkt. 10:15am, 2:15, 4:15pm; Frank Sinatra Sa 8–10pm
TALK	930	WRRF	‖	◇	🕐	**NEWS;** Spts.: Duke U.; R. Limbaugh M–F 1–4pm; Sally Jessy Raphael M–F 7–10pm
WILLIAMSTON AREA						
🥾	95.9	WPNC	‖			
🥾	98.9	WDRP	‖	◇	🕐	**SOUTHERN GOSP.** M–F 10am–2pm, M 6pm–12M, Tu–F 6–8pm; **BLACK GOSP.** Tu–F 8pm
☀️OLDIES	100.7	WTRG	‖‖	◇	AM & PM DRIVE	Morn. Humor; Dick Clark Su AM
☀️OLDIES	104.3	WCAS	‖‖	◇	AM DRIVE	**ADULT POPULAR; LITE HITS;** Morn. Humor; Spts.: Duke U.
WILLIAMSTON AREA CONTINUED ON THE NEXT PAGE						

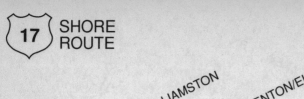

S ← WILLIAMSTON — EDENTON/ELIZABETH CITY

40   40

FORMAT ♪ TUNE TO	STATION	SIGNAL POWER	TRAFFIC REPORT	NEWS	SPECIAL PROGRAMMING
CONTINUATION OF WILLIAMSTON AREA					
Top40 103.7	WHTE	‖‖	◇	AM DRIVE	E. Carolina Top 25 Sa 10am–12N; C. Kasem Su 6–10pm; Future Hits Su 5–6pm
R&B 97.7	WDJB	‖			
EDENTON/ELIZABETH CITY AREA					
Adult Pop 99.1	WVOD	‖‖	◇	🕐	W. Cronkite M–F 7:25am, 12:30, 5:30pm; Class. Su 6am–1pm; Beach Music Su 4–8pm
Adult Pop 102.3	WZBO	‖			
Adult Pop 105.7	WRSF	‖‖	◇	MORE	News 12N; Dick Bartley Sa 7pm–12M; Charlie Bird's Beach Blast Su 6–10pm
🤠 99.3	WQDK	‖	🚗	MORE	News 12N, 12:30pm; Morn. Humor; Trading Post M–F 9–10am; Class. Su 8–9pm
R&B 93.7	WMYK	‖‖			**ADULT R & B**
🎓 89.9	WRVS	‖			Elizabeth State U.
††† 100.1	WBXB	‖	◇	AM & PM DRIVE	Morn. Humor; Christian Hits/Oldies; Children's Bible Hour; Inside Gospel
NORFOLK AREA					
Adult Pop 94.9	WJQI	‖‖	🚗	🕐	Morn. Humor; Love Songs 7pm–12M
Adult Pop 101.3	WWDE	‖‖	🚗	AM & PM DRIVE	Morn. Humor
Top40 104.5	WNVZ	‖‖			
Top40 105.3	WMXN	‖‖	🚗		**ADULT POPULAR;** Morn. Humor
🎸 92.1	WTZR	‖		SEE S.P.	News 6:30, 8:30am; New Mtl. Su 5–7pm; Dr. Demento Su 11pm–1am; Prgsv. Rock Su 9pm
🎸 98.7	WNOR	‖‖			**CLASSIC ROCK**

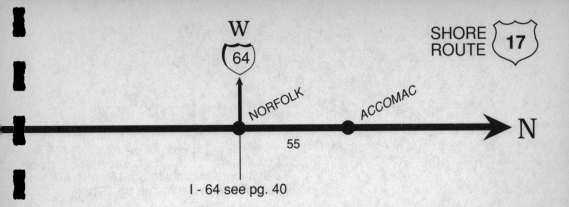

FORMAT ♪ TUNE TO		STATION	SIGNAL POWER	TRAFFIC REPORT	NEWS	SPECIAL PROGRAMMING
✌	106.9	WAFX	‖‖‖	🚗	🕐	News also on the 1/2 hour; Morn. Humor
👢	94.1	WKEZ	‖‖‖			
👢	97.3	WGH	‖‖‖	🚗	🕐	Morn. Humor; Ctry. Ctdwn. Su 9pm–12M
👢	100.5	WCMS	‖‖‖	🚗	MORE	News 12N, 3pm, Paul Harvey 9am, 12:30, 6pm; Bluegrass Su 7am & 11pm
OLDIES	95.7	WLTY	‖‖‖	🚗	AM DRIVE	Morn. Humor
OLDIES	96.5	WDCK	‖‖‖	🚗	AM DRIVE	Public Affairs Su 5:30–6am
R & B	102.9	WOWI	‖‖‖			
E ❋ Z	92.9	WFOG	‖‖‖	🚗	🕐	Morn. Humor; Sunday Morning Magazine 7–8am; Big Band Jump Sa 8–10pm
🎹	88.7	WFOS	‖‖‖	⚡	AM & PM DRIVE	JAZZ; Stk. Mkt. 12N; Detroit Symphony W 7pm; World's Greatest Orchestras Sa 7pm
🎹	90.3	WHRO	‖‖‖	🚗		NPR; APR; Opera Sa 1:30–5pm; With Hearts & Voice Su 12N–1pm; Pipedrms. Su 7–8pm
🎺	88.3	WHOV	‖	🚗	🕐	R & B; Hispanic Sa 8am–1pm; Reggae Su 6–10pm; Talk M–F 4pm; Gosp. Su 11am–1pm
🎺	91.1	WNSB	‖	🚗	🕐	UPI Roundtable; Blues; Misty Morning; Reggae Jamboree
ek-lek-tik	89.5	WHRV	‖‖‖	SEE S.P.		CLASS. M–F 9am–12N; JAZZ M–F 8pm–6am, Sa 8pm–12M, Su 12N–6pm; M.E. 6–8:30am
✝✝✝	96.1	WKSV	‖‖‖	🚗		CHRISTIAN CONTEMPORARY
✝✝✝	99.7	WYFI	‖‖‖	⚡	🕐	Turning Point 8:30pm; Insight for Living 10:30pm; Back to the Bible 9:30am
NEWS	1310	WGH	‖	🚗	ALL NEWS	SPORTS: U. of VA, NBA, Orioles, Local High School; Sportstalk M–F 5–8pm
ROUTE	850	WNIS	‖‖‖	🚗	🕐	News also on the 1/2 hr, Extended 6–9am; Stk. Mkt. :55 hourly; Spts.: Orioles, Redskins

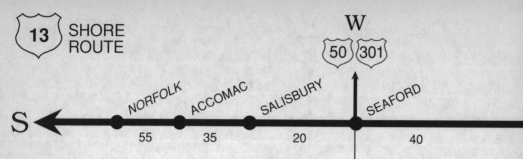

13 SHORE ROUTE

W 50 301

S ← NORFOLK · ACCOMAC · SALISBURY · SEAFORD

NORFOLK	ACCOMAC	SALISBURY	SEAFORD
55	35	20	40

To Baltimore Metro see pg. 168
To Washington Metro see pg. 218

FORMAT ♪ TUNE TO		STATION	SIGNAL POWER	TRAFFIC REPORT	NEWS	SPECIAL PROGRAMMING
ACCOMAC AREA						
![boot]	107.5	WKRE	|||	◇	MORE	News 12N; Agri-Net Farm Show 5:45am, 12:15pm; Ralph Emery 6:45am, 5:45pm
Lite Hits	103.3	WESR	||	◇	◷	P. Harvey M–F 12:06, 5:30pm; Spts.: Redskins; Farm News M–F 12:40pm
TALK	1330	WESR	||			
SALISBURY AREA						
Adult Pop	103.9	WOCQ	||	🚗	◷	Morn. Humor; C. Kasem Su 9am; P. Harvey M–F 8:30am, 12:06, 3:06pm, Sa 12:06pm
Adult Pop	104.7	WQHQ	|||			
Top 40	99.9	WKHI	|||	🚗	AM & PM DRIVE	Morn. Humor
![boot]	94.3	WICO	||	◇	◷	Agri. Reports 6–6:30am, 12:15pm; Ctry. Ctdwn. Sa 7pm–12M; Gospel Su 7–11am
Oldies	98.9	WSBY	||			
E ❄ Z	105.5	WDVH	||	◇	MORE	News 12N; Money Pro Report M–F 2pm; Peninsula Perspective Su 8am & 11am
🎹	89.5	WSCL	|||	◇	MORE	News 12N; Adventures in Good Music 7–8pm; Live from the Met Sa 1–5pm
🎺	91.3	WESM	|||	◇	AM & PM DRIVE	News Week on Air Su 1pm; Jazz from the City F 8–10pm; Strwy. to Heaven Tu, Thu 8pm
†††	102.5	WOLC	|||	◇	MORE	News 12N
SEAFORD AREA						
Adult Pop	96.7	WCEI	||			
Adult Pop	106.3	WCEM	||	◇	MORE	News 12N; Spts.: Orioles, Redskins; C. Kasem Top 40 Sa 2pm; D. Bartley Oldies Sa 7pm
🎸	93.5	WZBH	|||	◇	MORE	News 2pm, Su 9–10pm; New Rock Thu 11pm–12M; Jazz Su 11pm–1am

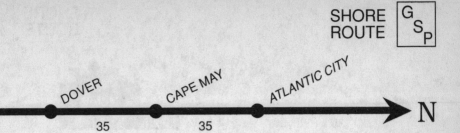

SHORE ROUTE G·S·P

DOVER — 35 — CAPE MAY — 35 — ATLANTIC CITY → **N**

FORMAT ♪ TUNE TO		STATION	SIGNAL POWER	TRAFFIC REPORT	NEWS	SPECIAL PROGRAMMING
🎩👢	100.9	WAAI	‖	◇⚡	MORE	News 12N; Ctry. Report M–F 9:40am, 5:40pm; Legendary Ctry. Sa 10–11am
Lite Hits	98.3	WECY	‖	◇⚡	MORE	**EASY LISTENING; TALK;** News 12N, 5pm; Marketplace 9–9:30am
E ❀ Z	92.7	WGMD	‖	🚗	🕐	News 12N, Bus. News on 1/2 hr. 6:30am–7:30pm; Spts. Updates thru day
WEST ON US 50 & 301 TO BALTIMORE SEE PAGE 168						
WEST ON US 50 & 301 TO WASHINGTON SEE PAGE 218						
DOVER AREA						
Adult Pop	97.7	WAFL	‖	🚗	AM & PM DRIVE	Morn. Humor; Dick Clark's Ctdwn. America Su 10am; Classic Lunch M–F 12N
🎩👢	94.7	WDSD	‖‖	◇⚡	MORE	News 12N; NASCAR Winston Cup Racing Su pm; Interstate Radio Network 12M–5am
NEWS	1600	WKEN	‖	◇⚡	MORE	Stk. Mkt., Commodities :40 6, 7, 8am; Spts.: NFL; Sally Jessy Raphael M–F 7–10pm
NORTH ON US 13 & 301 TO PHILADELPHIA SEE PAGE 212						
SHORE ROUTE CONTINUES ACROSS DELAWARE BAY						
CAPE MAY AREA						
Adult Pop	105.5	WBNJ	‖			
TOP 40	97.3	WBSS	‖‖	🚗		**R & B;** American Dance Trax Su 10pm–1am; Future Hits Su 5–6am; Top 20 Su 10am
🎸	100.7	WZXL	‖‖		AM DRIVE	Morn. Humor
E ❀ Z	94.3	WWOC	‖			
ek-lek´-tik	107.7	WSNJ	‖‖			
✝✝✝	102.3	WSJL	‖	🚗	SEE S.P.	News 7, 11am, 2, 3, 5pm; Children's Prog. Sa AM; Fam. Issues M–F 5:30am & 6pm

163

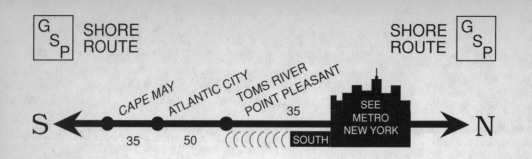

CAPE MAY   ATLANTIC CITY   TOMS RIVER   POINT PLEASANT

S ← 35   50   35   SOUTH   SEE METRO NEW YORK → N

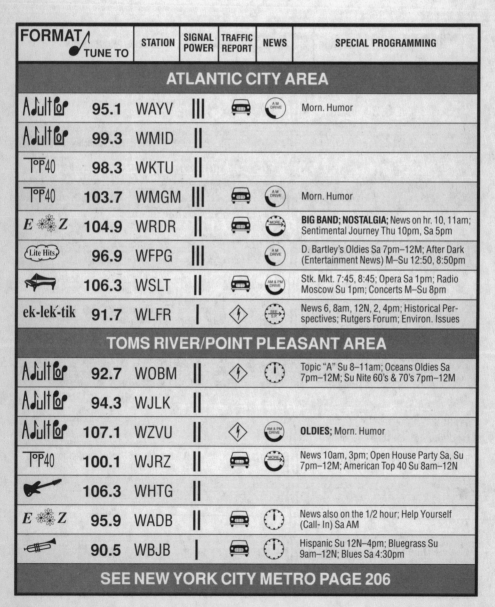

FORMAT TUNE TO		STATION	SIGNAL POWER	TRAFFIC REPORT	NEWS	SPECIAL PROGRAMMING
ATLANTIC CITY AREA						
Adult Cor	95.1	WAYV	|||	🚗	AM DRIVE	Morn. Humor
Adult Cor	99.3	WMID	||			
Top 40	98.3	WKTU	||			
Top 40	103.7	WMGM	|||	🚗	AM DRIVE	Morn. Humor
E ✿ Z	104.9	WRDR	||	🚗	MORE	**BIG BAND; NOSTALGIA;** News on hr. 10, 11am; Sentimental Journey Thu 10pm, Sa 5pm
(Lite Hits)	96.9	WFPG	|||		AM DRIVE	D. Bartley's Oldies Sa 7pm–12M; After Dark (Entertainment News) M–Su 12:50, 8:50pm
🎹	106.3	WSLT	||	🚗	AM & PM DRIVE	Stk. Mkt. 7:45, 8:45; Opera Sa 1pm; Radio Moscow Su 1pm; Concerts M–Su 8pm
ek-lek-tik	91.7	WLFR			◇	SEE S.P.	News 6, 8am, 12N, 2, 4pm; Historical Perspectives; Rutgers Forum; Environ. Issues
TOMS RIVER/POINT PLEASANT AREA						
Adult Cor	92.7	WOBM	||	◇	🕐	Topic "A" Su 8–11am; Oceans Oldies Sa 7pm–12M; Su Nite 60's & 70's 7pm–12M
Adult Cor	94.3	WJLK	||			
Adult Cor	107.1	WZVU	||	◇	AM & PM DRIVE	**OLDIES;** Morn. Humor
Top 40	100.1	WJRZ	||	🚗	MORE	News 10am, 3pm; Open House Party Sa, Su 7pm–12M; American Top 40 Su 8am–12N
🎸	106.3	WHTG	||			
E ✿ Z	95.9	WADB	||	🚗	🕐	News also on the 1/2 hour; Help Yourself (Call-In) Sa AM
🎺	90.5	WBJB			🚗	🕐	Hispanic Su 12N–4pm; Bluegrass Su 9am–12N; Blues Sa 4:30pm
SEE NEW YORK CITY METRO PAGE 206						

METRO

SECTION

ATLANTA

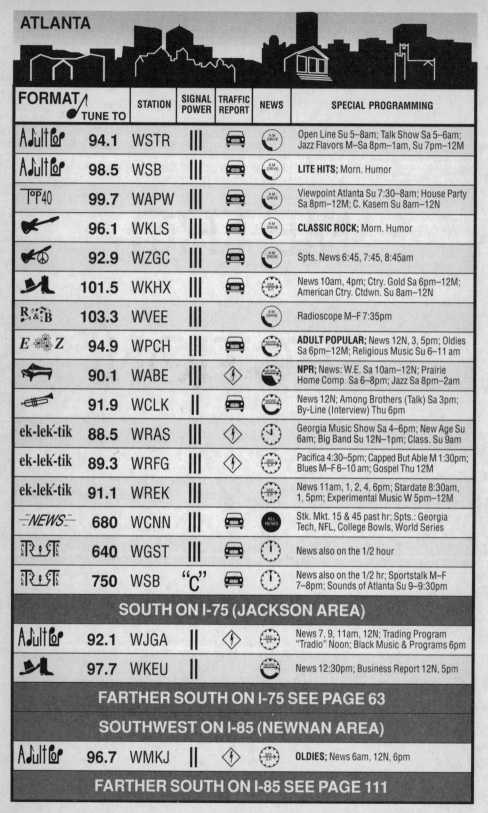

FORMAT ♪ TUNE TO		STATION	SIGNAL POWER	TRAFFIC REPORT	NEWS	SPECIAL PROGRAMMING
Adult Pop	94.1	WSTR	‖‖	🚗	A.M. DRIVE	Open Line Su 5–8am; Talk Show Sa 5–6am; Jazz Flavors M–Sa 8pm–1am, Su 7pm–12M
Adult Pop	98.5	WSB	‖‖	🚗	A.M. DRIVE	**LITE HITS;** Morn. Humor
TOP40	99.7	WAPW	‖‖	🚗	A.M. DRIVE	Viewpoint Atlanta Su 7:30–8am; House Party Sa 8pm–12M; C. Kasem Su 8am–12N
🎸	96.1	WKLS	‖‖	🚗	A.M. DRIVE	**CLASSIC ROCK;** Morn. Humor
🎸	92.9	WZGC	‖‖	🚗	A.M. DRIVE	Spts. News 6:45, 7:45, 8:45am
🤠	101.5	WKHX	‖‖	🚗	SEE S.P.	News 10am, 4pm; Ctry. Gold Sa 6pm–12M; American Ctry. Ctdwn. Su 8am–12N
R&B	103.3	WVEE	‖‖		A.M. DRIVE	Radioscope M–F 7:35pm
E❀Z	94.9	WPCH	‖‖	🚗	MORE	**ADULT POPULAR;** News 12N, 3, 5pm; Oldies Sa 6pm–12M; Religious Music Su 6–11 am
🎹	90.1	WABE	‖‖	⚡	MORE	**NPR;** News: W.E. Sa 10am–12N; Prairie Home Comp. Sa 6–8pm; Jazz Sa 8pm–2am
🎺	91.9	WCLK	‖	🚗	MORE	News 12N; Among Brothers (Talk) Sa 3pm; By-Line (Interview) Thu 6pm
ek-lek´-tik	88.5	WRAS	‖‖	⚡	🕐	Georgia Music Show Sa 4–6pm; New Age Su 6am; Big Band Su 12N–1pm; Class. Su 9am
ek-lek´-tik	89.3	WRFG	‖‖	⚡	SEE S.P.	Pacifica 4:30–5pm; Capped But Able M 1:30pm; Blues M–F 6–10 am; Gospel Thu 12M
ek-lek´-tik	91.1	WREK	‖‖		SEE S.P.	News 11am, 1, 2, 4, 6pm; Stardate 8:30am, 1, 5pm; Experimental Music W 5pm–12M
NEWS	680	WCNN	‖‖	🚗	ALL NEWS	Stk. Mkt. 15 & 45 past hr; Spts.: Georgia Tech, NFL, College Bowls, World Series
TALK	640	WGST	‖‖	🚗	🕐	News also on the 1/2 hour
TALK	750	WSB	"C"	🚗	🕐	News also on the 1/2 hr; Sportstalk M–F 7–8pm; Sounds of Atlanta Su 9–9:30pm

SOUTH ON I-75 (JACKSON AREA)

FORMAT ♪ TUNE TO		STATION	SIGNAL POWER	TRAFFIC REPORT	NEWS	SPECIAL PROGRAMMING
Adult Pop	92.1	WJGA	‖	⚡	SEE S.P.	News 7, 9, 11am, 12N; Trading Program "Tradio" Noon; Black Music & Programs 6pm
🤠	97.7	WKEU	‖		MORE	News 12:30pm; Business Report 12N, 5pm

FARTHER SOUTH ON I-75 SEE PAGE 63

SOUTHWEST ON I-85 (NEWNAN AREA)

FORMAT ♪ TUNE TO		STATION	SIGNAL POWER	TRAFFIC REPORT	NEWS	SPECIAL PROGRAMMING
Adult Pop	96.7	WMKJ	‖	⚡	SEE S.P.	**OLDIES;** News 6am, 12N, 6pm

FARTHER SOUTH ON I-85 SEE PAGE 111

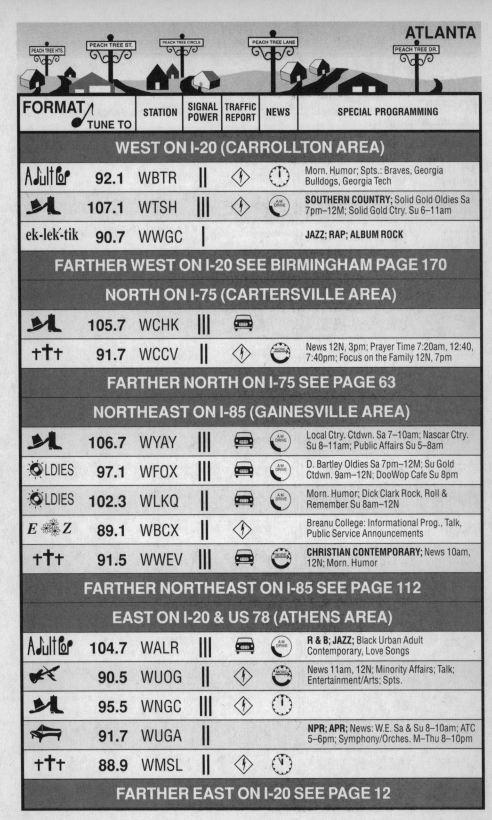

ATLANTA

FORMAT TUNE TO		STATION	SIGNAL POWER	TRAFFIC REPORT	NEWS	SPECIAL PROGRAMMING
WEST ON I-20 (CARROLLTON AREA)						
Adult Pop	92.1	WBTR	‖	◇	⊙	Morn. Humor; Spts.: Braves, Georgia Bulldogs, Georgia Tech
🤠	107.1	WTSH	‖‖	◇	AM DRIVE	**SOUTHERN COUNTRY;** Solid Gold Oldies Sa 7pm–12M; Solid Gold Ctry. Su 6–11am
ek-lek′-tik	90.7	WWGC	‖			**JAZZ; RAP; ALBUM ROCK**
FARTHER WEST ON I-20 SEE BIRMINGHAM PAGE 170						
NORTH ON I-75 (CARTERSVILLE AREA)						
🤠	105.7	WCHK	‖‖	🚗		
✝✝✝	91.7	WCCV	‖	◇	MORE	News 12N, 3pm; Prayer Time 7:20am, 12:40, 7:40pm; Focus on the Family 12N, 7pm
FARTHER NORTH ON I-75 SEE PAGE 63						
NORTHEAST ON I-85 (GAINESVILLE AREA)						
🤠	106.7	WYAY	‖‖	🚗	AM DRIVE	Local Ctry. Ctdwn. Sa 7–10am; Nascar Ctry. Su 8–11am; Public Affairs Su 5–8am
☀OLDIES	97.1	WFOX	‖‖	🚗	AM DRIVE	D. Bartley Oldies Sa 7pm–12M; Su Gold Ctdwn. 9am–12N; DooWop Cafe Su 8pm
☀OLDIES	102.3	WLKQ	‖	🚗	AM DRIVE	Morn. Humor; Dick Clark Rock, Roll & Remember Su 8am–12N
E ❄ Z	89.1	WBCX	‖	◇		Breanu College: Informational Prog., Talk, Public Service Announcements
✝✝✝	91.5	WWEV	‖‖	🚗	MORE	**CHRISTIAN CONTEMPORARY;** News 10am, 12N; Morn. Humor
FARTHER NORTHEAST ON I-85 SEE PAGE 112						
EAST ON I-20 & US 78 (ATHENS AREA)						
Adult Pop	104.7	WALR	‖‖	🚗	AM DRIVE	**R & B; JAZZ;** Black Urban Adult Contemporary, Love Songs
🎸	90.5	WUOG	‖	◇	MORE	News 11am, 12N; Minority Affairs; Talk; Entertainment/Arts; Spts.
🤠	95.5	WNGC	‖‖	◇	⊙	
🎹	91.7	WUGA	‖			**NPR; APR;** News: W.E. Sa & Su 8–10am; ATC 5–6pm; Symphony/Orches. M–Thu 8–10pm
✝✝✝	88.9	WMSL	‖	◇	⊙	
FARTHER EAST ON I-20 SEE PAGE 12						

FORMAT ♪ TUNE TO	STATION	SIGNAL POWER	TRAFFIC REPORT	NEWS	SPECIAL PROGRAMMING
A♪ult 🎵 92.3	WYST	|||	🚗	AM DRIVE	Morn. Humor; Oldies Sa 7–10pm; Public Affairs Su 6–10am
A♪ult 🎵 106.5	WWMX	|||	🚗	AM DRIVE	Morn. Humor
A♪ult 🎵 107.3	WRQX	||	🚗	AM DRIVE	**TOP 40;** Morn. Humor; American Top 40 Su 6–10pm; Live Line Su 10pm–1am
TOP40 95.5	WPGC	||	🚗	AM DRIVE	**R & B; CONTEMPORARY CROSSOVER;** Morn. Humor
TOP40 104.3	WBSB	|||	🚗	SEE S.P.	News 8:55am; Morn. Humor; C. Kasem Sa 9am–2pm, Su 12M–4am
🎸 97.9	WIYY	|||	🚗	AM DRIVE	Morn. Humor
🎸 101.1	WWDC	||	🚗	AM DRIVE	Stk. Mkt.
🎸 100.7	WGRX	|||	🚗	AM DRIVE	Morn. Humor; Comedy Line Su 10pm; Flashback Su 8am
🎸 89.7	WCVT	||	⬦	SEE S.P.	**JAZZ; CLASSICAL;** News 7am, 1, 3, 5pm; Spts.
🤠 93.1	WPOC	|||	⬦	🕐	P. Harvey 9am, 12:06, 6pm; Baltimore Ctdwn. Sa 10am–12:30pm; Top 10 at 9pm M–F
☀OLDIES 105.7	WQSR	|||	🚗	AM DRIVE	Morn. Humor; Forgotten 45's Su 7pm–12M; Dick Bartley Oldies Sa 7–11pm
R&B 95.9	WWIN	||	🚗	AM DRIVE	Morn. Humor; Inside 30 (Talk) Sa 7:30am; Gospel Su 6am; Money Matters Sa 8am
R&B 96.3	WHUR	||	🚗	AM DRIVE	**ADULT POPULAR;** Spts. Talk Su 6pm; Gospel Su 7–11am; Jazz Su 11am–3pm
R&B 102.7	WXYV	|||	🚗	SEE S.P.	News 6:30, 11:30am; Morn. Humor
Lite Hits 101.9	WLIF	|||	🚗	🕐	Stk. Mkt. 5 to the hour; Back to God Su 10–11am
E❋Z 99.5	WGAY	||	🚗	🕐	Stk. Mkt. 4:30pm; Matinee at One (Broadway Shows) Su 1pm
🎹 88.1	WJHU	|||	🚗	MORE	**NPR;** Stk. Mkt. 8:30am; Spts. News 7:35am
🎹 91.5	WBJC	|||		SEE S.P.	**APR;** MonitoRadio M–F 5–6am, 4–5pm; Opera Sa 1:30–5pm; Garrison Keillor Sa 6pm
🎺 88.9	WEAA	||		AM DRIVE	Gospel Su 5:30am–4pm; Oldies Sa 5:30–9am; Blues M 9–10pm
🎺 89.3	WPFW	||		SEE S.P.	News 7pm; World Music M–F 3–5:30pm; Morning Conversations M–F 9–10am
✝✝✝ 95.1	WRBS	|||	🚗	🕐	**INSPIR. MUSIC;** Focus on the Fam. M–F 10am, 12N; Gateway to Joy M–F 2:15pm
NEWS 1500	WTOP	"C"	🚗	ALL NEWS	Stk. Mkt. :25 & :55 each hour; Spts.: Orioles, NFL, Bullets, Playoffs, World Series
TALK 680	WCBM	||	🚗	🕐	News also on the 1/2 hr; Stk. Mkt. :10 6, 8, 11am, :30 1, 3, 5pm; Spts.: Horse Racing

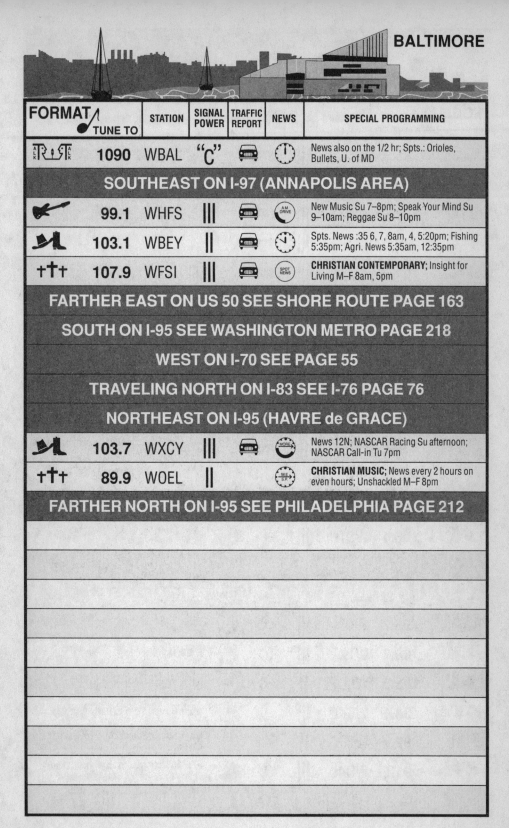

BALTIMORE

FORMAT ♪ TUNE TO	STATION	SIGNAL POWER	TRAFFIC REPORT	NEWS	SPECIAL PROGRAMMING
ROCK TALK SPORTS 1090	WBAL	"C"	🚗	🕐	News also on the 1/2 hr; Spts.: Orioles, Bullets, U. of MD
SOUTHEAST ON I-97 (ANNAPOLIS AREA)					
🎸 99.1	WHFS	‖‖	🚗	AM DRIVE	New Music Su 7–8pm; Speak Your Mind Su 9–10am; Reggae Su 8–10pm
👢🤠 103.1	WBEY	‖	🚗	🕐	Spts. News :35 6, 7, 8am, 4, 5:20pm; Fishing 5:35pm; Agri. News 5:35am, 12:35pm
✝✝✝ 107.9	WFSI	‖‖	🚗	SPOT NEWS	**CHRISTIAN CONTEMPORARY;** Insight for Living M–F 8am, 5pm
FARTHER EAST ON US 50 SEE SHORE ROUTE PAGE 163					
SOUTH ON I-95 SEE WASHINGTON METRO PAGE 218					
WEST ON I-70 SEE PAGE 55					
TRAVELING NORTH ON I-83 SEE I-76 PAGE 76					
NORTHEAST ON I-95 (HAVRE de GRACE)					
👢🤠 103.7	WXCY	‖‖	🚗	MORE	News 12N; NASCAR Racing Su afternoon; NASCAR Call-in Tu 7pm
✝✝✝ 89.9	WOEL	‖		SEE S.P.	**CHRISTIAN MUSIC;** News every 2 hours on even hours; Unshackled M–F 8pm
FARTHER NORTH ON I-95 SEE PHILADELPHIA PAGE 212					

BIRMINGHAM

FORMAT / TUNE TO		STATION	SIGNAL POWER	TRAFFIC REPORT	NEWS	SPECIAL PROGRAMMING
Adult Pop	96.5	WMJJ	|||	🚗	AM DRIVE	**OLDIES;** Lunchtime at the Oldies M–F 12N–1pm; Oldies Party M–F 7pm–12M
Top40	94.5	WAPI	|||	🚗	AM DRIVE	Morn. Humor; Shadoe Stevens Top 40 Su 10am–2pm
Top40	106.9	WKXX	|||	🚗	AM DRIVE	Hometown Ctdwn. Sa 10am–1pm; R. Dee Su 10am–2pm; Hangin' with Hlywd. Su 6–11pm
🎸	99.5	WZRR	|||	🚗	AM DRIVE	Stk. Mkt. during Morning Drive; Morn. Humor; Spts.: AL U.; Flashback Su 7–9pm
🤠	104.7	WZZK	|||	🚗	MORE	News 12N, 3pm; Morn. Humor; American Ctry. Ctdwn. Sa 8pm–12M, Su 8am–12N
R&B	107.7	WENN	|||	🚗	🕐	
🎹	90.3	WBHM	|||	◇	MORE	Stk. Mkt. 4:30pm; Thistle & Shamrock Sa 7–8pm; Pipedrms. Su 8–10pm; Folk Sa 8pm
✝✝✝	89.5	WBFR			◇	SPOT NEWS	**CHRISTIAN CONTEMPORARY;** Unshackled M–F 6:30–7pm; Morn. Clock M–F 6–8:30am
✝✝✝	91.9	WGIB	||	◇	🕐	**CHRISTIAN CONTEMPORARY;** Focus on the Family M–F 1:30pm, 10pm, Sa 1pm
✝✝✝	93.7	WDJC	|||	◇		**CHRISTIAN CONTEMPORARY;** Family News in Focus M–F 10:15pm; Talk M–F 12:30pm
TALK	960	WERC	||	🚗	🕐	Stk. Mkt. 5pm; Spts.: Birmingham Southern; Sportstalk M–F 5pm

SOUTH ON I-65 (CLANTON AREA)

🤠	97.7	WEZZ	||	◇	🕐	News also on 1/2 hr; Farm/Home News 5:30–5:55am; Spts. News 9:45–9:50am, 4:15pm
🤠	106.1	WSTH	|||	◇	SEE S.P.	News 11am, 5pm, Paul Harvey; Morn. Humor; Spts.; Larry King

FARTHER SOUTH ON I-65 SEE PAGE 42

SOUTHWEST ON I-20 & I-59 (TUSCALOOSA)

Adult Pop	95.7	WFFX	|||	◇	AM & PM DRIVE	Spts.: U. of AL; P. Harvey 7:30am, 12N, 4pm; C. Kasem Top 40 Su 10am
Top40	98.1	WTXT	|||	◇	AM DRIVE	**R & B;** Morn. Humor
🤠	105.5	WACT	||	◇	SPOT NEWS	Morn. Humor
OLDIES	94.1	WCKO	|||	◇	🕐	Morn. Humor; Markets; Spts.; Farm Reports
R&B	92.7	WTUG	||	🚗	AM DRIVE	Morn. Humor; Rap/Mix M–F 7pm–12M; Slow Love M–F 12M–5:30am; Pub. Affairs Sa 9am
🎹	91.5	WUAL	|||	◇	MORE	**NPR; JAZZ;** News also on the hour 11am, 1, 3pm; Variety, Humor Sa 5–8pm

FARTHER SOUTH ON I-59 SEE PAGE 31

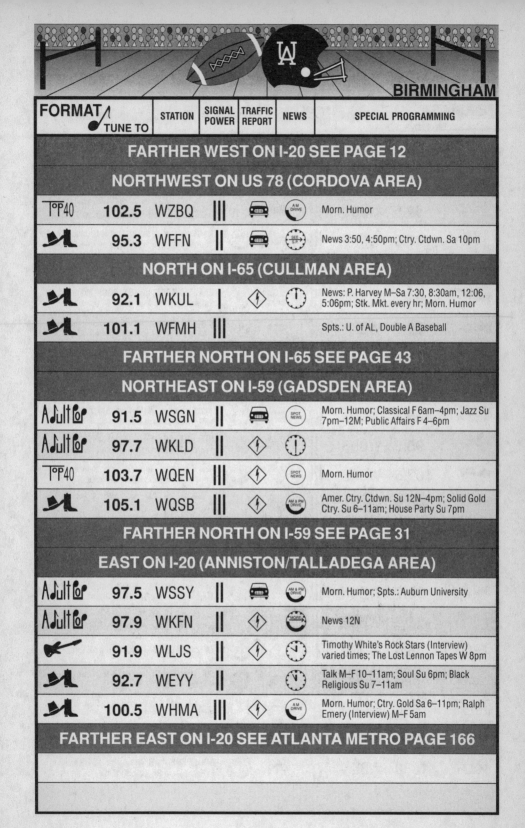

FORMAT ♪ TUNE TO	STATION	SIGNAL POWER	TRAFFIC REPORT	NEWS	SPECIAL PROGRAMMING

FARTHER WEST ON I-20 SEE PAGE 12

NORTHWEST ON US 78 (CORDOVA AREA)

TOP40	102.5	WZBQ	|||	🚗	A M DRIVE	Morn. Humor
🤠	95.3	WFFN	||	🚐	SEE S.P.	News 3:50, 4:50pm; Ctry. Ctdwn. Sa 10pm

NORTH ON I-65 (CULLMAN AREA)

🤠	92.1	WKUL			◇	🕐	News: P. Harvey M–Sa 7:30, 8:30am, 12:06, 5:06pm; Stk. Mkt. every hr; Morn. Humor
🤠	101.1	WFMH	|||			Spts.: U. of AL, Double A Baseball

FARTHER NORTH ON I-65 SEE PAGE 43

NORTHEAST ON I-59 (GADSDEN AREA)

Adult Cor	91.5	WSGN	||	🚗	SPOT NEWS	Morn. Humor; Classical F 6am–4pm; Jazz Su 7pm–12M; Public Affairs F 4–6pm
Adult Cor	97.7	WKLD	||	◇	🕐	
TOP40	103.7	WQEN	|||	◇	SPOT NEWS	Morn. Humor
🤠	105.1	WQSB	|||	◇	AM & PM DRIVE	Amer. Ctry. Ctdwn. Su 12N–4pm; Solid Gold Ctry. Su 6–11am; House Party Su 7pm

FARTHER NORTH ON I-59 SEE PAGE 31

EAST ON I-20 (ANNISTON/TALLADEGA AREA)

Adult Cor	97.5	WSSY	||	🚗	AM & PM DRIVE	Morn. Humor; Spts.: Auburn University
Adult Cor	97.9	WKFN	||	◇	MORE	News 12N
🎸	91.9	WLJS	||	◇	🕐	Timothy White's Rock Stars (Interview) varied times; The Lost Lennon Tapes W 8pm
🤠	92.7	WEYY	||		🕐	Talk M–F 10–11am; Soul Su 6pm; Black Religious Su 7–11am
🤠	100.5	WHMA	|||	◇	A M DRIVE	Morn. Humor; Ctry. Gold Sa 6–11pm; Ralph Emery (Interview) M–F 5am

FARTHER EAST ON I-20 SEE ATLANTA METRO PAGE 166

BOSTON

FORMAT ♪ TUNE TO		STATION	SIGNAL POWER	TRAFFIC REPORT	NEWS	SPECIAL PROGRAMMING
Adult Pop	98.5	WBMX	|||	🚗	MORE	News 12N, 2pm; Eat Your Heart Out (Review) Su 7:30–8am
Adult Pop	105.7	WVBF	|||	🚗	AM & PM DRIVE	Quiet Storm M–F 7pm–12M; C. Kasem Sa 6–9pm, Su 10am–1pm; Jazz Su 8–10am
Top 40	94.5	WZOU	|||	🚗	AM DRIVE	Amer. Top 40 Su 8am–12N; Rick Dee Sa 6–10am; Su Morn. Magazine Show 7:30am
Top 40	107.9	WXKS	|||	🚗	MORE	News also ten to the hr; Dance Classics Sa 10pm–1am; Evening Magazine M–F 6–9pm
🎸	92.9	WBOS	|||	🚗	AM & PM DRIVE	**ADULT POPULAR; JAZZ; NEW AGE;** Musical Starstreams Su 11pm–1am
🎸	104.1	WBCN	|||	🚗	AM DRIVE	**CLASSIC ROCK; PRGSV. ROCK;** Nocturnal Emissions (New Music) Su 8–10pm
🎸☮	100.7	WZLX	|||	🚗	AM DRIVE	Lost 45's Su 6–10pm; Dr. Demento Su 10pm–12M; Reelin' in the Years Su 1–4am
🎸	90.3	WZBC			◇		New Age Sa 10am–1pm; Su Morn. Ctry. 10am–2pm; Reggae Sa 1–5pm; Jazz Su 8–11pm
☀OLDIES	103.3	WODS	|||	🚗	AM & PM DRIVE	Little Walter Time Machine Su 8pm–12M; Elvis Only Su 8–9am; Thur. Nite Ctdwn. 8pm
(Lite Hits)	106.7	WMJX	|||	🚗	AM DRIVE	Jazz Su 8am–12N; Bedtime Magic M–F 8pm–12M; Bay State Forum Su 6–8am
🎹	90.9	WBUR	|||	🚗	MORE	**NPR;** W.E. Sa & Su 6–11am; Car Talk Sa 11am–12N, Su 6–7pm; Fresh Air M–F 4pm
🎹	102.5	WCRB	|||	◇	AM & PM DRIVE	N.E. Business Report 5:55pm; Symphony Concert M–F 9pm; Opera Sa 1:30pm
🎺	96.9	WCDJ	|||	🚗	AM DRIVE	
ek-lek-tik	88.1	WMBR					Blues Sa 12N–2pm; Oldies Sa 2–4pm; Gospel Su 8–10am; Classical Su 10am–12N
ek-lek-tik	88.9	WERS	|||			Spts. Su 7–7:30pm; Chagigah (Jewish) Su 8–11am
ek-lek-tik	89.7	WGBH	|||		MORE	**NPR;** Mktplace M–F 6–6:30pm; Blues F & Sa 10pm–1am; Folk Sa 12N–4:30pm
ek-lek-tik	91.9	WUMB					Acoustic; Folk M–F 5–8pm; Quiet Storm M–F 8pm–1am; Celtic Twilight Sa 5–9pm
ek-lek-tik	95.3	WHRB			◇	AM & PM DRIVE	**JAZZ; CLASSICAL; FOLK;** Spts.: Harvard
═NEWS═	590	WEEI	||	🚗	ALL NEWS	Stk. Mkt. 05 & 25 past the hour; Spts.: Celtics, Bruins
TALK	680	WRKO	"C"	🚗	🕐	Stk. Mkt. AM Drive; Spts.: Red Sox, Bruins; Spts. Call M–F 6–8pm
TALK	850	WHDH	"C"	🚗	🕐	Spts.: Patriots; Local & Syndicated Talk Hosts 24 hours a day
TALK	1030	WBZ	"C"	🚗	🕐	**ADULT POPULAR;** News also on 1/2 hr, Extended 4–6pm; Stk. Mkt. at news times

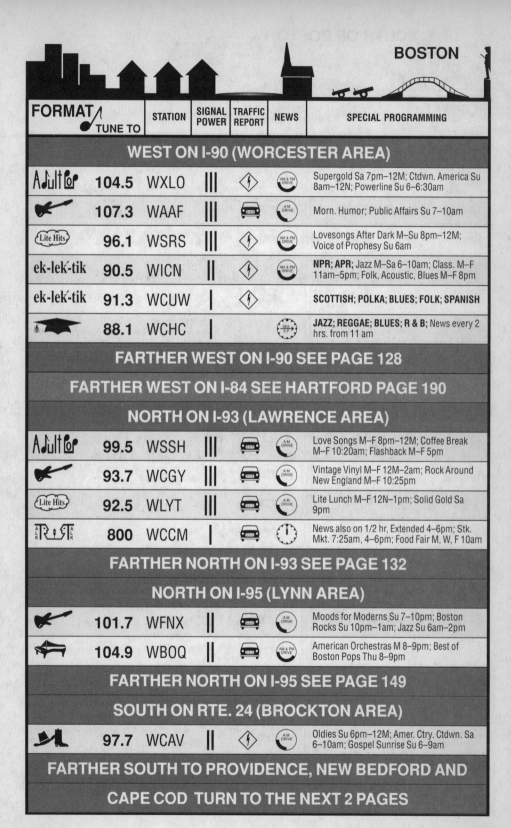

BOSTON

FORMAT / TUNE TO		STATION	SIGNAL POWER	TRAFFIC REPORT	NEWS	SPECIAL PROGRAMMING
WEST ON I-90 (WORCESTER AREA)						
Adult Pop	104.5	WXLO	|||	⚡	AM & PM DRIVE	Supergold Sa 7pm–12M; Ctdwn. America Su 8am–12N; Powerline Su 6–6:30am
🎸	107.3	WAAF	|||	🚗	AM DRIVE	Morn. Humor; Public Affairs Su 7–10am
Lite Hits	96.1	WSRS	|||	⚡	AM & PM DRIVE	Lovesongs After Dark M–Su 8pm–12M; Voice of Prophesy Su 6am
ek-lek´-tik	90.5	WICN	||	⚡	AM & PM DRIVE	**NPR; APR;** Jazz M–Sa 6–10am; Class. M–F 11am–5pm; Folk, Acoustic, Blues M–F 8pm
ek-lek´-tik	91.3	WCUW			⚡		**SCOTTISH; POLKA; BLUES; FOLK; SPANISH**
🎓	88.1	WCHC			SEE S.P.	**JAZZ; REGGAE; BLUES; R & B;** News every 2 hrs. from 11 am
FARTHER WEST ON I-90 SEE PAGE 128						
FARTHER WEST ON I-84 SEE HARTFORD PAGE 190						
NORTH ON I-93 (LAWRENCE AREA)						
Adult Pop	99.5	WSSH	|||	🚗	AM DRIVE	Love Songs M–F 8pm–12M; Coffee Break M–F 10:20am; Flashback M–F 5pm
🎸	93.7	WCGY	|||	🚗	AM DRIVE	Vintage Vinyl M–F 12M–2am; Rock Around New England M–F 10:25pm
Lite Hits	92.5	WLYT	|||	🚗	AM DRIVE	Lite Lunch M–F 12N–1pm; Solid Gold Sa 9pm
TALK	800	WCCM			🚗	🕐	News also on 1/2 hr, Extended 4–6pm; Stk. Mkt. 7:25am, 4–6pm; Food Fair M, W, F 10am
FARTHER NORTH ON I-93 SEE PAGE 132						
NORTH ON I-95 (LYNN AREA)						
🎸	101.7	WFNX	||	🚗	AM DRIVE	Moods for Moderns Su 7–10pm; Boston Rocks Su 10pm–1am; Jazz Su 6am–2pm
🎹	104.9	WBOQ	||	🚗	AM & PM DRIVE	American Orchestras M 8–9pm; Best of Boston Pops Thu 8–9pm
FARTHER NORTH ON I-95 SEE PAGE 149						
SOUTH ON RTE. 24 (BROCKTON AREA)						
👢	97.7	WCAV	||	⚡	AM DRIVE	Oldies Su 6pm–12M; Amer. Ctry. Ctdwn. Sa 6–10am; Gospel Sunrise Su 6–9am
FARTHER SOUTH TO PROVIDENCE, NEW BEDFORD AND						
CAPE COD TURN TO THE NEXT 2 PAGES						

SOUTH OF BOSTON

FORMAT TUNE TO		STATION	SIGNAL POWER	TRAFFIC REPORT	NEWS	SPECIAL PROGRAMMING
CONTINUATION OF BOSTON METRO						
SOUTHEAST ON MASS. RTE. 3 (PLYMOUTH AREA)						
Adult Pop	95.9	WATD	‖	🚗	🕐	News also on the 1/2 hr; Spts. Su 5pm; Irish Music Su 9am–12N; Oldies Sa 2pm–12M
OLDIES	99.1	WPLM	‖‖	🚗	🕐	**BIG BAND;** News also on the 1/2 hour; Stk. Mkt. 12:30, 5:30pm
SOUTH ON MASS. RTE. 140 (NEW BEDFORD AREA)						
Top 40	107.1	WFHN	‖	🚗	AM DRIVE	Rick Dee Su 8am–12N; Hot Mix Sa 8pm–12M
🎸	91.1	WSMU	‖	◇	🕐	Reggae Sa 8am–2pm; Folk Sa 2–8pm; Gosp. Su 8–11am; Jazz Su 11am–5pm; Bls. Su 5pm
🤠	98.1	WCTK	‖‖	🚗	AM & PM DRIVE	Amer. Ctry. Ctdwn. Su 9am–1pm; Nashville Live Su 8:30–10pm; Polish Time Su 7am
ek-lek´-tik	97.3	WJFD	‖‖	🚗	🕐	**PORTUGUESE;** Spts.: Portuguese; Talk (Live) M–F 10am–12N; Dedications Su 11am
TALK	1420	WBSM	‖	🚗	🕐	Extended News 12N–12:30pm; Spts.: Patriots; Talk Hosts M–F 6am–10pm
SOUTHWEST ON I-95 (PROVIDENCE AREA)						
Adult Pop	93.3	WSNE	‖‖	🚗	AM DRIVE	**OLDIES;** Supergold Sa 7pm–12M; Focus Su 7am; Jazz Su
Top 40	92.3	WPRO	‖‖	🚗	AM DRIVE	Morn. Humor; Hot Mix Sa 8pm–12M; American Top 40 Su 9am–1pm
Top 40	106.3	WWKX	‖	🚗	🕐	**DANCE MUSIC;** Stk. Mkt.
🎸	94.1	WHJY	‖‖	🚗	AM & PM DRIVE	Morn. Humor; Rick's Hard Rock Cafe M–F 12N–1pm
🎸	95.5	WBRU	‖‖	🚗	AM & PM DRIVE	**R & B; JAZZ**
OLDIES	101.5	WWBB	‖‖	🚗	🕐	Morn. Humor
Lite Hits	105.1	WWLI	‖‖	🚗	AM DRIVE	Morn. Humor; Night Lite M–F 9pm–12M
TALK	630	WPRO	‖	🚗	🕐	News also on the 1/2 hr; Stk. Mkt hrly; Spts.: Friars, Red Sox; Salty Brine M–F 5:30am
TALK	920	WHJJ	‖	🚗	MORE	Extended News 6–9am; Stk. Mkt. AM Drive; Spts.: Patriots, Celtics, Bruins, U. of RI, Rams
TALK	990	WALE	‖	🚗	🕐	Stk. Mkt. 7:52am, 5:55pm; Talk Hosts from 8am–6pm, 7pm–12M
FARTHER SOUTHWEST ON I-95 SEE PAGE 148						

FORMAT / TUNE TO		STATION	SIGNAL POWER	TRAFFIC REPORT	NEWS	SPECIAL PROGRAMMING
CAPE COD AND ISLANDS						
LOWER CAPE (FALMOUTH AREA)						
Adult Pop	101.1	WFAL	‖	⚡	AM DRIVE	Morn. Humor; American Dance Traxx Su 8–11pm; C. Kasem Su 8am–12N
🎸	92.7	WMVY	‖	⚡	MORE	News 12N; Oldies Sa 7pm–2am; Jazz Su 6am–12N; Clas. Su 8pm–12M; Fish Rpt. 9am
Lite Hits	101.9	WCIB	‖‖	⚡	AM DRIVE	P. Harvey 8:30am, 12:40, 5:50pm; Spts.: Bruins, Red Sox, Celtics; Lite Lunch M–F 12N
MIDDLE CAPE (HYANNIS/CHATHAM AREA)						
Adult Pop	106.1	WCOD	‖‖	🚗	AM & PM DRIVE	Morn. Humor
Top40	104.7	WKPE	‖‖	🚗	AM DRIVE	Amer. Top 40 Sa 6–10am; Weekly Top 40 Su 6–10am; Future Hits Su 11pm
🎸	102.9	WPXC	‖	🚗	MORE	News 12N; Live Lunch M–Sa 12N–1pm
OLDIES	96.3	WNTX	‖‖	⚡	AM & PM DRIVE	Wally O'Hara's People Su 7:30am; Live From the 60's Su 9pm–12M
Lite Hits	93.5	WFXR	‖	⚡	AM & PM DRIVE	Morn. Humor
Lite Hits	94.9	WOCB	‖‖	🚗	SEE SP	**TALK;** News 12N; Talknet daily 8pm–5am; Special of the Week Su 9am–12N
E ❄ Z	99.9	WQRC	‖‖	🚗	🕐	**CLASSICAL;** Boston Pops Sa 6:15pm; Boston Symphony Su 6:15am
🛋	107.5	WFCC	‖‖		MORE	News 10, 11am, 12N, 3pm; Symphony Orchestras M, W 8pm; Opera Sa 1:30pm
OUTER CAPE (PROVINCETOWN)						
ek-lek´-tik	91.9	WOMR	‖			**COMMUNITY RADIO;** Two Good Arms M 5:15pm; This Way Out M 5:30 pm

CHARLOTTE

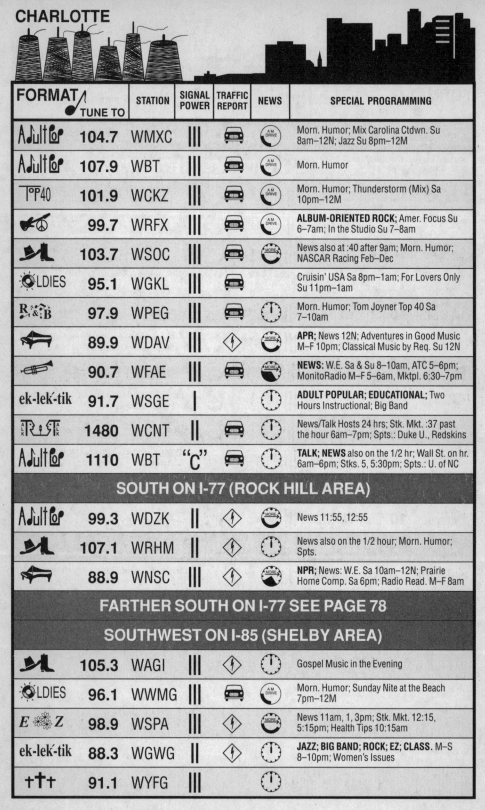

FORMAT / TUNE TO		STATION	SIGNAL POWER	TRAFFIC REPORT	NEWS	SPECIAL PROGRAMMING
Adult Pop	104.7	WMXC	|||	🚗	AM DRIVE	Morn. Humor; Mix Carolina Ctdwn. Su 8am–12N; Jazz Su 8pm–12M
Adult Pop	107.9	WBT	|||	🚗	AM DRIVE	Morn. Humor
Top40	101.9	WCKZ	|||	🚗	AM DRIVE	Morn. Humor; Thunderstorm (Mix) Sa 10pm–12M
🎸	99.7	WRFX	|||	🚗	AM DRIVE	**ALBUM-ORIENTED ROCK;** Amer. Focus Su 6–7am; In the Studio Su 7–8am
👢	103.7	WSOC	|||	🚗	MORE	News also at :40 after 9am; Morn. Humor; NASCAR Racing Feb–Dec
☀OLDIES	95.1	WGKL	|||	🚗		Cruisin' USA Sa 8pm–1am; For Lovers Only Su 11pm–1am
R&B	97.9	WPEG	|||	🚗	🕐	Morn. Humor; Tom Joyner Top 40 Sa 7–10am
🎹	89.9	WDAV	|||	◇	MORE	APR; News 12N; Adventures in Good Music M–F 10pm; Classical Music by Req. Su 12N
🎺	90.7	WFAE	|||	🚗	MORE	**NEWS:** W.E. Sa & Su 8–10am, ATC 5–6pm; MonitoRadio M–F 5–6am, Mktpl. 6:30–7pm
ek-lek-tik	91.7	WSGE				🕐	**ADULT POPULAR; EDUCATIONAL;** Two Hours Instructional; Big Band
RTLK	1480	WCNT	||	🚗	🕐	News/Talk Hosts 24 hrs; Stk. Mkt. :37 past the hour 6am–7pm; Spts.: Duke U., Redskins
Adult Pop	1110	WBT	"C"	🚗	🕐	**TALK; NEWS** also on the 1/2 hr; Wall St. on hr. 6am–6pm; Stks. 5, 5:30pm; Spts.: U. of NC

SOUTH ON I-77 (ROCK HILL AREA)

Adult Pop	99.3	WDZK	||	◇	MORE	News 11:55, 12:55
👢	107.1	WRHM	||	◇	🕐	News also on the 1/2 hour; Morn. Humor; Spts.
🎹	88.9	WNSC	|||	◇	MORE	**NPR;** News: W.E. Sa 10am–12N; Prairie Home Comp. Sa 6pm; Radio Read. M–F 8am

FARTHER SOUTH ON I-77 SEE PAGE 78

SOUTHWEST ON I-85 (SHELBY AREA)

👢	105.3	WAGI	|||	◇	🕐	Gospel Music in the Evening
☀OLDIES	96.1	WWMG	|||	🚗	AM DRIVE	Morn. Humor; Sunday Nite at the Beach 7pm–12M
E ❄ Z	98.9	WSPA	|||	◇	MORE	News 11am, 1, 3pm; Stk. Mkt. 12:15, 5:15pm; Health Tips 10:15am
ek-lek-tik	88.3	WGWG	||	◇	AM DRIVE	**JAZZ; BIG BAND; ROCK; EZ; CLASS.** M–S 8–10pm; Women's Issues
✝✝✝	91.1	WYFG	|||		🕐	

FORMAT ♪ TUNE TO	STATION	SIGNAL POWER	TRAFFIC REPORT	NEWS	SPECIAL PROGRAMMING
FARTHER SOUTHWEST ON I-85 SEE PAGE 113					
TRAVELING WEST ON I-40 SEE PAGE 24					
NORTH ON I-77 (STATESVILLE AREA)					
Adult Cor	99.5	WMAG	‖‖	🚗	AM & PM DRIVE	Morn. Humor; Sa Night at the Oldies 6–10pm
Adult Cor	100.3	WWWB	‖‖	🚗	AM DRIVE	Morn. Humor
Top40	98.7	WKSI	‖‖	🚗	AM & PM DRIVE	Morn. Humor
Top40	107.5	WKZL	‖‖	🚗	AM & PM DRIVE	Morn. Humor
🎸	95.7	WXRC	‖‖	◇	SPOT NEWS	**CLASSIC ROCK;** R & R Oldies Requests 12N; Psychedelic Psupper M–F 5pm
🤠	96.9	WTDR	‖‖	🚗	AM & PM DRIVE	Winston Cup Today M–S 6:15am; Amer. Ctry. Ctdwn. Su 8am–12N
🤠	104.1	WTQR	‖‖	🚗	MORE	News 12:30, 3:30pm; Amer. Ctry. Ctdwn. Sa 7–11pm; Bluegrass Express Sa 5–7pm
🤠	105.7	WFMX	‖‖	◇	AM DRIVE	World of Racing M–F 6:50, 11:30am, 4:30pm; Bluegrass F 8–11pm
☀OLDIES	93.1	WMQX	‖‖	🚗	AM DRIVE	
R&B	97.1	WQMG	‖‖	🚗	SEE S.P.	News 10am, 4pm; After Dark Su 8pm–12M; Gospel Su 6–10am; On the Move Sa 7am
R&B	106.5	WRDX	‖‖	🚗	AM & PM DRIVE	Sports; Beach Music
Lite Hits	102.9	WEZC	‖‖	🚗	AM DRIVE	Ctdwn. America Su 9pm–1am; Sunday Morning Sunrise (Religious Music) 6:30–10am
✝✝✝	88.1	WPAR	‖		🕐	**SOUTHERN GOSPEL** M–F 1–4pm; In Touch M–F 12:30–1pm; New Testament 8:30am
✝✝✝	94.1	WWGL	‖‖	◇	🕐	**SOUTHERN GOSPEL**
✝✝✝	95.5	WHPE	‖‖	◇	🕐	
TALK	1290	WHKY	‖	◇	🕐	Stk. Mkt. 5:15pm; Spts.: Local, Pro; C. Carter M–F 3–4pm; R. Limbaugh M–F 12:30–3pm
TALK	1490	WSTP	‖	◇	🕐	News also on the 1/2 hr; Bus. News 9am, 1, 5pm; Spts.: Catawba College, NC State
FARTHER NORTH ON I-77 SEE PAGE 78					
N.E. ON I-85 SEE WINSTON-SALEM/RALEIGH/DURHAM PG 220					
E. ON I-40 SEE WINSTON-SALEM/RALEIGH/DURHAM PG 220					

FORMAT TUNE TO		STATION	SIGNAL POWER	TRAFFIC REPORT	NEWS	SPECIAL PROGRAMMING
Adult Pop	100.3	WPNT	|||	🚗	AM DRIVE	**HOT ADULT POPULAR**
Adult Pop	101.1	WKQX	|||	🚗	AM DRIVE	Morn. Humor
Adult Pop	101.9	WTMX	|||	◇	MORE	News 12N; Morn. Humor
Adult Pop	102.7	WVAZ	|||	🚗	AM & PM DRIVE	**R & B; ADULT POPULAR;** First Day (Topics Relevant to the Black Community) Su 7am
Adult Pop	103.5	WFYR	|||	🚗	AM & PM DRIVE	
Top40	94.7	WYTZ	|||	🚗		Amer. Top 40 Su 9am–1pm; Insider Su 1–5pm; Open House Party Sa 6–11pm
Top40	96.3	WBBM	|||	🚗	AM & PM DRIVE	Morn. Humor
🎸	97.9	WLUP	|||		AM DRIVE	Lunchtime Roots(60's, 70's) M–F 12N–1pm; Three O'clock Rock Block M–F 3pm
🎸	105.9	WCKG	|||	🚗	AM DRIVE	Rock & Roll Diner 12N–1pm; Drive at 5 M–F 5–6pm; Psychedelic Psupper M–F 6–7pm
🎸	93.1	WXRT	|||	🚗	MORE	News 12N; Flashback Sa 8am–12N; Concert Su 8–9pm; Rock over London W 10–11pm
👢	99.5	WUSN	|||	🚗	AM & PM DRIVE	Cutting Edge(New Ctry.) Sa 11pm; US 99 Big 30 (Chicago Ctdwn.) Tu 7–9pm
☀OLDIES	104.3	WJMK	|||	🚗	AM DRIVE	Public Affairs Su 4:55–6am; Public Affairs/Religion Su 10am–12:45pm
R & B	107.5	WGCI	|||	🚗	SEE S.P.	Love Songs M–Thu 10pm–1am; News 6:45, 7:45am; Downside A & B (Rap) Sa 10pm
Lite Hits	93.9	WLIT	|||	🚗	AM DRIVE	
🎹	97.1	WNIB	|||			Adventures in Good Music M–F 7pm; Chicago Viewpoint Sa 6am
🎹	98.7	WFMT	|||		SEE S.P.	News 12N; Studs Terkel 5:30pm; Spoken Word (Drama) F 8pm, Su 3:30pm
🎺	91.5	WBEZ	|||	🚗	MORE	**NPR; TALK; NEWS**
🎺	95.5	WNUA	|||	🚗	AM & PM DRIVE	**ADULT POPULAR;** Soundscapes Su 8am–2pm; Musical Starstrms. Su 10pm–12M
ek-lek-tik	89.3	WNUR	||		AM & PM DRIVE	**ALT. ROCK; JAZZ; R & B** M–F
ESPAÑOL	105.1	WOJO	|||	🚗	🕐	Morn. Humor
✝✝✝	90.1	WMBI	|||	🚗	🕐	
✝✝✝	92.3	WYCA	|||			Ethnic Programs M, W, Thu, 1–4pm
✝✝✝	106.7	WYLL	|||	◇		Focus on the Family M–F 8am; Family News & Focus M–F 5:45pm

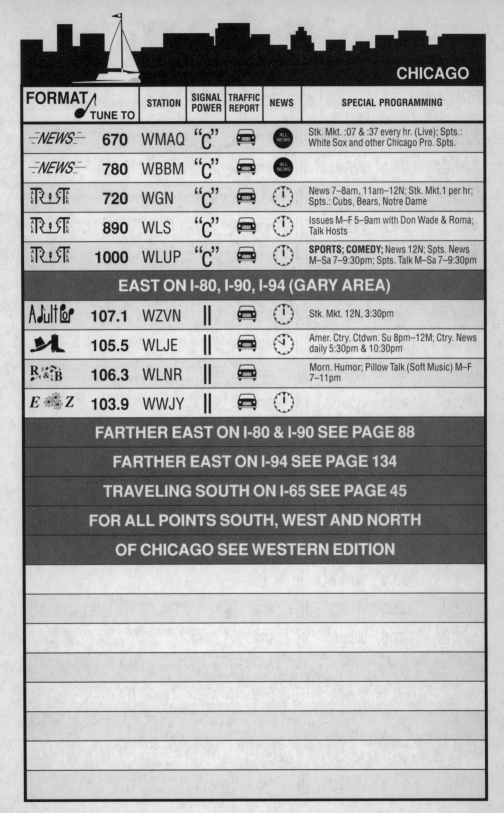

CHICAGO

FORMAT ♪ TUNE TO		STATION	SIGNAL POWER	TRAFFIC REPORT	NEWS	SPECIAL PROGRAMMING
═NEWS═	670	WMAQ	"C"	🚗	ALL NEWS	Stk. Mkt. :07 & :37 every hr. (Live); Spts.: White Sox and other Chicago Pro. Spts.
═NEWS═	780	WBBM	"C"	🚗	ALL NEWS	
TALK & TALK	720	WGN	"C"	🚗	🕐	News 7–8am, 11am–12N; Stk. Mkt.1 per hr; Spts.: Cubs, Bears, Notre Dame
TALK & TALK	890	WLS	"C"	🚗	🕐	Issues M–F 5–9am with Don Wade & Roma; Talk Hosts
TALK & TALK	1000	WLUP	"C"	🚗	🕐	**SPORTS; COMEDY;** News 12N; Spts. News M–Sa 7–9:30pm; Spts. Talk M–Sa 7–9:30pm
EAST ON I-80, I-90, I-94 (GARY AREA)						
Adult Pop	107.1	WZVN	‖	🚗	🕐	Stk. Mkt. 12N, 3:30pm
👢	105.5	WLJE	‖	🚗	🕐	Amer. Ctry. Ctdwn. Su 8pm–12M; Ctry. News daily 5:30pm & 10:30pm
R & B	106.3	WLNR	‖	🚗		Morn. Humor; Pillow Talk (Soft Music) M–F 7–11pm
E ❀ Z	103.9	WWJY	‖	🚗	🕐	

FARTHER EAST ON I-80 & I-90 SEE PAGE 88

FARTHER EAST ON I-94 SEE PAGE 134

TRAVELING SOUTH ON I-65 SEE PAGE 45

FOR ALL POINTS SOUTH, WEST AND NORTH

OF CHICAGO SEE WESTERN EDITION

CINCINNATI

FORMAT / TUNE TO		STATION	SIGNAL POWER	TRAFFIC REPORT	NEWS	SPECIAL PROGRAMMING
Adult Pop	94.1	WWNK	|||	🚗	AM DRIVE	Pillow Talk (Requests) M–Sa 7pm–12M; Religious Programming Su 7–10am
Adult Pop	98.5	WRRM	|||	🚗	AM & PM DRIVE	**LITE HITS;** Cincinnati After Dark (Jazz) Sa & Su 7pm–12M
Top40	101.9	WKRQ	|||	◇	🕐	News also at 20 past the hour; Morn. Humor
🎸	96.5	WZRQ	|||	🚗	AM DRIVE	Morn. Humor; Zaturday Nite Live (Local Bands) Sa 8pm
🎸	102.7	WEBN	|||	🚗	AM & PM DRIVE	Digital Classical Show Su 7–10am; Su Supplement 10pm–12M; Get Back Su 7–10pm
👢	105.1	WUBE	|||	🚗	AM DRIVE	Morn. Humor; Ctry. Ctdwn. Top 40 Su 9am–12N
OLDIES	94.9	WOFX	|||	🚗	AM DRIVE	**CLASSIC HITS**
OLDIES	103.5	WGRR	|||	🚗	AM & PM DRIVE	Morn. Humor; Public Affairs Su 6am
R&B	100.9	WIZF	||	🚗	MORE	News 11:50am, 1, 2, 3, 5:50pm; Su Jazz 10am–2pm; Club 100.9 (Rap) F–Sa 10pm
Lite Hits	92.5	WWEZ	|||	🚗	🕐	Stk. Mkt. PM; Requests M–F 12N–1pm; Religious Music Su 6–9am
🎹	90.9	WGUC	|||	🚗	SEE S.P.	**NPR; APR;** News: ATC M–F 5–6:30pm, Sa & Su 5–6pm; A Prairie Home Comp. Sa 6–8pm
🎺	91.7	WVXU	|||	🚗	MORE	**NPR;** News also on the hour; Bus. Report M–F 6–6:30pm; Autoline W & Sa 10–11am
ek-lek-tik	88.7	WOBO	||	◇	SEE S.P.	**COMMUNITY RADIO;** Stk. Mkt. 12N; News 9am; Spts.: University of Cincinnati
ek-lek-tik	89.7	WNKU	|||	🚗	MORE	**NPR; APR; FOLK; NEWS;** CBC Sunday Morning 9am–12N; Mtn. Stage Sa 4–6pm
🎺	107.1	WRBZ	||	🚗	AM & PM DRIVE	
✝✝✝	93.3	WAKW	|||	◇	🕐	
TRUST	1530	WCKY	|||	🚗	MORE	News also on hr. & 1/2 hr.; Spts.: U. of C, NFL, NCWA, Game of the Week, Updates 3–6pm
Adult Pop	700	WLW	"C"	🚗	🕐	**CTRY. 12M–5AM;** Stk. Mkt; Spts.: Xavier U, Reds, Sportstalk M–F 6–9pm, Su 9:30am

SOUTH ON I-75 SEE PAGE 68

SOUTH ON I-71 SEE LOUISVILLE METRO PAGE 194

WEST ON I-74 SEE INDIANAPOLIS METRO PAGE 192

NORTH ON US 127 (OXFORD/MIDDLETOWN)

| Top40 | 92.9 | WGTZ | ||| | ◇ | AM DRIVE | Morn. Humor; C. Kasem Su 9am–12N; Shadoe Stevens Su 5–9pm |

CINCINNATI

FORMAT ♪ TUNE TO	STATION	SIGNAL POWER	TRAFFIC REPORT	NEWS	SPECIAL PROGRAMMING
🎸 97.7	WOXY	‖	⚡	MORE	News 11:55am
🤠 105.9	WPFB	‖‖	🚗	MORE	News 12N; Morn. Humor; Ctry. Ctdwn. Su 7–10am
🎺 88.5	WMUB	‖‖	⚡	MORE	**NPR; APR;** News: Sa & Su 8–10am; MonitoRadio M–F 5am, 4pm; Swing Su 12N–5pm
NORTH ON I-75 (DAYTON AREA)
Adult Pop 107.7	WWSN	‖‖	🚗	AM DRIVE	Classic Lunch M–F 12N–1pm; Oldies (Live) Sa 9pm–2am; Miami Val. Viewpoint Su 8am
TOP40 95.3	WDJK	‖	🚗	🕐	Spts.; Public Affairs; Farm Reports
🎸 102.9	WAZU	‖‖		AM DRIVE	Morn. Humor
🎸 104.7	WTUE	‖‖	🚗	AM DRIVE	Morn. Humor; Reelin' in the Years Su 9am–12N; Rockline M 11:30pm–1am
🤠 99.1	WHKO	‖‖	🚗	MORE	News 12N, 2pm
OLDIES 103.9	WYMJ	‖	🚗	AM DRIVE	Morn. Humor; Miami Valley Forum Su 6–7am
R&B 88.9	WCSU	‖	⚡		**JAZZ;** Morn. Humor; Early AM Gospel
Lite Hits 99.9	WVUD	‖‖	🚗	🕐	**ADULT POPULAR;** Morn. Humor; Stk. Mkt. 10:55, 11:55am, 4:55pm
E ❄ Z 95.7	WCLR	‖‖	🚗	🕐	**OLDIES;** News also on the 1/2 hour; Stk. Mkt.; Farm Reports; Spts.
🛋 89.5	WDPR	‖			**OFF AIR:** 9:15am–4:30pm; Opera Sa 1:30–6pm; Orches./Symph. M–F 8–10pm
ek-lek-tik 91.3	WYSO	‖‖	⚡	MORE	**NPR; NEWS:** W.E. Sa 8–10am; Classical M–F 9–11am; Jazz, Blues M–Thu 7pm–12M
✝✝✝ 88.1	WQRP	‖	⚡	🕐	Preaching Programs; Western OH Reading for the Blind; Teaching Program
✝✝✝ 90.3	WCDR	‖‖	⚡	🕐	Turning Point M–F 8am; Focus on the Family M–F 8:30am; Cedarville Col. Chpl. M–F 11am
✝✝✝ 93.7	WFCJ	‖‖	⚡	MORE	News 1, 3pm
✝✝✝ 100.7	WEEC	‖‖	🚗	🕐	Farm Reports; Market Reports
TALK 1290	WHIO	‖	🚗	MORE	News on hr.; Spts.: Reds, U. of Dayton; R. Limbaugh M–F 10am–3pm; Talknet M–F 7–11pm
FARTHER NORTH ON I-75 SEE PAGE 68
N.E. ON I-71 OR EAST ON I-70 SEE COLUMBUS PAGE 186
WEST ON I-70 SEE INDIANAPOLIS PAGE 192

CLEVELAND

FORMAT / TUNE TO	STATION	SIGNAL POWER	TRAFFIC REPORT	NEWS	SPECIAL PROGRAMMING
Adult Pop — 104.1	WQAL	|||	🚗	🕐	**HOT ADULT POPULAR;** News also on the 1/2 hour; Morn. Humor
Adult Pop — 106.5	WLTF	|||	🚗	🕐	Morn. Humor; Cleveland Conversation; New Age Cleveland
Top40 — 107.9	WPHR	|||	🚗	🕐	News also 20 after the hour; Open House Party Sa & Su 7pm–12M; C. Kasem Su 9am
🎸 — 100.7	WMMS	|||	🚗		Morn. Humor; The Breakout (New Releases) Su 10–11pm; Talkback Su 11pm–12M
🎸 — 98.5	WNCX	|||	🚗	A.M. DRIVE	CD Hour M–F 11pm; Classics to Go 12N–1pm; Ten O'clock New Track Music M–F
— 99.5	WGAR	|||	🚗	AM & PM DRIVE	
OLDIES — 105.7	WMJI	|||	🚗	MORE	News 12N; Morn. Humor; Women's Connection Su 6am; Project Su 6:30am
R&B — 92.3	WJMO	|||	🚗	AM & PM DRIVE	**DANCE CONTEMPORARY;** Morn. Humor
R&B — 93.1	WZAK	|||	🚗	A.M. DRIVE	"Just the Two of Us" Sa 8am–2pm; On the Move Su 10am–3pm; Jazz Su 6–8pm
Lite Hits — 102.1	WDOK	|||	🚗		Jazz Su 9pm–12M; After Six (Love Songs) weeknights 7pm–12M
🎹 — 95.5	WCLV	|||	🚗	AM & PM DRIVE	Wall St. 5:55am, 5:55pm; Jazz Su 1–5am; Comedy & Broadway Sa 9pm–1am
ek-lek-tik — 88.7	WUJC	||	⚡		Eastwatch (Interview) Thu 10–10:30am; Ethnic Music Su 8am–8pm; Blues Tu 8–10am
ek-lek-tik — 90.3	WCPN	|||	🚗	MORE	**NPR; CLASS; JAZZ; FOLK; BLUEGRASS**
ek-lek-tik — 91.1	WRUW					**CLASS; JAZZ;** Case Western Reserve U.
🎺 — 107.3	WNWV	|||	🚗	MORE	News 10am, 4pm; Musical Starstreams Su 7–9am
🎓 — 89.3	WCSB			🚗		Morn. Humor; Ethnic Programs; Spts.; Farm Reports
✝✝✝ — 103.3	WCRF	|||	🚗	🕐	Morn. Humor; Stk. Mkt. 11:55am, 5:55pm; Farm Reports M–F 5:15am
NEWS — 1420	WHK	||	🚗	ALL NEWS	**TALK** M–F 7pm–5am; Stk. Mkt. four times an hour, Sa 7pm; Spts.: Vikings, Local
TALK — 1100	WWWE "C"		🚗	🕐	News also on the 1/2 hour; Stk. Mkt. :50 past hr. drive times; Spts.: Indians, CBS, Cavaliers
TALK — 1220	WKNR "C"		🚗		**SPORTS;** Stk. Mkt; Spts. Talk M–F 3–11pm (Different Hosts), Spts. Final M–F 11pm–6am
TALK — 1300	WERE	||	🚗	MORE	**NEWS;** Stk. Mkt. Drives; Spts.: N. Dame, M. Pollis M–F 10am–1pm, J. Rose M–F 1–4pm

SOUTH ON I-71 OR I-77 (AKRON AREA)

FORMAT / TUNE TO	STATION	SIGNAL POWER	TRAFFIC REPORT	NEWS	SPECIAL PROGRAMMING
Adult Pop — 92.5	WDJQ	|||	⚡	SEE S.P.	News at 20 and 40 after the hour; C. Kasem Sa 10am–2pm

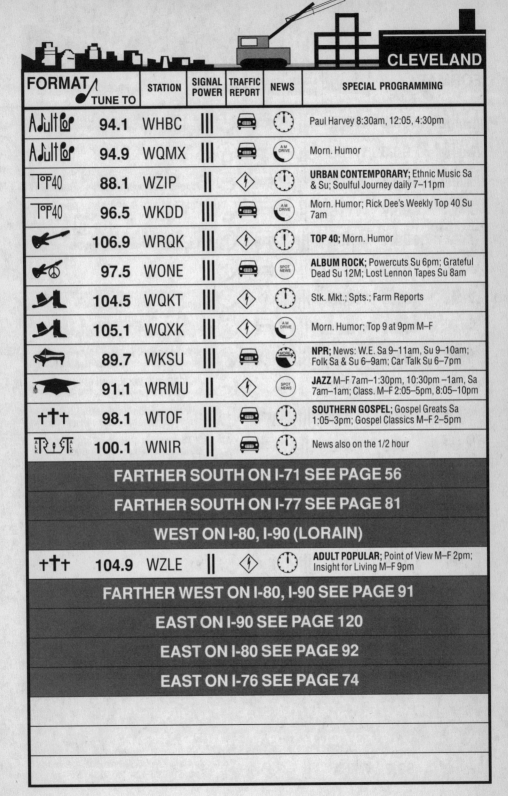

CLEVELAND

FORMAT / TUNE TO		STATION	SIGNAL POWER	TRAFFIC REPORT	NEWS	SPECIAL PROGRAMMING
Adult Pop	94.1	WHBC	|||	🚗	🕐	Paul Harvey 8:30am, 12:05, 4:30pm
Adult Pop	94.9	WQMX	|||	🚗	AM DRIVE	Morn. Humor
Top 40	88.1	WZIP	||	⚡	🕐	**URBAN CONTEMPORARY;** Ethnic Music Sa & Su; Soulful Journey daily 7–11pm
Top 40	96.5	WKDD	|||	🚗	AM DRIVE	Morn. Humor; Rick Dee's Weekly Top 40 Su 7am
🎸	106.9	WRQK	|||	⚡	🕐	**TOP 40;** Morn. Humor
🎸	97.5	WONE	|||	🚗	SPOT NEWS	**ALBUM ROCK;** Powercuts Su 6pm; Grateful Dead Su 12M; Lost Lennon Tapes Su 8am
👢	104.5	WQKT	|||	⚡	🕐	Stk. Mkt.; Spts.; Farm Reports
👢	105.1	WQXK	|||	⚡	AM DRIVE	Morn. Humor; Top 9 at 9pm M–F
🎹	89.7	WKSU	|||	🚗	MORE	**NPR;** News: W.E. Sa 9–11am, Su 9–10am; Folk Sa & Su 6–9am; Car Talk Su 6–7pm
🎓	91.1	WRMU	||	⚡	SPOT NEWS	**JAZZ** M–F 7am–1:30pm, 10:30pm –1am, Sa 7am–1am; Class. M–F 2:05–5pm, 8:05–10pm
✝✝✝	98.1	WTOF	|||	🚗	🕐	**SOUTHERN GOSPEL;** Gospel Greats Sa 1:05–3pm; Gospel Classics M–F 2–5pm
Talk Talk	100.1	WNIR	||	🚗	🕐	News also on the 1/2 hour

FARTHER SOUTH ON I-71 SEE PAGE 56

FARTHER SOUTH ON I-77 SEE PAGE 81

WEST ON I-80, I-90 (LORAIN)

✝✝✝	104.9	WZLE	||	⚡	🕐	**ADULT POPULAR;** Point of View M–F 2pm; Insight for Living M–F 9pm

FARTHER WEST ON I-80, I-90 SEE PAGE 91

EAST ON I-90 SEE PAGE 120

EAST ON I-80 SEE PAGE 92

EAST ON I-76 SEE PAGE 74

COLUMBIA

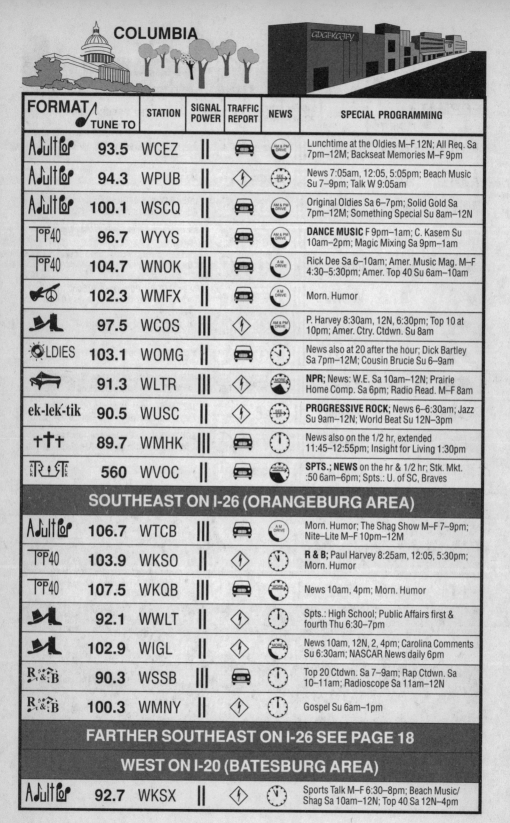

FORMAT / TUNE TO		STATION	SIGNAL POWER	TRAFFIC REPORT	NEWS	SPECIAL PROGRAMMING
Adult Pop	93.5	WCEZ	‖	🚗	AM & PM DRIVE	Lunchtime at the Oldies M–F 12N; All Req. Sa 7pm–12M; Backseat Memories M–F 9pm
Adult Pop	94.3	WPUB	‖	⚡	SEE S.P.	News 7:05am, 12:05, 5:05pm; Beach Music Su 7–9pm; Talk W 9:05am
Adult Pop	100.1	WSCQ	‖	🚗	AM & PM DRIVE	Original Oldies Sa 6–7pm; Solid Gold Sa 7pm–12M; Something Special Su 8am–12N
Top 40	96.7	WYYS	‖	🚗	AM & PM DRIVE	**DANCE MUSIC** F 9pm–1am; C. Kasem Su 10am–2pm; Magic Mixing Sa 9pm–1am
Top 40	104.7	WNOK	‖‖	🚗	AM DRIVE	Rick Dees Sa 6–10am; Amer. Music Mag. M–F 4:30–5:30pm; Amer. Top 40 Su 6am–10am
🎸	102.3	WMFX	‖	🚗	AM DRIVE	Morn. Humor
🤠	97.5	WCOS	‖‖	⚡	AM & PM DRIVE	P. Harvey 8:30am, 12N, 6:30pm; Top 10 at 10pm; Amer. Ctry. Ctdwn. Su 8am
☀OLDIES	103.1	WOMG	‖	🚗	🕐	News also at 20 after the hour; Dick Bartley Sa 7pm–12M; Cousin Brucie Su 6–9am
🛋	91.3	WLTR	‖‖	⚡	MORE	**NPR;** News: W.E. Sa 10am–12N; Prairie Home Comp. Sa 6pm; Radio Read. M–F 8am
ek-lek-tik	90.5	WUSC	‖	⚡	SEE S.P.	**PROGRESSIVE ROCK;** News 6–6:30am; Jazz Su 9am–12N; World Beat Su 12N–3pm
✝✝✝	89.7	WMHK	‖‖	🚗	🕐	News also on the 1/2 hr, extended 11:45–12:55pm; Insight for Living 1:30pm
TALK TALK	560	WVOC	‖	🚗	MORE	**SPTS.; NEWS** on the hr & 1/2 hr; Stk. Mkt. :50 6am–6pm; Spts.: U. of SC, Braves
SOUTHEAST ON I-26 (ORANGEBURG AREA)						
Adult Pop	106.7	WTCB	‖‖	🚗	AM DRIVE	Morn. Humor; The Shag Show M–F 7–9pm; Nite–Lite M–F 10pm–12M
Top 40	103.9	WKSO	‖	⚡	🕐	**R & B;** Paul Harvey 8:25am, 12:05, 5:30pm; Morn. Humor
Top 40	107.5	WKQB	‖‖	🚗	MORE	News 10am, 4pm; Morn. Humor
🤠	92.1	WWLT	‖	⚡	🕐	Spts.: High School; Public Affairs first & fourth Thu 6:30–7pm
🤠	102.9	WIGL	‖	⚡	MORE	News 10am, 12N, 2, 4pm; Carolina Comments Su 6:30am; NASCAR News daily 6pm
R & B	90.3	WSSB	‖‖	🚗	🕐	Top 20 Ctdwn. Sa 7–9am; Rap Ctdwn. Sa 10–11am; Radioscope Sa 11am–12N
R & B	100.3	WMNY	‖	⚡	🕐	Gospel Su 6am–1pm
FARTHER SOUTHEAST ON I-26 SEE PAGE 18						
WEST ON I-20 (BATESBURG AREA)						
Adult Pop	92.7	WKSX	‖	⚡	🕐	Sports Talk M–F 6:30–8pm; Beach Music/ Shag Sa 10am–12N; Top 40 Sa 12N–4pm

FORMAT 🎵 TUNE TO	STATION	SIGNAL POWER	TRAFFIC REPORT	NEWS	SPECIAL PROGRAMMING
R&B 95.3	WKWQ	‖	🚗	AM DRIVE	Walt Love's Ctdwn. Sa 6–8am; House Party F 10pm–2am

FARTHER WEST ON I-20 SEE PAGE 12

NORTHWEST ON I-26 (NEWBERRY AREA)

FORMAT	STATION	SIGNAL POWER	TRAFFIC REPORT	NEWS	SPECIAL PROGRAMMING
Adult Pop 106.3	WNMX	‖‖	🚐	🕐	**OLDIES;** News also on the 1/2 hour; Carolina Beach Music Su Afternoon
🎹 88.9	WNSC	‖‖	◇	MORE	**NPR;** News: W.E. Sa 10am–12N; Prairie Home Companion Sa 6pm; RadioReader M–F 8am

FARTHER NORTHWEST ON I-26 SEE PAGE 17

NORTH ON I-77 SEE CHARLOTTE METRO PAGE 176

EAST ON I-20 & US 76 (SUMTER AREA)

FORMAT	STATION	SIGNAL POWER	TRAFFIC REPORT	NEWS	SPECIAL PROGRAMMING
Adult Pop 99.3	WIBZ	‖	◇	🕐	Live from the Sixties Su 8–11am; Solid Gold Sa 7pm–12M; Shag Show Sa 3–7pm
👢 92.5	WHLZ	‖‖	◇	SPOT NEWS	Spts.: U. of South Carolina
R&B 101.3	WWDM	‖‖		AM & PM DRIVE	Kaleidoscope/Special Edit. Su 7–7:30pm; DM Connection (Request) M–F 12N–1pm
🎹 88.1	WRJA	‖‖	◇	MORE	**NPR;** News: W.E. Sa 10am–12N; Prairie Home Comp. Sa 6pm; Radio Read. M–F 8am

FARTHER EAST ON I-20 SEE I-95 PAGE 143

COLUMBUS

FORMAT / TUNE TO		STATION	SIGNAL POWER	TRAFFIC REPORT	NEWS	SPECIAL PROGRAMMING
Adult Pop	94.7	WSNY	‖‖	car	AM DRIVE	Morn. Humor
Adult Pop	98.9	WXMX	‖	car	AM DRIVE	Morn. Humor; Dick Bartley's Oldies Sa 7pm–12M
Top 40	97.9	WNCI	‖‖	car	AM DRIVE	**ADULT POPULAR;** C. Kasem Top 40 Su 9am–1pm; Shadoe Stevens Su 7–11pm
guitar	96.3	WLVQ	‖‖	car	AM DRIVE	Morn. Humor; Jazz Su 10am–12N
guitar peace	99.7	WMGG	‖‖	car	AM DRIVE	**ALBUM-ORIENTED ROCK;** Reelin' in the Yrs. Su 9am–12N; Desert Island Discs Su 6pm
boots	95.5	WHOK	‖‖	lightning	AM DRIVE	
OLDIES	92.3	WCOL	‖‖	car	SEE S.P.	News 6, 9am; Morn. Humor
OLDIES	103.1	WXLE	‖	lightning	AM DRIVE	Morn. Humor; Rock, Roll & Remember Su 8pm–12M; Supergold Sa 7pm–12M
E ❀ Z	97.1	WBNS	‖‖	car	clock	Stk. Mkt. 4:40, 5:30pm; Finance 1:30pm
piano	89.7	WOSU	‖‖	lightning	clock	All Classical Music
ek-lek-tik	90.5	WCBE	‖‖	car	MORE	**NPR;** News: W.E. Sa 8–10am, Su 11am–1pm; Folk & World Music M–F 9am–12N

SOUTH ON US 23 (CIRCLEVILLE)

FORMAT / TUNE TO		STATION	SIGNAL POWER	TRAFFIC REPORT	NEWS	SPECIAL PROGRAMMING
Top 40	94.3	WFCB	‖	lightning	MORE	News 12N; Stk. Mkt. 5:05pm; Solid Gold Sa 7pm–12M; C. Kasem Su 12N–4pm
boots	93.3	WKKJ	‖‖	lightning	AM DRIVE	**COUNTRY OLDIES;** Morn. Humor
trumpet	89.3	WVXC	‖	car	MORE	**NPR;** News also on the hour; Business Rpt. M–F 6–6:30pm; Autoline W & Sa 10–11am
✝✝✝	107.1	WTLT	‖	car	AM & PM DRIVE	**CHRISTIAN CONTEMPORARY;** Public Affairs Su 6–6:30am

SOUTHWEST ON I-71 (WASH. COURT HOUSE AREA)

FORMAT / TUNE TO		STATION	SIGNAL POWER	TRAFFIC REPORT	NEWS	SPECIAL PROGRAMMING
Adult Pop	102.3	WSWO	‖	lightning	SEE S.P.	News :04 every hour; Natural Outlook/Contact (Interviews, Talk) M–F 6:35pm
boots	105.5	WCHO	‖	lightning	clock	Farm Reports 6:45am, 12N, 1:57, 3:15pm; Spts. News 7:15, 8:15, 10:45am, 12:17pm
boots	106.7	WSRW	‖‖		clock	Morn. Humor; Spts.: Reds, Bengals; Country-Western Flashback Su 12N–6pm

FARTHER SOUTHWEST ON I-71 SEE CINCINNATI PAGE 180

WEST ON I-70 (LONDON AREA)

FORMAT / TUNE TO		STATION	SIGNAL POWER	TRAFFIC REPORT	NEWS	SPECIAL PROGRAMMING
guitar	102.9	WAZU	‖‖		AM DRIVE	Morn. Humor

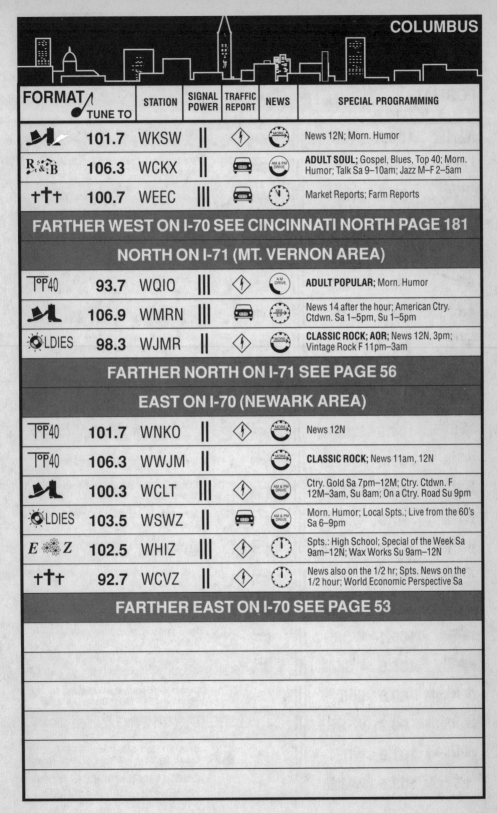

FORMAT / TUNE TO	STATION	SIGNAL POWER	TRAFFIC REPORT	NEWS	SPECIAL PROGRAMMING
🎵 101.7	WKSW	‖	◇	MORE	News 12N; Morn. Humor
R&B 106.3	WCKX	‖	🚗	AM & PM DRIVE	**ADULT SOUL;** Gospel, Blues, Top 40; Morn. Humor; Talk Sa 9–10am; Jazz M–F 2–5am
✝✝✝ 100.7	WEEC	‖‖	🚗	🕐	Market Reports; Farm Reports

FARTHER WEST ON I-70 SEE CINCINNATI NORTH PAGE 181

NORTH ON I-71 (MT. VERNON AREA)

FORMAT / TUNE TO	STATION	SIGNAL POWER	TRAFFIC REPORT	NEWS	SPECIAL PROGRAMMING
T°P40 93.7	WQIO	‖‖	◇	AM DRIVE	**ADULT POPULAR;** Morn. Humor
🎵 106.9	WMRN	‖‖	🚗	SEE S.P.	News 14 after the hour; American Ctry. Ctdwn. Sa 1–5pm, Su 1–5pm
☀LDIES 98.3	WJMR	‖	◇	MORE	**CLASSIC ROCK; AOR;** News 12N, 3pm; Vintage Rock F 11pm–3am

FARTHER NORTH ON I-71 SEE PAGE 56

EAST ON I-70 (NEWARK AREA)

FORMAT / TUNE TO	STATION	SIGNAL POWER	TRAFFIC REPORT	NEWS	SPECIAL PROGRAMMING
T°P40 101.7	WNKO	‖	◇	MORE	News 12N
T°P40 106.3	WWJM	‖		MORE	**CLASSIC ROCK;** News 11am, 12N
🎵 100.3	WCLT	‖‖	◇	AM & PM DRIVE	Ctry. Gold Sa 7pm–12M; Ctry. Ctdwn. F 12M–3am, Su 8am; On a Ctry. Road Su 9pm
☀LDIES 103.5	WSWZ	‖	🚐	AM & PM DRIVE	Morn. Humor; Local Spts.; Live from the 60's Sa 6–9pm
E ❄ Z 102.5	WHIZ	‖‖	◇	🕐	Spts.: High School; Special of the Week Sa 9am–12N; Wax Works Su 9am–12N
✝✝✝ 92.7	WCVZ	‖	◇	🕐	News also on the 1/2 hr; Spts. News on the 1/2 hour; World Economic Perspective Sa

FARTHER EAST ON I-70 SEE PAGE 53

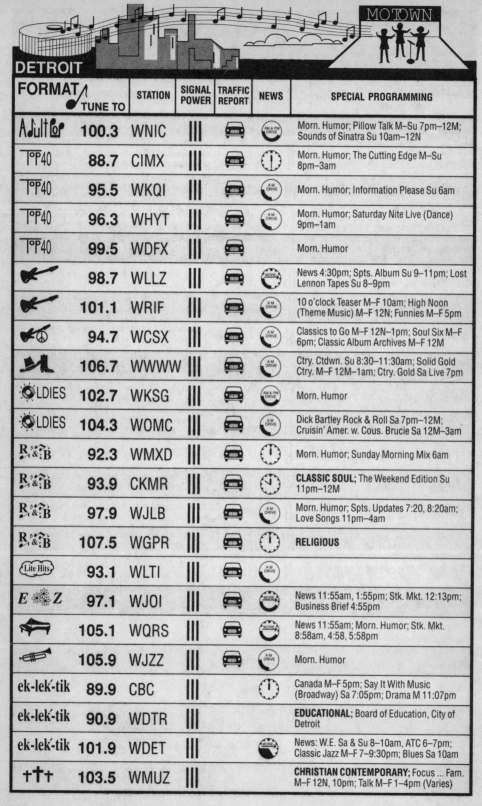

DETROIT

FORMAT ♪ TUNE TO	STATION	SIGNAL POWER	TRAFFIC REPORT	NEWS	SPECIAL PROGRAMMING
Adult ♪☎ 100.3	WNIC	|||	🚗	AM & PM DRIVE	Morn. Humor; Pillow Talk M–Su 7pm–12M; Sounds of Sinatra Su 10am–12N
TOP 40 88.7	CIMX	|||	🚗	🕐	Morn. Humor; The Cutting Edge M–Su 8pm–3am
TOP 40 95.5	WKQI	|||	🚗	AM DRIVE	Morn. Humor; Information Please Su 6am
TOP 40 96.3	WHYT	|||	🚗	AM DRIVE	Morn. Humor; Saturday Nite Live (Dance) 9pm–1am
TOP 40 99.5	WDFX	|||	🚗		Morn. Humor
🎸 98.7	WLLZ	|||	🚗	MORE	News 4:30pm; Spts. Album Su 9–11pm; Lost Lennon Tapes Su 8–9pm
🎸 101.1	WRIF	|||	🚗	AM DRIVE	10 o'clock Teaser M–F 10am; High Noon (Theme Music) M–F 12N; Funnies M–F 5pm
🎸☮ 94.7	WCSX	|||	🚗	AM DRIVE	Classics to Go M–F 12N–1pm; Soul Six M–F 6pm; Classic Album Archives M–F 12M
👢 106.7	WWWW	|||	🚗	AM DRIVE	Ctry. Ctdwn. Su 8:30–11:30am; Solid Gold Ctry. M–F 12M–1am; Ctry. Gold Sa Live 7pm
☀LDIES 102.7	WKSG	|||	🚗	AM & PM DRIVE	Morn. Humor
☀LDIES 104.3	WOMC	|||	🚗	AM DRIVE	Dick Bartley Rock & Roll Sa 7pm–12M; Cruisin' Amer. w. Cous. Brucie Sa 12M–3am
R&B 92.3	WMXD	|||	🚗	🕐	Morn. Humor; Sunday Morning Mix 6am
R&B 93.9	CKMR	|||	🚗	🕐	**CLASSIC SOUL;** The Weekend Edition Su 11pm–12M
R&B 97.9	WJLB	|||	🚗	AM DRIVE	Morn. Humor; Spts. Updates 7:20, 8:20am; Love Songs 11pm–4am
R&B 107.5	WGPR	|||	🚗	🕐	**RELIGIOUS**
Lite Hits 93.1	WLTI	|||	🚗	AM DRIVE	
E ❄ Z 97.1	WJOI	|||	🚗	MORE	News 11:55am, 1:55pm; Stk. Mkt. 12:13pm; Business Brief 4:55pm
🎹 105.1	WQRS	|||	🚗	MORE	News 11:55am; Morn. Humor; Stk. Mkt. 8:58am, 4:58, 5:58pm
🎺 105.9	WJZZ	|||	🚗	AM DRIVE	Morn. Humor
ek-lek'-tik 89.9	CBC	|||		🕐	Canada M–F 5pm; Say It With Music (Broadway) Sa 7:05pm; Drama M 11:07pm
ek-lek'-tik 90.9	WDTR	|||			**EDUCATIONAL;** Board of Education, City of Detroit
ek-lek'-tik 101.9	WDET	|||		MORE	News: W.E. Sa & Su 8–10am, ATC 6–7pm; Classic Jazz M–F 7–9:30pm; Blues Sa 10am
✝✝✝ 103.5	WMUZ	|||			**CHRISTIAN CONTEMPORARY;** Focus ... Fam. M–F 12N, 10pm; Talk M–F 1–4pm (Varies)

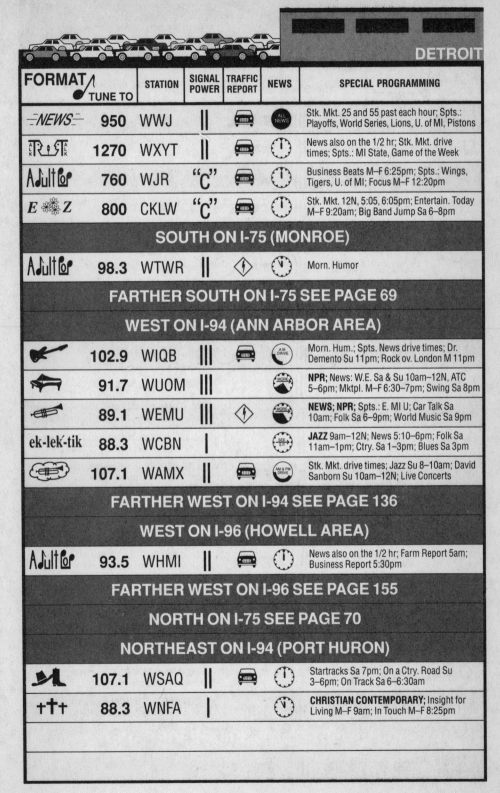

DETROIT

FORMAT / TUNE TO	STATION	SIGNAL POWER	TRAFFIC REPORT	NEWS	SPECIAL PROGRAMMING
═NEWS═ 950	WWJ	‖	🚗	ALL NEWS	Stk. Mkt. 25 and 55 past each hour; Spts.: Playoffs, World Series, Lions, U. of MI, Pistons
T·A·L·K 1270	WXYT	‖	🚗	🕐	News also on the 1/2 hr; Stk. Mkt. drive times; Spts.: MI State, Game of the Week
Adult Pop 760	WJR	"C"	🚗	🕐	Business Beats M–F 6:25pm; Spts.: Wings, Tigers, U. of MI; Focus M–F 12:20pm
E ❄ Z 800	CKLW	"C"	🚗	🕐	Stk. Mkt. 12N, 5:05, 6:05pm; Entertain. Today M–F 9:20am; Big Band Jump Sa 6–8pm
SOUTH ON I-75 (MONROE)					
Adult Pop 98.3	WTWR	‖	◇	🕐	Morn. Humor
FARTHER SOUTH ON I-75 SEE PAGE 69					
WEST ON I-94 (ANN ARBOR AREA)					
🎸 102.9	WIQB	‖‖‖	🚗	AM DRIVE	Morn. Hum.; Spts. News drive times; Dr. Demento Su 11pm; Rock ov. London M 11pm
🎹 91.7	WUOM	‖‖‖		MORE	**NPR;** News: W.E. Sa & Su 10am–12N, ATC 5–6pm; Mktpl. M–F 6:30–7pm; Swing Sa 8pm
🎺 89.1	WEMU	‖‖‖	◇	MORE	**NEWS; NPR;** Spts.: E. MI U; Car Talk Sa 10am; Folk Sa 6–9pm; World Music Sa 9pm
ek-lek'-tik 88.3	WCBN	‖		SEE S.P.	**JAZZ** 9am–12N; News 5:10–6pm; Folk Sa 11am–1pm; Ctry. Sa 1–3pm; Blues Sa 3pm
🎷 107.1	WAMX	‖	🚗	AM & PM DRIVE	Stk. Mkt. drive times; Jazz Su 8–10am; David Sanborn Su 10am–12N; Live Concerts
FARTHER WEST ON I-94 SEE PAGE 136					
WEST ON I-96 (HOWELL AREA)					
Adult Pop 93.5	WHMI	‖	🚗	🕐	News also on the 1/2 hr; Farm Report 5am; Business Report 5:30pm
FARTHER WEST ON I-96 SEE PAGE 155					
NORTH ON I-75 SEE PAGE 70					
NORTHEAST ON I-94 (PORT HURON)					
👢 107.1	WSAQ	‖	🚗	🕐	Startracks Sa 7pm; On a Ctry. Road Su 3–6pm; On Track Sa 6–6:30am
✝✝✝ 88.3	WNFA	‖		🕐	**CHRISTIAN CONTEMPORARY;** Insight for Living M–F 9am; In Touch M–F 8:25pm

HARTFORD & COASTAL AREAS

FORMAT ♪ TUNE TO		STATION	SIGNAL POWER	TRAFFIC REPORT	NEWS	SPECIAL PROGRAMMING
Adult Pop	93.7	WZMX	|||	🚗	A M DRIVE	Morn. Humor
Adult Pop	104.1	WIOF	|||	🚗	A M DRIVE	
Top 40	95.7	WKSS	|||	🚗	AM & PM DRIVE	**R & B;** Kiss Club F & Sa 9pm–1am; Amer. Dance Traxx Su 9pm–12M
Top 40	96.5	WTIC	|||	🚗	MORE	News 12N; Top 10 Tu 8pm; Public Affairs Su AM
🎸	105.9	WHCN	|||	🚗	MORE	News 10, 11:50am; Breakfast with the Beatles Su 11am–12N; Zep Set M–F 6–6:30pm
🎸	106.9	WCCC	|||	🚗	A M DRIVE	Morn. Humor; Pirate Radio Sa 7pm–12M
🤠	92.5	WWYZ	|||	🚗	MORE	News 3, 4pm; Weekly Ctry. Ctdwn. Su 9am–12N; Nashville Live Su 8:30–10pm
OLDIES	102.9	WDRC	|||	🚗	A M DRIVE	Morn. Humor
Lite Hits	100.5	WRCH	|||	🚗	AM & PM DRIVE	Pillow Talk nightly 10pm–1am
E ❄ Z	88.9	WJMJ	|||		🕐	**INSPIRATIONAL MESSAGES**
ek-lek-tik	91.3	WWUH	||	◇	SEE S.P.	News 12N; Jazz M–F 9am–12N, Tu–F 9pm–12M; New Age Su 10am; Portuguese Sa 7pm
✝✝✝	104.9	WIHS	||		🕐	**INSPIRATIONAL MUSIC;** Focus on the Family M–F 6:30pm; Key Life M–F 11:30am
TALK	1080	WTIC	"C"	🚗	🕐	**LITE HITS** 5:30–6pm; Stk. Mkt. every hr, 9:30am–6pm; Spts.: Red Sox, Whalers
TALK	1410	WPOP	||	🚗	🕐	Ext. News 6–9am, 12N–1pm, 4–7pm; Spts.: Huskies, U. of CT, Yankees, Patriots, Giants
SOUTH ON I-91 NEW HAVEN/MIDDLETOWN AREA						
Top 40	101.3	WKCI	|||	🚗	A M DRIVE	Open Hse. Prty. Sa & Su 7pm–12M; R. Dee Sa 6–10am, Su 8am; Party Amer. F 11pm–1am
🎸	99.1	WPLR	|||	🚗	A M DRIVE	For the People Su 6:30am
🎹	90.5	WPKT	|||	◇	MORE	**NPR; APR; NEWS:** W.E. Sa & Su 12N–1pm; Prairie Home Comp. Sa 6–8pm
ek-lek-tik	88.1	WESU				SEE S.P.	News 8:30am, 5:55pm; Italian Music daily 5–7am; R & B, Early 60's Su 3–5:30pm
ek-lek-tik	88.7	WNHU				SEE S.P.	**JAZZ; FOLK; NEW MUSIC;** News on the hour every two hours from 8am
ek-lek-tik	94.3	WYBC	||		SPOT. NEWS	**JAZZ; R & B; NEW AGE;** Electric Drum Sa 11am–12N; Heritage, Folk Su 5–7pm
SOUTHWEST ON I-95 BRIDGEPORT AREA						
Adult Pop	99.9	WEZN	|||	🚗	AM & PM DRIVE	Morn. Humor; Public Affairs Su 6:30am

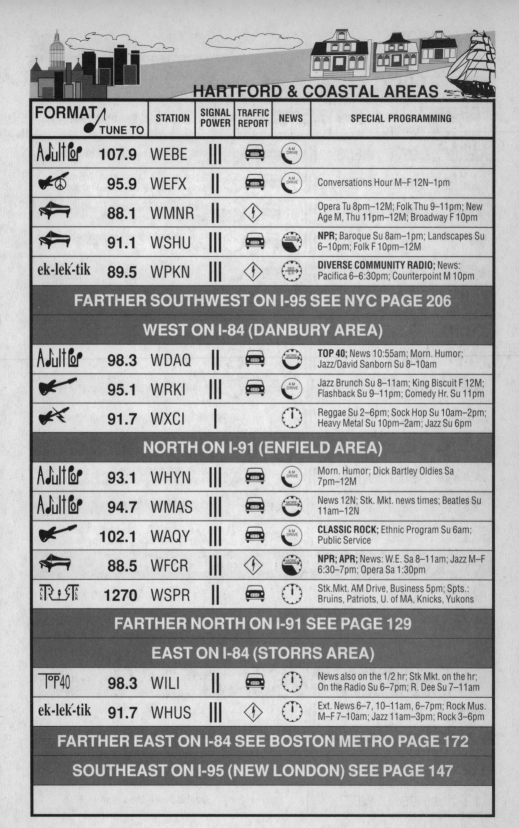

HARTFORD & COASTAL AREAS

FORMAT ♪ TUNE TO	STATION	SIGNAL POWER	TRAFFIC REPORT	NEWS	SPECIAL PROGRAMMING
Adult Pop 107.9	WEBE	|||	🚗	AM DRIVE	
95.9	WEFX	||	🚗	AM DRIVE	Conversations Hour M–F 12N–1pm
88.1	WMNR	||	◇		Opera Tu 8pm–12M; Folk Thu 9–11pm; New Age M, Thu 11pm–12M; Broadway F 10pm
91.1	WSHU	|||	🚗	MORE	**NPR;** Baroque Su 8am–1pm; Landscapes Su 6–10pm; Folk F 10pm–12M
ek-lek-tik 89.5	WPKN	|||	◇	SEE SP	**DIVERSE COMMUNITY RADIO;** News: Pacifica 6–6:30pm; Counterpoint M 10pm

FARTHER SOUTHWEST ON I-95 SEE NYC PAGE 206

WEST ON I-84 (DANBURY AREA)

FORMAT ♪ TUNE TO	STATION	SIGNAL POWER	TRAFFIC REPORT	NEWS	SPECIAL PROGRAMMING
Adult Pop 98.3	WDAQ	||	🚗	MORE	**TOP 40;** News 10:55am; Morn. Humor; Jazz/David Sanborn Su 8–10am
95.1	WRKI	|||	🚗	AM DRIVE	Jazz Brunch Su 8–11am; King Biscuit F 12M; Flashback Su 9–11pm; Comedy Hr. Su 11pm
91.7	WXCI				🕐	Reggae Su 2–6pm; Sock Hop Su 10am–2pm; Heavy Metal Su 10pm–2am; Jazz Su 6pm

NORTH ON I-91 (ENFIELD AREA)

FORMAT ♪ TUNE TO	STATION	SIGNAL POWER	TRAFFIC REPORT	NEWS	SPECIAL PROGRAMMING
Adult Pop 93.1	WHYN	|||	🚗	AM DRIVE	Morn. Humor; Dick Bartley Oldies Sa 7pm–12M
Adult Pop 94.7	WMAS	|||	🚗	MORE	News 12N; Stk. Mkt. news times; Beatles Su 11am–12N
102.1	WAQY	|||	🚗	AM DRIVE	**CLASSIC ROCK;** Ethnic Program Su 6am; Public Service
88.5	WFCR	|||	◇	MORE	**NPR; APR;** News: W.E. Sa 8–11am; Jazz M–F 6:30–7pm; Opera Sa 1:30pm
Talk 1270	WSPR	||	🚗	🕐	Stk.Mkt. AM Drive, Business 5pm; Spts.: Bruins, Patriots, U. of MA, Knicks, Yukons

FARTHER NORTH ON I-91 SEE PAGE 129

EAST ON I-84 (STORRS AREA)

FORMAT ♪ TUNE TO	STATION	SIGNAL POWER	TRAFFIC REPORT	NEWS	SPECIAL PROGRAMMING
TOP40 98.3	WILI	||	🚗	🕐	News also on the 1/2 hr; Stk. Mkt. on the hr; On the Radio Su 6–7pm; R. Dee Su 7–11am
ek-lek-tik 91.7	WHUS	|||	◇	🕐	Ext. News 6–7, 10–11am, 6–7pm; Rock Mus. M–F 7–10am; Jazz 11am–3pm; Rock 3–6pm

FARTHER EAST ON I-84 SEE BOSTON METRO PAGE 172

SOUTHEAST ON I-95 (NEW LONDON) SEE PAGE 147

INDIANAPOLIS

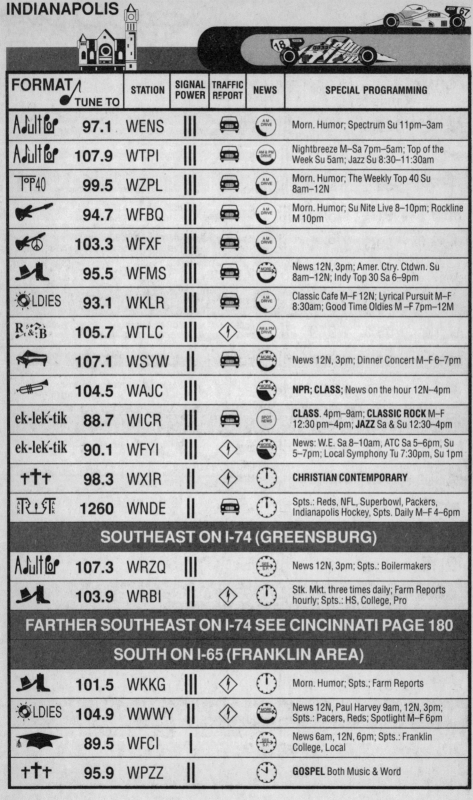

FORMAT ♪ TUNE TO		STATION	SIGNAL POWER	TRAFFIC REPORT	NEWS	SPECIAL PROGRAMMING
Adult Pop	97.1	WENS	|||	🚗	AM DRIVE	Morn. Humor; Spectrum Su 11pm–3am
Adult Pop	107.9	WTPI	|||	🚗	AM & PM DRIVE	Nightbreeze M–Sa 7pm–5am; Top of the Week Su 5am; Jazz Su 8:30–11:30am
Top40	99.5	WZPL	|||	🚗	AM DRIVE	Morn. Humor; The Weekly Top 40 Su 8am–12N
🎸	94.7	WFBQ	|||	🚗	AM DRIVE	Morn. Humor; Su Nite Live 8–10pm; Rockline M 10pm
🎸☮	103.3	WFXF	|||	🚗	AM DRIVE	
🤠	95.5	WFMS	|||	🚗	MORE	News 12N, 3pm; Amer. Ctry. Ctdwn. Su 8am–12N; Indy Top 30 Sa 6–9pm
OLDIES	93.1	WKLR	|||	🚗	AM DRIVE	Classic Cafe M–F 12N; Lyrical Pursuit M–F 8:30am; Good Time Oldies M–F 7pm–12M
R&B	105.7	WTLC	|||	◇	AM & PM DRIVE	
🎹	107.1	WSYW	||	🚗	MORE	News 12N, 3pm; Dinner Concert M–F 6–7pm
🎺	104.5	WAJC	|||		MORE	**NPR; CLASS;** News on the hour 12N–4pm
ek-lek-tik	88.7	WICR	|||	🚗	SPOT NEWS	**CLASS.** 4pm–9am; **CLASSIC ROCK** M–F 12:30pm–4pm; **JAZZ** Sa & Su 12:30–4pm
ek-lek-tik	90.1	WFYI	|||	◇	MORE	News: W.E. Sa 8–10am, ATC Sa 5–6pm, Su 5–7pm; Local Symphony Tu 7:30pm, Su 1pm
†T†	98.3	WXIR	||	◇	🕐	**CHRISTIAN CONTEMPORARY**
TALK	1260	WNDE	||	🚗	🕐	Spts.: Reds, NFL, Superbowl, Packers, Indianapolis Hockey, Spts. Daily M–F 4–6pm

SOUTHEAST ON I-74 (GREENSBURG)

FORMAT		STATION	SIGNAL POWER	TRAFFIC REPORT	NEWS	SPECIAL PROGRAMMING
Adult Pop	107.3	WRZQ	|||		SEE S.P.	News 12N, 3pm; Spts.: Boilermakers
🤠	103.9	WRBI	||	◇	🕐	Stk. Mkt. three times daily; Farm Reports hourly; Spts.: HS, College, Pro

FARTHER SOUTHEAST ON I-74 SEE CINCINNATI PAGE 180

SOUTH ON I-65 (FRANKLIN AREA)

FORMAT		STATION	SIGNAL POWER	TRAFFIC REPORT	NEWS	SPECIAL PROGRAMMING
🤠	101.5	WKKG	|||	◇	🕐	Morn. Humor; Spts.; Farm Reports
OLDIES	104.9	WWWY	||	◇	MORE	News 12N, Paul Harvey 9am, 12N, 3pm; Spts.: Pacers, Reds; Spotlight M–F 6pm
🎓	89.5	WFCI				SEE S.P.	News 6am, 12N, 6pm; Spts.: Franklin College, Local
†T†	95.9	WPZZ	||		🕐	**GOSPEL** Both Music & Word

FORMAT TUNE TO	STATION	SIGNAL POWER	TRAFFIC REPORT	NEWS	SPECIAL PROGRAMMING
	**FARTHER SOUTH ON I-65 SEE LOUISVILLE PAGE 194**				
	**S.W. ON IND. RTE. 37 (MARTINSVILLE/BLOOMINGTON)**				
TOP40	96.7	WBWB	‖		Morn. Humor
	92.3	WTTS	‖‖		
	102.3	WCBK	‖		News 10:30am, 12N, 3pm; Stk. Mkt. :40 10am–4pm, 5:30pm ; Spts. 7:30am, 12:01, 4:30pm
	103.7	WFIU	‖‖		**NPR; JAZZ;** News 11:55am, 3:25pm
	**WEST ON I-70 SEE PAGE 52**				
	**WEST ON I-74 SEE PAGE 57**				
	**NORTHWEST ON I-65 (LEBANON)**				
	100.9	WBCI	‖		News 12N, 5pm; Farm Reports 5:30–7am, Spts.: Indians, Local
	**FARTHER NORTHWEST ON I-65 SEE PAGE 45**				
	**NORTHEAST ON I-69 SEE PAGE 46**				
	**EAST ON I-70 (NEW CASTLE AREA)**				
AdultPop	97.9	WLHN	‖‖		Morn. Humor; Spts.: High School; Oldies Su night; Seventies Sa morning
AdultPop	101.3	WFMG	‖‖		**TOP 40**
AdultPop	104.1	WLBC	‖‖		**CLASSIC ROCK;** Morn. Humor; Stk. Mkt.; Spts.
TOP40	98.3	WZZY	‖		**ALBUM-ORIENTED ROCK;** News also on the 1/2 hour; Music Jam M–Su 6pm–6am
	96.1	WQLK	‖‖		Classic Diner 12N–1pm; King Biscuit Sa 11pm; Jazz Su 6–10am; Flashback Su 8pm
	100.3	WCNB	‖‖		Morn. Humor
	102.5	WMDH	‖‖		News 12N, 3pm
OLDIES	94.3	WRCR	‖		**SPORTS;** Farms News 05 to hr; Ctry. Sa 6am–12N; Wax Museum F, Sa 10:30pm–2am
	89.3	WVXR	‖		**NPR;** News also on the hour; Bus. Report M–F 6–6:30pm; Autoline W & Sa 10–11am
	**FARTHER EAST ON I-70 SEE CINCINNATI NORTH PAGE 180**				

FORMAT / TUNE TO		STATION	SIGNAL POWER	TRAFFIC REPORT	NEWS	SPECIAL PROGRAMMING
Adult Con	102.3	WLRS	‖	◇	🕐	Morn. Humor
Adult Con	103.9	WZKS	‖	🚗	A.M. DRIVE	Morn. Humor; Future Hits with Joel Denver Su 7–8am; C. Kasem Top 40 Su 8am–12N
Adult Con	106.9	WVEZ	‖	🚗	A.M. DRIVE	**CLASSIC HITS;** Morn. Humor
Top 40	99.7	WDJX	‖‖	🚗	A.M. DRIVE	Morn. Humor; Hot Mix Sa 10pm–2am; Top 40 Su 7–11am; Hitline USA Su 11pm
🎸	95.7	WQMF	‖‖	◇	A.M. DRIVE	Morn. Humor; Rockline M 11:30pm; Flashback Su 9–11am; In the Studio Thu 12M
🤠	97.5	WAMZ	‖‖	🚗	AM & PM DRIVE	Morn. Humor
OLDIES	103.1	WRKA	‖	🚗	AM & PM DRIVE	Morn. Humor; Supergold Sa 7pm–12M
E Z	101.7	WLSY	‖	🚗	MORE	**JAZZ** Su 10am–2pm; News 12N, 2, 3pm; Stk. Mkt. 6:15, 8:15am, 4:15, 5:15pm
🎺	89.3	WFPL	‖‖	◇	MORE	**NPR; APR;** News: W.E. Sa 8–10am, Su 10am–12N; Radio Reader M–F 11am
ek-lek´-tik	90.5	WUOL	‖‖	◇		Voices in Song Su 10:30am–12N; Cham. Mus. M–Su 12N; The Band Hour Sa 11am–12N
ek-lek´-tik	91.9	WFPK	‖‖	◇	AM & PM DRIVE	**APR;** Met Opera Sa 1:30pm; Pipedreams Sa 6:30–8pm; Hearts of Space Su 11pm–12M
✝✝✝	88.5	WJIE	‖‖	◇	🕐	Morn. Humor
Adult Con	840	WHAS	"C"	🚗	🕐	News also on the 1/2 hour; Spts.: U. of Louisville, U. of Kentucky
SOUTH ON I-65 (ELIZABETHTOWN AREA)						
Adult Con	100.1	WQXE	‖	◇	MORE	**TOP 40;** News 12N; American Top 40 Su 1–5pm; Lunchtime at the Oldies M–F 12N
Top 40	96.7	WOKH	‖	◇	🕐	**CLASSIC ROCK;** Sports Call M–F 7–8pm; National Music Survey Sa 9am–12N
🤠	106.3	WKMO	‖	🚗	🕐	Morn. Humor; Spts.; Farm Reports
Lite Hits	105.5	WASE	‖	◇	🕐	Morn. Humor; Live from the 60's Su 5pm; Supergold Sa 7pm; Dick Clark Su 8pm
🎹	90.9	WKUE	‖		MORE	**NPR;** News: W.E. Sa 7–8am, ATC Sa & Su 4–5pm; Big Band & Jazz Sa 6pm–5am
✝✝✝	90.1	WJCR	‖‖	◇		**SOUTHERN GOSPEL;** Ministry 7–7:15am, 8–8:45am; Prayerline 8–9pm

FARTHER SOUTH ON I-65 SEE PAGE 44

WEST ON I-64 SEE PAGE 32

FORMAT ♪ TUNE TO	STATION	SIGNAL POWER	TRAFFIC REPORT	NEWS	SPECIAL PROGRAMMING
NORTH ON I-65 (SCOTTSBURG AREA)					
Adult Pop 106.1	WINN	|||		🕐	Spts.: Reds; Hollywood Insider; Business Today; Health Watch
Top40 93.7	WZZB	|||	🚗	🕐	News also 10 after the hour; Spts.: Indiana U., Indy 500; Heat 30 Su 1–4pm
🤠👢 100.9	WMPI	||	◇	🕐	Morn. Humor
✝✝✝ 98.9	WSLM	|||	◇	SEE SP →	**SOUTHERN GOSPEL;** News 7, 10am, 12:30, 5pm; Bob Larson (Call-In) M–F 5pm
FARTHER NORTH ON I-65 SEE INDIANAPOLIS PAGE 192					
NORTHEAST ON I-71 (CARROLLTON AREA)					
Adult Pop 96.7	WORX	||	◇	MORE	**LITE HITS;** News 12:30pm; Stk. Mkt; Spts.: Local High School; Kidworx (Kids) Sa
Adult Pop 100.1	WIKI	||	◇	🕐	Dick Witty's Notebook (Nostalgia); WIKI-LAND History; Burley Tobacco
Top40 94.5	WLAP	|||	◇	AM DRIVE	**ADULT POPULAR;** Morn. Humor
🎸 98.1	WKQQ	|||		AM DRIVE	Block Party Sa 7pm–12M; Classic Cafe M–F 12N
🤠👢 92.9	WVLK	|||	🚗	🕐	Spts.: U. of KY; Ralph Emery Show 8:55pm; Amer. Ctry. Ctdwn. Sa 8pm, Su 12N
🤠👢 95.9	WKID	||	🚗	AM & PM DRIVE	Talk Line Su 5–8pm; General Store M–F 8:50am, 6:50pm; Farm Report M–F 6:16am
NEWS 91.3	WUKY	|||		MORE	**CLASS.** 9:30pm–5am; News: W.E. Sa 8–9am, Su 8–11am, ATC 5–6pm; Jazz Sa 8pm–7am
FARTHER NORTH ON I-71 SEE CINCINNATI PAGE 180					
EAST ON I-64 (SHELBYVILLE AREA)					
Adult Pop 105.7	WKXF	||	◇		**SOFT ROCK;** Spts.: University of Kentucky
🤠👢 101.3	WCKP	||	◇	MORE	News 12N; Agri. Stocks 12:35pm; Stk. Mkt. 5:15pm; On a Ctry. Road Su 3–6pm
FARTHER EAST ON I-64 SEE PAGE 33					

MEMPHIS

FORMAT / TUNE TO		STATION	SIGNAL POWER	TRAFFIC REPORT	NEWS	SPECIAL PROGRAMMING
Adult Pop	104.5	WRVR	‖‖	🚗	AM & PM DRIVE	Morn. Humor
Top 40	88.5	WQOX	‖	◇	🕐	**R & B;** MIAA Spts. F 6:30; Teen Talk M 5pm; Healthbeat W 8am
Top 40	99.7	WMC	‖‖	🚗	🕐	**ADULT POPULAR;** Morn. Humor
🎸	102.7	WEGR	‖‖	🚗	AM DRIVE	**CLASSIC ROCK;** Morn. Humor
🤠	105.9	WGKX	‖‖	🚗	🕐	Morn. Humor; Spts.: Memphis State
OLDIES	98.1	KPYR	‖‖	🚗	AM DRIVE	Morn. Humor
R & B	97.1	WHRK	‖‖	🚗	AM DRIVE	Morn. Humor; Power Line (Requests) M–F 9–11pm; Oldies Su 6–10pm
R & B	101.1	KHUL	‖‖	🚗		Morn. Humor
E ❀ Z	94.3	WEZI	‖	🚗	🕐	Stk. Mkt.; Wall St. Front Page 7:30am; Religious Music Su AM
🎹	91.1	WKNO	‖‖	◇	MORE	**NPR;** News: W.E. Sa & Su 7–9am, ATC 3–5pm
🎺	89.3	WLYX	‖	◇		**CLASSICAL; ALBUM ROCK**
🎺	91.7	WSMS	‖			Memphis State U.
ek-lek-tik	89.9	WEVL	‖‖	◇		News 8, 9, 10am; Ethnic Mixes M–F 10am; Memphis Blues & Gospel Train Thu 4–6pm
†††	107.1	KFTH	‖	🚗	🕐	Gospel Preaching & Teaching Ministries; Money Smarts; Be Aware (Public Affairs)
TALK	790	WMC	‖	🚗	SEE S.P.	News 6–9am, 12–1pm; Stk. Mkt; Spts.: Ole MS; Rush Limbaugh M–F 1–4pm
WEST ON I-40 (FOREST CITY AREA)						
Adult Pop	92.7	KWYN	‖	🚗	🕐	Morn. Humor; Talk Show 8:30am; Spts.; Business Reports
🤠	93.5	KBFC	‖	◇	🕐	Stk. Mkt.; Farm Reports; Spts.; Ethnic
FARTHER WEST ON I-40 SEE WESTERN EDITION						
NORTH ON I-55 (BLYTHEVILLE AREA)						
Top 40	101.9	KJBR	‖‖	🚗	AM DRIVE	Morn. Humor; Bulletin Board M–F 7am; Spts. Brief M–Sa 5pm; C. Kasem Su 9am–1pm
🤠	96.3	KHLS	‖‖	◇	SEE S.P.	News 8am, 12N, Paul Harvey; Spts.: Razorbacks, Cardinals; Farm Reports
🤠	107.9	KFIN	‖‖	◇	🕐	Morn. Humor; Farm Reports; Amer. Ctry. Ctdwn.; Business Briefing

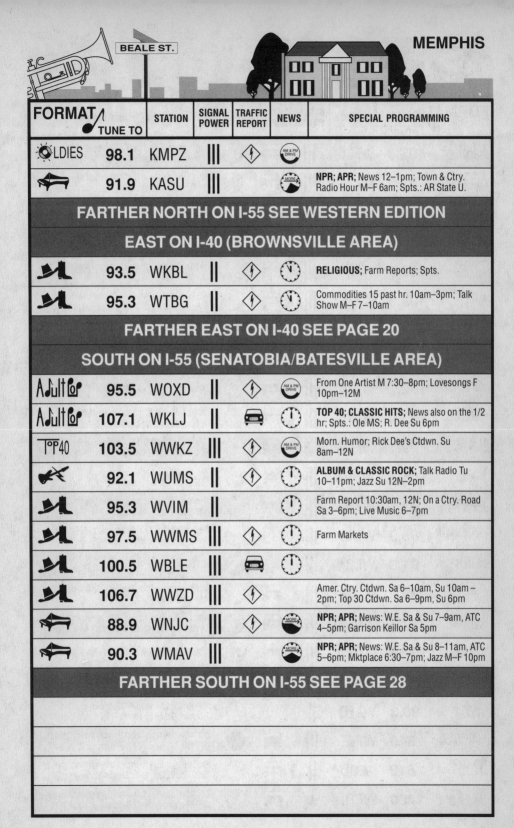

MEMPHIS

BEALE ST.

FORMAT ♪ TUNE TO		STATION	SIGNAL POWER	TRAFFIC REPORT	NEWS	SPECIAL PROGRAMMING
☀ OLDIES	98.1	KMPZ	‖‖	◇⚡	AM & PM DRIVE	
🎹	91.9	KASU	‖‖		MORE	**NPR; APR;** News 12–1pm; Town & Ctry. Radio Hour M–F 6am; Spts.: AR State U.

FARTHER NORTH ON I-55 SEE WESTERN EDITION

EAST ON I-40 (BROWNSVILLE AREA)

FORMAT ♪ TUNE TO		STATION	SIGNAL POWER	TRAFFIC REPORT	NEWS	SPECIAL PROGRAMMING
👢	93.5	WKBL	‖	◇⚡	🕐	**RELIGIOUS;** Farm Reports; Spts.
👢	95.3	WTBG	‖	◇⚡	🕐	Commodities 15 past hr. 10am–3pm; Talk Show M–F 7–10am

FARTHER EAST ON I-40 SEE PAGE 20

SOUTH ON I-55 (SENATOBIA/BATESVILLE AREA)

FORMAT ♪ TUNE TO		STATION	SIGNAL POWER	TRAFFIC REPORT	NEWS	SPECIAL PROGRAMMING
Adult Pop	95.5	WOXD	‖	◇⚡	AM & PM DRIVE	From One Artist M 7:30–8pm; Lovesongs F 10pm–12M
Adult Pop	107.1	WKLJ	‖	🚗	🕐	**TOP 40; CLASSIC HITS;** News also on the 1/2 hr; Spts.: Ole MS; R. Dee Su 6pm
TOP40	103.5	WWKZ	‖‖	◇⚡	AM & PM DRIVE	Morn. Humor; Rick Dee's Ctdwn. Su 8am–12N
🎸	92.1	WUMS	‖	◇⚡	🕐	**ALBUM & CLASSIC ROCK;** Talk Radio Tu 10–11pm; Jazz Su 12N–2pm
👢	95.3	WVIM	‖		🕐	Farm Report 10:30am, 12N; On a Ctry. Road Sa 3–6pm; Live Music 6–7pm
👢	97.5	WWMS	‖‖	◇⚡	🕐	Farm Markets
👢	100.5	WBLE	‖‖	🚗	🕐	
👢	106.7	WWZD	‖‖	◇⚡		Amer. Ctry. Ctdwn. Sa 6–10am, Su 10am– 2pm; Top 30 Ctdwn. Sa 6–9pm, Su 6pm
🎹	88.9	WNJC	‖‖	◇⚡	MORE	**NPR; APR;** News: W.E. Sa & Su 7–9am, ATC 4–5pm; Garrison Keillor Sa 5pm
🎹	90.3	WMAV	‖‖	◇⚡	MORE	**NPR; APR;** News: W.E. Sa & Su 8–11am, ATC 5–6pm; Mktplace 6:30–7pm; Jazz M–F 10pm

FARTHER SOUTH ON I-55 SEE PAGE 28

MIAMI

FORMAT / TUNE TO		STATION	SIGNAL POWER	TRAFFIC REPORT	NEWS	SPECIAL PROGRAMMING
Adult Cor	97.3	WFLC	|||	🚗	AM DRIVE	Lights Out Along the Coast 10pm–12M; Intracoastal Musicway F, Sa, Su 12M
Adult Cor	101.5	WLYF	|||	🚗	MORE	News on odd hrs; Stk. Mkt. 10:30am, 3:30pm, D. Jones 5:59, 11:59am, 4:29pm
Adult Cor	106.7	WJQY	|||	🚗	AM DRIVE	Morn. Humor
Top40	96.5	WPOW	|||	🚗	AM DRIVE	**DANCE; LATIN FREESTYLE;** Live Mix daily 8pm–2am; C. Kasem Su 8am–12N
Top40	100.7	WHYI	|||	🚗	SPOT NEWS	Morn. Humor; Joke Off F 8am; Blast Off F 5pm
🎸	103.5	WSHE	|||	🚗	AM DRIVE	All-Request Lunch 12N; 5 o'clock Whistle M–F 5pm; Z Rock Ctdwn. Su 7–11pm
🎸	94.9	WZTA	|||	🚗	AM DRIVE	King Biscuit Flower Hour M 10pm; Dr. Demento Su 12M; Acoustic Classics Su 9am
🤠	99.9	WKIS	|||	🚗	AM DRIVE	
OLDIES	102.7	WMXJ	|||	🚗	AM & PM DRIVE	Morn. Humor; Dick Clark Su 7–11am
OLDIES	105.9	WAXY	|||	🚗	🕐	**ADULT POPULAR;** Snacktime at the Oldies 3–5pm; Music for Lovers 7pm–12M
R&B	99.1	WEDR	|||	🚗	🕐	**RAP; BLACK OLDIES; JAZZ;** Your Personal Finance (4 times daily); Job Information AM
R&B	105.1	WHQT	|||	🚗	AM DRIVE	Morn. Humor
🎹	93.1	WTMI	|||	🚗	SEE S.P.	News 05 after the hr; Chicago Symphony Tu 8pm; On Your Toes Sa 7pm
ek-lek-tik	88.9	WDNA	|||		SEE S.P.	News: Pacifica 6–6:30pm; Jazz M–F 2–6pm, Sa & Su 3–6pm; Haitian Sa & Su 6–9am
ek-lek-tik	91.3	WLRN	|||		MORE	**NPR**
🎸	93.9	WLVE	|||	🚗	AM DRIVE	Morn. Humor; Brazilian Jazz Su 6–8pm; New Age Su 8–10pm
ESPAÑOL	92.3	WCMQ	|||	🚗	🕐	**ADULT POPULAR;** Bus. Rpt. 8:15am; Nocturno M–F 8pm; Noti-Musicales M–F 12N
ESPAÑOL	107.5	WQBA	|||	🚗	AM DRIVE	**ADULT POPULAR;** 60's & 70's M–F 9–10pm
✝✝✝	89.7	WMCU	|||	🚗	🕐	Morn. Humor; Miami Christian College
✝✝✝	90.3	WAFG	||		🕐	Insight for Living M–F 12:30pm, M–Thu 7:30pm; Grace to You M–Thu 8:30pm
NEWS	940	WINZ	|||	🚗	ALL NEWS	Stk. Mkt. 20 after and 10 to the hour; Spts.: FL State U.; Talknet 7pm–5am
TALK	610	WIOD	||	🚗	🕐	Ext. News 5:30–10am; Stk.Mkt. during News; Spts.: Dolphins, U. of Miami, Yankees
TALK	1400	WFTL			🚗	🕐	Stk. Mkt. 8, 10, 11am, 12N, 5pm; Sportstalk M–F 2–6am; N. Kent 6–10am; S. Kane 2–6pm

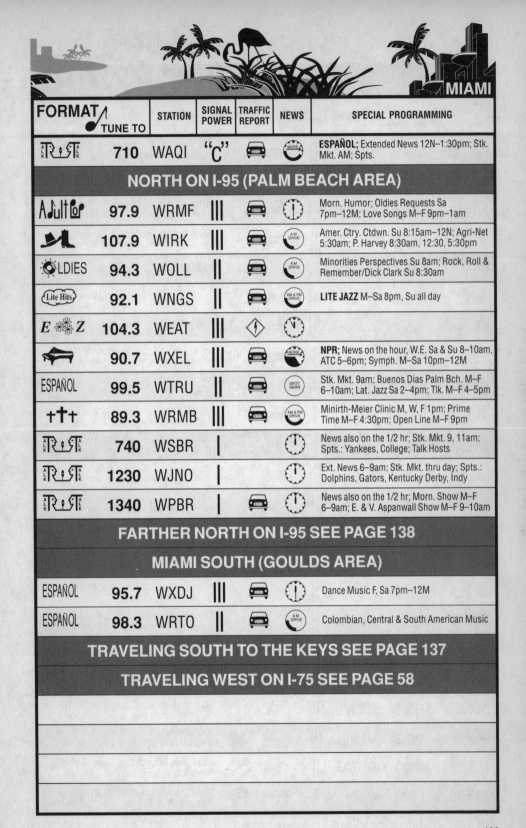

MIAMI

FORMAT / TUNE TO		STATION	SIGNAL POWER	TRAFFIC REPORT	NEWS	SPECIAL PROGRAMMING
TALK	710	WAQI	"C"	🚗	MORE	**ESPAÑOL;** Extended News 12N–1:30pm; Stk. Mkt. AM; Spts.
NORTH ON I-95 (PALM BEACH AREA)						
Adult Pop	97.9	WRMF	|||	🚗	🕐	Morn. Humor; Oldies Requests Sa 7pm–12M; Love Songs M–F 9pm–1am
(cowboy)	107.9	WIRK	|||	🚗	AM DRIVE	Amer. Ctry. Ctdwn. Su 8:15am–12N; Agri-Net 5:30am; P. Harvey 8:30am, 12:30, 5:30pm
☀OLDIES	94.3	WOLL	||	🚗	AM DRIVE	Minorities Perspectives Su 8am; Rock, Roll & Remember/Dick Clark Su 8:30am
(Lite Hits)	92.1	WNGS	||	🚗	AM & PM DRIVE	**LITE JAZZ** M–Sa 8pm, Su all day
E ❋ Z	104.3	WEAT	|||	◇	🕐	
(piano)	90.7	WXEL	|||	🚗	MORE	**NPR;** News on the hour, W.E. Sa & Su 8–10am, ATC 5–6pm; Symph. M–Sa 10pm–12M
ESPAÑOL	99.5	WTRU	||	🚗	SPOT NEWS	Stk. Mkt. 9am; Buenos Dias Palm Bch. M–F 6–10am; Lat. Jazz Sa 2–4pm; Tlk. M–F 4–5pm
✝✝✝	89.3	WRMB	|||	🚗	AM & PM DRIVE	Minirth-Meier Clinic M, W, F 1pm; Prime Time M–F 4:30pm; Open Line M–F 9pm
TALK	740	WSBR				🕐	News also on the 1/2 hr; Stk. Mkt. 9, 11am; Spts.: Yankees, College; Talk Hosts
TALK	1230	WJNO				🕐	Ext. News 6–9am; Stk. Mkt. thru day; Spts.: Dolphins, Gators, Kentucky Derby, Indy
TALK	1340	WPBR			🚗	🕐	News also on the 1/2 hr; Morn. Show M–F 6–9am; E. & V. Aspanwall Show M–F 9–10am
FARTHER NORTH ON I-95 SEE PAGE 138						
MIAMI SOUTH (GOULDS AREA)						
ESPAÑOL	95.7	WXDJ	|||	🚗	🕐	Dance Music F, Sa 7pm–12M
ESPAÑOL	98.3	WRTO	||	🚗	AM DRIVE	Colombian, Central & South American Music
TRAVELING SOUTH TO THE KEYS SEE PAGE 137						
TRAVELING WEST ON I-75 SEE PAGE 58						

FORMAT / TUNE TO	STATION	SIGNAL POWER	TRAFFIC REPORT	NEWS	SPECIAL PROGRAMMING
Adult Pop — 98.3	WDLT	‖	🚗	AM & PM DRIVE	Morn. Humor; Favorites of the 60's, 70's & 80's
Adult Pop — 99.9	WKRG	‖‖	🚗	AM DRIVE	Morn. Humor
Top40 — 97.5	WABB	‖‖	🚗	AM DRIVE	C. Kasem Su 9am; Open House Party Sa 6–11pm; R. Dee Su 6pm; S. Stevens Sa 6–10am
🎸 — 92.1	WZEW	‖	🚗	SPOT NEWS	**JAZZ; CLASSIC ROCK;** Jazz Brunch Su 9am–1pm; On the Edge W 10:30
🎸 — 104.1	WGCX	‖‖	⚡		**CLASSIC ROCK;** Morn. Humor
🤠 — 94.9	WKSJ	‖‖	🚗	MORE	News 12N; Spts.: U. of Alabama
OLDIES — 96.1	WAVH	‖‖	🚗	AM DRIVE	Inside the Hits M–F 6:45am; All-Request Lunch M–F 12N; Cruisin' Amer. Su 9am–12N
R&B — 92.9	WBLX	‖‖	🚗	🕐	Hot Lunch Music Mix 11:30am–12:30pm; Hot Nine at 9 9–10pm; Sp. Touch 11pm–1am
🎹 — 91.3	WHIL	‖‖		🕐	**APR;** MonitoRadio M–F 4:30–5pm; Mktpl. M–F 5–5:30pm; Opera Sa 1–4pm
TALK — 710	WKRG	‖	🚗	🕐	News also on 1/2 hr; Stk. Mkt. 20 & 40 after the hr; Spts.: Braves, Falcons, U. of S. AL

WEST ON I-10 (GULFPORT/BILOXI AREA)

FORMAT / TUNE TO	STATION	SIGNAL POWER	TRAFFIC REPORT	NEWS	SPECIAL PROGRAMMING
Adult Pop — 93.7	WQID	‖‖	🚗	🕐	Morn. Humor; C. Kasem Top 40 Su 6–10pm; Amer. Top 40 Su 6–10am; Hitline Su 10pm
Adult Pop — 107.1	WXLS	‖	⚡	AM & PM DRIVE	Stk. Mkt. 1:50pm; Sa & Su Evening Specials; Christian Contemporary Su 6–9am
Top40 — 107.9	WZKX	‖‖	⚡	AM DRIVE	Morn. Humor
🤠 — 99.1	WKNN	‖‖	⚡	MORE	News 12N; Morn. Humor
🤠 — 106.3	WGUD	‖	⚡	SPOT NEWS	Morn. Humor; Ctry. Top 10 Sa 9am, Su 11am; On a Ctry. Road Su 6pm
OLDIES — 102.3	WGCM	‖		AM DRIVE	Morn. Hum.; Supergold Sa 7pm–12M; Coast Cafe M–F 12N–1pm (Call–In) Menu of Oldies
R&B — 96.7	WQFX	‖	🚗	SPOT NEWS	Rap It Up Sa 10pm–12M; On the Move Sa 6–9pm; Walt Love Ctdwn. Sa 8–10am
R&B — 104.9	WKKY	‖	⚡	🕐	**TOP 40;** Morn. Humor
R&B — 105.5	WMMV	‖	🚗	🕐	Morn. Humor
🎹 — 90.3	WMAH	‖‖		MORE	**NPR; APR;** News: W.E. Sa & Su 8–11am, ATC 5–6pm, Marketplace M–F 6:30–7pm
✝✝✝ — 103.1	WOSM	‖	⚡	AM DRIVE	Spts.: Mississippi College, Ocean Springs, Sportsline
NEWS — 1460	WGUD	‖	⚡	ALL NEWS	Spts.: U. of MS, MS State, Local; Focus on the Family M–F 1:30pm

MOBILE

FORMAT♪ TUNE TO	STATION	SIGNAL POWER	TRAFFIC REPORT	NEWS	SPECIAL PROGRAMMING
FARTHER WEST ON I-10 OR I-12 SEE NEW ORLEANS PG 204					
NORTHEAST ON I-65 (BREWTON AREA)					
👢	106.3 WKNU	‖		SEE SEE	News 10am, 12N, 6pm, Paul Harvey; Spts.: U. of AL
FARTHER NORTH ON I-65 SEE PAGE 42					
EAST ON I-10 (PENSACOLA AREA)					
TOP40	100.7 WJLQ	‖‖		AM & PM DRIVE	
🎸	101.5 WTKX	‖‖		AM DRIVE	Nuts & Honey M–F 5:30–9am; Hot Lunch M–F 12N; Red Dog Saloon M-F 6pm (Class. Rock)
👢	102.7 WXBM	‖‖		AM DRIVE	Morn. Humor; Ctry. Ctdwn. Sa 6–9am, Su 9am–12N; On a Ctry. Road Su 6–9pm
👢	107.3 WOWW	‖‖		AM & PM DRIVE	Morn. Humor; Ctry. Ctdwn. Su 9am–12N; Trucking Music/Talk M–F 12M–5am
E ❀ Z	94.1 WMEZ	‖‖		MORE	News 12N
E ❀ Z	105.1 WKGT	‖		🕐	**BIG BAND;** Morn. Humor
🎹	88.1 WUWF	‖‖		MORE	**JZ.** M–F 10pm-1am, Sa 11pm-12M, Su 11pm; News: W.E. Sa & Su 7–9am, ATC 4–5:30pm
✝✝✝	89.5 WPCS	‖‖		SPOT NEWS	Focus on the Family M–F 2:30pm; Insight for Living M–F 9:30am, 6:30pm; Christian Music
✝✝✝	91.7 WEGS	‖‖			**SOUTHERN GOSPEL;** In Touch 9am; Focus on the Fam. 11am; Truths that Trans. 10am
FARTHER EAST ON I-10 SEE PAGE 2					

NASHVILLE

FORMAT ♪ TUNE TO		STATION	SIGNAL POWER	TRAFFIC REPORT	NEWS	SPECIAL PROGRAMMING
Adult Pop	100.1	WRLT	‖	🚗	AM DRIVE	**ALBUM-ORIENTED ADULT POPULAR;** Jazz Su 1am–2pm; Blues Su 2–3pm
Adult Pop	105.9	WLAC	‖‖	🚗	AM & PM DRIVE	Christian Contemporary Su 6–10am; Love Songs & Dedications M–Su 7pm–1am
Top40	107.5	WYHY	‖‖	🚗	AM DRIVE	C. Kasem Su 10am–2pm; Amer. Top 40 Sa 6–10am; Joel Denver's Future Hits Su 6–7am
🎸	103.3	WKDF	‖‖	🚗	SPOT NEWS	Morn. Humor
🎸☮	104.5	WGFX	‖‖	🚗	AM DRIVE	Morn. Humor
👢	95.5	WSM	‖‖	🚗	🕐	In the Black Su 5am; Men's 30 Su 5:30am
👢	97.9	WSIX	‖‖	🚗	🕐	News also on the 1/2 hour AM Drive; Morn. Humor
OLDIES	96.3	WRMX	‖‖	🚗	AM DRIVE	Lunchtime at the Oldies M–F 12N; Supergold Sa 7pm–12M; Live from the Sixties Su 9pm
R&B	92.1	WQQK	‖	🚗	AM DRIVE	Morn. Humor; Quiet Storm M–F 9pm–12M; Dance Party Sa 7pm–12M
Lite Hits	92.9	WZEZ	‖‖	🚗	SEE S.P.	News 6, 8, 10am, 12N, 2, 4pm; Focus Su 7:30am
🎹	90.3	WPLN	‖‖	◇	MORE	**NPR;** News 12N; Radio Reader 9am; BBC Newsreel 8am; Mktplace 5:35pm
🎓	88.1	WFSK	‖			**GOSPEL** 9am–3pm; **JAZZ** 3pm–12M; Fisk U.
🎓	91.1	WRVU	‖‖			**PROGRESSIVE ROCK; ECLECTIC; ETHNIC; BLUEGRASS; BLUES;** Vanderbilt U.
†††	89.1	WNAZ	‖	🚗	🕐	**CHRISTIAN CONTEMPORARY;** Spts. News 8:30am; Minirth-Meier Clinic 12N
TALK	1510	WLAC	"C"	🚗	🕐	**NEWS; RELIGION** 8pm–5am; Spts. 5–7pm; R. Limbaugh M–F 11am–1pm
👢	650	WSM	"C"	🚗	🕐	**NEWS; TALK;** News also on the 1/2 hour
SOUTH ON I-65 (COLUMBIA AREA)						
👢	94.3	WJJM	‖	🚗	🕐	News also on the 1/2 hour; Spts.: U. of TN, Local; Ctry. Ctdwn. Sa 7–8pm
OLDIES	101.7	WKOM	‖	◇	MORE	News 12N; Morn. Humor
FARTHER SOUTH ON I-65 SEE PAGE 44						
WEST ON I-40 (DICKSON AREA)						
👢	96.7	WHLP	‖	◇	MORE	News 12:30, 4:30pm; Spts.: Local; Farm Reports; Business Reports; Agri. Weather
OLDIES	105.1	WVRY	‖‖	🚗	AM DRIVE	Morn. Humor

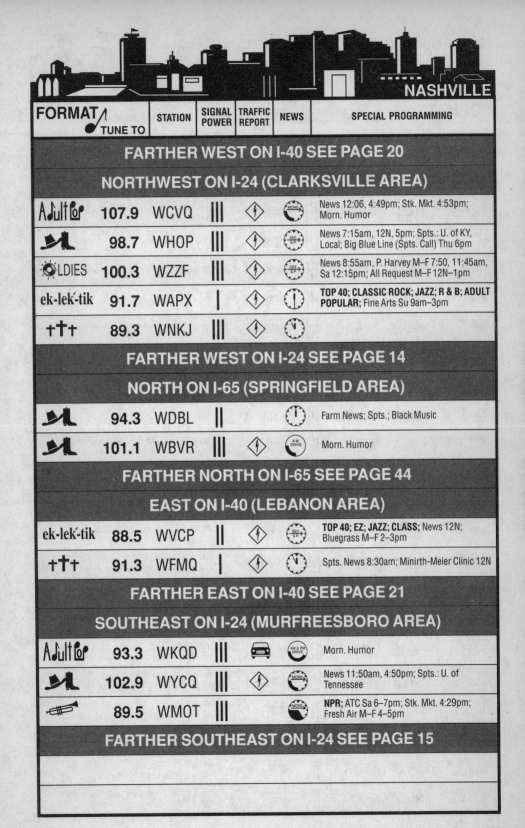

NASHVILLE

FORMAT / TUNE TO	STATION	SIGNAL POWER	TRAFFIC REPORT	NEWS	SPECIAL PROGRAMMING
FARTHER WEST ON I-40 SEE PAGE 20					
NORTHWEST ON I-24 (CLARKSVILLE AREA)					
Adult Pop · 107.9	WCVQ	‖‖	◇	MORE	News 12:06, 4:49pm; Stk. Mkt. 4:53pm; Morn. Humor
🤠 · 98.7	WHOP	‖‖	◇	SEE S.P.	News 7:15am, 12N, 5pm; Spts.: U. of KY, Local; Big Blue Line (Spts. Call) Thu 6pm
☀OLDIES · 100.3	WZZF	‖‖	◇	SEE S.P.	News 8:55am, P. Harvey M–F 7:50, 11:45am, Sa 12:15pm; All Request M–F 12N–1pm
ek-lek-tik · 91.7	WAPX	‖	◇		**TOP 40; CLASSIC ROCK; JAZZ; R & B; ADULT POPULAR;** Fine Arts Su 9am–3pm
✝✝✝ · 89.3	WNKJ	‖‖	◇		
FARTHER WEST ON I-24 SEE PAGE 14					
NORTH ON I-65 (SPRINGFIELD AREA)					
🤠 · 94.3	WDBL	‖			Farm News; Spts.; Black Music
🤠 · 101.1	WBVR	‖‖	◇	A.M. DRIVE	Morn. Humor
FARTHER NORTH ON I-65 SEE PAGE 44					
EAST ON I-40 (LEBANON AREA)					
ek-lek-tik · 88.5	WVCP	‖	◇	SEE S.P.	**TOP 40; EZ; JAZZ; CLASS;** News 12N; Bluegrass M–F 2–3pm
✝✝✝ · 91.3	WFMQ	‖	◇		Spts. News 8:30am; Minirth-Meier Clinic 12N
FARTHER EAST ON I-40 SEE PAGE 21					
SOUTHEAST ON I-24 (MURFREESBORO AREA)					
Adult Pop · 93.3	WKQD	‖‖	🚗	AM & PM DRIVE	Morn. Humor
🤠 · 102.9	WYCQ	‖‖	◇	MORE	News 11:50am, 4:50pm; Spts.: U. of Tennessee
🎺 · 89.5	WMOT	‖‖		MORE	**NPR;** ATC Sa 6–7pm; Stk. Mkt. 4:29pm; Fresh Air M–F 4–5pm
FARTHER SOUTHEAST ON I-24 SEE PAGE 15					

203

FORMAT / TUNE TO		STATION	SIGNAL POWER	TRAFFIC REPORT	NEWS	SPECIAL PROGRAMMING
Adult Pop	95.7	WMXZ	|||	🚗	AM DRIVE	Rick Dee Su 8am–12N; Louisiana Lagniappe (Public Affairs) Su 7–8am
Adult Pop	101.9	WLMG	|||	🚗	AM DRIVE	Morn. Humor; Dick Clark Sa 8pm–12M; Magic of New Orleans (Talk) Su 7am
Adult Pop	105.3	WLTS	|||	🚗	AM DRIVE	**LITE ROCK;** Morn. Humor; Super Gold Sa 7pm–12M
Top 40	93.3	WQUE	|||	🚗	AM DRIVE	**R & B;** Spot News
Top 40	97.1	WEZB	|||	🚗	🕐	Morn. Humor
🎸	92.3	WCKW	|||	🚗	MORE	News 2pm; Morn. Humor
🎸	99.5	WRNO	|||	🚗	🕐	
🎸	91.5	WTUL			◇	SEE S.P.	News 8am, 12N, 5pm; Class. M–Su 6–8am; Jazz M–Su 6–8pm; Reggae M 8–11pm
👢	101.1	WNOE	|||	🚗	🕐	Morn. Humor; Stk. Mkt; Entertainment Reports; Public Affairs; Spts.
OLDIES	104.1	KHOM	|||		MORE	News 12N; Morn. Humor
OLDIES	106.7	KQLD	|||	🚗	AM DRIVE	Class Reunion M–F 12N–1pm; Traffic Jam M–F 5–6pm; Your 9 at 9 M–F 9am
R & B	98.5	WYLD	|||	🚗	AM & PM DRIVE	Morn. Hum.; Mel. Moods M–Su 9pm–2am; Midday Slow Jam M–F 11:30am–12:30pm
🎹	89.9	WWNO	|||	🚗	MORE	**NPR; APR; JAZZ** M–Su 11pm–1am; News: W.E. Sa 7–9am, ATC Sa & Su 5–6pm
🎺	90.7	WWOZ	|||	🚗		**ECLECTIC;** Gospel Train Su 8:30–10am, 6:30pm; Cajun Su 11:30am–2:30pm
ek-lek-tik	88.3	WRBH	|||			**RADIO FOR THE BLIND;** Reading of Newspapers, Books, Magazines, etc.
💨	102.9	KNOK	|||	🚗	SEE S.P.	News :10 & :40; Breeze Special Su 6–8pm; Breeze Album Ctdwn. Su 8–9pm
✝✝✝	89.1	WBSN	|||	🚗	🕐	**CHRISTIAN CONTEMPORARY;** Ministry Talk daily 11am–12pm
R★S★	690	WTIX	||	🚗	MORE	**BUSINESS TALK;** Stk. Mkt. 4pm; Monkey Business (Theatre/Talent) M–S 7–8pm
R★S★	870	WWL	"C"	🚗	🕐	News also on the 1/2 hr; Stk. Mkt :55 5am–5pm; Spts.: Saints, LA U., Tulane; Talk Hosts
R★S★	1350	WSMB	||	🚗	🕐	News also on the 1/2 hr; Spts.: Tulane; Tom Fitzmorris & Gail DeLaughter M–F 6–9am
SOUTHWEST ON US 90 (HOUMA AREA)						
Adult Pop	106.3	KXOR	||	🚗	SEE S.P.	News 9, 11am, 1, 3pm, Paul Harvey 7, 7:30am, 12N; Morn. Humor
Top 40	96.7	KFXY	||		MORE	News 11:55am; Gospel Su 6–10am; Rockin' Amer. Top 30 Ctdwn. Sa 6–9am

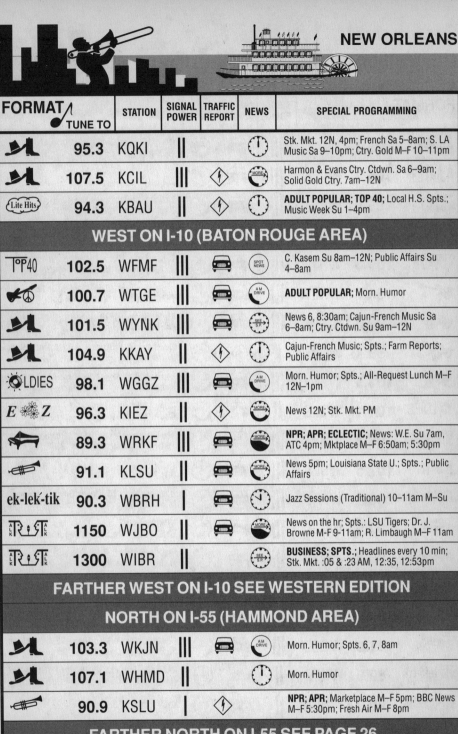

FORMAT ♪ TUNE TO		STATION	SIGNAL POWER	TRAFFIC REPORT	NEWS	SPECIAL PROGRAMMING
👢	95.3	KQKI	‖		🕐	Stk. Mkt. 12N, 4pm; French Sa 5–8am; S. LA Music Sa 9–10pm; Ctry. Gold M–F 10–11pm
👢	107.5	KCIL	‖‖	◇⚡	MORE	Harmon & Evans Ctry. Ctdwn. Sa 6–9am; Solid Gold Ctry. 7am–12N
Lite Hits	94.3	KBAU	‖	◇⚡	🕐	**ADULT POPULAR; TOP 40;** Local H.S. Spts.; Music Week Su 1–4pm
WEST ON I-10 (BATON ROUGE AREA)						
TOP40	102.5	WFMF	‖‖	🚗	SPOT NEWS	C. Kasem Su 8am–12N; Public Affairs Su 4–8am
🎸☮	100.7	WTGE	‖‖	🚗	A M DRIVE	**ADULT POPULAR;** Morn. Humor
👢	101.5	WYNK	‖‖	🚗	SEE S.P.	News 6, 8:30am; Cajun-French Music Sa 6–8am; Ctry. Ctdwn. Su 9am–12N
👢	104.9	KKAY	‖	◇⚡	🕐	Cajun-French Music; Spts.; Farm Reports; Public Affairs
OLDIES	98.1	WGGZ	‖‖	🚗	A M DRIVE	Morn. Humor; Spts.; All-Request Lunch M–F 12N–1pm
E ❀ Z	96.3	KIEZ	‖	◇⚡	MORE	News 12N; Stk. Mkt. PM
🛋	89.3	WRKF	‖‖	🚗	MORE	**NPR; APR; ECLECTIC;** News: W.E. Su 7am; ATC 4pm; Mktplace M–F 6:50am; 5:30pm
🎺	91.1	KLSU	‖	🚗	MORE	News 5pm; Louisiana State U.; Spts.; Public Affairs
ek-lek-tik	90.3	WBRH	‖	🚗	🕐	Jazz Sessions (Traditional) 10–11am M–Su
TALK	1150	WJBO	‖	🚗	MORE	News on the hr; Spts.: LSU Tigers; Dr. J. Browne M–F 9–11am; R. Limbaugh M–F 11am
TALK	1300	WIBR	‖		SEE S.P.	**BUSINESS; SPTS.;** Headlines every 10 min; Stk. Mkt. :05 & :23 AM, 12:35, 12:53pm
FARTHER WEST ON I-10 SEE WESTERN EDITION						
NORTH ON I-55 (HAMMOND AREA)						
👢	103.3	WKJN	‖‖	🚗	A M DRIVE	Morn. Humor; Spts. 6, 7, 8am
👢	107.1	WHMD	‖		🕐	Morn. Humor
🎺	90.9	KSLU	‖	◇⚡		**NPR; APR;** Marketplace M–F 5pm; BBC News M–F 5:30pm; Fresh Air M–F 8pm

FARTHER NORTH ON I-55 SEE PAGE 26

NORTH ON I-59 SEE PAGE 29

EAST ON I-10 SEE MOBILE PAGE 200

FORMAT ♪ TUNE TO		STATION	SIGNAL POWER	TRAFFIC REPORT	NEWS	SPECIAL PROGRAMMING
Adult Pop	105.1	WNSR	‖‖	🚗	MORE	News 12N, 3pm; Morn. Humor; Family Affairs Su 7am
Adult Pop	106.7	WLTW	‖‖	🚗	⏲	
Top 40	95.5	WPLJ	‖‖	🚗	A M DRIVE	Howard the Cab Driver Su 6–7am; On the Radio Su 8am; Hot Mix Sa 9pm
Top 40	97.1	WQHT	‖‖	🚗	A M DRIVE	**DANCE MUSIC;** Dance Party Sa 10pm–2am; Classics Showcase Su 8pm
Top 40	100.3	WHTZ	‖‖	🚗	A M DRIVE	C. Kasem Su 10am–2pm; Scott Shannon Sa 7–10am; Hitline USA Su 11pm–12M
🎸	102.7	WNEW	‖‖	🚗	⏲	High Voltage Su 11pm–1am; Mixed Bag Su 7–10am; Get the Led Out M–F 8pm
🎸	92.3	WXRK	‖‖	🚗	SPOT NEWS	Morn. Humor; Spirit of the 60's Sa 8–11am; The Sunday Show 8–11am
🎸	89.1	WNYU	‖	⚡	SEE S.P.	News 4, 4:52, 6:52pm; The Amusement Park W 7:30pm; Headphone Theatre Thu 7:30pm
👢	103.5	WYNY	‖‖	🚗	AM & PM DRIVE	Top 5 at 10pm M–F; New Music M 10:15pm; Hometown Ctdwn. Su 10:30am–1:30pm
☀ OLDIES	101.1	WCBS	‖	🚗	MORE	News 12N; Hall of Fame M–F 7–11pm; Top 20 Ctdwn. Sa & Su 5–7pm
R & B	98.7	WRKS	‖‖	🚗	⏲	The Week in Review Su 9am; Rap Show F, Sa 7pm–12M; Master Mix F, Sa 12M
R & B	107.5	WBLS	‖‖	🚗	⏲	Morn. Humor; Public Affairs Su 5:30–8am
E ❄ Z	93.1	WPAT	‖‖	🚗	⏲	Business News 25 after hr; Sinatra's Music & More Sa 7–9pm
🎹	93.9	WNYC	‖‖	🚗	MORE	**NPR;** News W.E. Sa 8–10am; Modern Times Sa 9–11pm; New Sounds M–F 11pm
🎹	96.3	WQXR	‖‖	🚗	⏲	Classic Jazz Su 6–7pm; Opera Sa 1:30–5pm, Su 8–11pm; My Music Sa 6:30–7pm
🎹	104.3	WNCN	‖‖	🚗	⏲	Morn. Humor; Chicago Symphony Orchestra Su 1pm
🎺	88.3	WBGO	‖‖	🚗	AM & PM DRIVE	**NPR; APR;** News: ATC 6–7:30pm; Stk. Mkt. 7:30, 8:30am, 5:04pm; Rhythm Sa 8am
🎺	101.9	WQCD	‖‖	🚗	A M DRIVE	New Age New York Su 10pm–12M; Cool Cuts Sa 9–10pm; Latin Quarter F 10pm–12M
ek-lek´-tik	89.9	WKCR	‖		SEE S.P.	**JAZZ; CLASSICAL; SPANISH; CTRY.; R & B;** News 5:50, 11:55am
ek-lek´-tik	90.3	WHCR	‖		SPOT NEWS	Latin Jazz Su–F 5–9pm
ek-lek´-tik	90.7	WFUV	‖‖	⚡	SEE S.P.	**APR;** Folk M–F 10am–2pm; Classical M–F 2:30–6pm; News M–F 5–6:15am, 6–7pm
ek-lek´-tik	91.5	WNYE	‖‖			**EDUCATIONAL; INSTRUCTIONAL;** French M–F 6:30–9am, 11pm–1am, Su 6:30–10am
ek-lek´-tik	99.5	WBAI	‖‖	⚡	MORE	News 1, 6pm; Multicultural Program W 8:30–9pm; Arts/Music Prog. M–F 4:30–6pm

FORMAT / TUNE TO		STATION	SIGNAL POWER	TRAFFIC REPORT	NEWS	SPECIAL PROGRAMMING
ek-lek´-tik	105.9	WNWK	|||		SPOT NEWS	FOREIGN LANGUAGES; ETHNIC; MULTICULTURAL MIXTURE; Interviews
ESPAÑOL	97.9	WSKQ	|||	🚗	🕐	TOP 40; Stk. Mkt. 7:30am
✝✝✝	94.7	WFME	|||	🚗	AM & PM DRIVE	
NEWS	880	WCBS	"C"	🚗	ALL NEWS	Stk. Mkt. :25 & :55 each hr; Spts.: Jets, St. John's; Spts. News :15 & :45 every hour
NEWS	1010	WINS	"C"	🚗	ALL NEWS	Stk. Mkt. Updates :26 & :56 each hour; Spts. :15 & :45 each hour
TALK	660	WFAN	"C"	🚗	🕐	SPORTS & SPORTSTALK: Mets, CBS, Knicks, NCAA Basketball Tourney, Rangers
TALK	710	WOR	"C"	🚗	🕐	News also on 1/2 hr.; Stk. Mkt. on all Newscasts; Talk 24 hours
TALK	770	WABC	"C"	🚗	🕐	Financial Report 8:05am; Money Talk M–F 6–10pm; Spts.: Devils, Yanks; Call-In all day
TALK	820	WNYC	||	🚗	MORE	News also on the hr; On the Line M–F 10am–12N; NY & Co.12N–2pm; Fresh Air 2pm
Adult Pop	1130	WNEW	"C"	🚗	🕐	ADULT STANDARDS until 7pm; SPORTS & TALK; Giants, N. Dame; Mkt. :06 hourly
E ❄ Z	1050	WEVD	"C"	🚗	🕐	ADULT STANDARDS; ETHNIC; Spts.: Islanders, Rutgers, B. Bresnan M–F 4–6pm
🎹	1560	WQXR	"C"	🚗	🕐	Stk. Mkt. on the hour
NEW YORK SOUTH						
Adult Pop	98.3	WMGQ	||	🚗	MORE	News 12N, 3pm; Oldies Sa 7pm–12M; Folk/Acoustic Su 8–10am; Jazz Su 7–8pm
ek-lek´-tik	88.7	WRSU				SEE S.P.	News 10am, 12N; Special/Ethnic Programs M–F 9–10am, 6–10pm, Su 6am–10pm
ek-lek´-tik	103.3	WPRB	|||	⬦	SEE S.P.	PROGRESSIVE ROCK; JAZZ; CLASS; News 6, 8, 10am, 12N, 2, 4, 6pm; Spts.: Princeton
✝✝✝	99.1	WAWZ	|||	⬦	🕐	CHRISTIAN CONTEMPORARY; Focus on the Family M–F 9am, 4:30pm

SOUTH ON US 1, N.J.T. (I-95) SEE PHILADELPHIA PAGE 212

SOUTH ON GARDEN STATE PKWY. SEE SHORE RTE. PG 164

TURN TO NEXT 2 PAGES FOR POINTS

WEST, NORTH, NORTHEAST AND EAST

NEW YORK CITY CONTINUED ON NEXT PAGE

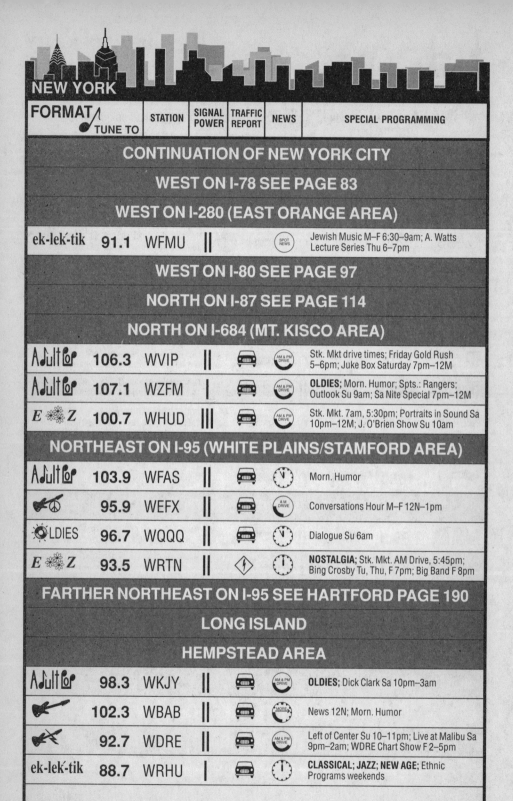

NEW YORK

FORMAT TUNE TO	STATION	SIGNAL POWER	TRAFFIC REPORT	NEWS	SPECIAL PROGRAMMING
CONTINUATION OF NEW YORK CITY					
WEST ON I-78 SEE PAGE 83					
WEST ON I-280 (EAST ORANGE AREA)					
ek-lek´-tik 91.1	WFMU	‖		SPOT NEWS	Jewish Music M–F 6:30–9am; A. Watts Lecture Series Thu 6–7pm
WEST ON I-80 SEE PAGE 97					
NORTH ON I-87 SEE PAGE 114					
NORTH ON I-684 (MT. KISCO AREA)					
Adult Pop 106.3	WVIP	‖	🚗	AM & PM DRIVE	Stk. Mkt drive times; Friday Gold Rush 5–6pm; Juke Box Saturday 7pm–12M
Adult Pop 107.1	WZFM	|	🚗	AM & PM DRIVE	**OLDIES;** Morn. Humor; Spts.: Rangers; Outlook Su 9am; Sa Nite Special 7pm–12M
E Z 100.7	WHUD	‖‖	🚗	AM & PM DRIVE	Stk. Mkt. 7am, 5:30pm; Portraits in Sound Sa 10pm–12M; J. O'Brien Show Su 10am
NORTHEAST ON I-95 (WHITE PLAINS/STAMFORD AREA)					
Adult Pop 103.9	WFAS	‖	🚗	🕐	Morn. Humor
✌ 95.9	WEFX	‖	🚗	AM DRIVE	Conversations Hour M–F 12N–1pm
☀OLDIES 96.7	WQQQ	‖	🚗	🕐	Dialogue Su 6am
E Z 93.5	WRTN	‖	◇	🕐	**NOSTALGIA;** Stk. Mkt. AM Drive, 5:45pm; Bing Crosby Tu, Thu, F 7pm; Big Band F 8pm
FARTHER NORTHEAST ON I-95 SEE HARTFORD PAGE 190					
LONG ISLAND					
HEMPSTEAD AREA					
Adult Pop 98.3	WKJY	‖	🚗	AM & PM DRIVE	**OLDIES;** Dick Clark Sa 10pm–3am
102.3	WBAB	‖	🚗	MORE	News 12N; Morn. Humor
92.7	WDRE	‖	🚗	AM & PM DRIVE	Left of Center Su 10–11pm; Live at Malibu Sa 9pm–2am; WDRE Chart Show F 2–5pm
ek-lek´-tik 88.7	WRHU	|	🚗	🕐	**CLASSICAL; JAZZ; NEW AGE;** Ethnic Programs weekends

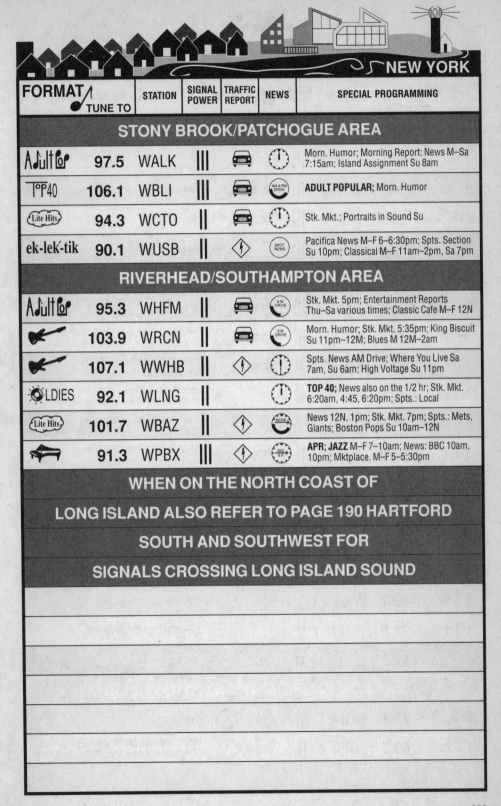

NEW YORK

FORMAT ♪ TUNE TO		STATION	SIGNAL POWER	TRAFFIC REPORT	NEWS	SPECIAL PROGRAMMING
STONY BROOK/PATCHOGUE AREA						
Adult Pop	97.5	WALK	|||	🚗	🕐	Morn. Humor; Morning Report: News M–Sa 7:15am; Island Assignment Su 8am
Top40	106.1	WBLI	|||	🚗	AM & PM DRIVE	**ADULT POPULAR;** Morn. Humor
Lite Hits	94.3	WCTO	||	🚗	🕐	Stk. Mkt.; Portraits in Sound Su
ek-lek-tik	90.1	WUSB	||	◇	SPOT NEWS	Pacifica News M–F 6–6:30pm; Spts. Section Su 10pm; Classical M–F 11am–2pm, Sa 7pm
RIVERHEAD/SOUTHAMPTON AREA						
Adult Pop	95.3	WHFM	||	🚗	AM DRIVE	Stk. Mkt. 5pm; Entertainment Reports Thu–Sa various times; Classic Cafe M–F 12N
🎸	103.9	WRCN	||	🚗	AM DRIVE	Morn. Humor; Stk. Mkt. 5:35pm; King Biscuit Su 11pm–12M; Blues M 12M–2am
🎸	107.1	WWHB	||	◇	🕐	Spts. News AM Drive; Where You Live Sa 7am, Su 6am; High Voltage Su 11pm
OLDIES	92.1	WLNG	||		🕐	**TOP 40;** News also on the 1/2 hr; Stk. Mkt. 6:20am, 4:45, 6:20pm; Spts.: Local
Lite Hits	101.7	WBAZ	||	◇	MORE	News 12N, 1pm; Stk. Mkt. 7pm; Spts.: Mets, Giants; Boston Pops Su 10am–12N
🎹	91.3	WPBX	|||	◇	SEE S.P.	**APR; JAZZ** M–F 7–10am; News: BBC 10am, 10pm; Mktplace. M–F 5–5:30pm

WHEN ON THE NORTH COAST OF

LONG ISLAND ALSO REFER TO PAGE 190 HARTFORD

SOUTH AND SOUTHWEST FOR

SIGNALS CROSSING LONG ISLAND SOUND

ORLANDO

FORMAT ♪ TUNE TO	STATION	SIGNAL POWER	TRAFFIC REPORT	NEWS	SPECIAL PROGRAMMING
Adult Pop 107.7	WMGF	‖‖	🚗	AM DRIVE	Morn. Humor
Top40 105.1	WOMX	‖‖	🚗	AM DRIVE	Morn. Humor; C. Kasem Su 9am–1pm; American Top 40 Su 7–11pm
Top40 106.7	WXXL	‖‖	🚗	AM DRIVE	Morn. Humor
🎸 96.5	WHTQ	‖‖	🚗	AM DRIVE	Morn. Humor
🎸 100.3	WDIZ	‖‖	🚗	MORE	News 10am
🤠 92.3	WWKA	‖‖	🚗	AM DRIVE	Morn. Humor
OLDIES 105.9	WOCL	‖‖	🚗	AM DRIVE	Morn. Humor; Live from the 60's Sa 10pm; Project 105.9 Su AM
🎹 90.7	WMFE	‖‖	🚗	MORE	**NPR; APR;** News: Evening Edition 4–5pm, W.E. Sa 8–10am; Mktpl. M–F 6:30pm
🎺 103.1	WLOQ	‖	🚗	🕐	**ADULT POPULAR; LITE HITS;** Morn. Humor; Stk. Mkt.; Spts.
ek-lek'-tik 89.9	WUCF	‖			Jazz M–F 9–11pm, Sa 5–8pm; Opera Sa 1:30pm; Ethnic Music Su 10am–9pm
ek-lek'-tik 91.5	WPRK	‖	◇	MORE	News 12N, 2, 5pm; Progressive Rock/Classic Rock M–F 8–11am; Class. M–Sa 11am–5pm
✝✝✝ 95.3	WTLN	‖	🚗	MORE	**TALK; MUSIC MINISTRIES;** News 1:55, 2:55pm
🚗 740	WWNZ	‖‖	🚗	MORE	**NEWS; SPTS.:** Dolphins, Magic, Hurricanes; Stk. Mkt. on hour; Sportstalk M–F 6pm
NORTHEAST ON I-4 & I-95 (DAYTONA BEACH AREA)					
R&B 101.9	WJHM	‖‖	🚗	AM DRIVE	**TOP 40;** Morn. Humor
Lite Hits 94.5	WWLV	‖‖	◇	MORE	News 10:55am, 12:55, 2:55pm; Stk. Mkt.
✝✝✝ 89.7	WJLU	‖	◇	🕐	Spts.; Religious Programs
✝✝✝ 91.5	WAPN	‖			**CHRISTIAN CONTEMPORARY**
FARTHER NORTH ON I-95 SEE PAGE 138					
EAST ON FLORIDA RTE. 50 (TITUSVILLE)					
🤠 98.1	WGNE	‖‖	◇	🕐	Morn. Humor
✝✝✝ 89.3	WPIO	‖		🕐	**INSPIRATIONAL MUSIC;** Prime Time Amer. M–F 4:30pm; Focus on the Family M–F 10am

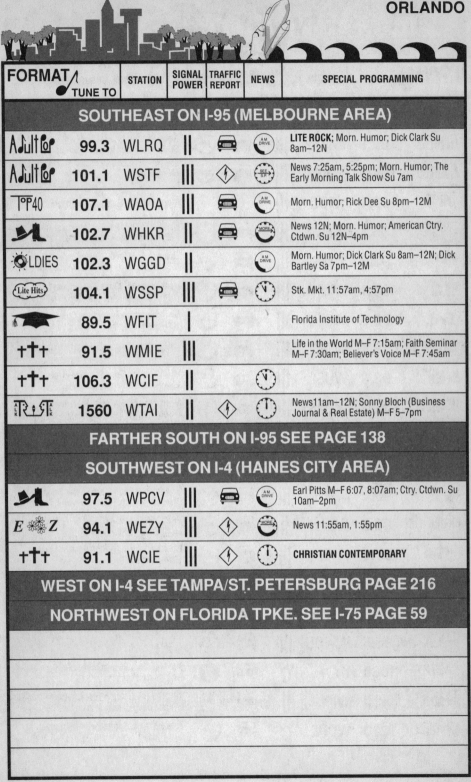

FORMAT ♪ TUNE TO	STATION	SIGNAL POWER	TRAFFIC REPORT	NEWS	SPECIAL PROGRAMMING
SOUTHEAST ON I-95 (MELBOURNE AREA)					
Adult Pop	99.3	‖	🚗	AM DRIVE	**LITE ROCK;** Morn. Humor; Dick Clark Su 8am–12N
Adult Pop	101.1	‖‖	◇⚡	SEE 57	News 7:25am, 5:25pm; Morn. Humor; The Early Morning Talk Show Su 7am
Top40	107.1	‖‖	🚗	AM DRIVE	Morn. Humor; Rick Dee Su 8pm–12M
🤠	102.7	‖	🚗	MORE	News 12N; Morn. Humor; American Ctry. Ctdwn. Su 12N–4pm
☀OLDIES	102.3	‖		AM DRIVE	Morn. Humor; Dick Clark Su 8am–12N; Dick Bartley Sa 7pm–12M
Lite Hits	104.1	‖‖	🚗	🕐	Stk. Mkt. 11:57am, 4:57pm
🎓	89.5				Florida Institute of Technology
✝✝✝	91.5	‖‖			Life in the World M–F 7:15am; Faith Seminar M–F 7:30am; Believer's Voice M–F 7:45am
✝✝✝	106.3	‖		🕐	
🛣	1560	‖	◇⚡	🕐	News11am–12N; Sonny Bloch (Business Journal & Real Estate) M–F 5–7pm
FARTHER SOUTH ON I-95 SEE PAGE 138					
SOUTHWEST ON I-4 (HAINES CITY AREA)					
🤠	97.5	‖‖	🚗	AM DRIVE	Earl Pitts M–F 6:07, 8:07am; Ctry. Ctdwn. Su 10am–2pm
E ✿ Z	94.1	‖‖	◇⚡	MORE	News 11:55am, 1:55pm
✝✝✝	91.1	‖‖	◇⚡	🕐	**CHRISTIAN CONTEMPORARY**
WEST ON I-4 SEE TAMPA/ST. PETERSBURG PAGE 216					
NORTHWEST ON FLORIDA TPKE. SEE I-75 PAGE 59					

PHILADELPHIA

FORMAT / TUNE TO	STATION	SIGNAL POWER	TRAFFIC REPORT	NEWS	SPECIAL PROGRAMMING
Adult Con. 100.3	WKSZ	|||	🚗	MORE	LITE HITS; News 12N, 5pm; Request Oldies Sa & Su 8pm–1am
Adult Con. 102.9	WMGK	|||	🚗	SEE S.P.	News 25 after hr; Breakfast with the Beatles Su 8–10am; Car Tunes M–F 5–6pm
Adult Con. 104.5	WYXR	|||	🚗	AM & PM DRIVE	Morn. Humor
Top 40 102.1	WIOQ	|||	◇		Morn. Humor; Local Ethnic Programs
Top 40 106.1	WEGX	|||	🚗	🕐	News also on the 1/2 hr; American Top 40 Su 4–8pm; All-Request Lunch M–F 12N
🎸 93.3	WMMR	|||	🚗	AM DRIVE	Ticket to Ride Su 8–10am; Rockers Su 11pm; MTV Music News M–F 9:20am, 3:10pm
🎸 94.1	WYSP	|||	🚗	AM DRIVE	Rockline M 11:30pm; All-Request Sa 7pm–12M; The Su Night Alternative 8–10pm
👢 92.5	WXTU	|||	🚗	AM DRIVE	Morn. Humor; Weekly Ctry. Ctdwn. Su 12N–3pm
☀OLDIES 98.1	WOGL	|||	🚗	AM DRIVE	98 Forum (Public Affairs) Su 7–8am
R&B 98.9	WUSL	|||	🚗	AM DRIVE	Morn. Humor; Quiet Storm M–Thu 10pm–2am, Su 7pm–12M
R&B 105.3	WDAS	|||	🚗	🕐	Morn. Humor; Stk. Mkt. AM Drive; Community Awareness (Talk) M–F 6–7pm
E❄Z 101.1	WEAZ	|||	🚗	AM DRIVE	Morn. Humor; Religious Programs Su
🐟 95.7	WFLN	|||	🚗	SEE S.P.	News 6:30, 9:30am, 3:30pm; Met Opera Sa 2pm; Philadelphia Orchestra Su 2pm
🎺 90.1	WRTI	|||	🚗	🕐	News also at 25 after hr; Reggae Sa 8am–12N; Blues Su 4–7pm; On the Line M–F 7–8pm
ek-lek-tik 88.5	WXPN	||	🚗	SEE S.P.	NPR; APR; News: ATC M–F 5–7pm; Car Talk Sa 11am; Afro Pop W 4pm
✝✝ 103.9	WIBF	|||	🚗	SPOT NEWS	ETHNIC; Thru the Bible 9am; Roy Masters 10am; Spanish Program 6:30pm
✝✝ 106.9	WKDN	|||	🚗	AM DRIVE	CHRISTIAN MUSIC; Morning Clock M–F 6–9am; Christian Home M–F 10am–12N
🗣 90.9	WHYY	|||	🚗	MORE	NEWS: ATC M–F 8–9:30pm, W.E. Sa 8–11am, Su 8–10am; Family Matters M 12N
🗣 96.5	WWDB	|||	🚗	🕐	
═NEWS═ 1060	KYW	"C"	🚗	ALL NEWS	Stk. Mkt. 25 & 55 past each hour; Spts. News 15 & 45 past each hour
🗣 610	WIP	||	🚗	🕐	SPORTS TALK: Spts.: Eagles, N. Dame, 76ers, Flyers, College; News also on the 1/2 hr.
☀OLDIES 1210	WOGL	"C"	🚗	AM DRIVE	Spts.: Phillies; Sportsline M–F 10pm–12M; 50's Friday 10am–10pm

FORMAT / TUNE TO		STATION	SIGNAL POWER	TRAFFIC REPORT	NEWS	SPECIAL PROGRAMMING
SOUTH ON I-95, I-295, N.J. TPK. (WILMINGTON AREA)						
Adult Pop	99.5	WJBR	|||	🚗	AM & PM DRIVE	Morn. Humor; Stk. Mkt. drive times; Focus on Delaware weekends
Top40	93.7	WSTW	|||	🚗	AM & PM DRIVE	**ADULT POPULAR;** Morn. Humor
🤠	103.7	WXCY	|||	🚗	MORE	News 12N; NASCAR Racing Su afternoon; NASCAR Call-In Tu 7pm
ek-lek´-tik	91.3	WXDR	I	◇		Jazz M–F 10pm–1am; Opera Su 12N; Folk M–F 9am–12N; Classical M–F 12N–2pm
✝✝✝	89.9	WOEL	II		SEE S.P.	**Sacred Christian Music;** News every 2 Hrs. on even hrs.; Gospel Hr. M–F 9:30am
NEWS	1450	WILM	I	🚗	ALL NEWS	Stk. Mkt. 2:20, 4:55, 5:20, 5:55pm; News/Talk 10:06-11:45am, 6:30-8pm; Spts. News 1/2 hr.
FARTHER SOUTH ON I-95 SEE BALTIMORE PAGE 168						
WEST ON I-76 SEE PAGE 77						
NORTH ON PA. TPK. EXT. SEE I-78 PAGE 82						
NORTHEAST ON I-95, I-295 & N.J. TPK. (TRENTON)						
Top40	97.5	WPST	|||	🚗	MORE	**ALBUM ROCK; CLASSIC HITS;** News 12N; American Top 40 Su 9am–1pm
☀OLDIES	101.5	WKXW	|||	🚗	🕐	**TALK;** Passion Phone M–F 8pm–12M
🐟	89.1	WWFM	I	◇		**JAZZ;** Public Affairs Sa 3–4pm, Su 11am–12N
ek-lek´-tik	91.3	WTSR	I	◇	SPOT NEWS	**REGGAE; GOSPEL; OLDIES; CLASSIC ROCK; JAZZ;** Spts: Trenton State College
ek-lek´-tik	103.3	WPRB	|||	◇	SEE S.P.	**PROGRESSIVE ROCK; JAZZ; CLASS;** News 6, 8, 10am, 12N, 2, 4, 6pm; Spts.: Princeton
✝✝✝	94.5	WCHR	|||	◇	MORE	News 12N, 12:30, 1, 1:30, 2, 3:30pm
FARTHER NORTH ON US 1 & N.J. TPK. SEE N.Y.C. PG 206						
EAST ON ATLANTIC CITY EXP. SEE SHORE RTE. PG 164						

PITTSBURGH

FORMAT / TUNE TO		STATION	SIGNAL POWER	TRAFFIC REPORT	NEWS	SPECIAL PROGRAMMING
Adult Pop	96.1	WHTX	|||	🚗	AM DRIVE	Morn. Humor
Top 40	93.7	WBZZ	|||	◇	AM DRIVE	C. Kasem Top 40 Su 8am–12N
Top 40	100.7	WMXP	|||	🚗	AM DRIVE	Casey Kasem Top 40 Sa 6–10am; Hot Mix Sa 9pm–1am; UK Chart Attack Su 7–8am
🎸	102.5	WDVE	|||	🚗	SPOT NEWS	Su Morn. Show, 2nd Su of month 8–10am; Home Grown (Bands) 3rd Su of month 10pm
🎸☮	96.9	WMYG	|||	🚗	AM DRIVE	Morn. Humor
🤠	107.9	WDSY	|||	🚗	AM & PM DRIVE	Home Grown Ctry. Su 10–11pm; Ctry. Ctdwn. Sa 6–9am; Ctry. Gold Sa 7pm–12M
☀ OLDIES	94.5	WWSW	|||	🚗	AM & PM DRIVE	Morn. Humor
R&B	105.9	WAMO	|||	🚗		Morn. Humor
Lite Hits	92.9	WLTJ	|||	🚗	AM & PM DRIVE	Morn. Humor; Stk. Mkt. drive times; Week Watch Su 8:30am
Lite Hits	99.7	WSHH	|||	🚗	🕐	Stk. Mkt. 7, 8am, 5, 6pm; Wish for Lovers Daily 9pm–12M; Wish on B'dwy. Su 9–10am
E 🌼 Z	104.7	WEZE	|||	🚗	MORE	News 12N, 3, 5pm; Local Cultural Prog.; Arts Features Su 12N–1pm; Lifestyles Features
🎹	89.3	WQED	|||	🚗	🕐	
🎺	90.5	WDUQ	|||	◇	MORE	**NPR;** News: W.E. Sa & Su 8–10am; Music from India Su 6–8pm; Car Talk Sa 10am
ek-lek-tik	91.3	WYEP	|||	◇	SEE S.P.	Pacifica News M–F 5:30–6pm; Mktplace M–F 5–5:30pm; World Music M–F 6–8pm
✝✝✝	101.5	WPIT	|||	🚗	🕐	**CHRISTIAN CONTEMPORARY;** Insight for Living M–F 9:30am; D. Hatch (Talk) M–F 5pm
TALK	1250	WTAE	||	🚗	🕐	Ext. News 6–10am & on 1/2 hr; Stk. Mkt. 05 after hr; Spts.: Steelers, U. of Pittsburgh
NEWS	1410	KQV	||	🚗	ALL NEWS	Stk. Mkt. 20 & 50 after the hr; Spts.: Duquesne, CBS Football, Notre D. football
Adult Pop	1020	KDKA	"C"	🚗	🕐	**TALK** M–F 6pm–5am; News also on the 1/2 hr; Stk. Updates 4–6pm; Spts.: Pirates, Penn.

SOUTHEAST ON I-76 (NEW STANTON AREA)

FORMAT / TUNE TO		STATION	SIGNAL POWER	TRAFFIC REPORT	NEWS	SPECIAL PROGRAMMING
Top 40	107.1	WSSZ	||	🚗	🕐	
☀ OLDIES	103.9	WLSW	||	◇	MORE	News 11:50am, 3:20, 4:50pm; Stk. Mkt. 12N

FARTHER EAST ON I-70 SEE PAGE 54

FARTHER EAST ON I-76 SEE PAGE 74

214

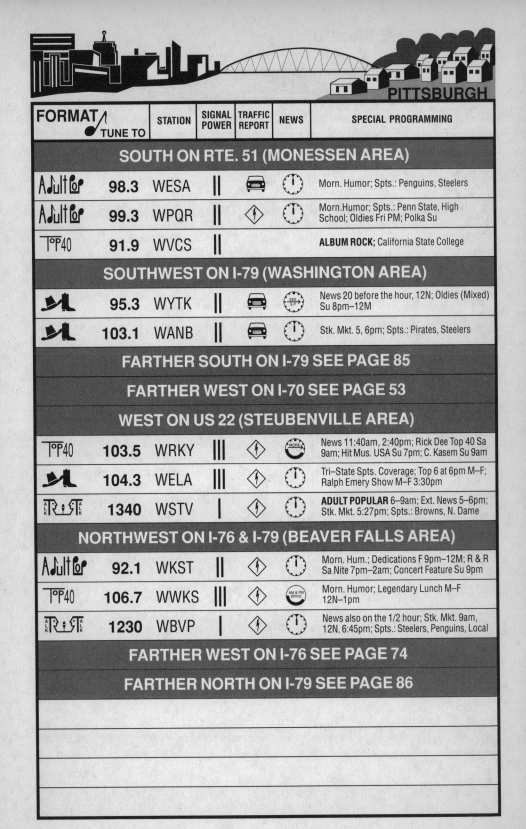

PITTSBURGH

FORMAT / TUNE TO		STATION	SIGNAL POWER	TRAFFIC REPORT	NEWS	SPECIAL PROGRAMMING
SOUTH ON RTE. 51 (MONESSEN AREA)						
Adult Pop	98.3	WESA	‖	🚗	🕐	Morn. Humor; Spts.: Penguins, Steelers
Adult Pop	99.3	WPQR	‖	◇	🕐	Morn. Humor; Spts.: Penn State, High School; Oldies Fri PM; Polka Su
Top40	91.9	WVCS	‖			**ALBUM ROCK;** California State College
SOUTHWEST ON I-79 (WASHINGTON AREA)						
🤠	95.3	WYTK	‖	🚗	SEE S.P.	News 20 before the hour, 12N; Oldies (Mixed) Su 8pm–12M
🤠	103.1	WANB	‖	🚗	🕐	Stk. Mkt. 5, 6pm; Spts.: Pirates, Steelers
FARTHER SOUTH ON I-79 SEE PAGE 85						
FARTHER WEST ON I-70 SEE PAGE 53						
WEST ON US 22 (STEUBENVILLE AREA)						
Top40	103.5	WRKY	‖‖	◇	MORE	News 11:40am, 2:40pm; Rick Dee Top 40 Sa 9am; Hit Mus. USA Su 7pm; C. Kasem Su 9am
🤠	104.3	WELA	‖‖	◇	🕐	Tri–State Spts. Coverage; Top 6 at 6pm M–F; Ralph Emery Show M–F 3:30pm
Talk Tri St	1340	WSTV		◇	🕐	**ADULT POPULAR** 6–9am; Ext. News 5–6pm; Stk. Mkt. 5:27pm; Spts.: Browns, N. Dame
NORTHWEST ON I-76 & I-79 (BEAVER FALLS AREA)						
Adult Pop	92.1	WKST	‖	◇	🕐	Morn. Hum.; Dedications F 9pm–12M; R & R Sa Nite 7pm–2am; Concert Feature Su 9pm
Top40	106.7	WWKS	‖‖	◇	AM & PM DRIVE	Morn. Humor; Legendary Lunch M–F 12N–1pm
Talk Tri St	1230	WBVP		◇	🕐	News also on the 1/2 hour; Stk. Mkt. 9am, 12N, 6:45pm; Spts.: Steelers, Penguins, Local
FARTHER WEST ON I-76 SEE PAGE 74						
FARTHER NORTH ON I-79 SEE PAGE 86						

TAMPA/ST. PETERSBURG

FORMAT ♪ TUNE TO		STATION	SIGNAL POWER	TRAFFIC REPORT	NEWS	SPECIAL PROGRAMMING
Adult Pop	93.3	WFLZ	|||	🚗	AM & PM DRIVE	Morn. Humor
Adult Pop	95.7	WNLT	|||	🚗	AM DRIVE	Morn. Humor
Adult Pop	100.7	WUSA	|||	🚗	🕐	News also on the 1/2 hour; Morn. Humor
Top 40	104.7	WRBQ	|||	🚗	AM DRIVE	**ADULT POPULAR;** Spts.: Buccaneers, Yankees
🎸	94.9	WYNF	|||	🚗	MORE	News 12N; Morn. Humor; All Req. M–Sa 9pm; Wax Mus. Su 9am–12N; Pwrcts. Su 6–8pm
🎸	97.9	WXTB	|||	🚗	AM DRIVE	Morn. Humor; Tampa Bay Rocks Su 9–11pm; Public Service Su 6:30am
👢	99.5	WQYK	|||		MORE	News 12N; Morn. Humor
☀OLDIES	92.5	WYUU	|||	🚗	AM DRIVE	Cruisin' America/Cousin Brucie Sa 6–10am; Live from the 60's Su 9am–12N
Lite Hits	107.3	WWRM	|||	🚗	AM DRIVE	Spectrum Su 7am
🎹	89.7	WUSF	|||	🚗	MORE	**NPR; APR;** News: W.E. Sa 8–9am, ATC Sa & Su 5–6pm; Prairie Home Comp. Sa 6pm
ek-lek-tik	88.5	WMNF	|||	⬦	MORE	News also 4:30pm; Talk Show M–F 10am, 6:30pm; Women's Show Sa 10am
†††	90.5	WBVM	|||	🚗		**CHRISTIAN CONTEMPORARY;** Focus on the Family M–F 7:30pm
†††	91.5	WLPJ					**ADULT POPULAR; INSPIRATIONAL;** Christian Hard Rock F 7pm–1am
†††	91.7	WFTI	||		🕐	News also on the 1/2 hour; Sacred Classical Music Su 4pm
†††	101.5	WKES	|||			**CHRISTIAN TRAD.;** Focus on the Family M–F 5:30pm; Insight for Living M–F 8:30am
NEWS	570	WTKN	||	⬦	ALL NEWS	News also on the hr. 6pm–6am; Stk. Mkt. 3x an hr; Spts.: Gators, Magic & Cardinals
TALK	970	WFLA	||	🚗	🕐	News also on the 1/2 hr.; Stk. Mkt. Updates 24 hrs; Spts.: Major League Baseball; Talk Hosts
TALK	1430	WLKF	||	⬦	🕐	Stk. Mkt. 12N; Spts.: U. of FL, Dolphins, High School; Investment Strategies Sa 10am–12N

TAMPA/ST. PETERSBURG

FORMAT ♪ TUNE TO		STATION	SIGNAL POWER	TRAFFIC REPORT	NEWS	SPECIAL PROGRAMMING
SOUTH ON I-75 (SARASOTA AREA)						
👢	92.1	WCTQ	‖	◇	🕐	John Madden Spts. 8:30pm
☀OLDIES	106.3	WSRZ	‖		AM DRIVE	Live at the Oldies Sa 7–11pm; Class Reunion (Oldies) Su 9pm; Dr. Demento Su 10pm
E ✿ Z	103.3	WDUV	‖‖	◇	🕐	Stk. Mkt. on the half hour every other hour
🎺	102.5	WHVE	‖‖	🚗	AM DRIVE	Su Brunch 7am–2pm; Suncoast Jazz Affair Su 7pm–12M; Digital Wavelengths M 10pm
✝✝✝	88.1	WJIS	‖‖	🚗	MORE	**CHRISTIAN CONTEMPORARY; JAZZ;** News 12N; Focus on the Family ⸱⸱ u 10:30am, 8pm
✝✝✝	105.5	WKZM	‖	◇	🕐	Action Interview Tu & Thu 10⸱⸱ Community News Daily 9:45am
FARTHER SOUTH ON I-75 SEE PAGE 59						
NORTHWEST ON US 19 (NEW PORT RICHEY)						
E ✿ Z	105.5	WGUL	‖	◇	🕐	**BIG BAND; SWING; SHOW TUNES; SOFT JAZZ;** News also on the 1/2 hour
E ✿ Z	106.3	WLVU	‖	◇	🕐	**ALL VOCALS FROM MEMORY LANE**
NORTH ON I-75 SEE PAGE 59						
EAST ON I-4 (LAKELAND AREA)						
👢	97.5	WPCV	‖‖	🚗	AM DRIVE	Morn. Humor; American Ctry. Ctdwn. Su 10am–3pm; Nashville Live Sa 10:30pm
E ✿ Z	94.1	WEZY	‖‖	◇	MORE	News 11:55am, 1:55pm
✝✝✝	91.1	WCIE	‖‖	◇	🕐	**CHRISTIAN CONTEMPORARY**
✝✝✝	91.9	WYFO	‖	◇	🕐	**CHRISTIAN MUSIC;** Focus on the Family M–F 2:30pm; Back to the Bible M–F 9:30am
FARTHER EAST ON I-4 TO ORLANDO SEE PAGE 210						

WASHINGTON

FORMAT TUNE TO		STATION	SIGNAL POWER	TRAFFIC REPORT	NEWS	SPECIAL PROGRAMMING
Adult Pop	94.7	WLTT	III	🚗	AM & PM DRIVE	LITE HITS; LITE ROCK
Adult Pop	97.1	WASH	III		AM DRIVE	LITE HITS; Morn. Humor
Adult Pop	102.3	WMMJ	II	🚗	AM DRIVE	BLACK-ORIENTED ADULT POPULAR; Dance Party Oldies Sa 7–10pm
Adult Pop	107.3	WRQX	III	🚗	AM DRIVE	TOP 40; Morn. Humor; American Top 40 Su 6–10am; Live-Line Su 10pm–1am
TOP40	95.5	WPGC	III	🚗	AM DRIVE	R & B; CONTEMPORARY CROSSOVER
TOP40	105.1	WAVA	III	🚗	AM DRIVE	Morn. Humor; Top 40 Su 8–10pm; Take One (Public Affairs) Su 5am
🎸	101.1	WWDC	III	🚗	AM DRIVE	Stock Market
🎸	105.9	WCXR	III	🚗	AM DRIVE	Morn. Humor
🎸	106.7	WJFK	III	🚗	AM DRIVE	TALK: 6–10:30am; Rckln. M 11pm–12:30am; Flashback Su 8–10am; New Music Thu 11pm
🎩👢	98.7	WMZQ	III		AM DRIVE	American Ctry. Ctdwn. Su 8am
OLDIES	104.1	WXTR	III	🚗	🕐	Morn. Humor; D. Clark Rock, Roll & Rem. Su 8am–12N; Supergold Sa & Su 7pm–12M
R&B	93.9	WKYS	III	🚗	MORE	Morn. Humor; News 2:50pm
R&B	96.3	WHUR	III	🚗	AM DRIVE	ADULT POPULAR; Spts. Talk Su 6pm; Gospel Su 7–11am; Jazz Su 11am–3pm
E ❀ Z	99.5	WGAY	III	🚗	🕐	Stk. Mkt. M–F 4:30pm; Matinee at One (Broadway Shows) Su 1pm
🎹	90.9	WETA	III	🚗	SEE S.P.	NPR; NEWS: ATC M–F 5–6:30pm, W.E. Su 11am–12N, MonitoRadio M–F 4:30–5pm
🎹	91.9	WGTS	II	◇		RELIGIOUS
🎹	103.5	WGMS	III	◇	MORE	News 10am, 12N, 2pm; Stks., Bus. Report M–F 6:50pm; Rpt. on Congress 6:40pm
🎺	89.3	WPFW	III		SEE S.P.	News 7pm; World Music M–F 3–5:30pm; Morning Conversations M–F 9–10am
🎺	90.1	WDCU	II	◇		TALK; Gospel Sa & Su 6–11am; Hispanic, African Sa 11am–3pm; Jazz Sa 3–7pm
🎺	100.3	WJZE	III	🚗	AM DRIVE	Morn. Humor
ek-lek´-tik	88.5	WAMU	III	🚗	MORE	NPR; APR; News: W.E. Sa 9–11am, ATC Sa & Su 6–7pm; Car Talk Sa 8–9am
NEWS	1500	WTOP	"C"	🚗	ALL NEWS	Stk. Mkt. :25 & :55 each hour; Spts.: Orioles, Bullets, NFL, Playoffs, World Series
NEWS	1580	WPGC	III	🚗	ALL NEWS	BUSINESS; Stk. Mkt.; Local, Political News; Talknet M–F 7pm

FORMAT / TUNE TO		STATION	SIGNAL POWER	TRAFFIC REPORT	NEWS	SPECIAL PROGRAMMING
TALK/TALK	630	WMAL	‖	🚗	🕐	**INFO; NEWS;** News also on 1/2 hr; Spts.: Redskins, Capitols; Spts. Call M–F 7pm
TALK/TALK	980	WWRC	‖	🚗	🕐	**NEWS;** Morn. Humor; Stk. Mkt. hourly; Talknet M–Su 7pm–5am
TALK/TALK	1050	WNTR	ǀ	🚗	🕐	**NEWS Related Issues;** Bottom Line M–F 4–7pm; Doug Stephan M–F 6–10am
EAST ON US 50 (ANNAPOLIS AREA)						
🎸	99.1	WHFS	‖‖	🚗	AM DRIVE	New Music Su 7–8pm; Speak Your Mind Su 9–10am; Reggae Su 8–10pm
🤠	103.1	WBEY	‖	🚗	🕐	Spts. News :35 6, 7, 8am, 4, 5:20pm; Fishing News 5:35pm; Agri. News 5:35am, 12:35pm
†††	107.9	WFSI	‖‖	🚗	SPOT NEWS	**CHRISTIAN CONTEMPORARY;** Insight for Living M–F 8am, 5pm
EAST ON US 50 SEE SHORE ROUTE PAGE 163						
SOUTH ON I-95 SEE PAGE 146						
WEST ON I-66 (WARRENTON)						
Adult Pop	94.3	WQRA	‖	⬦	🕐	Gospel Train, Su 6–11am
☀OLDIES	107.7	WMJR	‖‖	🚗	AM & PM DRIVE	Solid Gold Sa 7pm–12M; Req. Special Su 7pm–12M; Sold Gold Scrapbk. Su 9am–2pm
FARTHER WEST ON I-66 SEE I-81 PAGE 101						
NORTHWEST ON I-270 SEE I-70 PAGE 55						
NORTH ON I-95 SEE BALTIMORE METRO PAGE 168						

WINSTON-SALEM HIGHPOINT

FORMAT / TUNE TO		STATION	SIGNAL POWER	TRAFFIC REPORT	NEWS	SPECIAL PROGRAMMING
WESTERN AREA (WINSTON-SALEM)						
Adult Cor	99.5	WMAG	|||	🚗	AM & PM DRIVE	Morn. Humor; Sa Night at the Oldies 6–10pm
Adult Cor	100.3	WWWB	|||	🚗	AM DRIVE	Morn. Humor
Top40	107.5	WKZL	|||	🚗	AM & PM DRIVE	Morn. Humor
🎸	92.3	WKRR	|||	◈	AM DRIVE	Morn. Humor; Electric Lunch 12N; Monday Nite Classic CD 10pm
🤠	104.1	WTQR	|||	🚗	MORE	News 12:30, 3:30pm; Amer. Ctry. Ctdwn. Sa 7–11pm; Bluegrass Express Sa 5–7pm
OLDIES	93.1	WMQX	|||	🚗	AM DRIVE	
OLDIES	98.3	WTHP	||	◈	🕐	Spts.: NC State, Local; Dick Bartley Oldies Sa 7pm; New Gold on CD M–F 12:40pm
R&B	90.5	WSNC	||	🚗	🕐	**GOSPEL; JAZZ;** Fair Dollar daily 10:30am, 1:30, 5:30pm; Health Tips M, W, F 8:10am
🎹	88.5	WFDD	|||	◈	MORE	**NPR; JAZZ** M–Thu 10pm–12M, F 8pm–7am, Su 8–11pm; News: W.E. Sa 8–10am
✝✝✝	94.1	WWGL	|||	◈	🕐	**SOUTHERN GOSPEL**
✝✝✝	95.5	WHPE	|||	◈	🕐	
FARTHER WEST ON I-40 & I-85 SEE CHARLOTTE PAGE 176						
CENTRAL AREA (GREENSBORO/BURLINGTON)						
Top40	98.7	WKSI	|||	🚗	AM & PM DRIVE	Morn. Humor
🎸	93.9	WZZU	|||	🚗	AM DRIVE	
🤠	101.1	WPCM	|||	◈	AM & PM DRIVE	Ctry. Gold Spotlight Sa 9am–12N; CD Album Hour Su 6–7pm; Ctry. Calendar Su 9:20am
R&B	90.1	WNAA	|||	◈	🕐	**JAZZ; GOSPEL; RAP;** In Black America F 10:30am; Jazz from the City Su 4–6pm
R&B	97.1	WQMG	|||	🚗	SEE S.P.	News 10am, 4pm; Pwr. aft. Drk. Su 8pm–12M; Gospel Su 6–10am; On the Move Sa 7am
R&B	102.1	WJMH	|||	🚗	AM DRIVE	Morn. Humor; Straight Talk Su 7:30am; Oldies Su 8–10pm
Lite Hits	94.5	WWMY	|||	🚗	MORE	News 11am, 12N, 3, 4pm; Stk. & Bus. Rpt. 4:30, 5:30pm; Sunday Over Easy 7am–12N
ek-lek´-tik	90.9	WQFS			◈		New Music Review Su 11pm–12M; Rush Hr. Blues M–F 5–6pm; Reggae Lnch. Splash 12N

GREENSBORO DURHAM RALEIGH

FORMAT / TUNE TO	STATION	SIGNAL POWER	TRAFFIC REPORT	NEWS	SPECIAL PROGRAMMING
EASTERN AREA (RALEIGH/DURHAM)					
Adult Pop — 101.5	WRAL	|||	🚗	AM & PM DRIVE	Morn. Humor; Dick Bartley's Rock & Roll Oldies Sa 7pm–12M
Top 40 — 105.1	WDCG	|||	🚗	AM DRIVE	Morn. Humor; Open House Party Sa & Su 7pm–12M; C. Kasem Top 40 Su 6–10am
🎸 106.1	WRDU	|||	🚗	AM DRIVE	Class. 9 at 9am M–F; Vintage Block M–F 6pm; Short Order Lunch M–F 12N; Jazz Su 7am
🎸 88.1	WKNC	||		MORE	R & B; News 12:30pm; Spts. NC U; Christian Rock Su 12N; Jazz Su 3pm
🎸 88.7	WXDU			◇	SEE S.P.	News 11am, 2, 5pm; Jazz M–F 5–8pm, Su 12N–3pm; Women's Mus. Sa 3–6pm; Blues Sa 3pm
🎸 89.3	WXYC					**INTERNATIONAL MUSIC;** Northern Hemis. Su 6pm; Backyard Barbecue Su 8pm
🤠 94.7	WQDR	|||	🚗	🕐	Morn. Humor; Farm Reports M–F 5–6am; Spts.: U. of NC
☀️OLDIES 100.7	WTRG	|||	◇	AM & PM DRIVE	Morn. Humor; Dick Clark Su AM
☀️OLDIES 104.3	WCAS	|||	◇	AM DRIVE	**ADULT POPULAR; LITE HITS;** Morn. Humor; Spts.: Duke U.
R&B 97.5	WQOK	|||	🚗	AM DRIVE	Hot Mix M–F 6pm, Sa 10pm–12M; Quiet Storm M–F 5–6pm; Gospel M–F 5–6am
R&B 107.1	WFXC	||		🕐	**OLDIES;** Morn. Humor; The Ctdwn. Sa 10am–12N; Around the Triangle Su 10–11am
Lite Hits 96.1	WYLT	|||	🚗	🕐	Morn. Humor; Lite Nite Lovesongs M–F 7pm–12M
🎹 89.7	WCPE	|||		SEE S.P.	News BBC 7, 9am, 12N, 6pm; Adven. in Good Music M–Sa 11am–12N; Opera Thu 7pm
🎺 88.9	WSHA	|||	🚗	🕐	African Music Sa 3–6pm; Reggae Sa 9am–3pm; Latin Music Sa 6–9pm
🎷 103.9	WNND	||	🚗	🕐	Stk. Mkt. drive times; Jazz Trax Su 7pm–12M; Musical Starstreams Su 8–10am
✝✝✝ 92.5	WYFL	|||	◇	🕐	Stock Market 6pm
—NEWS— 91.5	WUNC	|||	🚗	MORE	**NPR; APR; CLASS; JAZZ;** News: W.E. Sa & Su 10am–12N; Car Talk Sa 12N
TALK 680	WPTF	"C"	🚗	🕐	Stk. Mkt. :50 6, 8am, 2, 3, 4, 5pm; Spts.: NC State U., Redskins, CBS

FARTHER NORTHEAST ON I-85 SEE PAGE 113

FARTHER EAST ON I-40 SEE PAGE 24

NORTH OR SOUTH ON I-95 SEE PAGE 144